MYTH AND POETICS

A series edited by

GREGORY NAGY

The Ravenous Hyenas and the Wounded Sun:
Myth and Ritual in Ancient India
by Stephanie W. Jamison

Also in the series

The Language of Heroes:
Speech and Performance in the Iliad
by Richard P. Martin

Greek Mythology and Poetics
by Gregory Nagy

Homer and the Sacred City
by Stephen Scully

Poetry and Prophecy:
The Beginnings of a Literary Tradition
edited by James Kugel

Epic Singers and Oral Tradition
by Albert Bates Lord

The Traffic in Praise:
Pindar and the Poetics of Social Economy
by Leslie Kurke

THE RAVENOUS HYENAS AND THE WOUNDED SUN

Myth and Ritual in Ancient India

STEPHANIE W. JAMISON

CORNELL UNIVERSITY PRESS

ITHACA AND LONDON

First published 1991 by Cornell University Press.
First printing, Cornell Paperbacks, 2011
International Standard Book Number 0-8014-2433-X
Library of Congress Catalog Card Number 90-55723
Printed in the United States of America
Librarians: Library of Congress cataloging information appears on the last page of the book.

♾ The paper in this book meets the minimum requirements of the American National Standard for Information Sciences—Permanence of Paper for Printed Library Materials, ANSI Z39.48-1984.

ISBN: 978-0-8014-7732-4

For Calvert

yato hi bhartā mama sā gatir dhruvā

MBh.III.281.28

Contents

Foreword

Gregory Nagy

Myth and Ritual in Ancient India, by Stephanie W. Jamison, is a crucial volume in the Myth and Poetics series. My goal, as series editor, is to encourage work that helps to integrate literary criticism with the approaches of anthropology and that pays special attention to problems concerning the nexus of ritual and myth. The first two books in the series, Richard P. Martin's *The Language of Heroes* (1989) and my own *Greek Mythology and Poetics* (1990), set the groundwork for a broadened understanding of the very concepts of myth and ritual as reflected in the specific cultural context of ancient Greek poetics. A major problem for Hellenists, however, is that the corpus of attested Greek literature, in all its vastness, seldom provides explicit testimony about the relationship of myth and ritual. The corpus of Indic literature, by contrast, which is even more vast, abounds with such testimony. Jamison's book offers a masterly analysis in depth.

In the case of ancient Greek literature, the lack of explicit evidence concerning the relationship of myth and ritual is at least compensated for by a core of implicit evidence, recoverable from the application of comparative linguistics to the traditional poetics of the Greeks. The very word "myth," as derived from Greek *mūthos,* is a case in point: the history of the meaning of this word brings to life, in microcosm, the relationship between myth and ritual in ancient Greek society. It also affects our own understanding of myth as a concept. At earlier stages of Greek literature, *mūthos* referred to myth conveyed by song, poetry, and prose, as it was performed in the context of ritual. At later stages, the performance of myth in Classicized traditions of song, poetry, and prose tended to become divorced from the performance of myth in ritual. As a consequence, the truth-value of the word *mūthos* became destabilized. Already in the second half of the fifth century before our era, it was reaching negative levels of connotation comparable to what we inherit in our own casual usage of the word "myth" in situations where we are referring to what is not true. No such divorce took place in Indic literature, where the truth-value of myth is continually reinforced by its explicit symbiosis with ritual. Moreover, the strikingly rich syntax of Indic ritual is matched by an equally rich syntax of myth, which invites in-depth exploration on the level of form as well as content. Such a tradition, in its distinctness from Greek literature in particular and most other forms of Western literature in general, promises radically new perspectives for the literary critic. Stephanie Jamison's *Myth and Ritual in Ancient India* gives the general reader a sharp view of this literature in all its challenging complexity.

Acknowledgments

It is a great pleasure to have the opportunity to thank the many who have instructed, helped, and encouraged me in this enterprise. Chief among them are Stanley Insler and my husband, Calvert Watkins. Stanley Insler is primarily responsible for whatever Vedic I know. Over the course of nearly twenty years he has shaped my scholarly methodology, watched over my philological development, prodded me back to the path when I have wandered into technical thickets, and most of all taught me, by example, that it is scrupulous philological techniques that allow us to approach our texts afresh and pose—and answer—imaginative questions about them. He gave an earlier draft of this book an intensive reading, and his many suggestions are noted throughout the book. But I owe him a debt in every line that cannot possibly be sufficiently acknowledged.

It is likewise impossible to acknowledge how much I owe to Calvert Watkins. He has taught me how to look at the verbal shape of ancient texts and how to talk about what we see there. This book could not have been written—or even conceived—without the example of his seemingly effortless, but searching responses to texts all over the Indo-European world. He has also been an unfailing source of personal encouragement and support and has, with tireless patience, talked through, read, and reread every word of this work—and everything else I have written. His mark, too, is on every line.

I am also happy to thank Gregory Nagy for first suggesting that I write this book, for his continual encouragement along the way, and for many suggestions he made about a previous version. Michael

Witzel, Hanns-Peter Schmidt, and Alf Hiltebeitel, the reader for Cornell University Press, also generously read this earlier version, and their helpful suggestions have led to many improvements.

I have also had the benefit of discussions with many people on general and specific issues relating to this book. I cannot name them all, but I think particularly of Rosemary Hale, Mark Hale, Joel Brereton, and Chris Minkovsky—and Kristine Forsgard, who introduced me to the hyena literature.

I would also like here, perhaps unorthodoxly, to acknowledge my debt to the dead. The scholars who led the way in the nineteenth and early twentieth centuries are commonly conceived of as the scholars (or the giants, if we are being generous) on whose shoulders we rest. But the metaphor that imposes itself on me is different: I feel part of an atelier of an Old Master. Sometimes I paint a pleasing tree or a mountain or a distant building, but I am simply filling in a picture that has been sketched out or well structured by those who came before. There are too many names to mention, from the beginning of Western Vedic studies, but W. Caland stands supreme, of the more recent of the older practitioners. I also think that A. B. Keith, who gave us so many usable texts and general treatments of them, is undervalued, presumably because of the superficial contempt he affects for the texts. (But could he have spent so much care and intelligence without some respect for the texts? And can those who evince more respect for the texts claim as large a contribution to our understanding of them? I cannot.) I hesitate to mention other names (for fear of omitting some), but my appreciation of all Vedic scholars increases as the years go by: H. Oldenberg, K. F. Geldner, J. Eggeling, and so on, not to mention W. D. Whitney, A. Weber, and many others.

Finally, I want to express my appreciation for, and sense of connection with, the composers of the Brāhmaṇas. When I first read this sort of text, I must confess that I resisted it, thinking it the most sterile and tedious of styles. But I have gradually come greatly to appreciate, and feel part of, the intellectual tradition of the Brāhmaṇa authors. I am not a poet: I can enjoy the talents and artistic sincerity of a Rig Vedic poet, but I cannot emulate it or imagine how it feels to be part of this creative tradition. I am a scholar (though not a theologian), and I can appreciate internally the intellectual effort and acuity employed to make sense of the religious traditions that confronted the scholar of the Brāhmaṇa period. I would hope to have in some measure the same controlled intelligence, the flashes of insight, and the empathy that these ancient scholars brought to bear on the tradition they were trying to explain, and I would also hope that they would appreciate the fact that this tradition remains an absorbing intellectual puzzle to this day.

S. W. J.

Abbreviations

Texts

The order given here and in the glossary is that of the Roman alphabet, with long vowels following the corresponding short vowels and *ś* following *s*.

AB	Aitareya Brāhmaṇa
AiĀr	Aitareya Āraṇyaka
AV	Atharva Veda
AVP	Atharva Veda Paippalāda
AVŚ	Atharva Veda Śaunaka
ĀpDS	Āpastambha Dharma Sūtra
ĀpGS	Āpastambha Gṛhya Sūtra
ĀpŚS	Āpastambha Śrauta Sūtra
ĀśvŚS	Āśvalāyana Śrauta Sūtra
BĀU	Bṛhad Āraṇyaka Upaniṣad
BDS	Baudhāyana Dharma Sūtra
BGS	Baudhāyana Gṛhya Sūtra
BhārŚS	Bhāradvāja Śrauta Sūtra
Brāh.	Brāhmaṇa
Bṛhaddev.	Bṛhaddevatā
BŚS	Baudhāyana Śrauta Sūtra
BYV	Black (Kṛṣṇa) Yajur Veda
DS	Dharma Sūtra
GautDS	Gautama Dharma Sūtra
GB	Gopatha Brāhmaṇa
GobhGS	Gobhila Gṛhya Sūtra
GS	Gṛhya Sūtra
HirŚS	Hiranyakeśin Śrauta Sūtra
JB	Jaiminīya Brāhmaṇa

JGS	Jaiminīya Gṛhya Sūtra
KapS	Kapiṣṭhala Saṃhitā
KauṣUp	Kauṣītaki Upaniṣad
KāṭhĀ	Kāṭhaka Āraṇyaka
KāṭhGS	Kāṭhaka Gṛhya Sūtra
KātyŚS	Kātyāyana Śrauta Sūtra
KB	Kauṣītaki (or Śāṅkhāyana) Brāhmaṇa
KS	Kāṭhaka Saṃhitā
LāṭyŚS	Lāṭyāyana Śrauta Sūtra
MBh.	Mahābhārata
MDŚ	Mānava Dharma Śāstra
MS	Maitrāyaṇī Saṃhitā
MŚS	Mānava Śrauta Sūtra
PāraskGS	Pāraskara Gṛhya Sūtra
PB	Pañcaviṃśa Brāhmaṇa (or Tāṇḍya Mahābrāhmaṇa)
Pp	Pada Pāṭha
RV	Rig Veda
RV Kh	Rig Veda Khila
Sāy.	Sāyaṇa
SV	Sāma Veda
ŚāṅkhŚS	Śāṅkhāyana Śrauta Sūtra
ŚB	Śatapatha Brāhmaṇa
ŚBK	Śatapatha Brāhmaṇa Kāṇva
ŚBM	Śatapatha Brāhmaṇa Mādhyaṃdina
ŚS	Śrauta Sūtra
TĀr	Taittirīya Āraṇyaka
TB	Taittirīya Brāhmaṇa
TS	Taittirīya Saṃhitā
VaikhŚS	Vaikhānasa Śrauta Sūtra
VādhS	Vādhūla Sūtra
Vālakh.	Vālakhilya
VārŚS	Vārāha Śrauta Sūtra
VāsDS	Vāsiṣṭha Dharma Sūtra
Vi.Smṛ	Viṣṇu Smṛti
VS	Vājasaneyi Saṃhitā
WYV	White (Śukla) Yajur Veda
Yājñ.Smṛ	Yājñavalkya Smṛti
YV	Yajur Veda

Publications

Abh. Preuss. Akad. d. Wiss.	*Abhandlungen der Preussischen Akademie der Wissenschaft*
AO	*Acta Orientalia*
BB	*Beiträge zur Kunde der indogermanischen Sprachen*
ÉVP	*Études védiques et pāṇinéennes* (Renou 1955–69)
EWA	*Etymologisches Wörterbuch des Altindoarischen* (Mayrhofer 1986–)
IIJ	*Indo-Iranian Journal*
Ind. Stud.	*Indische Studien*

Ind. Taur.	*Indologica Taurinensia*
JAOS	*Journal of the American Oriental Society*
KEWA	*Kurzgefasstes etymologisches Wörterbuch des Altindischen* (Mayrhofer 1956–80)
KZ	*Zeitschrift für vergleichende Sprachforschung auf dem Gebiete der indogermanischen Sprachen*
MSS	*Münchener Studien zur Sprachwissenschaft*
PAPS	*Proceedings of the American Philosophical Society*
WZKM	*Wiener Zeitschrift für die Kunde des Morgenlandes*
ZDMG	*Zeitschrift der Deutschen Morgenländischen Gesellschaft*

THE RAVENOUS HYENAS AND THE WOUNDED SUN

Introduction

The literature on mythology and ritual is dauntingly vast; just the definition of these deceptively straightforward terms has engaged many minds and filled many pages.[1] Nonetheless, even the primary data about these subjects, from numerous cultures and eras, have barely begun to be assembled and their significance and singularity appreciated. Among these primary sources, no doubt the greatest legacy from the ancient world concerning myth and ritual comes to us from Vedic India, from the first period of attested Indian literature. Yet for those outside Indology proper this great storehouse of materials is perhaps the least known and used of the ancient traditions—for reasons partly intrinsic to the texts themselves.

The Vedic texts cover approximately one thousand years (1500?–500? B.C.) and are of an amplitude that can only amaze those accustomed to the more restricted scope of Classical texts specifically devoted to ritual. They consist of many thousands of pages. The texts are of various types and offer us a variety of vantage points on ritual and mythology. For ritual we have not only the liturgy itself, but explication of, and speculation about, the ritual, and, at the end of the Vedic period, manuals exhaustively detailing the astounding complexities of ritual praxis.

[1]Though it is not my purpose to add to this discussion, it is probably useful for the reader to know what *I* mean by these terms. For purposes of this work, a *myth* is a story/narrative that involves divine or semidivine figures as major (but not necessarily the only) participants. *Ritual* is patterned and repeated religious observance that involves physical activity and the manipulation of objects as well as words.

The value of these bodies of texts for the general study of ritual should be obvious: we have voluminous evidence of both the action and the words of ritual performance, and numerous, sophisticated, contemporary justifications of, and speculations on, the reason for both. Despite the great time span these texts fill, they are all concerned with the same body of rituals or, at the very least, the same unbroken ritual tradition.

The texts are of equal value for the study of the relations between ritual and myth, for mythology is a major component of the texts, particularly of the first two types. For mythology we have stories about, and characterizations of, the gods, from various periods, told in various styles—from the most elegant and elaborate poetry to prose of an almost awkward simplicity—for a variety of reasons, usually to please and celebrate the gods or to explain some detail of ritual practice. Moreover, very few myths are related just once. A single text can have several versions of (or simple allusions to) one myth; different texts can each have their own version(s).

Each *type* of text, liturgical, exegetical, and explanatory, has a number of representatives, so that we have not only gross differences in style, purpose, and point of view, but also subtle variations on almost identical themes. It is this almost prismatically split vision of a single ritual event or a single myth that is one of the chief values (and the chief difficulty) of Vedic for the general study of ritual.

Given the diversity and richness of the material, why has it had comparatively little impact on the general study of myth and ritual?[2] One answer is that the Vedic tradition is simply a victim of its own vigor, the florid proliferation of texts. The material is so vast and detailed and there are so many parallels, so many different treatments of the same myth or ritual, so many necessary cross-references that it is difficult even for a specialist to control it all, and almost impossible for a nonspecialist to know where to begin. Many of the most important texts have not been translated (into *any* modern language); many are badly edited and almost unavailable. Even texts that have been faithfully translated plunge the reader into a welter of ritual minutiae with little framework to make sense of the details. General treatments of particular rituals (including translators' annotations) or of the ritual

[2]With rare but important exceptions, like the seminal work of Hubert and Mauss on sacrifice (1898), which relies heavily on the landmark work of S. Lévi 1898, as well as on other, technical works on Vedic sacrifice.

in general[3] simply compound this problem in a way, with a daunting array of multiple references for each position of the hands, each libation, each recited verse. An example chosen almost at random from the introduction to a text edition will demonstrate how quickly the non-initiate can become lost:

> The Kāṇvas and the Baudhāyanīyas again agree in prescribing that the moistening of the left whisker during the apsudīkṣā should take place *yajuṣā* or *tūṣṇīm*.[4]

But this situation is not beyond remedy: it is possible for the specialist to make the richness of these texts available to those outside the narrow Vedic circle, and now, especially, in the current scholarly climate of keen interest in the general relations between myth and ritual,[5] there is a strong incentive to do so. I hope that this work will make a small contribution in this direction, alongside those of others who work or have worked in this area.

This book does not purport to be a comprehensive work on Vedic mythology and its place in the ritual. Though an up-to-date treatment of these topics is badly needed, it is probably premature to hope for one now. Nor does it approach the topic with the elaborate theoretical apparatus of any of the prevailing modern schools of mythology or religion. I have sought neither abstract structures nor extra-Indic thematic parallels. What I have tried to do, instead, is to treat the myths exactly as they are presented to us—not detaching them from their ritual context or surpressing their ritualistic references, not paraphrasing the language in which they are related. (Nonetheless, one cannot proceed without some methodological biases; I discuss mine below.)

It would be the work of a lifetime to demonstrate the interrelations of myth and ritual in the whole Vedic corpus. Fortunately, more restricted case studies can confront us with many of the fundamental issues in Vedic religion and mythology, and connect us directly with the web of other myths and other rituals that makes the seemingly chaotic jumble of Vedic texts a harmonious whole. Accordingly, I devote the greater part of this work to two complementary case stud-

[3]E.g., Hillebrandt 1897.

[4]Caland 1926, Intro, p. 97.

[5]Among the many who work in this field, I will only mention, for the domain of Classical Greece, W. Burkert, M. Detienne, J.-P. Vernant, and G. Nagy, but this is meant just as the beginning of a long and honorable list.

ies, focussing on two separate myths attested in various versions in both poetry and prose. I hope to have produced in this way a work of use and interest also to specialists in Vedic religion, by elucidating some ill-studied and ill-understood myths found in fragments scattered throughout Vedic literature: their narrative structure, their place and function in the ritual. Both studies directly address the interrelations between myth and ritual in these texts, for to me it becomes clearer and clearer that neither strand is intelligible without the other. Vedic mythology and ritual are interpenetrated and ultimately inseparable, though it is possible to focus on one or the other for a certain time.

Yet it is remarkable how often, even in Indological circles, the study of myth and the study of ritual have proceeded in almost complete independence, even to the present day. Sometimes this separation is accompanied by a perfunctory nod to the importance of the other strand. Quite as often, it seems, the separation is a matter of principle: the relations between myth and ritual that are so inescapable in the texts are considered too cozy to be legitimate. They are held to be secondary and artificial, each strand tainting the pure tradition of the other. It is still all too possible to extract the myth from the ritual, or the ritual from the myth—to treat ritual as an arid mechanism contaminating the fresh, ingenuous imagination of myth, or myth as a childish interruption of the serious business of ritual.

This is not the place to detail the history of this disagreement[6] or to contribute polemics of my own; it will be enough if I can demonstrate that studying the two strands in conjunction illuminates aspects of each that would otherwise remain in darkness. Thus the peculiar fitness of

[6]As recent representatives of the "isolationist" position, for the strict separation of myth and ritual, one might cite F. Staal for ritual (e.g., 1979, boldly entitled "The Meaninglessness of Ritual") and W. D. O'Flaherty for myth/folklore (e.g., 1985, esp. pp. 12ff. [taking up Oertel 1899]).

There are, on the other hand, many exceptions to this isolationist tendency, many scholars who allow the evidence of myth to color their interpretation of ritual or vice versa. Among older scholars we can pick out, for example, S. Lévi and M. Bloomfield; among more recent ones, F. B. J. Kuiper, J. C. Heesterman, H.-P. Schmidt, U. Schneider, H. Falk. (This is by no means meant as an exhaustive list.) Even among scholars with "integrationist" tendencies, there are great differences—in how they view the interrelations between myth and ritual and between different chronological strata of Vedic texts, in which methods they consider appropriate and which illegitimate for approaching the data, in what preconceived structures (if any) they attempt to fit the Vedic evidence, in how much reliance they have on allied disciplines such as anthropology, sociology, historical linguistics and philology, comparative religion. Particular similarities and differences between my approach and the approaches of various of these scholars will become clearer in the detailed treatments that follow.

restricted case studies rather than a general survey: this will allow us to try to *demonstrate,* extensively and repeatedly, the interpenetration of myth and ritual, rather than simply *asserting* it and thereby merely adding another layer of acrimony to this long-term debate.

But first, in order to make this book of utility and accessibility to the non-Vedicist, I will devote the next several sections to a brief introduction to Vedic literature and religion.

What follows is intended to be a straightforward, unadorned, and (if this is possible) noncontroversial introduction to Vedic literature and religion. It provides, for those with little or no familiarity with Vedic India, some general orientation in the texts, the gods, and the religious practices of this period. It is not intended for specialists, who will find nothing new here; I trust that these Vedic adepts will forgive the inevitable glossing over of difficult and debated issues in the interests of brevity and clarity. I will also dispense here for the most part with references to the secondary literature on each point. Most of the information is distilled from the standard general treatments,[7] the introductions and textual comments of translators and editors of the various texts, monographs and articles on more specific issues (such as particular rituals, particular divinities), as well as the floating body of lore and opinion that any student of Vedic partakes of from teachers and colleagues—in my case, my views have been particularly shaped by my teacher, Stanley Insler, as well as, more recently, by my colleague, Michael Witzel. The principal source of information is, of course, the primary texts themselves.

A. "Vedic"

We must first roughly define the term *Vedic.* Vedic India is the first India we know, at least verbally, and indeed to a great extent it is its language that demarks what is Vedic. Vedic or Vedic Sanskrit is a language markedly more archaic than either Epic Sanskrit, the language of the two epics, the Mahābhārata and the Rāmāyaṇa, or the very similar later Classical Sanskrit, the learned language whose norms were established by the great grammarian Pāṇini (c. 500 B.C.). Vedic

[7]Such as Hillebrandt 1897; Oldenberg 1917; Keith 1925; Renou 1954.

was also still a living language: unlike Classical Sanskrit, whose grammar has been artificially fixed for the last twenty-five hundred years, Vedic Sanskrit continued to change and develop. The language of our earliest Vedic text is quite different from that of the latest ones; indeed, late Vedic looks very much like what became grammatically codified as Classical Sanskrit.

It is not merely the language that defines Vedic but also its culture. Given the nature of our evidence, what we primarily know about this culture is its religion. Political, social, economic, and quotidian matters we know in general only as they were filtered through a religious lens, but "religion" here is to be broadly defined. It profoundly affected most areas of what might today be considered secular life, and we are therefore luckily in possession of much incidental information in these areas.

The religion is in essence a highly developed ritualism, with a particularly remarkable respect for the power of the word. It is closely related both in its general outlines and in many striking particulars to ancient Iranian religion, as we know it from texts in the oldest Iranian language, Avestan. Like the Vedic language, Vedic religion changed in the course of the period, primarily in two seemingly contradictory directions, both contained within essentially the same community: on the one hand, toward increasing elaboration of the rituals; on the other, toward a more mystical, less physical, interpretation of them, leading to the speculations of the Upaniṣads, which close the Vedic period. But the roots of both changes can be seen in the earliest texts, and there is a strong continuity of tradition.

Both language and religion must belong to people. The people in this case were the speakers of an Indo-European language, who penetrated into India probably in the second millennium B.C., appearing first in northwest India, in the Punjab, but slowly spreading south and east. These people are often referred to in Indological literature as "Aryans," from the Sanskrit self-designation ā́rya-. This word identifies collectively the members of the three major divisions of society, a social organization most likely inherited from Indo-European models, and distinguishes them from members of indigenous social systems. The term has none of the perverted racial overtones found in its modern usage outside Indology. It is simply a sociocultural label, and will be so used in this work.

By language as well as religion, these people were most closely related to the Iranians.[8] Sanskrit and its descendant languages form with the Iranian languages (Old Iranian—Avestan, Old Persian—and the medieval and modern Iranian languages) the important Indo-European subgroup known as Indo-Iranian.

As with much of the rest of pre-Mogul Indian history, putting firm dates to the Vedic period is a difficult and risky matter, and many absurdities have been committed in this enterprise. We may suggest, with some trepidation, that the Vedic period lasted roughly a thousand years, from about 1500 B.C. to about 500 B.C.,[9] but any such pronouncement should be taken as tentative and approximate. In studying Vedic India, it is well to keep in mind Witzel's statement: "Even after some 150 years of studying the texts, a dark mist still covers the whole Vedic period, which makes it very difficult to make out who did what, where, and at what time."[10] The only material we can rely on is the texts.

B. The Texts

All of Vedic literature was entirely oral, and what has survived is entirely (or almost entirely) religious in character. Let us briefly examine each point in turn.

Both the composition and the transmission of all the vast body of Vedic literature were oral throughout the Vedic period, and for a considerable time afterward. Writing was not known or (later) was disregarded. Obviously, this circumstance deeply affected the form of the texts;[11] it also has important social implications. To begin with the latter, the preservation of the texts depended on a disciplined and diligent transmission by memory across many generations. This was ac-

[8]Indeed the word *Iran* is ultimately derived from a cognate of Sanskrit ā́rya- just discussed. Cf. Middle Persian ērān(šahr), along with earlier Avestan airiia-, Old Persian ariya-. For further discussion, see Mayrhofer, *EWA*, sub ā́rya-.

[9]For recent and illuminating discussion of the localization of the Vedic people(s) at various points in their history and on their dating, also with reference to archeological findings, see Witzel 1987 and 1989.

[10]Witzel 1989, p. 102.

[11]Here and in what follows I use certain terms that may evoke in the reader's mind a written rather than oral tradition—terms like *text, canon, recension*. It should be borne in mind that such terms, with minor adjustment, are also appropriate to oral transmission and fixation.

complished through the various theological schools, which developed ingenious methods for memorizing and passing on texts with little or no alteration, even when their language was no longer entirely understood. It also meant that texts that were not adopted into the canon of one or another of these schools had little chance of surviving, at least in the linguistic form in which they were first composed.

What about their form? To those whose sense of oral literature has been shaped by the generous measures of Homeric epic, Vedic literature may look somewhat alien. Though much of it is in verse, it is poetry of a different stripe from epic—condensed, elliptical, grammatically scrambled. The language is formulaic in the broad sense, but it makes surprisingly little use of metrically fixed and verbally frozen formulae in the strict sense. On the other hand, it seems likely that, rather than undergoing continual recreation in performance, the form of each separate poem was fixed relatively early, in some instances at the time of first composition, and then passed on without variation, even during the early Vedic period, when oral hymnal composition was still a living practice.[12]

There is also a vast body of prose, much of it expository. This was a bit more flexibly transmitted than the poetry, but the remarkable agreements in wording across theological schools indicate that much of this prose was transmitted with little variation allowed from very early times.

That all (or almost all) of preserved Vedic literature concerns religion is somewhat predictable given that its transmission was in the hands of the theological schools. Needless to say, we cannot infer that there was no secular literature, merely that it did not survive or not in a form recognizably Vedic.

This religious literature is, more specifically, *ritual* literature. We can divide this ritual literature into two major types. The first consists of words to be used in the performance of the ritual, that is, liturgical material *internal* to the ritual.[13] Almost all of the verse and some of the prose fit into this category. The second type consists of material about the ritual, *external* to its performance, commentary in the broadest sense. This is almost entirely in prose, though in various different types of often mannered prose, depending on the type of commentary.

[12]On this sort of fixed oral transmission, see, e.g., Nagy 1990, pp. 40–42.

[13]Here and in what follows I use the term *liturgy* to refer to the fixed verbal portion of a ritual performance.

Vedic literature has traditionally been catalogued into Vedas, Brāhmaṇas, Āraṇyakas (and Upaniṣads), and Sūtras, in roughly that chronological order. This is a useful, more or less accurate, but not adequate categorization. We must first distinguish text *types,* that is, styles and contents appropriate to these labels, and only then the individual texts, since the individual texts may mix text types, or their traditional names may misrepresent what sort of text type they are.

The *veda-* (or *mantra-*) text type consists of collections of liturgical material used in the performance of rituals.

The *brāhmaṇa*-text type consists of ritual exegesis, in relatively straightforward prose. These commentaries do not, except incidentally, tell us what happens in the ritual. Rather, they presuppose knowledge of the ritual and comment on the reasons for, significance of, and good or bad outcome from, ritual activity and speech, or they dispute about the exactly proper manner of performing some ritual activity. The commentary ranges far afield; the justification or explanation for a ritual action may be, for example, practical, etymological, cosmic, or mythic—or each in turn.

The *āraṇyaka*-text type develops the cosmic side of brāhmaṇa explanations into esoteric speculation about some of the more cryptic of the rituals. In certain ways, the āraṇyaka-text type seems like a lopsided brāhmaṇa with a mystic bent. The doctrines expounded in these texts were considered to be so powerful that it was dangerous to divulge them in inhabited places, hence the literal meaning of the term āraṇyaka, a text to be recited 'in the wilderness, away from habitation', "Forest Book."

The *sūtra*-text type is a departure from this development, both in style and in content. Its style differs from the generally simple and serviceable prose of the brāhmaṇa-text type in that it is more condensed, elliptical, and syntactically inflexible. Its contents are, in contrast, the most straightforward of the text types. The ritual (or Śrauta) Sūtras give minutely detailed descriptions of rituals, with little or no comment. These are, as it were, rule books, manuals of procedure. Thus it is only at the end of the Vedic period that we get a full, extensive notion of what actually goes on in a ritual, as opposed to what the mantras (liturgical utterances) hinted at or the commentators chose to focus on. Some of the consequences of this situation for the study of Vedic ritual we will examine below.

The text types provide a genre-based classification of Vedic texts, whose rough chronology is veda/mantra, brāhmaṇa, āraṇyaka, sūtra.

It is not only chronology that sets off the first three types from the last, but also their supposed origins. The first three types of text are considered, at least in the later tradition, to be "revealed," divinely inspired: the technical term is *śruti* 'hearing (from the gods)' (hence not composed by mortals). The seers whose names are attached to particular poems merely received them as messages from divine sources. In contrast, the fourth text type, the Sūtra, belongs to the division of knowledge known as *smṛti* 'remembrance', traditional lore that has mortal origins. Other smṛti texts include the ghṛya and dharma texts to be discussed below.

There is another important dimension in Vedic textual classification, that of the theological schools. Each of these schools, under whose control the texts were transmitted, began as a set of adherents to *a* particular Veda and became further splintered as time went on. Besides preserving this text, the school (or Śākhā, lit. 'branch') produced in the course of time a set of associated exegetical texts proper to that Veda. Thus, a particular Brāhmaṇa or Sūtra is not a general work on general Vedic ritual but a work belonging to a particular Veda and a particular theological school. Each Veda can (and usually does) spawn more than one school. Thus we get a vertical configuration schematically of the following type:

VEDA A		VEDA B	
School (Śākhā) A1	*School A2*	*School B1*	etc.
Brāhmaṇa A1	Brāhmaṇa A2	Brāhmaṇa B1	
Āraṇyaka A1	Āraṇyaka A2	etc.	
Śrauta Sūtra A1	Śrauta Sūtra A2		

As must be clear, the central texts in this system are the Vedas.

1. *The Vedas*

There are four Vedas, the Rig Veda, the Sāma Veda, the Yajur Veda, and the Atharva Veda, but the texts are not exactly parallel and equal in age and importance.

The oldest and most important in Vedic ritualism (and in later Indian religion) is the *Rig Veda* (RV). This is a collection (Saṃhitā) of *ṛc*'s 'verses' forming hymns that are addressed primarily to various deities and that are recited during ritual. They were composed in a variety of meters and by a variety of bards or bardic families over a period of several hundred years, at the very least, given the development in language and the evidence of tradition and variation in compositional practice. The Rig Veda is divided into ten books or Maṇḍalas. Maṇḍalas II–VII constitute the so-called Family Books, since each is attributed to a different bardic family. This is the core of the oldest Rig Veda. Maṇḍala VIII has various smaller family collections. All of the aforementioned books contain hymns addressed to a variety of gods, especially Agni and Indra. By contrast, Maṇḍala IX consists of hymns, presumably extracted from the rest of the collection, addressed solely to the god Soma Pavamāna, the deified intoxicating drink of the important soma sacrifice. Books I and X contain smaller collections, as in VIII, and also some miscellaneous appended material. Book X, especially, has a number of linguistically "late" or "popular" hymns, some with apparently secular character. When, where, and in how many stages the collection of the Rig Veda (as opposed to the composition of the individual hymns) was made and fixed is a difficult question.[14]

The standard translation of the Rig Veda is that of Geldner (into German);[15] there is also a substantially complete translation into French by Renou.[16] Unfortunately there exists no complete modern translation into English, though W. D. O'Flaherty has recently translated a portion of the hymns.[17]

The *Sāma Veda* (SV) is the collection of *sāmans* or 'chants,' also to be performed in the course of the ritual. The sāmans themselves are tunes, melodies to which a variety of different verses can be sung. The texts of the sung verses, that is, the verbal part of the Sāma Veda, are almost entirely extracted from the Rig Veda, though in performance they were modified and adapted in somewhat florid, almost operatic ways to the chanting mode. Because almost all of the Sāma Veda material is repeated from the Rig Veda, it is of little interest to us here, but the subsequent literature of the Sāma Veda schools is of considerable importance, particularly their Brāhmaṇas, as we will see.

[14]On these questions one can consult, among other works, Oldenberg 1888 and Renou 1947.

[15]Geldner 1951.

[16]Renou 1955–69, in the series *Études védiques et pāṇinéennes* (Renou, *ÉVP*).

[17]O'Flaherty 1981.

The *Yajur Veda* (YV) collects the third form of sacral utterance in the ritual beside the ṛc and sāman, namely, the *yajus*. This is a short prose formula used of the ritual ministrant, the objects being manipulated in the ritual, or the offerings being made. Unlike the recitation of ṛc's and the chanting of sāmans, which function, as it were, as separate verbal performances embedded in, but distinct from, ritual activity, the yajus is tied to this realm of activity and almost incidental to it. In fact it is the priest in charge of this activity, the Adhvaryu, who ordinarily pronounces the yajus. The form of the Yajur Veda is somewhat complex, and we will defer discussion of it for a short while.

The *Atharva Veda* (AV) stands a little apart from the other three Vedas. Though we can, I think, reasonably call it a ritual text under the characterization of ritual given in n. 1, it is not generally concerned with the great, solemn, śrauta rituals on which the other three Vedas converge. Instead, it is a collection of hymns in great part devoted to magical (black and white) and healing rites, affording to some degree a homely and practical view of Vedic society almost impossible to glimpse in the other texts of high culture.

There are two extant recensions of this Veda, differing from each other not only in arrangement but in phraseology and in materials included. Currently the more usable recension is that ordinarily known as the Śaunaka recension (AVŚ). A complete English translation of this text by W. D. Whitney exists,[18] and a partial translation by M. Bloomfield[19] remains valuable. The other, the Paippalāda recension (AVP), was until recently known only in a very corrupt and almost unusable manuscript from Kashmir. The discovery of a much better version preserved in Orissa will now allow the Paippalāda version to take its proper place in the Vedic canon. The editing and publication of the AVP based on both versions is a very eagerly awaited event in Vedic studies.

The language of the Atharva Veda and of the mantra material of the Yajur Veda is linguistically the oldest Vedic we have, after the Rig Veda.

2. *The Yajur Veda and the Brāhmaṇas*

In the Yajur Veda we meet the circumstance in which the distinction between veda-text type and Veda becomes important, for the material

[18] Whitney 1905.
[19] Bloomfield 1897.

found in the Yajur Veda is not entirely veda-text type but is also in part brāhmaṇa-text type. Moreover, it is somewhat misleading to call it *a* Veda: it appears more like a mini Veda industry.

The Yajur Veda is divided into two branches: the *Black (Kṛṣṇa) Yajur Veda* (BYV) and the *White (Śukla) Yajur Veda* (WYV). The Black Yajur Veda is a blend: interspersed with the collections of yajus's for which the Veda is named are lengthy passages of expository prose of brāhmaṇa-text type. In other words, the Black Yajur *Veda* contains its own *Brāhmaṇa*. The White Yajur Veda, in contrast, looks like a proper Veda, since it contains only mantras; its Brāhmaṇa is separate. Yet it is generally considered that this separation is secondary, that the mantras of the WYV were abstracted from a text that would have looked more like the BYV.

These two picturesque designations, Black and White, are ordinarily thought to refer to the arrangement of the texts: the White YV is perspicuous, hence White; the Black YV is mixed up, hence Black.

The Veda proper of the White Yajur Veda is generally known as the *Vājasaneyi Saṃhitā* (VS). It exists in two very similar recensions, the Mādhyaṃdina and the Kāṇva. There is a rather unsatisfactory English translation by Griffith.[20] Its Brāhmaṇa, one of the largest and most important of these texts, is the *Śatapatha Brāhmaṇa* (ŚB), the 'Brāhmaṇa of the Hundred Paths' (after the number of its 'lessons'). It also exists in two similar recensions, likewise called Mādhyaṃdina and Kāṇva (ŚBM and ŚBK). The one ordinarily referred to is the Mādhyaṃdina, edited by A. Weber and translated into English by Eggeling.[21] The Kāṇva[22] and the Mādhyaṃdina recensions are virtually identical in their later books (ŚBK VIII–XVI, ŚBM VI–XIV) and very similar in the earlier books. Nonetheless, their differences in wording can be illuminating. In the rest of this work, a passage identified only as ŚB will be from the Mādhyaṃdina recension, but I will occasionally contrast ŚBM and ŚBK versions or preferentially cite the ŚBK version when it provides a clearer picture than the ŚBM.

The Black YV is more complex. It exists in three major versions. These are quite similar to each other, but they are not close enough to be considered mere recensions, for their brāhmaṇa portions, especially, take independent and often opposing positions. The three are the *Taittirīya Saṃhitā* (TS), the *Maitrāyaṇī Saṃhitā* (MS), and the *Kāṭhaka*

[20]Griffith 1899.

[21]Eggeling 1882–1900 (in five volumes).

[22]Edited by Caland 1926a.

Saṃhitā (KS), the latter two often agreeing with each other against the TS. (There is also a fragmentarily and corruptly preserved fourth version, very close to the KS, known as the *Kapiṣṭhala Saṃhitā*.) Of the three major versions, only the TS has been translated (into English, by Keith), which is a pity, since the MS and the KS are often fuller and more archaic in appearance than the TS.[23] The prose of the brāhmaṇa portion of these texts is the oldest expository prose we have in Sanskrit, older than that of the texts specifically called Brāhmaṇas (for example, the Śatapatha Brāhmaṇa of the other branch, the White YV), and its exposition of the ritual and narration of myths is therefore of central importance for our understanding of Vedic religion.

Though the prose portions of the Taittirīya Saṃhitā serve as its primary Brāhmaṇa, there also exists a Taittirīya *Brāhmaṇa* (TB) with additional commentary (and mantras). It is unfortunately a late and inferior product. It has been partly translated (into English) in a series of articles by P.-E. Dumont.[24] Neither the Maitrāyaṇi Saṃhitā nor the Kāṭhaka Saṃhitā has a surviving separate text called a Brāhmaṇa.

There are two Brāhmaṇas of the Rig Veda, the *Aitareya Brāhmaṇa* (AB) and the *Kauṣītaki* (or *Śāṅkhāyana*) *Brāhmaṇa* (KB), of which the Aitareya is the older and the more extensive. Both have been translated into English by Keith.[25]

The major Brāhmaṇas of the Sāma Veda are the *Jaiminīya Brāhmaṇa* (JB) and the *Pañcaviṃśa Brāhmaṇa* (or *Tāndya Mahābrāhmaṇa*) (PB). The former is a voluminous, frequently corrupt, and very interesting text, whose riches remain difficult of access. Caland edited and translated significant portions of it (into German),[26] as did, to a lesser extent, Oertel in a series of articles.[27] A complete edition of the work did not appear until 1954,[28] but this edition has not solved all the many textual problems endemic to this Brāhmaṇa. Among more recent partial translations of this work is that of W. D. O'Flaherty,[29] which contains some of the narrative portions of the text (though most of her selections were

[23]The TS was edited by Weber, and both the MS and the KS by von Schroeder. The translation is Keith 1914.

[24]The articles date from 1948 to 1969 and appear primarily in *PAPS*, vols. 92–113.

[25]Keith 1920.

[26]Caland 1919.

[27]These articles appeared between 1897 and 1907, primarily in *JAOS*, under the title "Contributions from the Jaiminīya Brāhmaṇa to the History of the Brāhmaṇa Literature."

[28]Raghu Vira and Lokesh Chandra 1954.

[29]O'Flaherty 1985a.

already translated by Caland or Oertel). The Pañcaviṃśa Brāhmaṇa is a more accessible text (in the English translation by Caland),[30] but also unfortunately far less discursive and younger than the JB.

The AV has a very late and inferior, almost imitation Brāhmaṇa, the *Gopatha Brāhmaṇa* (GB).

Given the mythological and ritual focus of this work, the Āraṇyakas and the Upaniṣads will be of little relevance, and I accordingly omit particular discussion of them here.

3. *The Sūtras*

The ritual (Śrauta) Sūtras (ŚSs) are, however, of some importance, in particular those of the Yajur Veda, since these concern themselves with the physical activity of the ritual, for which we have no other evidence. There are a number of Śrauta Sūtras, testifying to a further splintering of the Vedic Śākhās. I will mention here only those that will be of special relevance later.

Not surprisingly, the Yajur Veda, particularly the Black YV (and of that, particularly the Taittirīya Saṃhitā) is especially well provided with Śrauta Sūtras. To the TS belong the relatively early *Baudhāyana Śrauta Sūtra* (BŚS),[31] the *Vādhūla ŚS*, and the later, but important *Āpastambha ŚS* (ĀpŚS)[32] with a number of other related ŚSs (Bhāradvāja, Hiranyakeśin, Vaikhānasa). To the Maitrāyaṇī Saṃhitā belong the *Mānava ŚS* (MŚS)[33] and the *Vārāha ŚS*. To the White YV (specifically ŚBM) belongs the *Kātyāyana ŚS*.

The Rig Veda has two Śrauta Sūtras, *Āśvalāyana ŚS* (to the Aitareya Brāhmaṇa) and *Śāṅkhāyana ŚS* (to the Kauṣītaki Brāhmaṇa).

The Śrauta Sūtras of the Jaiminīya Brāhmaṇa (Lāṭyāyana ŚS etc.) are less useful for our purposes.

As to the AV, in contrast to the unimportance of its Brāhmaṇa, its principal Sūtra, the *Kauśika Sūtra,* is a rich and fascinating sourcebook on magical practices.[34]

There are two final divisions of literature that should be mentioned here, the *Gṛhya Sūtras* (GSs) and the *Dharma Sūtras* (DSs). Though in the form we have them their language is not strictly Vedic, much of the

[30]Caland 1931.
[31]Not translated but easily usable in the edition of Caland 1904–13.
[32]Translated into German by Caland 1921–28.
[33]Edited and translated into English by van Gelder 1961–63.
[34]Edited by M. Bloomfield 1889 and partially translated in Caland 1900.

material contained in them and even much of their phraseology must be old.[35] The Gṛhya Sūtras treat the rites of the domestic cult, the private ritual behavior undertaken without the elaboration and expense of the great public śrauta rituals. Since almost every aspect of daily life, as well as every major and minor rite of passage, is governed by, or requires, a ritual action, the picture of domestic life in the Gṛhya Sūtras is a remarkably full one. The Dharma Sūtras concern the realm of customary law, broadly defined, and so afford us insights into social life and relations that neither the public nor the private ritual texts grant.

The Gṛhya and Dharma Sūtras belong, at least nominally, to many of the same schools that also produced the Śrauta Sūtras. Thus, for example, beside the Baudhāyana Śrauta Sūtra, there are also a Baudhāyana *Gṛhya* Sūtra (BGS) and a Baudhāyana *Dharma* Sūtra (BDS).

Following is a simplified schema of the principal Vedas and their schools:

	RIG VEDA		YAJUR VEDA			SĀMA VEDA		ATHARVA VEDA
VEDAS:			*White YV*	*Black YV*				
	RV		*VS*	*TS*	*MS*	*KS*	*SV*	*AV*
BRĀHMAṆAS:	AB	KB	ŚB	TB	—	JB	PB	[GB]
ŚRAUTA SŪTRAS:	Āśv	Śāṅkh	Kāty	Baudh Vādh Āp etc.	Mān Vār	Lāṭy etc.		Kauś

C. Vedic Ritual

Before we examine what characterizes Vedic religious practice, we should consider briefly what features it lacks. First and foremost is the complete absence of temples or other buildings permanently devoted

[35]For a detailed case of the latter, see Chap. 8, B.1–B.2, below.

to religious performances. This is not to say that a ritual can be performed anywhere, at any time. Rather, a sacrificial ground must be chosen and prepared by careful measurement and demarcation, with different portions within that ground devoted to different functions. Their shapes and the distances between them are minutely prescribed. There may also be temporary structures (such as the Sadas 'shed' necessary for certain rituals). But the fact remains that the site of worship is not permanently fixed, and there is no building to become the focus of its own cult associations or to be adorned and decorated.

Moreover, there is no evidence for icons or images representing gods or their attributes. There are, of course, physical objects used in the ritual, but these are of a practical and necessary sort: baskets, pots, cups, and so forth to contain and transport the substances to be offered, spoons and ladles for dipping out liquids, a spade for digging, a wooden sword for drawing lines on the ground, a post for tying up the animal victim, and similar objects. Though these are addressed and often propitiated in the course of ritual, they do not in general have an independent divine status. Moreover, they are ordinarily newly made for each ritual, of homely materials, so that they do not acquire the status of ancient and hallowed objects on which precious materials are lavished. Furthermore, given the absence of writing, there are, needless to say, no venerated physical representatives of holy scriptures.

In other words, Vedic religion is the ideally portable religion. The liturgy is in the heads of the practitioners; the implements are the same as, or similar to, those needed in everyday life; the service can be performed wherever a suitable piece of ground can be found. Though assembling the materials and men for some of the great rites described in the Śrauta Sūtras probably assumes a more settled population, it is not hard to see the roots of Vedic religious practice in the steady movement of its practitioners' perpetually advancing Indo-European ancestors.

The central physical focus of Vedic ritual is fire. We can see this focus evidenced in a variety of ways. First, the principal act of almost all Vedic rituals, that for which all the other actions and words are mobilized, the act which the ritual carefully prepares for and leads away from, is the offering of various edible or drinkable substances into the fire. On the one hand, the simplest ritual, to be performed twice daily in both the domestic and the solemn cult, is the offering of milk (and similar products) in the fire. This is called the *Agnihotra* or 'fire offering'. The fire (or fires) must be kept burning constantly. On the other hand, even the most elaborate of the śrauta rituals can be in some sense reduced to this—offering into the fire. The elaboration consists of complexity in the obtaining and preparation of the offering, in the preparation of the participants, in the praise of the god(s) for whom the offering is intended, and so on. The central act is still the same.

Fire—the number of fires—is the single technical criterion that distinguishes domestic (gr̥hya) and solemn (śrauta) rites. In gr̥hya rituals there is one fire, but śrauta rituals require three (even when the rituals are substantially the same in gr̥hya and śrauta versions, as in the daily Agnihotra). These three fires are called the *Gārhapatya* (householder's fire), the *Āhavanīya* (the fire 'to be offered into', which functions as its name implies), and the *Dakṣiṇāgni* (southern fire). In order to perform śrauta rites, one must "establish" these three fires through a special ritual knows as the *Agnyādheya* 'establishment of the fires'; one who has done this becomes an *Āhitāgni* (one 'having established fires') and is thereafter eligible to perform the śrauta rites. Because of the trouble and expense required to maintain the three fires and perform the more elaborate rituals, most people who were by birth entitled to have three fires would nonetheless presumably have contented themselves with one fire and the simpler gr̥hya observances. Technically, a man belonging to any of the three Aryan classes, brāhmaṇa, kṣatriya, and vaiśya, which together constitute the so-called twice born, was eligible, but surely only a fraction would have chosen to or could afford to.

The central importance of the fire(s) is also clear from the arrangement of the sacrificial ground in the śrauta rituals. The simplest form of this ground, and that which serves as basis and model for the other versions, contains essentially only the three fires. The Gārhapatya, which is round, and the Āhavanīya, which is square, are aligned on a west-east axis, with the Dakṣiṇāgni (half-moon shaped) to the south of the line (as its name implies) and closer to the Gārhapatya than to the Āhavanīya. (See figure 1.) Between the Āhavanīya and the Gārhapatya a space of roughly hourglass shape is shallowly dug out. This is called the *Vedi*, usually, if misleadingly, translated 'altar'. The Vedi is strewn with grass (this "strew" is called the *barhis*) for the gods to sit on. In practical terms, the implements and offerings are placed there ready for use.

The strew as comfortable seat for the visiting gods, as well as the central act of offering consumable substances in the fire, should make clear on what model the ritual is conceived, that of a formal meal given to a visiting dignitary. The gods are invited to attend. They travel to

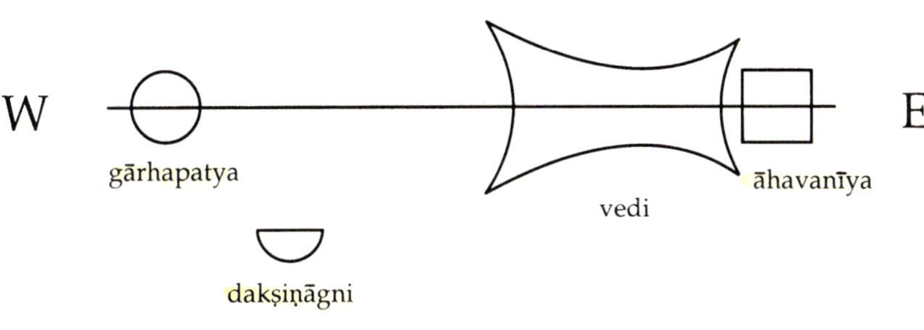

Figure 1. The Ritual Ground

the place of worship and sit in the place of honor. They are entertained by praise and song and offered food in the form of oblations: each offering in the fire is made to a particular god or set of gods, and they are urged to partake of it. They are entertained again and sent away with due formality. This delicately calibrated ceremony is meant to evoke from the honored divine guests generosity and benevolence, in the form of worldly goods, success, and protection from misfortune. There are of course other purposes for, and interpretations of, the ritual, often cosmic in scope—nothing so culturally central can have only one meaning. But in the actual form of the ritual, the concept of a good-humored social occasion with a mutually satisfactory exchange of benefits never seems far from the surface.

Who derives these benefits? Let us now look more closely at the mortal participants in the ritual. The person who derives *all* the spiritual benefit from the ritual (and the bad luck, if it goes wrong) is called the *Yajamāna*, often translated 'sacrificer' and literally a participle meaning 'worshipping on his own behalf'. These renderings are somewhat misleading, for it is important to keep in mind that the Yajamāna actually does very little in the ritual but pay for it. He is an Āhitāgni who hires the requisite number of priests to perform a particular ritual. The priests do almost all of the actual ritual work; the Yajamāna attends, along with his wife, and occasionally he (or she) is alloted a relatively minor task. In addition, for many rituals the Yajamāna must previously undergo an elaborate and sometimes arduous consecration (*Dīkṣā*), from which he is released at the conclusion of the rite.

The officiating priests derive none of the spiritual benefits from the worship they perform, but they can to some degree control how these benefits are allotted. If they feel hostility towards the Yajamāna for whom they are acting, they can perform certain actions in such a way as to make the Yajamāna "worse off," as the Brāhmaṇas frequently tell us. Furthermore, even tiny oversights or unavoidable accidents in the performance of the ritual, unintended by the priest, may drain the ritual of benefit to the Yajamāna and make him worse off. There are extensive lists of expiations (*Prāyaścitti*) to set right these mistakes and ensure the favorable outcome of the ritual.

Why does the Yajamāna undertake this expensive, inconvenient, and risky enterprise? In part simply to maintain the continued favor of the gods and generalized good fortune. But he may also have certain rituals performed for special desires (such as for sons or success in battle), and people of great importance, especially kings, may mount one of the especially elaborate ritual spectacles in order to consolidate, display, or extend their power.

What the priests get out of their ritual performance is simply wages or something very close to that notion. The Yajamāna "gives" to each participating priest a *Dakṣiṇā* or 'priestly gift'. What the Dakṣiṇā should be is usually prescribed by the ritual, though clearly some Yajamānas were more munificent than others. Most generally, Dakṣiṇās consist of livestock and/or gold, though cleverly appropriate Dakṣiṇās were designed for the more outré rituals.

Let us now examine the divisions of the priesthood, for most śrauta rituals require more than one priest. (A conspicuous exception is the daily Agnihotra, which needs only one, the Adhvaryu.) There is a bewildering array of priestly titles in Vedic literature, but most of them designate minor acolytes. Priests fall into four main groups, distributed according to the four Vedas, and each group has a leader, a chief representative. Most rituals require the cooperation of three or four of these groups, each performing the role assigned to it by its Veda. Thus, in having a ritual performed, the Yajamāna is assembling a disparate collection of professionals, engineering something of a social feat.

The Brahman[36] is the representative of the Atharva Veda (or sup-

[36]Brahman here is the name of a priest, not the nearly identical name of the highest Aryan class.

posed representative), for, as we saw above, the AV stands rather to one side of the system. In śrauta ritual the Brahman oversees the whole operation, mostly in silence, watching for slips and omissions and authorizing certain actions. He is not specialized in function, as the other priests are, and it is highly unlikely that he originally "belonged" to the Atharva Veda. Instead it is likely that this pairing was made secondarily, for symmetry and to provide a place for the Atharva Veda (and its adherents) in the śrauta ritual. This assignment probably reflects one of the major changes in the ritual between our earliest texts and those later ones in which ritual praxis is spelled out.

The other three groups of priests are divided among the Rig Veda, the Sāma Veda, and the Yajur Veda, and each is responsible for, and representative of, one of the three types of sacral utterance that together form the verbal sector of Vedic ritual. So far we have concentrated on what happens in a ritual, not what gets said, but verbal behavior is at least as important (and, I would say, more so) as physical activity. As we will see again and again below, a correctly made verbal formulation conveys extraordinary power on its formulator; a skillful, artful, and novel hymn particularly pleases the gods and makes them generous; "truth" keeps the cosmos functioning, and "untruth" disturbs its harmonies. The Vedic people profoundly did not believe that "sticks and stones may break my bones, but words can never hurt me": in most instances they would rather confront a cudgel than a curse. This aspect of Vedic (and Indo-European) society has been amply discussed and documented; it is now a commonplace of the field.

The chief priest representing the Rig Veda in śrauta ritual is the *Hotar,* who recites the *śastra,* a grouping of ṛc's extracted from the Rig Veda and arranged for a particular ritual purpose. Though it is clear that in the early Vedic period hymns were freely composed, perhaps for each new ritual occasion or for particularly important ones, sometimes probably as part of a poetic contest or competition, by the time of the ritual set down in the brāhmaṇa and sūtra texts, the verses appropriate for particular occasions had become fixed, with the Rig Veda a canonical scripture, not an expandable collection. The Hotar is thus a rote reciter, not a composer, of verses. He has various assistants, who may help him recite and who have other duties. They will not concern us here.

The Sāma Veda is represented by the *Udgātar,* who is responsible for singing the *stotra,* a group of ṛc's (most derived from the Rig Veda) set to sāman melodies and sung as a unit. The stotra often forms a larger verbal complex with the śastra of the Hotar. Like the Hotar, the Udgātar has assistants, whom we will pass over in silence.

The *Adhvaryu* is the chief priest of the Yajur Veda and is responsible for the third type of sacral utterance, the yajus, but in a sense uttering the yajus is the least of his duties, for the Adhvaryu (along with his assistants) is the performer of most ritual *actions*—the preparation of the ground, the implements, and the oblations, the offering of the oblations, and so on. Some of his assistants will be important below; I mention here only the *Pratiprasthātar,* a sort of duplicate Adhvaryu, who steps in when identical and nearly simultaneous actions are required at different parts of the ritual ground.

All three forms of sacral utterance are not employed in all śrauta ritual. The simpler rituals make do with r̥c and yajus, and, for their utterance, Hotar and Adhvaryu. It is only the soma sacrifices that require the operatic flourishes of the sāman and its performer, the Udgātar.

Rituals are often classified according to the identity of their most important offering. The offering of this chief oblation will generally occur at the exact center of the ritual, for Vedic rituals are bilaterally symmetrical, leading up to and away from the climactic moment. The simplest of the categories is *Haviryajña*s, with oblations of vegetable and dairy products; also technically considered Haviryajñas are animal sacrifices, but it is convenient to treat these separately. And finally *Somayajña*s, with oblations made with the intoxicating or inspiriting drink soma. These oblations are not mutually exclusive. Animal sacrifices also include offerings of the other Haviryajña classes, and the soma sacrifice has both offerings of that sort and animal sacrifices embedded in it.

Of the Haviryajña oblations, the dairy products include clarified butter (ghee), milk, various types of curds, and so on. Vegetative offerings include gruel and cakes made of various types of meal. In the animal sacrifice, the animal (usually a goat) or animals are dismembered after being killed, and various parts of the animal are cooked and offered, the first being usually the omentum.

Soma is the most highly prized of the oblations. As mentioned above, an entire Maṇḍala of the Rig Veda is devoted to extolling it. It was originally a drink, prepared from a plant (also called soma), with the power to produce both remarkable physical strength and poetic inspiration, or so the poets would have us believe. The procurement and preparation of soma for the ritual was an elaborate affair; particularly prominent events were pressing the soma, straining it through a sheep's fleece, and mixing it with milk. Descriptions of these events recur constantly in the Rig Veda, phrased with all the artistry and ingenuity that the poets could command. The use of this drink in this ceremony goes back to the Indo-Iranian period, since Avestan texts preserve accounts of similar rituals involving the etymologically cognate *haoma*. Unfortunately, the identity of this plant is unknown (though much debated); substitutes for it had to be employed already in the Vedic period.

As I have already implied several times, many of the basic actions and patterns of Vedic ritual are common to *all* the rituals or to large groups of them. In particular, certain rituals serve as the type or model of a group of variants, which differ from each other only in matters like the number and identity of the śastras and stotras or the divinities to which certain oblations are offered. Thus, in theory, the number of Vedic rituals is infinitely expandable: one can keep the fixed elements of the model and vary the optional ones without limit. Moreover, rituals can be nested or embedded in other rituals, building larger and increasingly intricate ritual structures. We have already noted, for example, that animal sacrifices form part of the soma sacrifice. The lengthy rituals are in great part assemblages of smaller, self-contained ritual units. The following selection of rituals gives some indication of the variety of Vedic ritual practice.

Many of the *Haviryajñas* are regular, relatively frequent observances determined by the rhythm of the year:

Agnihotra. The twice-daily (early morning and evening) offering into the fire.

Darśapūrṇamāsa. 'New (and) full moon' sacrifice. Offerings every two weeks of the lunar month on the day of the new and full moon. This ritual serves as the model for the class of rituals known as *Iṣṭis*.

Cāturmāsyāni. 'Four-monthly' sacrifices. These are the three seasonal sacrifices, celebrated every four months, as their name implies: *Vaiśvadeva* in the spring, *Varuṇapraghāsa* in the rainy season, *Sākamedha* in the autumn. Each has its peculiar characteristics, some appropriate to the season. The Varuṇapraghāsa will be of special interest to us below.

Āgrayaṇa. 'First fruits' sacrifice. Offered at harvest, before partaking of the crop.

There are numerous other Iṣṭis, created on the model of the Darśapūrṇamāsa, performed for particular desires. These are known collectively as *Kāmyā* Iṣṭi or 'wish offerings'.

Paśubandha. 'Animal sacrifice'. This is technically reckoned a Haviryajña, conforming to the pattern of the Darśapūrṇamāsa. But, as its chief oblation is an animal, which must be killed, this sacrifice introduces additional ritual machinery and participants. The ritual ground is enlarged (as it is in the soma sacrifice), and a post (Yūpa) is required to which the victim is tied. This post is cut and shaped with due ceremony. Most important, the inauspicious act of slaughter, bringing death in contact with the rest of ritual activity, must be delicately controlled, confined, and deprived of its bad consequences.

The model for soma sacrifices is the so-called *Agniṣṭoma*, a type of 'one day' (*Ekāha*) soma sacrifice. This designation is somewhat misleading, since all soma sacrifices are preceded by some days of preparation as well as by the consecration (Dīkṣā) of the Yajamāna. What the term means is that the soma is pressed and offered only on one day in a series of three pressings. The three pressings are characteristic of all soma sacrifices and are called the *Prātaḥsavana* (early-morning pressing), the *Mādhyaṃdinasavana* (midday pressing), and the *Tṛtīyasavana* (third [or evening] pressing).

There are a number of variants on the one-day soma sacrifices, as well as multiday types, some lasting up to a year, or indeed many years (at least theoretically). Sacrifices of twelve days or more are known as *Sattras* ("Sittings" or "Sessions").

A number of important and elaborate rituals incorporate soma sacrifices and conform to their model. I mention here only the *Rājasūya* (consecration of the king) and the *Aśvamedha* (horse sacrifice). The purpose of the former is to invest a newly crowned king with religious authority. The latter can be performed only by a king, to consolidate and increase his power. It is in essence an animal sacrifice (or set of animal sacrifices) with a horse as chief victim. But before the horse is slaughtered (with extensive ceremony), it is set free to roam at will for a year, with a large entourage to follow and protect it. One lurid feature of the sacrifice itself is the copulation of the chief queen with the dead horse, after it has been sacrificed.

A ritual that stands slightly apart from the system just outlined is the *Agnicayana* (piling of the fire altar). Rather than using the ordinary ritual ground, soma sacrifices can employ a raised fire altar of bricks, the construction of which is the object of another extremely elaborate rite. The bricks are of various shapes and designations, and are piled in intricate patterns accompanied by the usual complex of actions and utterances. This ritual has given rise to an especially large amount of esoteric speculation in later texts.

A question we must briefly raise here is to what extent this entire elaborate system was in place from the earliest period and how much was manufactured in the Brāhmaṇa or even the Sūtra period. This is a question without a satisfactory answer (at least so far), because of the nature of our evidence—that we get complete descriptions of rituals only at the end of the period (in the Sūtras), while our earliest evidence, the Rig Veda, is ritual-internal and indeed represents only one of the strands of ritual performance, namely, verbal recitation. Clearly we cannot use arguments from silence: that a detail is not mentioned in the Rig Veda does not mean it was unknown in that period.

What is also clear is that many of the technical terms of later practice appear already in the RV, for example, names of priests, of rites, of offerings, of the three pressings, of types of verbal performance, and that, for instance, an entire hymn is devoted to an ordered account of the Aśvamedha. We are therefore entitled to assume that much of the ritual structure, in some form, was in place, at least in the late RV period, often in considerable detail. What we cannot know is how much detail was already present, how frozen in form it was, whether the technical terms mean the same thing as they do later, and what restructuring may have occurred, especially in the roles of the priests, as freely composed poetry gave way to rote recitation. At the very least, it seems likely that the later (post-RV) ritual has become both more elaborate and less flexible than that mirrored so darkly in the text of the Rig Veda. Nonetheless, when Rigvedic verses can easily be interpreted in the light of later ritual procedure, I think we should not hesitate to do so.

It is important to note, however, a change or at least an evolution in attitude with regard to the power of the ritual: in Brāhmaṇic speculation the ritual comes to be more and more *the* compelling mechanism in the cosmos, to which even the gods are subject. The Brāhmaṇic universe (and quite possibly the universe of the Vedas) is intellectually structured as a set of homologies linking the divine or cosmic realm, the human realm, and the ritual realm. Participants and objects in the ritual stand for, embody, and indeed actually *become* participants and objects in the larger sphere of human life and in the cosmos, so that, for example, a golden ornament used in the ritual can represent both wealth and prosperity (in the human sphere) and the sun (in the cosmic sphere). Statements of these equivalences form a large part of Brāhmaṇic discourse.

Manipulation of participants and objects in the interior of the ritual ground can produce parallel effects on their equivalents in the larger realms. In other words, the performance of the ritual is a way of exerting control on the unruly human and natural forces in the universe by controlling their representatives within the restricted compass of the ritual ground. Microcosm controls macrocosm. Because of the power of the ritual to effect this control, it becomes an independent and ultimately transcendent force, almost another, separate *actor* akin to the gods. The figure of Prajāpati, whom we will discuss below, in part embodies this power of the sacrifice.

D. Vedic Mythology

This brief account of Vedic mythology, that is, of the principal deities and their principal characteristics and exploits, is again not meant as an exhaustive catalogue, much less as a comprehensive treatment of this vast and much-discussed subject. I will also refrain, as far as possible, from discussing the "meaning" or "symbolism" of particular myths and divinities. I want merely to provide something akin to the list of dramatis personae at the beginning of a play, before we plunge into the particular dramas we are going to examine in the rest of this work.

What we know about Vedic mythology is very much controlled, indeed severely limited, by the nature of our evidence. As in the case of the ritual, the very great distinction in *types* of texts from different periods makes it difficult to know whether the variation in treatment of a god or a story results from real change and development over time or simply from a different viewpoint, the different shaping each type of text gives its subject matter. As with the ritual, I think there are enough broad-based similarities in mythological treatment across the different text types to allow us, with due caution, to interpret details from the Vedas in light of Brāhmaṇic evidence (and vice versa). There are, however, some instances where we must reckon with extensive underlying differences (e.g., in the conflict of the Devas and the Asuras, described below).

For Vedic mythology our evidence comes essentially from the Vedas and the Brāhmaṇas (and to a far lesser extent the Āraṇyakas). The Sūtras, those no-nonsense technical handbooks, provide us with relatively little. The evidence of both veda and brāhmaṇa texts is quite extensive, but, not surprisingly, there are difficulties of interpretation. For one thing, in neither type of text do we ordinarily find a complete story. The myths were clearly too well known to require straight narrative retelling. In veda text, stories are only alluded to, often as elliptically and enigmatically as possible for artistic effect. Events may be chronologically scrambled, participants may be unnamed, and so on. The purpose of telling or alluding to a myth is to please and celebrate the gods involved. Since the gods presumably know their own exploits, they do not need and would not enjoy a flat-footed chronological account of the myth, but they do listen with a connoisseur's appreciation to a poet cleverly ringing changes on it.

In brāhmaṇa text, myths often have a more coherent *appearance,* but, I fear, this coherence is usually illusory. The stories may seem to have a chronological narrative line, but they often begin in the middle and stop abruptly, somewhere short of the end. They are often interrupted by long passages of ritual exegesis and then picked up without warning. In other words, they are mythological fragments, and they cannot be used as raw data without evaluation and interpretation anymore than the veda tales can. Myths are almost always told in brāhmaṇic text to explain a ritual or some part of one; therefore, what is focussed on may not be determined by purely narrative considerations.

Before proceeding to a directory of divinities, I should say a word about one prominent approach to Vedic mythology, which has a number of adherents, namely, "trifunctionalism." For many decades Vedic mythology has furnished much of the evidence for a "trifunctional" analysis of Indo-European ideology, an analysis associated especially with Georges Dumézil. In brief, this theory sees all aspects of the culture of the Indo-Europeans (and its daughter cultures) as reflecting a social and ideological division into three major classes or "functions": priest (first function), warrior (second function), and, roughly, agriculturist (third function). This division matches neatly the division of Aryan society in India into brāhmaṇa, kṣatriya (or rājanya), and vaiśya. In terms of mythology, most gods will be associated primarily with one function, and mythological events will represent aspects of the function(s) of their participants, for example, strained or harmonious relations between functions.

This approach has yielded a number of important insights into Vedic religion; indeed sometimes the Vedic material itself imposes a trifunctional interpretation.[37] But trifunctional analyses can also be overly schematic; often other aspects of a god or a tale are more prominent and lead to more interesting interpretations. Though my approach makes relatively little use of the trifunctional model, I hope my work will be seen as complementary, not contradictory, to the trifunctional view.

I present first the three gods to whom the majority of Rigvedic hymns are addressed, then an assortment of other gods, in rough (and subjectively determined) order of prominence. The list is otherwise unordered and mixes what we might term "ritual" gods with gods of action, gods of the ethical and conceptual sphere, and gods representing natural phenomena. There is no organized and hierarchical pantheon in Vedic mythology, and no overarching organizing principle. I would like to emphasize particularly this last point, for the search for, and insistence on, such a principle skewed much of the nineteenth- and early twentieth-century work on Vedic mythology, and makes many of the standard treatments from that period works only to be used with a cautious awareness of this bias.[38] Their principle was that of nature mythology: that every god must represent a natural phenomenon or force. It is undeniable that certain Vedic gods do so, as their transparent names indicate, but other gods had to be forced into this system, with unfortunate results, including a set of "solar" deities who have about as many solar characteristics as I do. Much of the work in Vedic mythology in the last fifty years or so has been devoted to providing alternate interpretations for gods who do not easily fit the nature-mythology paradigm.

The name of the god *Agni* is identical with the common noun agni- 'fire', and there is little about this god that is not interpretable in the framework of deified Fire. This includes fire in all its aspects, including the destructive and uncontrollable, but the god Agni is viewed primarily as the ritual fire. As a god, Agni is viewed as the eater of oblations and as the mediator between the human realm on earth and the divine realm in heaven. Agni both carries the consumed oblations to heaven with his smoke and conveys the other gods to the actual place

[37]For an example, see Chap. 4, B, below.
[38]Such as Macdonell 1897; Keith 1925; and Hillebrandt 1927–29.

of worship. A particularly interesting narrative-myth about Agni concerns his flight and concealment, from fear of the dangerous job of conveying the oblations. He is ultimately found and coaxed to return. Agni also has a number of important epithets, emphasizing various aspects of his personality or activities.

Indra is without doubt and by far the most vividly realized god in the Vedic pantheon. He is the embodiment of the powerful Aryan warrior, and his main activity is smashing with his cudgel (*vajra*) foes, obstacles, and resistances to the relentless progress of the warriors he champions. He often derives strength for these conflicts by drinking soma. The most famous and endlessly retold episode is Indra's defeat of *Vṛtra* (Obstacle), who is conceived of as a snake surrounding and confining the vital waters, which Indra's deed releases. Another very well-known story is his opening of the cave of *Vala* to free a herd of stolen cows hidden there. There are numerous other less-famous opponents, and an assortment of other cosmogonic activities. He is sometimes aided by other gods, for example, the Maruts. The number of stories about Indra, notwithstanding a certain monotony of bashing and smashing in the narrative line, really qualify as an Indra cycle. One myth from this cycle forms the basis for our first case study.

Soma is a god especially dependent on the ritual. He represents the deified soma drink, the major oblation in the elaborate soma rituals, as well as the plant from which it is made. The many hymns in his honor primarily describe the preparation of this drink, with Soma portrayed as a swift steed or other animate being. An important myth about Soma concerns the stealing of Soma from heaven.

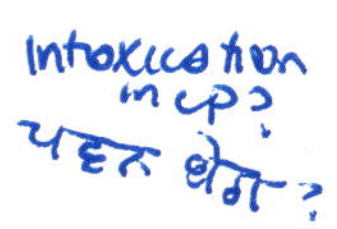

Three complementary gods form the core of a group of divinities called the *Ādityas* or 'Sons of *Aditi*', a goddess whose primary deed was giving birth to those gods.[39] They both embody and oversee the various types of relationships that bind men in society.

The most prominent of the three is *Varuṇa,* a stern but just king figure, who guards commandments, that is, the responsibilities imposed on an inferior by a superior. Varuṇa is also closely associated with *ṛta-* 'truth'.

Mitra is Varuṇa's almost inseparable partner; indeed Mitra is barely to be found without Varuṇa. Mitra is the embodiment of the common noun mitra- 'contract' or, better, 'alliance', that is, relationships of mutual responsibility.

[39]On this myth, see below, Chap. 7, C.2.

Mitra and Varuṇa have little dynamic mythology; few stories involve them as principal actors. But their status in the Rig Veda as ethical figures, as guardians of right and punishers of wrong, is very prominent. This is especially true of Varuṇa. No other god inspires the same moral awe, and some of the most powerful and affecting Rigvedic poetry is directed to Varuṇa. One notable feature of Mitra-Varuṇa mythology is their "spies": the sun and other heavenly bodies see all human actions and can report infractions to this pair.

Aryaman is a more shadowy figure than Mitra and Varuṇa, though frequently joined with them. He is the representative of custom, of the collective social traditions that characterize the Aryan community. As such he is prominent in, for example, the marriage ceremony.

Other gods are occasionally designated Ādityas, but these three constitute the defining nucleus of the group in early Vedic.[40]

The *Aśvins* are twin divinities whose speciality is healing and rescuing those in distress, and, as we will see, their good deeds also win them some desirable privileges. They are often portrayed as young and handsome.

The *Maruts* are likewise young, a group of spirited youths without individual identities. They often aid Indra in his martial exploits, and they seem the very model of a warrior band, arrayed for battle.

The only prominent goddess in the Vedic pantheon (besides Aditi) is the young and beautiful *Uṣas* 'Dawn', who inspired the Rigvedic poets to particularly appealing descriptive flights. Other deified natural phenomena in this sphere include *Sūrya* 'Sun' (who will form the subject of our second case study); *Dyaus* 'Heaven, Sky' (or Dyaus Pitar 'Father Sky') and his consort, *Pr̥thivī* 'Earth', who has complementary maternal characteristics; the *Āpas* 'Waters', an undifferentiated group of female divinities; *Vāyu* or *Vāta* 'Wind'; and *Parjanya* 'Thunder'.

Certain gods are merely deified roles or concepts, like *Savitar* 'Impeller'. Some of these, like *Tvaṣṭar* 'Fashioner', acquire a certain amount of personality. See the tale of Tvaṣṭar's son below.[41] But others, like *Bhaga* 'Portion', can scarcely be distinguished from the common nouns that name them.

A curious god is *Pūṣan,* who possesses a rather unattractive appearance but seems especially engaged in guarding and forwarding

[40]My treatment of the Ādityas, individually and collectively, depends crucially on J. P. Brereton 1981.

[41]Chap. 3, A.

many of the aspects of daily human life. His role in the marriage ceremony will be examined briefly in Part II.

The two great gods of later Hinduism, Viṣṇu and Śiva, do not have the same prominence in Vedic, though they certainly appear there (Śiva under his name Rudra, rather than his epithet, Śiva 'Kindly'). *Viṣṇu*'s principal exploit in Vedic is the 'Three Strides', which win and define the three worlds or realms of the gods. *Rudra* is primarily a fear-inspiring god, who needs frequent propitiation, but, as we will see, his violent propensities can be justly employed.

This brief catalogue gives some idea of the range and identities of the Vedic gods we will meet most frequently in the succeeding pages. The gods can also be referred to in groups. The texts often refer simply to the *Deva*s or gods—deva- is the ordinary, unmarked word for 'god'. Their collective totality can also be underlined by the term *Viśve Devās* 'all the gods' or the 'All Gods'. We have already noted one smaller group among the gods, the Ādityas; others include the *Vasu*s and the *R̥bhu*s.

As discussed above, we can often assume an underlying identity or strong similarity in veda and brāhmaṇa mythology, though much also has changed its focus and perhaps its nature in the later texts. Two major novelties in brāhmaṇa mythology should be noted here.

One is an extremely prominent mythic theme, comprehending a number of myths and myth fragments, namely, the relentless hostility between the Devas and their eternal and (almost) equal opponents, the Asuras, in a seemingly infinite number of episodes that all begin, 'The Devas and the Asuras were contending'. The Asuras, as the gods' enemies, are the mirror image of the gods, so that every divine characteristic and activity has its Asuric opposite. The Asuras are usually bested in each encounter, but the balanced conflict nonetheless persists endlessly. This perpetual war described so often in the brāhmaṇa texts is, surprisingly, not represented in the Rig Veda. Yet, disturbingly, the word asura- exists there, as an epithet meaning 'lord' and applied to a number of the Devas. This contradiction has always troubled Vedic studies; we will refer to it in Part II.

The other major novelty in the brāhmaṇa texts is the emergence of a new divine figure, *Prajāpati* 'Lord of Creatures', who is the ultimate creator of everything, though he otherwise lacks much personal definition. The word prajāpati is occasionally an epithet of gods in the Rig Veda, and he begins to emerge as a distinct figure in the late Rig Veda.

Afterwards he comes to represent a rather abstract divinity embodying the concept of the ritual. But, as we will see in Part II, he can appropriate for himself mythic material once belonging to other, more individually realized gods.

Besides these thoroughly divine figures, there are a number of semi-divine personages and families. Most common are the legendary, originally mortal originators or early practitioners of Vedic religion: priestly families like the *Bhr̥gus,* whom we will encounter in Part I, or 'seers' (*r̥ṣis*) like *Atri,* who is a principal actor in our second case study. The most important of these seers form a group called the *Saptarṣi* or 'Seven Seers'.

E. The Case Studies

The two case studies are of what we might term "minor" myths, but they are minor *only* in the amount of space they occupy in the Vedic corpus. Though each is told a number of times, in a number of texts, neither has anything like the prominence of the familiar warhorses of Vedic mythology, such as Indra's slaying of Vr̥tra. But these myths are not minor in their concerns. Starkly and in narrow compass, they grapple with many of the most fundamental issues for Vedic people (or any people, for that matter): birth, successful or not; death, often violent; sexuality, also often violent; family relations, often hostile; offenses against the moral order and retribution for them; the loss and restoration of power; the paradox that good and desirable things often come from bad and blameworthy actions; not to mention the origin and maintenance of the sacrifice and of the cosmos and the puzzles posed by frightening, unpredictable, and uncontrollable cosmic events—a litany of "major" concerns that inform many other Vedic myths, whether they are commonly or rarely told.

The first study, 'Indra fed the Yatis to the hyenas', concerns an ill-understood myth, rarely treated in Western secondary literature—or rather a set of fragments of a myth, preserved in some eight short passages in two brāhmaṇic traditions, and possibly in a few glancing references in the hymns. It is a curious story: Indra, the great hero, the warrior god of ancient India, feeds a group of his devotees, the Yatis, to a group of wild beasts, the Sālāvr̥kas, probably hyenas. The Yatis appear to be priests, and they seem to have been slain while performing a ritual. About the Yatis and the Sālāvr̥kas very little else is known.

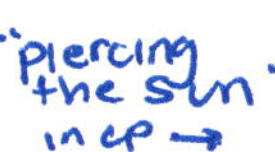

Indra, however, is perhaps the major figure of Vedic mythology, and this story raises questions about Indra's integrity—and piety—also raised elsewhere. The texts give us no direct answers. However, it is possible to reconstruct more of a coherent narrative for this event than the fragments at first glance seem to allow, and to approach an answer to the question: why did Indra so mistreat his friends?

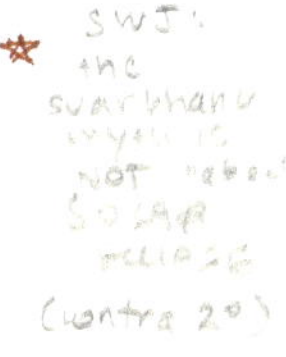

The second study, 'Svarbhānu pierced the sun with darkness', concerns a myth rather better attested than that of Indra and the Yatis. It is found in at least seven Brāhmaṇas, distributed among all four Vedas, and in addition there is a version in the Rig Veda that is far more discursive than the usual Rigvedic mythical allusions. Also in contrast to the Yati story, the Svarbhānu myth is well known and frequently treated in Western secondary literature, and has almost always been taken (indeed up to the present day) as a myth about the solar eclipse. The story is this: a supposed demon Svarbhānu wounds/pierces the sun with darkness, and it no longer shines. A priest named Atri and/or a god or gods remove the darkness and fix the sun in heaven again, accomplishing this by some sort of ritual means.

Both studies will be conducted in the same manner, using the same methods:

(*a*) First we must assemble and confront all the different versions or fragmentary versions and try to reconcile and combine the details each contributes, in order to construct a self-consistent and coherent story. This procedure involves in both cases beginning with the prose versions, as these are somewhat clearer and more discursive. But the more enigmatic evidence of the hymns crucially illuminates the narrative entity that emerges from comparison of the prose versions.

(*b*) At all times we must pay strict attention to the language in which the myth is told. Many apparently innocent and neutral phrases in Vedic have precise idiomatic uses that give clues to which activity is really involved. Moreover, these phrases can recur at crucial points in other myths and in the ritual, so that apparently unrelated myths or rituals will be linked by characteristic verbal echoes that underscore thematic parallels.

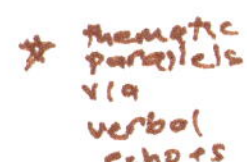

(*c*) At the same time we must pursue all the ritual connections of the myth. These include: (1) ritualistic details embedded in the narrative of the myth (these details are particularly striking in the first myth because the slaughter happens in the midst of a ritual, on the ritual ground), (2) the setting of the myth in the text as a whole (where, in what part[s] of what ritual[s] is the myth related?), (3) the justification of the myth in the text (what reason[s] are given for telling the myth at that point in the exegesis?).

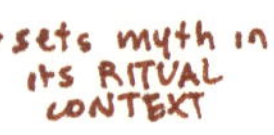

Thus, my approach here is to begin with a myth and set it in its ritual context; it would, however, be possible to proceed in the opposite direction, to focus on a ritual and examine the cluster of myths that support and illuminate it.

We must also set our chosen myths into the context of Vedic myth in general. Here I will make some brief observations about the structure of Vedic myth, both verbal and thematic.

The verbal form of a Vedic myth has some striking features, which are particularly clear in the myths told in prose. Most Vedic prose myths, no matter how many times they are told and in what disparate collection of texts, begin with an invariant or almost invariant first sentence. This first sentence formulaically encapsulates the myth, announces the most important action in it. The remainder of the myth is more fluid (though verbal agreements between versions are not rare); it selects (and perhaps embellishes) details from the story, whether chronologically earlier or later in the narrative than the first sentence. The details chosen are those most relevant to the ritual context at hand.

The first sentence will be identical for different Śākhās of the same Veda and for Brāhmaṇas belonging to different Vedas. In other words, not merely the narrative kernel of the story but the exact wording of it predates the Brāhmaṇa period. Indeed, in the case of the Svarbhānu myth, the Rigvedic version begins with a barely scrambled variant of the first sentence. Clearly the verbal form of this story goes all the way back to the Rigvedic period, and the syntactic relation between the prose and verse versions of the first sentence may suggest that the prose form is older.

We need no further evidence than this verbal inflexibility to demonstrate that investigating its language is crucial to understanding a myth, that its language *is* the myth, in some sense, not an accidental form that the myth has assumed and can as easily abandon.[42]

Although striking verbal agreements between versions may continue beyond the first sentence, there is often significant variation. Vedic myth has much the same type of structure as Vedic ritual. We noted above that a set or class of Vedic rituals are often systematically related

[42] We might frivolously put forth an example of this phenomenon from American children's literature: the banal morality tale "The Little Engine That Could" cannot be transformed into "The Small Able Engine," despite apparently identical semantics.

to each other: they share the same basic structure, the same fixed set of principal events arranged in a fixed order. But they differ from each other in certain optional elements: they may add additional events at certain, allowably open places in the proceedings, and there are other places in the ritual where a choice among different options may be made.

Different versions of a Vedic myth display this same type of structure. Within a basically fixed narrative structure, different versions include or omit certain optional episodes or details, or focus especially on one episode. They can also show systematic variation at particular points in their structure, reflecting a choice of various alternatives based on their appropriateness to the exegetical point. One of the places in myth most open to this systematic variation is what I will call the "ritual remedy," the mechanism that sets the story to rights. This remedy will often differ depending on what weapons are considered most effective in each separate tradition; for example, someone will often "see a sāman" in a Sāma Veda text at the point where in a Yajur Veda text he will offer an oblation. This sort of variation often leads investigators to conclude that myths found in the Brāhmaṇas have been utterly transformed and subordinated to sectarian concerns. When we examine these circumstances, however, we see that the opportunities for choice are really quite constrained.

Vedic myth parallels the structure of Vedic ritual in another important way. Just as certain larger ritual structures are assembled from smaller, self-contained rituals or parts of rituals, for example, the soma sacrifice incorporating animal sacrifices, there are certain thematic building blocks that function as episodes in a number of Vedic myths, with different gods filling the roles of the fundamental participants. A few of these thematic units are (*a*) a god or a substance or a quality goes away and "enters" something else, and must be removed and recovered for the world to continue; (*b*) two rival sets of beings run a race for some disputed stake; (*c*) a god is recruited to help in an enterprise; he demands a share, and is given one, in the ritual; then he helps.

Besides these narrative units in which the identity of the participants is less important than their roles and thematic relations, there is a small but very prominent group of mythic formulae in which the participants (or major participant) are fixed. I will call these "vehicle myths," and despite apparent identity of structure, they differ profoundly from the type of limited "minor" myth that forms the principal subject of this work. These myths, too, begin with an invariant first sentence, but this sentence announces a whole cycle, a succession of episodes of infinite or at least indefinite number. These more general myths or mythic cycles are applicable to a large set of ritual contexts, and the episode and details chosen vary accordingly. These more general mythic cycles can be seen as the controlling, vehicle myths both of the cosmos and of the ritual. Perhaps the three most important are (*a*) Prajāpati created the creatures; (*b*) the gods and the Asuras were in contention; (*c*) Indra slew ______ (Vṛtra, e.g.).

Because of their very prominence, they have attracted to themselves all manner of additional material—narrative incidents, ritual applications, linguistic flourishes. They are elastic and adaptable to any need; when an explanation is required for a ritual fact, a source for a hymn or a prayer, a home for an orphaned story fragment, they are pressed, indeed manipulated, into service. It is for this reason especially that I have chosen to concentrate on less common and more restricted myths, for they are more likely to be free of such accretions.

I approach this material with some general assumptions and principles about mythology and ritual, which it is as well to state at the outset. I see these principles as discovery procedures—much as the assumption of regular sound change is a discovery procedure in classical historical linguistics. In other words, these principles and assumptions shape particular questions about the texts and force us to ask these questions.

The first principle is one I heard most straightforwardly stated by George S. Lane at the University of North Carolina in the summer of 1972 in his Tocharian class. After a student's particularly incoherent translation from the Tocharian, Lane said with plaintive exasperation, "These things are supposed to make sense." This seems a simple thing to say; indeed at the time it seemed to me simpleminded. But over the years it has come to seem a profoundly important and all too often ignored assumption about ancient texts. We are often willing to exempt these texts from the necessity of "making sense." Sometimes we do so quite consciously, with a boastful pride, under a principle of enlightened cultural tolerance, of not imposing Western, rational categories on the products of other cultures. We see these texts as arising from a different mind-set or worldview, not constrained by the logical straitjacket that the Western philosophical tradition has created. We see them as reflecting dreams, archetypes, unconscious desires and fears, or whatever else is not subject to the pressure of conscious thought.

And we take pride in making no attempt to analyze them, ask about motive, or cause and effect, or coherence in story line or application, thus avoiding pedantic, Western narrowness.

Yet I think that not asking these questions is patronizing and displays more Western cultural arrogance than asking them. It assumes that cultures laboriously composed and carefully preserved texts that were little more than babble, that they poured out the disordered contents of their minds without realizing that they could shape this mental chaos in order to express what happens next or to express why it does. In other words, this assumes that there are cultures that, in their most cherished verbal expressions, do not attempt to communicate, do not try to make sense. I doubt this. Needless to say, we must try to make sense of the texts in their context, not in ours. We must recognize different styles, strategies, and conventions for expressing sense. We must realize that we will sometimes fail to see the sense because we lack sufficient information or because we cannot make the necessary imaginative leap. But I think we must grant that there is sense to be grasped.

For myths or mythological fragments, making sense requires asking a number of questions. Why is this story being told at this particular point in the larger text? What is the plot, the narrative line? Very often a myth will not be narrated in a straight, temporal line, but I think we are entitled to assume that such a narrative line lies behind the myth as we have it. If we search for one, we can often construct a coherent story that accounts for all the scattered allusions and fragmentary mentions of a mythic episode, without contradiction. What are the cause-and-effect relations between different actions in the story? If action *b* follows after action *a*, is there a sensible causal relation between them? If there seems not to be, further investigation will often show a causal connection that we at first missed.

In other words, I assume that simple daily experience imposes on all peoples two perceptions: that some events happen after other events (linearity) and that sometimes, but not always, an event *a* which happens before event *b* is the cause of *b* (causality). Cultures may simultaneously have other perceptions about the relations among events, and may in fact invest a good deal of sophisticated argument in trying to deny or downplay the perceptions just expressed, but I think the simplest and most straightforward human perception begins here. I further think that myth will on some level reflect these perceptions.

In other words, myth should have both an underlying internal coherence—it should be paraphrasable as a story, no matter how convoluted that story may be—and it should make sense in its culture—it should have an intelligible relation with the lives of the people who tell and hear the myth.

My second assumption is that references to the external world are as observationally accurate as they can possibly be for a culture without modern technology and sophisticated science. Another patronizing assumption we often make about ancient cultures is that they contemplated their world with dulled or blinkered senses, deprived of the clarity that modern science brings. This assumption is not usually stated as such, but it can be discerned behind the absurd modern interpretations of myths (indeed of single words) that we are willing to accept.

Let me construct a hypothetical case. The daily progress of the sun across the sky is an apparent fact that all people recognize; it has received myriad mythic treatments in myriad cultures: as a bright chariot wheel, for example. None of these, of course, is "scientifically" accurate. But I think we may assume that they are all observationally accurate—that the myths all involve a progress from east to west. If a modern scholar analyzing an ancient myth took it as treating or being about a normal daily solar passage from west to east, we are entitled to reject his interpretation. People just don't get that wrong.

This may seem an extreme case, but absurdities not much less extreme abound in natural interpretations of myths, as I will show, for example, of the so-called eclipse myth of Svarbhānu.[43] We seem to be willing to believe that ancient cultures simply did not pay attention to what went on around them. Yet, on the other hand, there is a commonplace that ancient or primitive man was "closer to nature" than our urbanized and mechanized societies. It is a commonplace worth bearing in mind. People who live by their herds and their fields are likely to notice a good deal more than we do about (1) weather and astronomical phenomena in general, (2) animal physiology, (3) animal behavior, both of domestic animals and of wild ones, potential predators, (4) plant growth and characteristics. If in interpreting a myth, a ritual, or even an item of vocabulary, we are forced to attribute to its culture an opinion about any part of the natural world that clearly contradicts ordinary observation, we should abandon or alter our interpretation.[44]

[43] And as I have shown for a single word, a body part, elsewhere (Jamison 1987).

[44] This is, of course, not to say that *un*natural things are not depicted in myth: miraculous transformations, prodigious feats, and so on. But these departures from nature will be drawn attention to; they will be the *point* of the tale.

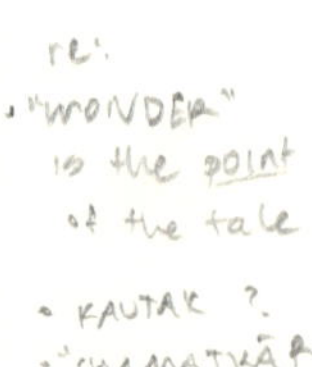

My final and perhaps most important principle concerns language. As I have already indicated, I assume that the language in which a myth is told is an integral part of the telling, not a gauzy verbal garment that can be removed without damage to the real meaning of the myth. The clues to contemporary understanding of myth often lie in its vocabulary and phraseology, which have complex and suggestive relationships with similar vocabulary and phraseology elsewhere. Examining other instances of the same words and phrases will often allow us to see these associations.

I think this is probably true of all mythology: that the verbal expression is of major importance and that abstracting themes or archetypes or patterns from their verbal expression does violence to the "meaning" of the myth. But it is especially and centrally true for Vedic India because of the extreme prominence and prestige of the word in this culture. Many have written about this ascendancy of the word, and I will not repeat their arguments in detail. I will just mention some of the most obvious evidence.

First, of course, the Vedic hymns themselves: the earliest text we have in this language, the Rig Veda, is the highly wrought, very self-conscious and sophisticated creation of an organized set of professional poets. The way something is said is as important as what is said.

Moreover, the central role of speech is discussed often and explicitly in both poetry and prose; a prominent goddess is Vāc, Speech, and the realm of words, or verbal behavior, is at least as important as that of physical activity in the ritual.

Finally, we can point to evidence from the myths themselves. In different texts, of different schools and vastly different ages, myths are presented in the same or almost the same words, especially at the beginning of the story, as we have noted. Not only the myth but its verbal expression has been carefully guarded.

Words in a sense must do double duty in this culture, standing in for visual art as well as doing their own job. In the absence of decorated or visually inspiring temples, indeed of temple buildings at all, in the presumable absence of images of the gods or their exploits, of any religiously inspired visual object, save for the ritual implements, words must serve as a pictorial substitute, as a sort of verbal iconography—capable of signalling the characteristics and deeds of the divinities and the relations among them and between the divine and the human. They must also have been the only stable guide to the mazy simultaneity of ritual action. As such, every association, every relationship signalled by words would be grasped and held onto, and we ignore this valuable aid at the risk of misunderstanding or simply not understanding the mythic elements being expressed.

Though not as reliable an index as verbal echoes and agreements, there is another type of similarity that can aid our analysis, what I will call "parallelism," a rough-and-ready structuralism. Different stories or ritual episodes, with differently identified participants, often show the same configuration of roles, of narrative events, of striking incidental details, or of thematic concerns. When these similarities are salient or far-reaching enough, I think we are entitled to confront the two stories or episodes to see if they illuminate each other, if they are comparable or even superimposable. Indeed, often the similarities of these apparently distinct stories will also be signalled by covert verbal links. Obviously the methodological problem with this technique is the delicate one of deciding how much agreement is required for two episodes to qualify as parallel; in this matter I try to err on the side of caution.

In the case studies I have attempted to be as explicit as possible both in expounding the mythic or ritual subject matter and in laying out the steps in my argument. One of the results of this explicitness is the sheer length of the treatments, which far exceeds that of the myths they seek to explain. Exegetical prolixity is a trait that goes all the way back to the Brāhmaṇas, I would point out in my defense. But, though explicit, the exposition may not always be simple to follow, partly because of my methods and partly because of the subject.

First, many arguments depend on the meaning and context of Sanskrit words, for reasons I have just given. All Sanskrit words and passages are translated into English, and these verbal arguments should be intelligible to those without Sanskrit.[45] But verbal arguments may strike the nonspecialist as "harder" than thematic ones. Nonetheless, these arguments must be there: we cannot skip over the words and think we have got to the myth.

Moreover, though the two myths form the primary organizing principle of the book, they are not the only myths we will meet. They cannot be understood in isolation, cut off from the web of Vedic myths that treat the same issues and use the same key words. So there will be digressions concerning other myths as well as the details of numerous

[45] I also draw attention here to the Glossary of Technical Terms at the close of this work.

rituals. When one does this sort of investigation, every wisp of a clue seems suddenly to lead to a piece of another myth or another ritual that unexpectedly illuminates the original subject. I have tried to give some of the feeling that one has in discovering these hidden bonds, these secret parallels, and some of the flavor of the discoveries lies precisely in the twisted trails that lead to them.

I would finally point out that if the subject is complex and difficult, this is its intention. As the Brāhmaṇas tell us so often, 'the gods love the obscure' (parókṣakāmā hí deváḥ), and in investigating Vedic matters, we must learn to cultivate at least that divine taste.

PART I

INDRA AND THE YATIS

CHAPTER I

The Texts

'Indra and the Yatis' forms a minor part of the Indra cycle, occasionally alluded to or briefly narrated in the BYV Saṃhitās and the Brāhmaṇas. Though the tale is mentioned far more rarely than many of Indra's famous exploits, and the narrative line is sketchy at best, the details are more vivid than in many Brāhmaṇa stories. The myth has been known to the West since the beginning of Vedic studies. It attracted Weber's attention in 1850, and he returned to it several times; it was treated as well by scholars like Oertel, von Schroeder, and E. Washburn Hopkins.[1] But very little attention has been paid to it since, until the recent articles of Dange and Bodewitz,[2] and so, for good or ill, it has escaped treatment at the hands of modern schools of mythological studies.

There are two main strains of the myth, one found in the Black Yajur Veda Saṃhitās, particularly the Maitrāyaṇī Saṃhitā and the Kāṭhaka and Kapiṣṭhala Saṃhitās,[3] the other in the Brāhmaṇas of the Sāmaveda. There is no unambiguous mention of the myth in earlier literature, the Rig Veda or Atharva Veda, though both the Yatis and the Sālāvr̥kas are marginally found there, each in conjunction with Indra.

In the BYV the story is partly related in eight separate passages, four

[1]Weber 1850, 1855, 1873; Oertel 1898; von Schroeder 1909a; Hopkins 1909.

[2]Dange 1980–81; Bodewitz 1984.

[3]The Kapiṣṭhala Saṃhitā is in general a fragmentary and corrupt version of the Kāṭhaka Saṃhitā and gives very little evidence independent of it. Hence, the two texts can be referred to together.

in the KS (two of these with KapS parallels), two each in the MS and TS. In addition there is a mere allusion to it in another TS passage.

MS I.10.12 índro vaí yátīnt sālāvṛkeyébhyaḥ prā́yachat téṣāṁ vā́ etā́ni śīrṣā́ṇi yát kharjū́rāḥ somapīthó vā́ eṣò 'syā́ údaiṣad yát karī́rāṇi

Indra handed over the Yatis to the Sālāvṛkeyas. Their heads are (now) kharjūra (plants). The soma-drink that went up from this (earth?) is (now) karīra (fruits).

MS III.9.3 índro vaí yátīnt sālāvṛkeyébhyaḥ prā́yachat téṣāṁ vā́ eṣá brahmacārī́ camasā́dhvaryur āsīd yò 'yáṁ hariṇás tásya yáḥ somapīthá ā́sīt sá svajò 'bhavat tásmād dhariṇā́ḥ svajā́ṃ khādati somapīthó hy ásyaiṣá sá yátra camasā́ṃ nyaùbjat táto rohítako [sic] 'jāyata tásmād raúhītakas tásmād rohī́take-rohītake svajā́ḥ

Indra handed over the Yatis to the Sālāvṛkeyas. The cup-adhvaryu was their student, a certain Hariṇa (personal name, pun on animal name)—his soma-drink became a viper(?). Therefore hariṇas eat vipers—because it (the viper) was its (Hariṇa's/the hariṇa's) soma-drink. Where he overturned the cup a rohītaka tree arose. Therefore (the Yūpa 'sacrificial post') is made of rohītaka (wood). Therefore, there's a viper in every rohītaka tree. [Because the soma-drink/viper was in the cup/rohītaka tree.]

KS VIII.5 indro vai yatīn sālāvṛkeyebhyaḥ prāyacchat teṣām adyamānānāṁ syūmaraśmir ṛṣir aśvaṃ prāviśat tasmād aśvas svaṁ śakṛd upajighrati kaś cid [better reading KapS VII.1 kac cid] ṛṣiṃ cāgniṃ ca na nirāsthā3m iti

Indra handed over the Yatis to the Sālāvṛkeyas. Of them being eaten, the ṛṣi Syūmaraśmi entered a horse. Therefore a horse sniffs its own excrement (thinking), "Have I not expelled the/an ṛsi and Agni/the fire?"

KS XI.10 yátīn vaí sālāvṛkeyā́ ādaṁs téṣāṁ śīrṣā́ṇi párāpataṁs té kharjū́rā abhavan yás somapīthás sá ūrdhvó 'patat tā́ni karī́rāṇi

The Sālāvṛkeyas ate the Yatis. Their heads flew off and became kharjūra (plants). The soma-drink flew straight up. (It became) these karīra (fruits).

KS XXV.6 (= KapS XXXIX.4) yatīn vai sālāvṛkeyā ādaṁs ta ādīyamānās saṃmṛśyamānā uttaravedim̐ samudakrāmaṁs tān nābhyadhṛṣṇuvaṁs teṣām eko 'smayata tata enān abhyadhṛṣṇuvaṁs teṣām ekaikam āvarham ādaṁs tasmān na moghahāsinā bhavyam

The Sālāvṛkeyas ate the Yatis. They (the Yatis) being taken, being seized, went up to/upon the Uttaravedi (upper altar). They (the Sālāvṛkeyas) did not dare against them. One of them (the Yatis?) smiled. Then they dared against them. Tearing them off (the Uttaravedi?) one by one, they ate them. Therefore, there is to be no foolish laughing.

KS XXXVI.7 yatīn vai sālāvṛkeyā ādaṁs teṣām etāni śīrṣāṇi yat kharjūrās somapītha eṣa udīṣati yat karīrāṇi

The Sālāvṛkeyas ate the Yatis. Their heads are (now) kharjūra (plants). The soma-drink that goes up is the karīra (fruits).

TS II.4.9.2 yátīnām adyámānānām̐ śīrṣā́ṇi párāpatan té kharjū́rā abhavan téṣām̐ rása ūrdhvò 'patat tā́ni karī́rāṇy abhavan

Of the Yatis being eaten the heads flew away. They became these kharjūra (plants). Their sap flew straight up. It became these karīra (fruits).

TS VI.2.7.5 índro yátīnt sālāvṛkébhyaḥ prā́yachat tā́n dakṣiṇatá uttaravedyā́ ādan yát prókṣaṇīnām ucchíṣyeta tád dakṣiṇatá uttaravedyaí ní nayed yád evá tátra krūrā́ṃ tát téna śamayati

Indra handed over the Yatis to the Sālāvṛkas. They ate them to the south/right of the Uttaravedi. What is left of the sprinkling waters he should bring to the south/right of the Uttaravedi. What is cruel there he thus appeases.

Of the SV Brāhmaṇas, the JB and PB each contain an elaborate account of the tale, and both texts mention it on several other occasions.

JB I.185 indro yatīn sālāvṛkebhyaḥ prāyacchat / teṣām adyamānānāṃ trayaḥ kumārāḥ paryaśiṣyanta rāyovājaḥ pṛthuraśmir bṛhadgiriḥ / ta indram astuvan / tān abravīt kiṃkāmā mā kumārās stutheti / bibhṛhy eva no maghavann ity abruvan / tān antarāṃsayor adhyāsyata / tā asya tisraḥ kakubho 'lambhanta . . .

I.186 tān abravīt kiṃkāmo vā ekaḥ kiṃkāma ekaḥ kiṃkāma eka iti / so 'bravīd rāyovājaḥ paśukāmo 'ham asmīti / tasmā iḷāṃ prāyacchat / paśavo vā iḷā / athābravīt pr̥thuraśmiḥ kṣatrakāmo 'ham asmīti / tasmai kṣatraṃ prāyacchat / sa eva pr̥thur vainyaḥ / athābravīd br̥hadgirir annādyakāmo 'ham asmīti / tasmā athakāram [?] prāyacchat / annam vā athakāraḥ[4]

Indra handed over the Yatis to the Sālāvr̥kas. Of them being eaten, three boys were left: Rāyovāja, Pr̥thuraśmi, and Br̥hadgiri. They praised Indra. He said to them: "With what desire do you boys praise me?" "Bear/support us, O Maghavan," they said. He threw them up between/over? his shoulders. They clung to his three humps.[5] . . .

He said to them, "What wish does this one have? What wish this one? What wish this one?" Rāyovāja said, "I want cattle." He (Indra) gave him iḷā (the refreshing drink). The iḷā is really cattle. Then Pr̥thuraśmi said, "I want dominion." To him he gave dominion. He thus (became) Pr̥thu Vainya. Then Br̥hadgiri said, "I want food/the eating of food." To him he gave ______ (?). For ______ is food.

PB XIII.4.17 indro yatīn sālāvr̥keyebhyaḥ prāyacchat teṣāṃ traya udaśiṣyanta pr̥thuraśmir br̥hadgirī rāyovājas te 'bruvan ko na imān putrān bhariṣyatīti aham itīndro 'bravīt tān adhinidhāya paricāryācarad[6]

[4]This is essentially the text of the Crit. Ed., with the addition of mā in I.185, and kṣatrakāmo and kṣatraṃ (as in PB XIII.4.17) rather than kṣetra-, both following Oertel 1898, p. 123. The portion of I.185 left out is textually more disturbed. On the problems see Oertel, ad loc.; Hoffmann 1960a, pp. 9–10 (1975, pp. 85–86); and Bodewitz 1984, pp. 67ff. That portion concerns the three kakubhs and does not contribute much to the understanding of our myth (though it does have to do, somewhat indirectly, with the question of how Indra feeds the boys).

A textual crux remains in the final part of I.186: athakāram, which surely cannot be right. Oertel edits atha kāmam (and indeed one manuscript reads athakāmam). This makes better sense: 'He gave him his wish', but there is a syntactic problem. Atha never appears in second (or third) position of its clause, as it would here in this case. Moreover, the last sentence is missing from Oertel's version; it would presumably have to be annam vā atha kāmaḥ, which would be very strange, since atha would appear noninitial in its clause and it would be repeated for no obvious semantic reason.

One manuscript reads (possibly, as far as I can gather from the apparatus of the Crit. Ed.) rathakāram: 'he gave him the making/maker of chariots'. We would need to understand more about rathakāra- than we do at present to accept this reading. (On rathakāra- see now Minkowsky 1989.)

[5]This is Oertel's translation. Hoffmann instead suggests "Diese drei Höcker hingen an ihm" (These three humps hung on him) (1960a, p. 9 [1975, p. 85]), but Bodewitz has convincingly argued against this interpretation (1984, pp. 68f.) in favor of Oertel's.

[6]Following Caland 1931, ad loc.

vardhayaṁs tān vardhayitvābravīt kumārakā varān vṛṇīdhvam iti kṣatraṃ mahyam ity abravīt pṛthuraśmis tasmā etena pārthuraśmena kṣatraṃ prāyacchat . . . brahmavarcasaṃ mahyam ity abravīd bṛhadgiris tasmā etena bārhadgireṇa brahmavarcasaṃ prāyacchat . . . paśūn mahyam ity abravīd rāyovājas tasmā etena rāyovājīyena paśūn prāyacchat

Indra handed over the Yatis to the Sālāvṛkeyas. Three of them were left: Pṛthuraśmi, Bṛhadgiri, and Rāyovāja. They said, "Who will bear/support us (as) sons?" "I," said Indra. Putting them up (on his back), serving them, he set about raising them. Having raised them he said, "Boys [notice tender kumāraka-], choose yourself boons." "(Give) me dominion," said Pṛthuraśmi. He gave him dominion with this Pārthuraśma (Sāman). . . . "(Give) me brahmaṇic glory," said Bṛhadgiri. He gave him brahmaṇic glory with this Bārhadgira (Sāman). . . . "(Give) me cattle," said Rāyovāja. He gave him cattle with this Rāyovājīya (Sāman).

PB VIII.1.4 indro yatīn sālāvṛkebhyaḥ prāyacchat teṣāṃ traya udaśiṣyanta rāyovājo bṛhadgiriḥ pṛthuraśmis te 'bruvan ko naḥ putrān bhariṣyatīti aham itīndro 'bravīt tāṁs trikakub adhinidhāyācarat sa etat sāmāpaśyad yat trikakub apaśyat tasmāt traikakubham

.5 sa ātmānam eva punar upādhāvat . . . sa etena ca pragāthenaitena [ca][7] sāmnā sahasraṃ paśūn asṛjata tān ebhyo prāyacchat te pratyatiṣṭhan

Indra handed over the Yatis to the Sālāvṛkeyas. Three of them were left: Rāyovāja, Bṛhadgiri, and Pṛthuraśmi. They said, "Who will bear/support us (as) sons?" "I," said Indra. The Trikakubh, putting them up (on his back), went about. He saw this sāman. In that the Trikakubh saw (it), therefore (is it called) the Traikakubha (Sāman).

He resorted again to himself. . . . With this pragātha [just quoted] and this sāman, he created a thousand cattle. He gave these to them (the boys). They (thus) got firm standing.

PB XIV.11.28 (≅ XIX.4.7) indro yatīn sālāvṛkeyebhyaḥ prāyacchat tam aślīlā vāg abhyavadat so 'śuddho 'manyata sa etac chuddhāśuddhīyam apaśyat tenāśudhyat

[7] Restoration suggested by Caland 1931, ad loc.

Indra handed the Yatis over to the Sālāvṛkeyas. An ugly voice addressed him, and he considered himself unclean. He saw this Śuddhāśuddhīya (Sāman). With it he became clean.

PB XVIII.1.9 indro yatīn sālāvṛkeyebhyaḥ prāyacchat tam aślīlā vāg abhyavadat sa prajāpatim upādhāvat tasmā etam upahavyaṃ prāyacchat taṃ viśve devā upāhvayanta

Indra handed over the Yatis to the Sālāvṛkeyas. An ugly voice addressed him. He had recourse to Prajāpati. He (Prajāpati) gave him this Upahavya (rite). The All-gods invited [upa √hvā, cf. Upahavya] him (again) (to the soma sacrifice).

PB XIX.4.7 indro yatīn sālāvṛkeyebhyaḥ prāyacchat tam aślīlā vāg abhyavadat so 'śuddho 'manyata sa ete śuddhāśuddhīye apaśyat tābhyām aśudhyat

Indra handed over the Yatis to the Sālāvṛkeyas. An ugly voice addressed him, and he considered himself unclean. He saw these (two) Śuddhāśuddhīya (Sāmans). With them he became clean.

The myth is alluded to in other Brāhmaṇa texts, and later, but its actual content seems to have been forgotten. We will have occasion to make reference to altered versions of the myth in two later texts, the Bṛhaddevatā (Bṛhaddev.) and the Mahābhārata (MBh.).

Bṛhaddev. III.132 tritaṃ gās tv anugacchantaṃ, krūrāḥ *sālāvṛkīsutāḥ*
kūpe prakṣipya gāḥ sarvās, tat evāpajahrire[8]

The cruel sons of the Sālāvṛkī, having thrown Trita, who was following the cows, into a well, carried off all the cows.

MBh. I.71.25 dānavās taṃ tataḥ kacam / /
.26 gā rakṣantaṃ vane dṛṣṭvā, rahasy ekam amarṣitāḥ
jaghnur bṛhaspater dveṣād, vidyārakṣārtham eva ca
hatvā śālāvṛkebhyaś ca, prāyacchaṃs tilaśaḥ kṛtam
.27 tato gāvo nivṛttās tā, agopāḥ svaṃ niveśanam

[8]The last pāda is a syllable short, unless one reads eva apa . . .

The Dānavas, then having seen Kaca guarding cows in the forest alone and in secret, killed him without remorse, from hatred of Bṛhaspati and to guard the (secret) knowledge.
Having killed him, they handed him, made into sesame-seed-sized pieces, over to the Śālāvṛkas. Then the cows, without a herdsman, returned to their own dwelling.

The focuses of the two main Vedic textual traditions differ sharply. The BYV versions, though different in detail, all concentrate on the act itself, the actual slaughter of the Yatis and the fate of their persons and implements. Each account is short, almost telegraphic, but on reading all the accounts together one gets a picture of terror and confusion, of an act in the course of happening, that seems to me rare in early Vedic literature. In contrast, the two narratives in the SV Brāhmaṇas dispose of the act in a single sentence; their concern is entirely the fate of the three surviving Yatis.

Needless to say, in both the YV and the SV Brāhmaṇas the telling of the myth is subordinated to the ritual preoccupations of the text. In the YV the myth is introduced to account for particular ritual actions or implements employed at that moment in the ritual performance; in the SV Brāhmaṇas it explains the origin of various sāmans.

Confronting the two traditions we see that the YV version is earlier and more of a piece. The bulk of the SV story concerns the granting of boons to the three survivors and seems somewhat irrelevant to the murderous act that begins it. This subsequent story (or part of it) may have been originally separate and later attached to the bare incipit of the Sālāvṛka tale. The YV in general knows nothing but the act, relates nothing but it and its immediate consequences, rather in the manner of the Vṛtra-slaying myth. But the SV and YV versions do share several features: an identical first sentence and some covert thematic parallels that we will examine later.

Whenever all three sets of participants in the story are mentioned, the narrative always begins with the same sentence, invariant in both order and vocabulary:

MS I.10.12 índro vaí yátīnt sālāvṛkeyébhyaḥ prā́yachat

Indra handed over the Yatis to the Sālāvṛkeyas.

[= MS III.9.3; KS VIII.5 (= KapS VII.1); TS VI.2.7.5; JB I.185; PB VIII.1.4, XIII.4.17, XIV.11.28 (= XIX.4.7), XVIII.1.9.[9]]

The complete agreement of all versions on this sentence contrasts with the relative fluidity of the rest of their treatments; the sentence would appear to be quite old in Vedic, predating the rigid division into Śākhās. The fact that the myth *must* be introduced in this fashion suggests that the precise wording of the sentence is important, that it is

[9]Three of the KS versions and one in TS do not mention Indra. The KS passages (XI.10, XXV.6, XXXVI.7) all begin with the invariant sentence

yátīn vaí sālāvr̥keyā́ ādan

The Sālāvr̥keyas ate the Yatis,

while TS II.4.9.2 begins

yátīnām adyámānānāṁ śīrṣā́ṇi párāpatan

Of the Yatis being eaten, the heads flew off.

The same myth is clearly meant, however, as the remainder of these versions closely parallels the versions with Indra. For example, KS XXXVI.7 continues

teṣām etāni śīrṣāṇi yat kharjūrāḥ

Their heads are (now) kharjūra (plants),

which is identical (save for the absence of vaí) with the second sentence of MS I.10.12:

índro vaí yátīnt sālāvr̥keyébhyaḥ prā́yachat téṣāṁ vā́ etā́ni śīrṣā́ṇi yát kharjū́rāḥ.

The absence of Indra in these passages has led Dange (1980–81, pp. 113ff.; see also Appendix below) to argue that Indra is an intrusion in the story, a secondary signal of "divine participation" (p. 115), and that the Yatis were originally responsible for their own fate. But this seems very unlikely, as Bodewitz (1984, pp. 66f.) also points out. The majority of the passages mention Indra; the first sentence with Indra is found in all Vedic texts that have the myth (including KS and TS). The deed is also assigned to Indra in the indrasya kilbiṣāṇi (Indra's misdeeds) passages, starting with TS. On the other hand, the version without Indra is confined to the YV, primarily the KS.

Moreover, the two versions are hardly incompatible: the Indra-less first sentence is simply the logical second sentence of the other version: 'Indra gave the Yatis to the Sālāvr̥keyas. The Sālāvr̥keyas ate them.' Indeed, something close to the Indra-less TS version begins the second sentence of the KS version with Indra:

KS VIII.5 indro vai yatīn sālāvr̥keyebhyaḥ prāyacchat teṣām adyamānānām . . .

As Bodewitz sensibly says, "The fact that Indra is not mentioned in some contexts does not prove much. Well-known myths, stories, topics, or passages are often abridged. *The ritualistic texts only use what is relevant for the context*" (my italics; p. 67). For more on Dange's and Bodewitz's views of this myth, see Appendix.

a formulaic encapsulation of the entire myth, much as *áhann áhim* 'He smashed the serpent'[10] encapsulates the Vr̥tra-slaying myth.[11]

Indeed this sentence is remarkably persistent. Although the actual content of our myth seems to have been forgotten relatively early, it continues to be mentioned in the lists of Indra's misdeeds we will discuss later on. In these lists this sentence, the only echo remaining of the myth, remains invariant. And even in the MBh., where a fractured version of the myth is briefly told, with Indra and the Yatis replaced by quite different participants, the verbal echo remains.

MBh. I.71.26 śālāvr̥kebhyaś ca prāyacchan

And they (the Dānavas) handed (him = Kaca) over to the Śālāvr̥kas.

As in the Vr̥tra myth, we enter the story at the moment of the act itself, but unlike the Vr̥tra myth, we are never told directly, here or elsewhere, what might have motivated the action—why Indra should wish to harm the Yatis. Again in contrast to the Vr̥tra slaying, the action is somewhat ambiguous. In the formulaic summary of the Vr̥tra slaying, the verb is *áhan* 'he smashed', the heroic verb par excellence, but here the verb is *prāyacchat* 'hold forth, hand over': Indra performs not a heroic but an apparently craven act of betrayal. He does not smash the Yatis himself, but sets a pack of wild animals to do the job.

In approaching this myth we will first examine in more detail the two unfamiliar participants, the Yatis and the Sālāvr̥k(ey)as, and their relations with Indra. These investigations will show that the myth depicts an act of a very different type from that which a superficial reading suggests. Then we will focus on the ritual or rituals depicted in the myth from two points of view: first, how the ritual activity is disturbed and emperiled by the slaughter of the Yatis, second, how the Yatis' rituals succeed notwithstanding, or perhaps because of, their own deaths. Both of these approaches will require an exacting attention to verbal and ritual detail and some further knowledge about the geography of the ritual ground. Finally, we will turn to the versions of the myth in which some Yatis survive.

[10]This particular formula, and its equivalents in other Indo-European traditions, is extensively discussed by Watkins 1987.

[11]For general discussion of first sentences, see the Introduction.

CHAPTER 2

The Participants

A. The Yatis

1. Ritualists or Shamans?

When we examine our scanty evidence concerning the character of the Yatis, Indra's act in the myth seems even less explicable than it does at first glance. Though the myth is absent from the RV, the Yatis do occasionally appear there, and in connection with Indra. They are, in fact, his friends and clients. There are three occurrences of the plural to yati- in the RV.[12] Two depict the Yatis and Indra in a mutually beneficial relationship:

RV VIII.6.18 yá indra yátayas tvā, bhŕ̥gavo yé ca tuṣṭuvúḥ

[12]Singular yáti- occurs twice in the RV (VII.13.1, IX.71.1, the latter with metrical irregularity) as an attributive, probably meaning 'leading, leader' or the like, with no apparent connection to our passages. A Yati or Yatis also appear parallel to Bhr̥gu in an AV passage, with variants elsewhere:

AVŚ II.5.3 índras turāṣā́ṇ mitró vr̥tráṃ yó jaghā́na yatī́r ná
bibhéda valáṃ bhŕ̥gur ná sasahé śátrūn máde sómasya

The other versions (SV II.304, ŚāṅkhŚS IX.5.2, ĀśvŚS VI.3.1) read mitró *ná* and *yátir* ná, surely the correct readings as Whitney (AV, ad loc.) and von Schroeder (1909a, p. 10, n. 1) saw. The last three syllables of each of the first three pādas, mitró ná, yátir ná, and bhŕ̥gur ná, are all patterned interpolations: the same metrical structure is found in the two preceding verses. See Whitney's introduction to the hymn for further discussion. Given the peculiar structure of the verse, no conclusions about the Yatis can be drawn, save that they (/he) are associated with Bhr̥gu, as in the passages quoted in the body of the text.

O Indra, which Yatis and which Bhr̥gus praised thee . . .

RV VIII.3.9 tát tvā yāmi suvī́ryam̧, tád bráhma . . . /
yénā yátibhyo bhŕ̥gave dháne hité, yéna práskaṇvam
ā́vitha

I implore you (Indra) for that good manliness, that formulation . . .
With which (you came with help) for the Yatis, for Bhr̥gu when the
prize was set, with which you helped Praskaṇva.

Note the presence in both passages of Bhr̥gu or the Bhr̥gus; this association is also found in a relatively common YV mantra:

MS I.4.1 iṣṭó yajñó bhŕ̥gubhir draviṇodā́ yátibhir āśīrdā́ vásubhiḥ

This worship has been performed by the Bhr̥gus, the wealth-granting (worship) by the Yatis, the wish-granting (worship) by the Vasus. [Cf. MS II.12.3; KS V.4, XVIII.18; KapS XXIX.6.[13]]

It is primarily this habitual association with the somewhat better-known Bhr̥gu family that allows the character of the Yatis to be more narrowly defined. The Bhr̥gus appear to be ancient ritualists, especially connected with the original establishment of fire in the cult, and often mentioned in conjunction with other priestly families, the Aṅgirases, the Atharvans, and so on.[14] The passages so far quoted suggest that the Vedic Yatis are completely parallel to the Bhr̥gus, performing the usual cultic services of praise (√*stu* [*tuṣṭuvuḥ,* RV VIII.6.18]) and worship (√*yaj* [*iṣṭó yajñáḥ* MS I.4.1 etc.]) and receiving the gods', particularly Indra's, aid in return (RV VIII.3.9). As we will see, our YV mythological passages overwhelmingly support the view of the Yatis as ritualists.

However, this is not at all the common interpretation of the Yatis, who generally are taken as magicians or heterodox ascetics, the very antithesis of orthodox priests. This misinterpretation seems to result in part from confusion with later *yati-* 'ascetic', a common noun derived from √*yam* 'hold, control', first found in this meaning in the Up-

[13]VS XVIII.56 contains more or less the same mantra, but without the Yatis.

[14]Cf. Macdonell and Keith 1912, sub Bhr̥gu; Keith 1925, pp. 223ff.; Bergaigne 1878–83, vol. 1, pp. 52ff.; Hillebrandt 1927–29, p. 88.

aniṣads. It also can be traced to an excessively creative reading of the passage containing the third appearance of the Yatis in the RV:

RV X.72.7 yád devā yátayo yáthā, bhúvanāny ápinvata
átrā samudrá ā́ gūḷhám, ā́ sū́ryam ajabhartana

[Geldner:] Als ihr Götter *wie Zauberer* die Welten anschwelltet, da holtet ihr die im Meere versteckte Sonne.
[When, O gods, like magicians you swelled the worlds, then you brought the sun hidden in the ocean.]

The rendering of Yati as 'Zauberer' (magician) seems to go back to Weber, and the identification with later yati- 'ascetic' was argued by Bergaigne for precisely this passage.[15] But the most enthusiastic proponent of this doctrine was von Schroeder in a 1909 article,[16] which is worth looking at partly as a cautionary example of scholarly history.

The article is careful, and von Schroeder is aware of most of the relevant passages concerning the Yatis. He recognizes the close association of the Yatis with the Bhr̥gus (pp. 9, 11), and the fact that both groups appear to be 'priestly families' ("ein . . . priesterliches Geschlecht") or 'priestly orders' ("eine bestimmte Priesterordnung") (p. 10). But he progresses from this unimpeachable description to one far less defensible: that they are shamans, Zauberpriester, engaged in a world-creating dance (p. 14), a dance possibly alluded to in the previous verse:

RV X.72.6 yád devā adáḥ salilé, súsaṃrabdhā átiṣṭhata
átrā vo nr̥tyatām iva, tīvró reṇúr ápāyata

[Geldner:] Als ihr Götter damals in der Flut euch fest aneinanderhaltend standet,
da ging von euch heftiger Staub *wie von Tanzenden*.

[When you gods stood holding each other fast in the flood, then thick dust came from you, *as from dancers*.]

Von Schroeder considers this verse an image reflecting the conception of primitive peoples ("in der Vorstellung primitiver Völker") of the magical power of dance ("die zaubermächtige Gewalt des Tanzes").

[15]Weber 1873, p. 145; Bergaigne 1878–83, vol. 1, p. 132; vol. 2, p. 321, n. 5.
[16]Von Schroeder 1909a.

One sees here the overhasty readiness of many scholars of this period to ascribe almost any detail in an ancient text to a vaguely defined primitive mind and primitive religion. Note, moreover, that the dancers of verse 6 are only in a simile: the gods are not dancing, but are compared to dancers—and only because of the dust stirred up by their activity. (Geldner notes this in passing.) This puts the Yatis of verse 7 one further step removed from the dancers: *both* groups are in similes. The gods are compared in successive verses to dancers ("thick dust came from you, *as* from dancers") and to Yatis ("*like* Yatis, you swelled the worlds"), but this in no way implies that the Yatis are dancers, that the activity the gods are engaged in is dancing, that such a dance would be shamanistic and/or world-creating, and least of all, that the Yatis are shamans. But such are von Schroeder's conclusions.[17]

Rather than assuming that any people who can 'swell' the beings must be sorcerers, shamans, it behooves us to look elsewhere for evidence of *how* they swelled the world. We must try to fit this enigmatic simile concerning the Yatis into the other evidence about them, rather than bending that evidence to fit an outdated notion of the religion of "primitive" peoples. Our myth will in fact provide the key for interpreting this RVic verse.

2. *Death at the Ritual*

The myth not only provides evidence that the Yatis were ritual priests but it makes dramatically clear that the Yatis were beset by beasts while performing a ritual. Their violent death seems all the more shocking because it interrupts and profanes the ritual and desecrates the ritual ground. Of the eight YV passages, six clearly show the Yatis being attacked in the midst of a ritual, three quite vividly.

Let us look first at the most complex of these passages, MS III.9.3. It concerns itself especially with the fate of the Yatis' Camasādhvaryu, their 'cup-adhvaryu' or 'priest of the drinking vessels', the title of a

[17]Unfortunately, as too often happens, von Schroeder's careful consideration of the textual evidence has been forgotten; what has endured is an unchallenged and unexamined identification of the Yatis as shamans—an identification that has had remarkable staying power. It has recently been asserted without question or discussion by both O'Flaherty (1981, pp. 39–40) and Varenne (1982, p. 209). But this is the entire sum of evidence that it rests on: two unconnected similes in a cryptic hymn. (However, Brown [1965, p. 30] translates X.72.7 simply 'like zealous priests', with no implication of magic.) Both Dange and Bodewitz maintain the connection of our Yatis with later yati- 'ascetic'. See Appendix below.

minor functionary employed only in the ritual. The passage mentions a vivid detail: his overturned cup and the spilled soma, a sign of the violent disruption of a ritual act. The Camasādhvaryu is their Brahmacārin, their student, again showing the Yatis holding an appropriately priestly place in orderly Vedic society.

MS III.9.3 índro vaí yátīnt sālāvr̥keyébhyaḥ prā́yachat *téṣām̐ vā́ eṣá brahmacārī́ camasā́dhvaryur āsīd* yò 'yám̐ hariṇás tásya *yáḥ somapīthá ā́sīt sá svajò 'bhavat* tásmād dhariṇā́ḥ svajáṃ khādati somapīthó hy ásyaiṣá *sá* yátra camasáṃ nyaùbjat táto rohī́tako 'jāyata tásmād raúhītakas tásmād rohī́take-rohītake svajáh

Indra handed over the Yatis to the Sālāvr̥keyas. *The cup-adhvaryu was their student,* a certain Hariṇa—*his soma-drink became a viper(?).* Therefore hariṇas eat vipers—because it (the viper) was its (Hariṇa's/the hariṇa's) soma drink. *Where he overturned the cup* a rohītaka tree arose. Therefore (the Yūpa 'sacrificial post') is made of rohītaka (wood). Therefore, there's a viper in every rohītaka tree. [Because the soma-drink/viper was in the cup/rohītaka tree.]

This passage involves some philological uncertainties, as well as larger questions of interpretation.[18] The major philological question is the meaning (or meanings) of the word hariṇá-. This word ordinarily means 'deer, gazelle' in Vedic (insofar as it is possible to tell), but in this passage it seems to have two values, at least one of them not 'deer'. Its primary value, the reason for its appearance in the passage, must be as a proper name, the name of the Yatis' Camasādhvaryu. I conclude this on the basis of structural parallelism: whenever the Yatis are treated not as a group but individually, they are given names.[19]

KS VIII.5 teṣām adyamānānām̐ *syūmaraśmir* r̥ṣir aśvaṃ prāviśat

Of them being eaten, the seer Syūmaraśmi entered a horse.

JB I.185 teṣām adyamānānāṃ trayaḥ kumārāḥ paryaśiṣyanta *rāyovājaḥ pr̥thuraśmir br̥hadgiriḥ*

[18] As it turns out, my independent translation of this passage generally agrees with that of Caland (in his translation of the ĀpŚS, ad VII.1.16), which I came across only after my interpretation had been formed.

[19] Except in KS XXV.6.

> Of them being eaten three boys were left over: Rāyovāja, Pr̥thuraśmi, Br̥hadgiri.
> [Cf. PB XIII.4.17.]

But as the explanatory sentence in MS III.9.3

> tásmād dhariṇáḥ svajáṃ khādati
>
> Therefore the hariṇá eats the viper[20]

shows, the personal name cannot be its only value here: it must be punning on the name of some animal. Despite the usual meaning of hariṇá-, both Caland and the Sanskrit dictionary of Monier-Williams[21] interpret hariṇá- in just this passage as 'ichneumon, mongoose' (ordinarily nakulá-), presumably because of the mongoose's famous snake-killing powers, already announced in the AV:

> AV VI.139.5 yáthā nakuló vichídya . . . áhim
>
> As a mongoose, having cut apart a snake . . .

Deer do not have a similar reputation in Vedic texts.

The identification of hariṇá- as mongoose is perfectly possible on etymological grounds. Hariṇá- is in origin a color term ('tawny' or the like) related to hári- (the standard designation of Indra's bay [steeds]), and the same color term could easily be applied to different animals of the same shade: it could as well be applied to a mongoose as to a deer.[22]

However, H.-P. Schmidt has pointed out to me (pers. comm.) that in Iranian and Near Eastern sources, as well as Christian ones, snake-

[20]On the precise identification of the svajá-, see n. 87.

[21]Caland in his translation ad ĀpŚS VII.1.16; Monier-Williams s.v.

[22]Some supporting evidence comes from the reverse situation. In the TS the word nakulá- 'mongoose', which seems *not* to be originally a color term (cf. Mayrhofer, *KEWA*, sub nakulá-), must refer to a color, not an animal, since it appears in the middle of an extensive list (at least thirteen terms) of colors:

> TS VII.3.18.1 . . . babhráve sv͡āhā nakul͡āya sv͡āhā róhitāya sv͡āhā
>
> . . . Hail to the brown. Hail to the mongoose(-colored). Hail to the red. . . .

This might indicate that the mongoose was often enough referred to as the 'tawny one' (hariṇá-) that its real name could also be interpreted as a color term.

killing ability *is* attributed to deer and similar animals. He cites the following Pahlavi (Middle Persian) passage from the Indian Bundahišn:

> Ind. Bundahišn XIX.26 gāv-i kōfīg pāzūn āhūg gōr abārīg dadān hamāg mār xvarēnd
>
> The mountain-ox, the capricorn (or ibex), the gazelle, the onager, and other deer eat all snakes.

R. Ettinghausen has explored the ample visual evidence for the "snake-eating stag" in Oriental sources and concluded that the image has its roots in folklore about a large variety of wild goat, *Capra magaceros* (called mārkhor 'snake-eater' in Persian), of the high mountains; he believes that the source for this belief was India.[23] The image of a snake-eating deer does appear in Indian art, of non-Muslim as well as Muslim inspiration.[24]

Hence it is possible that hariṇá- in this passage does have its usual meaning, 'deer' or similar, and is a valuable but isolated verbal reference to this folk belief. I do not see a principled way to decide this issue.[25]

The passage thus presents us with three transformations:

Hariṇa	⇛	mongoose/gazelle
soma-drink	⇛	viper
cup	⇛	rohītaka tree

The larger question, of course, is why these elements of the story should be transformed into these particular things, beyond the convenience of explaining the hostility between snake and mongoose/gazelle. The reason for the cup becoming the rohītaka tree is obvious: the cup is wooden. The same transformation (though into a different tree)

[23]Ettinghausen 1955 (1984, pp. 674–92).

[24]However, since these images are some millennia later than the text in question, we cannot attribute too much weight to their evidence.

[25]Verbal arguments cut both ways. On the one hand, if at all possible we should prefer to interpret a single word in the same way whatever the context. This consideration would favor the gloss 'gazelle'. On the other, the only snake-eating animal for which we have Vedic textual evidence is the mongoose.

also occurs in an AB story, in which the gods on their way to heaven knock over (ni √ubj as here) their cups:

AB VII.30 tatraitāṃś camasān nyubjaṃs [*sic*—*nyaubjaṃs] te nyagrodhā abhavan

They overturned their cups there. They became nyagrodha (trees).[26]

Hariṇa presumably becomes a mongoose at least in part because of his name. But why should the pure ritual substance, soma, become a dangerous snake? The answer to this important question must be deferred for some time.[27]

Thus one important passage (MS III.9.3) shows the Sālāvr̥ka attack occurring in the middle of a soma sacrifice. Two passages depict the destruction as occurring near or even *on* the Uttaravedi, the 'further' or 'upper' altar used in the most solemn rites. The KS passage is particularly striking.

TS VI.2.7.5 índro yátīnt sālāvr̥kébhyaḥ prā́yachat *tā́n dakṣiṇatá uttaravedyā́ ādan* yát prókṣaṇīnām ucchíṣyeta tád dakṣiṇatá uttaravedyaí ní nayed yád evá tátra krūráṃ tát téna śamayati

Indra handed over the Yatis to the Sālāvr̥kas. *They ate them to the south/right of the Uttaravedi.* What is left of the sprinkling waters he should bring to the south/right of the Uttaravedi. What is cruel there he thus appeases.

KS XXV.6 (= KapS XXXIX.4) yatīn vai sālāvr̥keyā ādaṁs *ta ādīyamānās saṃmr̥śyamānā uttaravediṁ samudakrāmaṁs* tān nābhyadhr̥ṣṇuvaṁs teṣām eko 'smayata tata enān abhyadhr̥ṣṇuvaṁs *teṣām ekaikam āvarham ādaṁs* tasmān na moghahāsinā bhavyam

The Sālāvr̥keyas ate the Yatis. *They (the Yatis) being taken, being seized, went up to/upon the Uttaravedi.* They (the Sālāvr̥keyas) did not dare against them. One of them (the Yatis?) smiled. Then they dared against them. *Tearing them off (the Uttaravedi?) one by one, they ate them.* Therefore, there is to be no foolish laughing.

[26]This AB tale also concerns the possession of the somapītha, the 'soma-drink'.
[27]See Chap. 3, A, below.

Three other passages mention their somapītha 'soma-drink', which makes sense only in a ritual context, since soma is only consumed during ritual performance.

MS I.10.12 índro vaí yátīnt sālāvr̥keyébhyaḥ prā́yachat téṣāṁ vā́ etā́ni śīrṣā́ṇi yát kharjū́rāḥ *somapīthó vā́ eṣò 'syā́ údaiṣad* yát karī́rāṇi

Indra handed over the Yatis to the Sālāvr̥keyas. Their heads are (now) kharjūra (plants). *The soma-drink that went up from this (earth?)* is (now) karīra (fruits).

KS XXXVI.7 yatīn vai sālāvr̥keyā ādaṁs teṣām etāni śīrṣāṇi yat kharjūrās *somapītha eṣa udīṣati* yat karīrāṇi

The Sālāvr̥keyas ate the Yatis. Their heads are (now) kharjūra (plants). *The soma-drink that goes up* is the karīra (fruits).

KS XI.10 yátīn vaí sālāvr̥keyā́ ādaṁs téṣāṁ śīrṣā́ṇi párāpataṁs té kharjū́rā abhavan *yás somapīthás sá ūrdhvó 'patat* tā́ni karī́rāṇi

The Sālāvr̥keyas ate the Yatis. Their heads flew off and became kharjūra (plants). *The soma-drink flew straight up.* (It became) these karīra (fruits).

3. *The Yatis' Killing: A Sin of Indra's?*

Given the shocking desecration attendant on the Yatis' murder, one might expect this to be considered one of Indra's excesses, an essentially blameworthy action to be accepted, reluctantly, only from an uncontrollable warrior god. And so it becomes later, in the indictments against Indra that become a fashionable topos beginning in later Vedic texts. But it is a mystery of some note that in the early Brāhmaṇa period this is not the attitude: what little evidence there is suggests that the deed was positively regarded.

The best evidence we have for the Vedic attitude toward this deed comes from examining other of Indra's activities with which it is equated. In the TS the destruction of the Yatis is expressly likened to the slaying of Vr̥tra and to this alone.[28]

[28]This equivalence was already noted by Hopkins 1909, p. 50, n. 2.

TS III.3.7.3 yád índro vṛtrám áhann amedhyám̥ tád yád yátīn apā́vapad[29] amedhyám̥ tád átha kásmād aindró yajñá ā́ saṁsthā́thor íty āhur

"In that Indra smashed Vṛtra there is impurity. In that he scattered/destroyed the Yatis there is impurity. Then why does the worship belong to Indra up to (its) completion?" they say.

From the word amedhyá-, roughly translated here 'impurity', one might assume that the acts are receiving a morally negative valuation, but such a surmise would badly distort the meaning of amedhyá-. This word, often parallel with ayajñiyá- 'not fit for (contact with) the worship',[30] is a morally neutral way of referring to substances and acts that should not be part of the ritual sphere, whatever their use and value in the profane world. What is amedhyá- can be rendered médhya- 'ritually pure' by a simple purificatory act. After examining all examples of amedhyá- in the BYV Saṃhitās, I have found none that involved a moral judgement.

The substances deemed amedhyá- include certain parts of the earth, certain parts of plants, beans, and notably, certain parts of the body.[31] The activities include the daily life of the rājanya (member of the warrior class), the ritual washing by the sacrificer's wife of the dead victim at the animal sacrifice (even though this is ritually prescribed), and the practice of medicine.[32]

What links some of these activities and substances is their contact or equivalence with death or with the interior parts of a being (often after death). The sacrificer's wife touches the dead animal; the doctor is presumably in continual contact with the dead and dying and with their bodily secretions. The hair and beard, which several texts call amedhyá-, are so considered because they are 'dead skin'.

[29]Note the idiom apa √vap 'scatter away, destroy', rather than the otherwise canonical pra √yam/dā 'give, hand over'. The substitution is presumably necessary because the Sālāvṛkas are not mentioned.

[30]E.g., MS I.8.7, KS XXX.8.

[31]Parts of the earth: quite frequently, e.g., TS VI.2.3.2, VI.2.4.5; MS III.2.3; KS XXV.5. Parts of plants: TS II.6.4.2. Beans: TS V.1.8.1; KS XX.8. Parts of the body: e.g., TS VI.1.1.2, VI.1.3.4; MS III.6.2; and esp. KS XXXIV.8, which lists twelve amedhya- parts of man, the first six of which are a slightly altered version of the Vedic "canonical creature" (see Jamison 1986, esp. pp. 174f.).

[32]Life of rājanya: MS I.8.7. Washing of the victim: MS III.10.1. Medicine: TS VI.4.9.2.

TS VI.1.1.2 mṛtā́ vā́ eṣā́ tvā́g amedhyā́ yát keśaśmaśrú

This is dead, impure skin, namely, the hair and beard.[33]

The amedhyá- nature of the two deeds mentioned in TS III.3.7.3, the smashing of Vṛtra and the destruction of the Yatis, must also lie in this: Indra, by killing them, had contact with death and quite literally with the blood of his victims. He should not, without subsequent purification, have any part in the ritual. This connection is spelled out in the KS with regard to the slaying of Vṛtra (though it is the earth, not Indra, who is rendered impure here).

KS XXXI.8 indro vai vṛtram ahaṁs tasyemāṃ lohitam anuvyadhā-vat tad amedhyābhavat

Indra smashed Vṛtra. His (Vṛtra's) blood flowed forth along this (earth). Then she (the Earth) became impure.[34]

Thus the assignment of the term amedhyá- to the Yati killing is a simple statement of ritual cause and effect, not a condemnation of the deed.

What should engage our attention in TS III.3.7.3 is that the Yati episode is equated with the killing of Vṛtra, Indra's most celebrated exploit, the most praised and praiseworthy deed of any figure in Vedic mythology. If the Yati episode forms a pair with it here, then it seems unlikely that the Yati killing was, at the time, considered an embarrassing example of Indra run amuck. Instead it presumably shares the positive valuation of the Vṛtra slaying.

This attitude changes relatively rapidly. We can see it change in the course of the Vedic period. A catalogue of Indra's misdeeds comes to be a formulaic commonplace in later Vedic texts; these indictments have been treated by Oertel under the heading of indrasya kilbiṣāṇi 'Indra's misdeeds'.[35] It is important to note the progression in these passages. In AB VII.28, we have perhaps the first of these formal indictments of Indra, drawn up in this case by the gods. Both the Vṛtra slaying and the Yati episode are included, along with undeniable exam-

[33]Cf. MS III.6.2, KS XXII.13.

[34]It is in fact this impurity arising from Vṛtra's blood that seems to be referred to in the other passages just mentioned concerning the amedhyá of the earth.

[35]Oertel 1898, pp. 118–25.

ples of culpable behavior like the slaying of Viśvarūpa.[36] The common denominator here is presumably again the automatic impurity arising from blood guilt, not the goodness or wickedness of the action.

AB VII.28 yatrendraṃ devatāḥ paryavr̥ñjan viśvarūpaṃ tvāṣṭram abhyamaṃsta *vr̥tram astr̥ta yatīn sālāvr̥kebhyaḥ prādād* arurmaghān avadhīd br̥haspateḥ pratyavadhīd iti tatrendraḥ somapīthena vyārdhyata

When the gods excluded Indra, (saying), "He has dishonored Viśvarūpa, son of Tvaṣṭar. *He has laid Vr̥tra low. He has handed over the Yatis to the Sālāvr̥kas.* He has slain the Arurmaghas. He has struck against Br̥haspati," then Indra was deprived of soma-drinking.

Note also the consequences of his actions. The gods excluded him (paryavr̥ñjan) from the ritual and deprived him of soma-drinking (somapītha-). But this is precisely the unavoidable result of these deeds: the contact with blood and death rendered Indra amedhyá-, ayajñiyá-, and, by the unbending rules of ritual activity, he could not take part in the ritual. The gods are not being capricious or morally judgmental. They have no choice but to exclude him.

Others who are or become amedhyá-, for whatever reason, are not allowed to drink soma. In particular, the Aśvins, the physicians of the gods (and highly valued as such), are non-soma-drinking (ásomapa-) because of their profession.

MS IV.6.2 átha vā́ etaú tárhi devā́nāṃ bhiṣájā āstām aśvínā ásomapau

Then there were at this time these two physicians of the gods, the Aśvins, (who were) non-soma-drinking.

TS VI.4.9.1–2 taú devā́ abruvann ápūtau vā́ imaú manuṣyacaraú/ bhiṣájāv íti tásmād brāhmaṇéna bheṣajáṃ ná kāryàm ápūto hy èṣò 'medhyó yó bhiṣák

The gods said about these two, "These two are unpurified, going about among men (as) physicians." Therefore medicine is not to be practiced by a Brahman. For that one is unpurified, impure—namely, the physician.
[See also KS XXVII.4.]

[36]See Chap. 3, A, below.

The Aśvins bargain for (and receive) somapīthá- 'soma-drinking' in exchange for a particular act of healing, but they must be purified of their amedhyá- before they can participate in the ritual.

> MS IV.6.2 taú vaí bahiṣpavamānénaivá pāvayitvā́ tā́bhyāṃ pūtā́bhyāṁ yajñíyābhyāṃ (KS XXVII.4 medhyābhyāṃ] bhūtā́bhyāṃ gráham agṛhṇan
>
> Having purified the two (Aśvins) with the Bahiṣpavamāna (Stotra), they drew a cup (of soma) for the two, having become purified and fit for contact with the worship.

In other words, the exclusion of the Aśvins from soma-drinking has the same cause as Indra's: amedhyám, even though the reason for this amedhyám is universally valued. We cannot interpret Indra's exclusion in AB VII.28 as morally motivated.

Contrast, however, this AB passage with the following JB passage (and the later passages modelled on it).[37] First, note that the slaying of Vṛtra has been removed from the list, while that of the Yatis remains. The criterion on which these later lists are based does seem now a moral valuation, not an automatic assignment of impurity for bloodshed. And indeed the frame of the passage is couched in moral terms, not on the automatic and morally neutral exclusion from ritual. The indictment here is delivered by the creatures, and this time the deeds are explicitly called kilbiṣāṇi 'misdeeds, offenses'. Notice the frame of the passage: indraṃ vai bhūtāni paryacakṣata . . . etebhyo devakilbiṣebhyaḥ (the creatures condemned Indra . . . for these *offenses against the gods*). The Vṛtra slaying has been removed from the list because it is precisely *not* an 'offense against the gods', but the opposite; the Yati affair remains, I would say, because the story, or its import, has been forgotten. Its likeness to the Vṛtra slaying is no longer apparent.[38]

> JB II.134 indraṃ vai bhūtāni paryacakṣata triśīrṣāṇaṃ tvāṣṭram avadhīd *yatīn sālāvṛkebhyaḥ prādād* arurmukhān avadhīd bṛhaspateḥ pratyava-

[37] KauṣUp III.1; ŚaṅkhŚS XIV.50.1–2; cf. Oertel 1898.

[38] Dumézil, working with Oertel's indrasya kilbiṣāṇi materials, inter alia, interprets the passages as depicting the predictable but culpable excesses of a second-function warrior, showing the inevitable hostility between first- and second-function figures (1956, pp. 66ff.; 1968, pp. 113–15; 1985, pp. 79–86, esp. 83–84; etc., and cf. Littleton 1982, pp. 120–22). Although some of the accounts of Indra's behavior may reflect such attitudes, it is important to note with some care how each text treats the deeds. The accounts and attitudes are not uniform, as I hope I have shown.

dhīt . . . namucer āsurasya śiraḥ prāchaitsīd ity etebhyo devakilbiṣe bhyaḥ.

The creatures condemned Indra for these offenses against the gods: "He has slain the three-headed son of Tvaṣṭar. *He has handed over the Yatis to the Sālāvṛkas.* He has slain the Arurmukhas. He has struck against Bṛhaspati. . . . He has cut off the head of Namuci, the Āsura."

Thus, although in later Brāhmaṇic literature Indra's treatment of the Yatis can be condemned, in the earlier texts it seems almost to be celebrated. And even in these later texts it is generally only the automatic blood guilt that is emphasized: passages like JB II.134 are rare. Though elsewhere in the SV Brāhmaṇas the killing of the Yatis makes Indra feel unclean, this seems nothing more than the amedhyám of the TS passage, impurity brought on by any killing:

PB XIV.11.28 indro yatīn sālāvṛkeyebhyaḥ prāyacchat tam aślīlā vāg abhyavadat so 'śuddho 'manyata

Indra handed over the Yatis to the Sālāvṛkeyas. An ugly voice addressed him, and he considered himself impure.
[= PB XIX.4.7; cf. XVIII.1.9.]

Indra quickly acquires a sāman and is purified.

The striking phrase aślīlā vāk 'ugly speech/voice'[39] seems in the PB to be a sort of external, verbal embodiment of the internal state of amedhya (a word that does not occur in the PB). In other texts aślīlā also often refers to verbal phenomena, especially unfavorable rumor or report.[40]

The gods several times in the JB have the same feeling of impurity about the killing of their traditional enemies, the Asuras, a deed that is always considered positive. The internal correspondent, amedhya-, appears in the following passage:

JB I.121 devā vā asurān hatvāpūtā ivāmedhyā amanyanta

[39]Hopkins (1909, p. 50) translates aślīlā as 'unauspicious', but the word actually refers to physical ugliness, as shown by

ŚB III.1.2.16 tásmād ápy aślīlám suvā́sasaṃ didṛkṣante

Therefore (people) like to see even an ugly person well-dressed.
Cf. also AB I.25.

[40]Cf. MS II.3.9 ≅ KS XII.10; MS II.5.2; MS III.1.9, III.6.7 ≅ KS XIX.10, XXIII.6.

> The gods, having slain the Asuras, considered themselves unpurified, impure, as it were.

Hence, like the gods in this passage, Indra's feeling impure in the PB passages results from his contact with death, not from feelings of guilt or remorse about killing the Yatis.

In sum, though the Yati episode brings about ritual impurity, this impurity is the automatic result of any killing, good or bad. The destruction of the Yatis is unambiguously treated as a blameworthy excess of Indra's only after its content has been forgotten. In earlier texts it is assimilated to the benevolently regarded Vr̥tra slaying. So far we have seen nothing about the deed that justifies this tolerance, but now I can suggest some possible reasons why Indra is less to be blamed than we might suppose.

B. The Sālāvr̥keyas

1. *Hyenas and Their Young*

Let us now turn to the third major set of actors—the Sālāvr̥kas or Sālāvr̥keyas. This animal is ordinarily identified as a hyena, a jackal, or some variety of wild dog; Weber in 1850 suggested 'werewolf'. Modern sources seem to favor 'hyena'.[41] Etymology is no help: the second compound member, -vr̥ka- (wolf), obviously suggests an animal similar to a wolf, but the first member of the compound is obscure,[42] and

[41]'Werewolf': Weber 1850, p. 413; 'hyena': e.g., Mayrhofer, *KEWA*, sub sālāvr̥ka-.

[42]None of the attempts to etymologize this element seems to me successful. The standard older etymology begins with the form śālā-, which is frequent in later texts. However, the Vedic texts have only sālā- (with rare manuscript variants: one JB manuscript has śālā- in JB II.134, quoted above). The later palatal *ś* results from the common confusion of sibilants in this period, and any etymology should thus begin with the plain dental sibilant *s*. This makes the usual connection (cf., e.g., Monier-Williams sub sālā-) with śālā- 'house, room' unlikely—which is just as well, since the required semantic equation 'house-wolf' = 'hyena/jackal' is unappealing.

K. Hoffmann's proposal (reported by Mayrhofer, *KEWA*, vol. 3, p. 462) *salā́vr̥ka- 'laufe-Wolfe', with *salā́- presumably from an l-form of √sr̥ 'run,' is no more attractive semantically, though its phonology is better. Thieme's (1954, p. 554, n. 3; p. 562, n. 2 [cf. Mayrhofer, *KEWA*, vol. 3, p. 327]) attempt to see a color word as first member makes better sense, but suffers from the fact that the other purported Sanskrit lexical relatives begin with *ś*. In principle, I think it unlikely that a satisfactory etymology can be found for this semantically charged word, which is a likely subject for taboo deformation.

even for the -vr̥ka- part we must reckon with the possibility of borrowing cum folk etymology.

It is always difficult to make such identifications without precise behavioral or anatomical descriptions. However, 'hyena' seems to fit the behavior of the animals in the myth in some striking ways, insofar as information on the characteristics and behavior of hyenas is available (or available to me). There are three varieties of hyena: the striped hyena (*Hyaena hyaena*), the spotted hyena (*Crocuta crocuta*), and the brown hyena (*Hyaena brunnea*). Only the striped hyena is (now?) found in India, the other two only in sub-Saharan Africa. The subspecies of the striped hyena found in India is *Hyaena hyaena hyaena*, one of the larger of the subspecies.[43]

Unfortunately, almost all careful studies of hyenas concern the spotted hyena. "The life of the striped and brown hyenas is a much greater mystery than that of the spotted hyena."[44] Information available about the striped hyena is scanty and often contradictory, and tends to be contrastive (of the form "unlike the spotted hyena, the striped hyena . . .") and to concern striped hyenas in Africa, where the habitat is quite distinct from that of India and where, in particular, the striped hyena must compete with its larger cousin, the spotted hyena.[45] Several recent studies treat the striped hyena in Israel,[46] but again this habitat is quite unlike that of India. I have so far been unable to locate any studies specifically concerning Indian hyenas, apart from a very brief summary by Krishnan[47] and occasional anecdotal accounts of hyena behavior.[48] A very useful and informative survey of our knowledge of the striped hyena is given by Rieger.[49]

The studies just cited[50] state emphatically that difference in habitat, in particular the availability of food and presence or absence of competing predators, as well as the difference in size among the subspecies,

[43]Rieger 1979, p. 81.

[44]Grzimek 1975, p. 192.

[45]Cf. esp. Kruuk 1976.

[46]Ilani 1975 (a somewhat popular treatment); D. W. Macdonald 1978; Skinner and Ilani 1979.

[47]Krishnan 1972. The section on hyenas consists of only two pages (pp. 40–41) and is based on a very small number of sightings. Krishnan himself states, "The striped hyena in India has not received the serious attention of naturalists" (p. 41).

[48]Primarily in the *Journal of the Bombay Natural History Society;* for references, see Rieger 1979.

[49]Rieger 1979.

[50]Esp. those of D. W. Macdonald (1978, pp. 196–97) and Rieger (1979, p. 81).

causes very different behavioral and social patterns among different populations of striped hyenas. Indeed, both Macdonald and Rieger produce counterevidence to some of the claims about striped hyena behavior resulting from studies of East African hyenas.[51] Macdonald speaks of "the flexibility of hyaena social behavior and organization."

Moreover, the recent studies of *spotted* hyenas by Kruuk and van Lawick-Goodall and of *brown* hyenas by M. and D. Owens[52] have exploded some long-held beliefs about these animals. For example, the spotted hyena is far more of a predator and less of a scavenger than previously thought. (Lions are frequently scavengers of hyena kills.[53]) It seems likely that received information in the literature about *striped* hyenas will be equally subject to review once the animal is studied more closely. Indeed this is already happening. The speed with which even a small amount of close observation changes received opinions about the animal can be gauged by the following (perhaps slightly overdramatized) statement of Ilani: "During the subsequent hour and one-half all of our previous notions about the social behavior of [striped] hyenas were discarded."[54]

For information I have drawn on several animal encyclopedias[55] and the just mentioned studies of Macdonald, Rieger, Krishnan, Ilani, and Skinner and Ilani, as well as those of Kruuk, van Lawick-Goodall, and Owens and Owens (these last primarily for spotted and brown hyenas). When information is not available about the striped hyena, I have, with some trepidation, used the corresponding data about the spotted and/or brown hyena.

For the similarity between the Sālāvr̥kas' behavior and the characteristics of hyenas, note first the KS passage about the Yati's ill-timed smile:

KS XXV.6 (= KapS XXXIX.4) tān nābhyadhr̥ṣṇuvaṁs teṣām eko

[51]E.g., Kruuk 1976. In particular, Kruuk, among others, asserts that striped hyenas are extremely solitary in comparison with their gregarious cousins, the spotted hyenas (1975, p. 78; Kruuk 1976; Grzimek 1975, p. 193). But D. W. Macdonald observed nonsolitary striped hyenas in more than half of his sightings (1978, p. 195), and he describes very elaborate greeting, grooming, and playing behavior. Cf. also Ilani 1975, pp. 15–16; Rieger 1979, pp. 81, 88, and 92. Rieger (p. 92) considers the larger subspecies (including the *Hyaena hyaena hyaena* of India) to be more likely to and able to form stable family groups.

[52]Kruuk 1972; van Lawick-Goodall 1971; Owens and Owens 1984.

[53]Kruuk 1972, p. 129; Kruuk 1975, pp. 15, 44f.; van Lawick-Goodall 1971, pp. 181f.

[54]Ilani 1975, p. 16.

[55]Grzimek 1975; Walker 1983; D. Macdonald 1984; Whitfield 1984.

'smayata tata enān abhyadhṛṣṇuvaṁs teṣām ekaikam āvarham ādaṁs tasmān na moghahāsinā bhavyam

They (the Sālāvṛkeyas) did not dare against them. One of them (the Yatis?) smiled. Then they dared against them. Tearing them off (the Uttaravedi?) one by one, they ate them. Therefore, there is to be no foolish laughing.

This may be indirectly designed to recall the hyenas' "laugh" (although apparently the "laugh" is especially characteristic of the spotted hyena; the striped hyena is much less noisy[56]).

Another possible piece of evidence for the Sālāvṛka as hyena is the mantra with which one addresses a Sālāvṛkī (the feminine stem to Sālāvṛka) to avert evil omen in the BŚS:

BŚS IX.18 yadi sālāvṛkī vāśyeta tām anumantrayate dīrghamukhi durhaṇv iti

If a Sālāvṛkī should howl, one should address her with the mantra "O you of the long muzzle and the terrible jaw."

The Macmillan animal encyclopedia describes hyenas this way: "They have massive heads; indeed the jaws of the spotted hyena, the largest member of the group, are the most powerful of any mammal. All hyenas are able to crush the biggest bones of their prey to extract the marrow."[57]

Some grammatical observations and some further mythological passages may help explain why Indra gives the Yatis to these beasts. First,

[56]Cf. Grzimek 1975, p. 192; Walker 1983, p. 1060; D. Macdonald 1984, p. 156. Ilani (1975), Kruuk (1976, p. 104), and Rieger (1979, p. 92) all remark on the relative silence of the striped hyena, but all also distinguish various cries they do make. Though Rieger states that striped hyenas "vocalize only on rare occasions," he has distinguished eight different vocalizations. Unfortunately his data on vocalizations are as yet unpublished (as far as I know). Kruuk mentions a number of cries, including a "giggle" similar to that of the spotted hyena. Ilani classifies four types of cries, including "short and very hard sounds that may have inspired the legend of the laughing hyena," though he feels that the sounds are "not at all like laughter." Most important, Krishnan, writing of the striped hyena in India, says, "The vocalization associated with the hyena is its discordant, cackling 'laughter,' which seems to be indulged in when it is excited." (I am, however, a little suspicious of how much this statement rests on field observation and how much on generalized popular knowledge of hyena lore, since Krishnan's report is otherwise so thin.)

[57]Whitfield 1984, p. 98; cf. also, e.g., Walker 1983, p. 1058; Ilani 1975, p. 11.

the grammar: our mythological passages give these animals one of two names, sālāvr̥ká- or sālāvr̥keyá-. With the exception of one TS passage, the earliest versions of the myth, those of the BYV, use sālāvr̥keyá-, as does PB in four of its five occurrences.[58] It is easy to conceive how sālāvr̥ká- could have been substituted for sālāvr̥keyá- in later versions of the myth. Since the beasts are characteristically in the dative plural in the first-sentence encapsulation of the myth, the fuller dative plural form sālāvr̥keyébhyaḥ seems a likely candidate for haplology (loss of a repeated syllable) to sālāvr̥kébhyaḥ.

The derivational difference is significant. The morphological shape of sālāvr̥ká- has no necessarily associated semantic value, but that of sālāvr̥keyá- does. The suffix -eyá- in conjunction with vr̥ddhi (lengthening of the vowel in the initial syllable) serves primarily to form patronymics and, especially, *metronymics,* that is, to designate the offspring of a person or animal and especially offspring in relation to their mother.[59] Compare, for example, already RV gārṣṭeyá- 'born of a heifer': gr̥ṣṭí- 'heifer'; āditeyá- (once, beside very common ādityá-) 'son of Aditi'; sārameyá- 'offspring of Saramā' (the 'divine bitch'). This derivational process remains productive, for example, in the MBh., where the Pāṇḍavas are also often called Kaunteya- 'son(s) of Kuntī', and other examples such as gāṅgeya- 'son of Gaṅgā' (e.g., MBh. I.93.44) are frequently met.

Sālāvr̥keyá- is then best taken as '*young* hyena', and it implies reciprocally a mother, feminine sā̆lāvr̥kī-. So, the earliest versions of the myth refer almost without exception to young animals, and should be translated 'Indra handed the Yatis over to the *young* Sālāvr̥keyas, the young hyenas'. That the mother-child relation is being emphasized in these passages may be signalled by a passage cited above from the later Br̥haddevatā (a sort of versified commentary on the RV), where the animals are called explicitly sālāvr̥kī-sutāḥ 'the *sons* of the *female hyena*' (III.132).[60]

[58]Sālāvr̥ká- is found in TS VI.2.7.5, PB VIII.1.4, in the JB and AB versions, in the indictments discussed above, and outside the myth in RV, AV, and post-Vedic texts.

[59]Wackernagel-Debrunner, *AIG,* vol. 2.2, p. 506.

[60]However, the rest of the story has been assimilated to another myth, that of Trita in the well. The sālāvr̥kīsutāḥ are Trita's attackers.

Br̥haddev. III.132 tritaṃ gās tv anugacchantaṃ, krūrāḥ *sālāvr̥kīsutāḥ*
kūpe prakṣipya gāḥ sarvās, tat evāpajahrire

The cruel sons of the hyena, having thrown Trita, who was following the cows, into a well, carried off all the cows.

What about their mother? The feminine stem does exist, in two forms: salāvṛkī́ (MS, TS, etc.) and sālāvṛkī́- (KS/KapS etc.); indeed she seems almost the only form of the adult animal that does exist. In Vedic prose the masculine sālāvṛká- occurs only in our myth (where it seems to result from haplology); in many later texts even in lists of masculine animals the feminine sālāvṛkī will appear, as in the following catalogues of ill-omened cries:

> ĀpŚS XV.19.4 atha yadi gṛdhraḥ *salāvṛkī* bhayeḍako dīrghamukhy ulūko bhūtopasṛṣṭaḥ śakunir vā vadet
>
> If a vulture, a (female) Salāvṛkī, a wild ram, a Parra-bird, an owl, one possessed by a Piśāca, or a Śakuni-bird should call
>
> ĀpDS I.10.19 *salāvṛky*-ekasṛka-ulūka-śabda-
>
> The noise of a (female) Salāvṛkī, of a solitary jackal, of an owl. [Cf. also BŚS IX.18 quoted above.]

The animal seems characteristically female: this is a grammatical reason for favoring 'hyena' as a gloss, as it recalls the curious fact that Greek ὕαινα 'hyena' is also always feminine. The association of the animal with females is also evident in a famous passage from the RVic Purūravas and Urvaśī hymn. The nymph Urvaśī urges the mortal Purūravas not to kill himself from love of her, with the cold comfort of verse 15:

> RV X.95.15 ná vaí straíṇāni sakhyā́ni santi, sālāvṛkā́ṇāṃ hṛ́dayāny etā́
>
> Truly, there are no friendships with women; they have the hearts of hyenas.

Though the form here is masculine, the personality is typed as female.

The gender agreement between Greek and Sanskrit might at first seem merely a curious grammatical accident, but in fact it seems to reflect important features of hyena physiology and social organization. First, among striped hyenas the sexes look very much alike: "In their natural state it is only possible to tell them apart when the female suckles its young and the teats are extended. The male has a very small scrotum which makes it hard to identify."[61] If only female sexual characteristics are ever readily identifiable, it is easy to understand why the female should come to stand for the entire race.[62]

The prominence of the female physiologically is matched in the organization of hyena societies, which seem to show female dominance. Walker asserts that female dominance is the rule among striped hyena. Most other sources are silent on this issue, though Rieger states: "I know of three [striped] hyaena males that were clearly subordinate to their females, but no information of males dominating their females are [*sic*] known to me." Among spotted hyenas this dominance is quite clearly described by Kruuk; for example: "If the sexes meet, males step aside."[63] Indeed, the social structure of spotted and brown hyenas seems to revolve around females: there is a communal den, consisting of the females and their cubs—adult males are seldom seen there. Skinner and Ilani refer to this den among our striped hyenas as a "maternity den" (p. 231).[64]

[61]Ilani 1975, p. 11.

[62]Among spotted hyenas the female has some physiological features that set her even further apart. The female is much larger than the male (Kruuk 1975, p. 76). (Among striped hyenas the sexes are the same size [so Walker 1983, pp. 1059f.] or the males are slightly larger [Rieger 1979, p. 89; Kruuk 1976, p. 105; 7–12 percent—D. Macdonald 1984, p. 157].) Moreover, in spotted hyenas the female genitalia mimic in a rather amazing fashion those of the male: "The clitoris can be erected to the same extent as the penis" (Kruuk 1975, p. 75); indeed, "the clitoris looks exactly like a penis, and, as well as this, the female also has a sham scrotum, looking very masculine indeed, but with nothing significant inside it. This is the structure which brought into the world the story of hyaenas being hermaphrodite; it goes back to the days of Aristotle, and is still current in Africa today" (Kruuk 1975, p. 75). Unfortunately in our striped hyena "the sexual organs are conventional" (D. Macdonald 1984, p. 157; cf. Grzimek 1975, p. 191).

The alternative explanation of the feminine gender of ὕαινα (Ernout and Meillet 1959, s.v. volpēs)—"Le genre féminin que présentent plusieurs des noms de l'animal . . . est, comme dans le dérivé gr. ὕαινα, un moyen de marquer du mépris pour une bête sans courage" (The feminine gender that several animal names show is, as in the derivative, Greek ὕαινα, a way of marking scorn for a beast without courage.)—may tell us more about the attitudes of the writers of this dictionary than of the speakers of the original language.

[63]Walker 1984, p. 1060; Rieger 1979, p. 89; Kruuk 1975, p. 77.

[64]Spotted: Kruuk 1972, p. 234; van Lawick-Goodall 1971, pp. 159–161, 180. Brown: Owens and Owens 1984, pp. 255f., 260f. Striped: Skinner and Ilani 1979, p. 231. Among striped hyenas, however, the father does seem to be more in evidence and more involved in the care of the young, at least at the beginning of the cubs' life. Cf. Ilani 1975, p. 15; Rieger 1979, p. 89.

2. Indra and the Mother Hyena

The female hyena, then, is a formidable animal, and the predominance of the feminine stem sălāvr̥kī in Vedic is not surprising. The extent of her power is suggested by several briefly narrated stories in Vedic prose, one of which will, unexpectedly, give us the clue to Indra's participation in the Yati story. In one a rejected Dakṣiṇā (the 'present' or 'fee' given to the priests officiating at a ritual) becomes a Sālāvr̥kī and destroys the Asuras.[65] More important for us is one of the many tales of the gods' winning the world away from the Asuras. In two passages in the BYV, in a story structurally parallel to the strides of Viṣṇu[66] (and immediately preceding it in the MS version), a Salāvr̥kī circles the world three times to make it entirely the gods' territory. In both passages the story is told apropos of the demarking of the Vedi (altar).

> MS III.8.3 ásurāṇāṁ vā́ iyám ágra āsīd yā́van niṣádya parā́paśyaṁs tád devā́nāṃ té devā́ḥ salāvr̥kī́m abruvan yā́vad iyā́ṃ tríḥ samantā́ṃ paryéti tád asmā́kam íti sā́ vā́ imā́ṃ tríḥ samantā́ṃ páryait tád vaí devā́ imā́m avindanta

> In the beginning this (earth) was the Asuras'. (Only) as much as they saw while sitting down was the gods'. The gods said about a/the Salāvr̥kī: "As much as she goes around completely three times (will be) ours." She went around this (earth) completely three times. In this way the gods acquired this (earth).

This circling of the world by the Salāvr̥kī may be a reflection of hyena marking behavior, either of a clan territory or of a more limited area. Spotted hyena clans inhabit a well-defined territory, whose boundaries are clearly marked by laying down scent. "Small parties of [spotted] hyenas regularly 'patrol' the borders." More important for our purposes, Macdonald repeatedly observed among striped hyenas what he calls a "circular tour" during feeding. "Typically a feeding hyena would break off from its meal and make a 'circular tour' (of about

[65]KS XXVIII.4/KapS XLIV.4, ĀpŚS XIII.7.12; for more on this myth, see Chap. 3, B.2.

[66]In one of the most popular and enduring stories in Indian mythology, the god Viṣṇu, often in the guise of a dwarf, makes three massive strides, which cover the earth, the atmosphere, and heaven, thus winning all the worlds for the gods.

25m. radius) around the feeding site. Sometimes these tours were associated with scent-marking activity, but mostly they had no obvious function although they might happen every 5–10 minutes."[67]

The TS version of this story has a surprising twist: Indra makes himself into the Salāvṛkī and wins the world:

> TS VI.2.4.3–4 ásurāṇā́ṃ vā́ iyám ágra āsīd yā́vad ā́sīnaḥ parāpáśyati tā́vad devā́nāṃ té devā́ abruvann ástv evá no 'syām ápī́ti kíyad vo dāsyāma íti yā́vad iyā́ṁ salāvṛkī́ tríḥ parikrā́mati tā́van no dattéti sá índraḥ salāvṛkī́ rūpáṃ kṛtvémā́ṃ tríḥ sarvátaḥ páryakrāmat
>
> In the beginning this (earth) was the Asuras'. (Only) as much as one sees while sitting down, so much was the gods'. The gods said, "Let there be (a share) for us in this (earth) also." "How much shall we give you?" "As much as this Salāvṛkī goes around three times, that much give us." *Indra, having made himself a Salāvṛkī in form, went around this (earth) completely three times.*[68]

I would suggest that this same transformation is involved in the Yati story, that it is Indra in the form of a Salāvṛkī, a female hyena, who gives the Yatis to the Sālāvṛkeyas, feeding them to the young hyenas that are structurally and grammatically his/her offspring. So the action would be appropriate in some sense, proper parental behavior to provide live food for the helpless but developing young to practice their hunting skills on. Although I have no indication that striped hyenas ordinarily feed *live* food to their young, they are particularly well known for carrying food to their cubs. According to Rieger, cubs start eating meat at about thirty days (while still suckling). The adults carry food back to the den. "The *female* prepares meat for her offspring by cutting it into pieces and dropping them beside the cubs" (my italics).[69]

[67]Spotted: Kruuk 1975, p. 66. Striped: D. W. Macdonald 1978, p. 195.

[68]A disguised form of this story also appears in the TĀr.

> TĀr. I.6.3 etayaivendraḥ salāvṛkyā saha / asurān parivṛścati
>
> With this (verse) Indra, together with the female Salāvṛkī, 'cuts around' the Asuras.

The verb pari √vraśc means literally 'cut around, carve' (cf. ŚB VI.7.2.8) and must refer to the Salāvṛkī's 'running circles' around the Asuras and demarking the world as the gods'. But the transformation of Indra into a female hyena is too radical for this later text, and she is demoted to Indra's companion.

[69]Striped hyenas carrying food: Skinner and Ilani 1979, p. 231; cf. Walker 1983, p. 1060. Female preparing meat: Rieger 1979, p. 89. Brown hyena mothers also bring food

Kruuk observed both this behavior and, with older cubs, the mother's taking the cubs along on searches for food, rather like Indra/Salāvṛkī and her Sālāvṛkeyas: "In striking difference with the spotted hyaena, the striped hyaena *female* also regularly took meat to her offspring, carried in the mouth. . . . When cubs were over six months old, they began to accompany their *mothers* on foraging expeditions" (my italics). Macdonald also describes an apparent family group, with two parents and two relatively grown littermates, feeding together.[70]

As a motherly act of nurture, Indra's action may not inspire the horror that the desecration of the ritual and betrayal of the Yatis might be expected to evoke. In other words, under this interpretation, this is not a story of Indra, the violent warrior, callously handing over the Yatis to a pack of ravening beasts, but rather of Indra, in the guise of a protective mother, feeding her cubs. The evidence just presented for this mythic complex is, to some degree, indirect, but it seems to me persuasive. We already saw that the stem sālāvṛkeyá- found in most versions of the myth identifies the young of a mother; but the myth on its surface lacks this implied mother figure. On the other hand, elsewhere Indra is transformed into a female Salāvṛkī́, an appropriate mother for our Sālāvṛkeyas. One need only superimpose these two facts to achieve the identification here suggested. And once we have made this identification, we find other evidence to support it. First, stories of Indra's transformations are legion, and in a number of them he becomes a female, though usually to work mischief.[71]

Then let us look at the verb in the initial sentence of our myth, prá̄yacchat. I have already noted that it is a surprisingly nonheroic verb. It also turns out to be a completely nonviolent verb. Pra √yam is never used, unless here, to consign an object to its doom, nor is it used of betrayal or deliberate destruction. Pra √yam is quite a benign idiom ordinarily; in fact, with pra √dā it forms a suppletive system in the simple meaning 'give, proffer'. Pra √yam supplies the transitive present; pra √dā the passive, causative, transitive aorist, and nominal

to their cubs (Owens and Owens 1984, p. 260). But among spotted hyenas meat is apparently seldom or never brought to the cubs; they have to follow along on hunts and learn to make their way to the kill (cf. Kruuk 1972, p. 172; Kruuk 1975, p. 70; van Lawick-Goodall 1971, pp. 196f. [mothers sometimes bring back bones for cubs]; D. Macdonald 1984, p. 157).

[70]Kruuk 1976, pp. 105–6; D. W. Macdonald 1978, p. 195.

[71]As discussed recently by O'Flaherty 1985b; cf. also Oertel 1898, p. 120; Hoffmann 1960b (1975, pp. 114f.); and texts such as KS XIII.5, MS II.5.5.

forms. Even though outside of this idiom the present dadāti occurs freely, it is seldom found with pra.[72] One example of the interchange is

MS III.9.4 eté vā́ amúṣmiṃl loké 'nnasya pradātā́ras té 'smā ánnaṃ práyachanti

They are the *givers of food* in yonder world. They *give food* to him.

Various nouns serve as objects to these verbs, many of the usual gifts desired by Vedic people, both material and spiritual. One of the common objects is 'food' ánnam (as above) or 'the eating of food' annā́dyam. The Yatis as object of prā́yachat can serve merely as a particular type of food. The verb shows that the emphasis is not on the destruction of the Yatis but on the feeding of the Sālāvr̥keyas. One might translate this sentence fully as: 'Indra (in the shape of a female hyena) gave the Yatis (as food) to the young hyenas'.

There is other evidence for Indra's parental role. One of the two occurrences of sālāvr̥ká- in the RV is the following curious passage in an Indra hymn.[73]

RV X.73.3 r̥ṣvā́ te pā́dā prá yáj jígāsy, ávardhan vā́jā utá yé cid átra
tvám indra sālāvr̥kā́n sahásram, āsán dadhiṣe aśvínā́vavr̥tyāḥ

[Geldner:] Hoch sind deine Füsse, wenn du ausschreitest; die Vājas stärkten (dich) und welche (Götter) sonst noch dabei (waren).
Du Indra hast tausend Wölfe in den Mund gesteckt; du mögest die Aśvin herbringen.
[High are your feet when you go forth. The Vājas strengthened (you) and which (gods) (were) also there.

[72]Pāṇini teaches the suppletion between √dā and present yacchati (VII.3.78), but does not confine it to the preverb pra.

In this connection it should be noted that in a few versions of the indrasya kilbiṣāṇi indictments, all of Indra's misdeeds are mentioned in the aorist. In these the verb for the Yati episode is prādāt, the aoristic counterpart of imperfect prāyacchat in this lexeme. Otherwise the abbreviated mention conforms to the prototype first sentence of the myth: so AB VII.28 (/JB II.134) yatīn sālāvr̥kebhyaḥ prādāt. Other versions of the indictment, couched in the imperfect, maintain pra √yam: KauṣUp III.1 prāyaccham; ŚāṅkhŚS XIV.50.1–2 prāyacchat.

[73]Note in passing that this hymn is adjacent to the one containing the peculiar Yati reference X.72.7; however, the Anukramaṇī (RV index) assigns these two hymns to different poets, and so their juxtaposition is probably accidental. The other occurrence of sālāvr̥ká- in the RV was discussed above.

You Indra have put a thousand wolves in your mouth. You should bring the Aśvins hither.]

Geldner claims (in his note to the passage) that the only point of the (italicized portion of the) passage is to emphasize how large Indra's mouth is (as compared to his feet!); the Sālāvr̥kas are mentioned because their jaws are especially fearful. He explicitly denies that the passage has anything to do with our "well-known saga" ("Mit der bekannten Sage . . . hat die Stelle nichts zu tun"). But this seems ingenuous at best. There are many ways in the RV to express vastness, but the number of wolves that will fit into a space is not one of them. And of course the Sālāvr̥kas are not wolves anyway. The word sālāvr̥k(ey)á- is rare enough in Vedic that the image intended in this passage must be specific. The image is too striking, poetically disruptive, to be merely a nonreferential spatial measure.

I think this may be a glancing reference to Indra's career as mother Salāvr̥kī: picking her young up by the scruff of the neck and carting them around. Hyenas are distantly related to cats, and they do (at least spotted and brown ones) carry their young in their mouth. Owens and Owens relate a remarkable tale of a female carrying her six-week-old cub in her mouth to the communal den, a distance of about two miles.[74] The image of some variety of feline carrying her young in her mouth is found explicitly in another Vedic text, as an image of gentleness.

PB VII.9.11 yathāṅkulī putrān saṃdaśyāsaṃbhindatī harati yathā vāto 'psu śanair vāti

Even as an aṅkulī [= mārjārī 'female cat', according to Sāyaṇa] picking up her offspring with her teeth (but) not biting carries them, even as the wind blows softly on the water [so is the sāman to be sung].

Of course, as Geldner suggests, the RVic passage is also a measure of Indra's prodigious powers—unlike a normal animal he could carry a thousand young at a time—but the mythological kernel must be there to have made this image intelligible to contemporary audiences.

The last evidence for Indra as hyena parent comes from the Sā-

[74]Related to cats: Kruuk 1972, p. 6; Ilani 1975, p. 11. Carrying young in their mouths: van Lawick-Goodall 1971, pp. 155f., 159f., 178ff., and photograph no. 14; Grzimek 1975, pp. 187, 193; Owens and Owens 1984, pp. 255f.

maveda Brāhmaṇa version of our myth. It is indirect, but offers a strong thematic parallel to the YV situation. Note especially the PB passage; the JB version is similar, though less explicitly parental. In both stories three Yatis remain after the Sālāvṛkeyas feed—a number that makes the denouement of both versions strongly trifunctional.[75] They are young (the JB calls them kumārāḥ 'boys'), and they ask Indra to raise them as sons (so the PB). He agrees, lifts them up, and carries them about until they are grown, whereupon he grants each a wish and settles them down in prosperity.

> PB XIII.4.17 indro yatīn sālāvṛkeyebhyaḥ prāyacchat teṣāṃ traya udaśiṣyanta pṛthuraśmir bṛhadgirī rāyovājas te 'bruvan *ko na imān putrān bhariṣyatīti aham itīndro 'bravīt tān adhinidhāya paricaryācarad vardhayaṁs* tān vardhayitvābravīt kumārakā varān vṛṇīdhvam iti

> Indra handed over the Yatis to the Sālāvṛkeyas. Three of them were left: Pṛthuraśmi, Bṛhadgiri, and Rāyovāja. They said, "*Who will bear/support us (as) sons?" "I", said Indra. Putting them up (on his back), serving them, he set about raising them*. Having raised them he said: "Boys [notice tender kumāraka-], choose yourself boons."

> JB I.185 indro yatīn sālāvṛkebhyaḥ prāyacchat / teṣām adyamānā-nāṃ trayaḥ kumārāḥ paryaśiṣyanta rāyovājaḥ pṛthuraśmir bṛhadgiriḥ / ta indram astuvan tān abravīt kiṃkāmā mā kumārās stutheti *bibhṛhy eva no maghavann ity abruvan tān antarāṃsayor adhyāsyata . . .*[76]

> Indra handed over the Yatis to the Sālāvṛkas. Of them being eaten, three boys were left: Rāyovāja, Pṛthuraśmi, and Bṛhadgiri. They praised Indra. He said to them, "With what desire do you boys praise me?" *"Bear/support us, o Maghavan," they said. He threw them up between (/over?) his shoulders. . . .*

In context it makes little sense that the remaining defenseless Yatis should praise Indra and ask for his care, after he has just fed their relatives to the hyenas. It makes even less sense for Indra to embark on the arduous task of raising them (on his back!) if he had systematically tried to eradicate their family.[77] But this does makes sense as a trans-

[75]For more on this version, see Chap. 4, B.

[76]Text following Oertel 1898, p. 123.

[77]Bodewitz (1984, p. 67) is also troubled by this, but reaches quite different conclusions about its causes. See Appendix.

posed echo of Indra's parental behavior towards the Sālāvr̥keyas. Notice the emphasis on Indra's physically carrying the boys, reminiscent of RV X.73.3 above. It may be that the story of the three boys and the three boons was grafted onto the Sālāvr̥keya story precisely because of this underlying parallelism.[78]

[78]There is one last passage involving Indra and the Sālāvr̥kas, in the AV; it is difficult to fit it in with the other evidence about their relations.

AV II.27.5ab táyāhám̐ śátrūnt sākṣa [Whitney—sākṣya], índraḥ sālāvr̥kā́m̐ iva

With this (plant) will I overcome (my) rivals, like Indra the Sālāvr̥kas.

No other passages depict a hostile relation between Indra and the hyenas. Perhaps this refers obscurely to a portion of the myth in which Indra as Salāvr̥kī defeats and dominates adult male hyenas. Without further evidence this passage must remain unexplained.

CHAPTER 3

The Ritual in the Myth

Positing a transformation of Indra into a mother hyena helps clarify his relation with the young hyenas, but leaves unexplained why the Yatis are the chosen food and why the feeding occurs in the midst of a ritual. Let us begin with the Yatis. Here I can point out two ways to mitigate the horror of the ritual desecration associated with their death. First, the sudden attack of the Sālāvr̥keyas seems to have forced the Yatis into committing a set of ritual flaws. Though to modern eyes these are scarcely their fault, to the ritualist the motivation or cause of such flaws is of no interest; they all demand their expiation, their Prāyaścitti, and in this case the harsh Prāyaścitti may be the death of the person who committed the error.

Second, and in a more positive vein, the Yatis, strict ritualists as we have seen, may actually have accomplished the ritual objectives they had set themselves, by their own deaths. These two approaches overlap to some degree.

A. The Yatis' Ritual Flaws

Some of the ritual flaws, depicted in the KS, are quite obvious.

KS XXV.6 (= KapS XXXIX.4) ta ādīyamānās saṃmr̥śyamānā *uttaravediṁ samudakrāmaṁs* tān nābhyadhr̥ṣṇuvaṁs *teṣām eko 'smayata* tata enān abhyadhr̥ṣṇuvan . . . tasmān na moghahāsinā bhavyam

They (the Yatis) being taken, being seized, *went up to/upon the Uttaravedi*. They (the Sālāvr̥keyas) did not dare against them. *One of them (the Yatis?) smiled*. Then they dared against them. . . . Therefore, there is to be no foolish laughing.

Their taking refuge on the Uttaravedi is surely an unseemly act, clambering up on the altar, violating sacred space. We have also already mentioned the ill-timed and no doubt nervous smile that gave the Sālāvr̥keyas the courage to attack them on the Uttaravedi. The smile breaks the solemnity of the ritual vow of silence, when only words prescribed by the ritual may be spoken and only in prescribed tones of voice.[79]

Then in the MS the cup overturns, and Hariṇa spills the precious soma, a grave violation indeed.

MS III.9.3 *sá yátra camasám̥ nyaùbjat* táto rohítako 'jāyata

Where he overturned the cup a rohītaka tree arose.

The ritual manuals all have elaborate treatments of the expiations necessary for spilling any of the liquids used in sacrifice.[80]

A final violation, perhaps the worst, is not immediately discernible, but emerges from close examination of the words used in the telling of the myth. In the three passages above treating the fate of the Yatis' somapītha 'soma-drink', it 'goes' or 'flies' up:

MS I.10.12 somapīthó vā́ eṣò 'syā́ údaiṣad yát karī́rāṇi

The soma-drink that went up from this (earth?)[81] is (now) karīra (fruits).

KS XXXVI.7 somapītha eṣa udīṣati yat karīrāṇi

The soma-drink that goes up is the karīra (fruits).

[79]Indeed this passage introduces a prescription against laughing in the ritual. The requirement vācaṃ √yam 'restrain/hold speech' is a common part of much Vedic ritual activity, and particular types of speech, such as √jap 'murmer, whisper' are frequently part of the stage directions for given utterances.

[80]Cf., e.g., for the spilling of soma ĀpŚS IX.17.3, XIV.28.2–6; MŚS III.6.21; for other ritual liquids, e.g., ĀpŚS IX.6.1ff., IX.13.1ff.; MŚS III.1.31, III.2.2, 4, 5, 10.

[81]On asyā́(s) in this passage, see n. 85.

KS XI.10 yás somapīthás sá ūrdhvó 'patat tā́ni karī́rāṇi

The soma-drink flew straight up. (It became) these karīra (fruits).

In a fourth passage the liquid is called instead rása- 'sap', but its transformation is identical, and the verb complex is the same as in KS XI.10:

TS II.4.9.2 tésāṁ rása ūrdhvò 'patat tā́ni karī́rāṇy abhavan

Their "sap" flew straight up. (It) became these karīra (fruits).

Rása- is here then just a designation for somapīthá-.[82]

Now somapīthá-, though rare and apparently semantically neutral in RV and AV, is a charged word in Vedic prose; it does not refer merely to soma or a measured amount of it. Rather, one might say, it refers to soma in its relation to the participants in the ritual. Though sometimes it is simply the physical drink they consume at a ritual performance, it is often instead an abstraction: the power or privilege of drinking soma, in other words the abstract quality that allows one to participate fully in the most solemn rites. Here is one from among many such passages:

TS II.1.5.5–6 yá ā́ tṛtī́yāt púruṣāt sómaṃ ná píbed víchinno vā́ etásya *somapīthó* yó brāhmaṇáḥ sánn ā́ / tṛtī́yāt púruṣāt sómaṃ ná píbatīndrāgnī́ evá svéna bhāgadhéyenópadhāvati tā́v evā́smai *somapīthám* prá yacchata upaínaṁ *somapīthó* namati

One who for three generations [so Keith] should not (have) drunk soma, his 'soma-drinking' is cut off. One who, though being a

[82]Rása- is used as a byword for soma elsewhere in Vedic. For example, in the AB passage in which the gods overturn their (soma) cups (quoted in part above), what spills from these cups is called rasa, and when one eats the vegetation that this rasa turned into one 'mysteriously' obtains somapītha. This passage thus makes explicit the identity of rasa and somapītha.

AB VII.30 tatraitāṃś camasān nyubjan [*sic*—*nyaubjan] . . .

They overturned their cups there.

.31 teṣāṃ yaś camasānāṃ *raso* 'vāṅ ait ta 'varodhā abhavann atha ya ūrdhvas tāni phalāni . . . yo nyagrodhasyāvarodhāṃś ca phalāni ca bhakṣayaty upāha parokṣenaiva *somapītham* āpnoti

The *sap* of these cups that went downward became the descending growths [of the nyagrodha tree] and that which (went) upward (became) these fruits. Who eats the downward growths and the fruits of the nyagrodha tree, he mysteriously obtains *soma-drinking*.

Brahman, does not drink for three generations has recourse to Indra and Agni with their own share [i.e., he offers soma to them]. They grant 'soma-drinking' to him. 'Soma-drinking' bows down to him.

As this passage shows, the possession of somapītha can be hereditary. It can also be bestowed on someone for exceptional merit: an often told myth involves the twin Aśvins, the healers of the gods. Though they begin as non-soma drinkers, they bargain for somapīthá in exchange for one or another act of healing.[83]

MS IV.6.2 tā́ abrūtāṃ bhāgó nā astv íti vṛṇā́thām íty abruvaṁs tā́ abrūtāṃ gráhaṃ nau gṛhṇantu *somapīthám áśnavāvahā* íti

(The Aśvins) said, "Let us have a share." "Choose," said (the gods). They said, "Let them draw a cup for us. *Let us attain the soma-drinking.*"

It is also a quality of which one can be deprived for various mistakes and excesses. Indeed, Indra himself is on several occasions so deprived. We saw one example above, where the gods exclude Indra from soma-drinking for the totality of his offenses. The usual expression is, as there, somapīthena vyr̥dhyate '(PN) is deprived of soma-drinking'.

The ambiguity between concrete and abstract somapītha is often deliberately played upon, and I think it is here in our passages as well. Abuse of the concrete somapītha leads to deprivation of the abstract somapītha. For the Yatis the clue to what kind of abuse lies in the verb.

The ūrdhvó 'patat of KS XI.10 (yás somapīthás sá ūrdhvó 'patat) / TS II.4.9.2 (téṣāṁ rása ūrdhvò 'patat) may seem a colorless descriptive expression, 'flew (straight) up, erect', but comparison of another occurrence in Vedic prose shows the contrary. It is a euphemism for vomiting, as we can see by examining several accounts of another, well-known Indra episode, the killing of Viśvarūpa, Tvaṣṭar's son.

In this story, after Indra kills Viśvarūpa, the enraged Tvaṣṭar refuses to allow Indra to drink soma, but Indra by force (or guile) acquires some of Tvaṣṭar's soma anyway. Having drunk it, without permission

[83]For their non-soma-drinking state, cf., e.g., MS IV.6.2 devā́nāṃ bhiṣájā āstām aśvínā ásomapau 'The Aśvins were the healers of the gods, (and) non-soma-drinking'. It is, of course, ironic that what makes them unfit for soma-drinking in the first place—their practice of medicine—affords them the leverage to bargain for the privilege, by significant acts of healing.

or invitation,[84] he vomits it and is again deprived of somapītha. Let us examine an MS version of this in a Kāmyā Iṣṭi 'special rite' for the recovery of a soma vomiter:

> MS II.2.13 índro vaí tváṣṭuḥ sómam apibad ánupahūyamānas tásyordhváḥ *somapīthò* 'patat té śyāmā́kā abhavant somapīthéna vā́ eṣá vyr̥̀dhyate *yáḥ sómam̐ vámiti*
>
> Indra drank Tvaṣṭar's soma without being invited. *His soma-drink 'flew straight up'* (and) became these millet (grains). He is deprived of soma-drink(ing) *who vomits soma.*

The verb is ūrdhváḥ . . . apatat, exactly the verb in the KS and TS passages about the Yatis, and the parallelism of ūrdhváḥ . . . apatat and vámiti here and in the following passages imposes the correct interpretation of this euphemism. The phrase ūrdhváḥ √pat 'fly straight up' is thus a Sanskrit expression exactly parallel to English 'throw up'. The word ūrdhvá- is explicitly used with √vam in a TS version of the same episode:

> TS II.3.2.5–6 índraḥ / tváṣṭuḥ sómam abhīṣáhāpibat . . . sá indriyéṇa somapīthéna vyàrdhyata sá *yád ūrdhvám udávamīt* té śyāmā́kā abhavan
>
> Indra drank Tvaṣṭar's soma by force. . . . He was deprived of his Indriyan strength and soma-drink(ing). *What he vomited upward* became these millet (grains).

The KS also attests to vomiting in this tale.

> KS XI.1 indro vai tvaṣṭus somam anupahūto 'pibat . . . sa yat *parāvamīt* te śyāmākāḥ
>
> Indra, uninvited, drank Tvaṣṭar's soma. . . . What he *vomited forth* became these millet (grains).

In the Yati passage KS XI.10, yá somapīthás sá ūrdhvó 'patat must also mean '(Their) soma-drink was vomited' (and similarly TS

[84]One might note in passing that upa √hvā 'invite to' seems to be the opposite of vi √r̥dh 'deprive of' somapītha-. A complete discussion of the attainment, possession, and loss of somapītha- is beyond the scope of this work; suffice it to say that it is a theme of great importance, running through a number of apparently disparate myths.

II.4.9.2), as in MS II.12.13 just quoted. The apparently similar expression ud √īṣ 'go up' in MS I.10.12[85] and KS XXXVI.7 presumably also means the same thing. But this lexeme is very rare (c. five other occurrences in all of Vedic), and unfortunately I can find no other passages where it clearly means 'vomit'.

So, one or more of the Yatis, in the panic of the Sālāvṛkeyas' attack, vomited the soma he had just ritually consumed. Vomiting soma is a serious offense and requires not merely an expiatory action or Prāyaścitti, but a separate expiatory ritual, the Sautrāmaṇī, which will be discussed later.[86]

Indra's sad state after drinking soma illicitly now allows us to explain a puzzling detail in a passage discussed earlier. Recall MS III.9.3, in which the somapīthá of the unfortunate Camasādhvaryu Hariṇa was transformed into a snake (svajá-).

> MS III.9.3. téṣāṁ vā́ eṣá brahmacārī́ camasā́dhvaryur āsīd yò 'yáṁ hariṇás tásya yáḥ somapīthá ā́sīt sá svajò 'bhavat tásmād dhariṇā́ḥ svajā́ṃ khādati somapīthó hy ásyaiṣá
>
> The cup-adhvaryu was their student, a certain Hariṇa—his soma-drink became a viper(?). Therefore hariṇas eat vipers—because it (the viper) was its (the hariṇa's) soma-drink.

Why should this central ritual substance become this fearsome animal? As the story of Indra and Tvaṣṭar's soma shows, if someone has no right to the abstract somapītha 'the right/privilege of drinking soma', drinking the concrete somapītha makes him sick: he literally cannot keep it in his body. In MS III.9.3 the soma is showing this dangerous aspect: it has become venomous, a poisonous snake, with the potential to cause serious injury. But because the snake was originally Hariṇa's

[85]There is a slight textual problem also with MS I.10.12: in somapīthó vā́ eṣò 'syā́ údaiṣat, the asyā́(ḥ) has no clear referent and no parallel in the KS passages (KS XXXVI.7 somapītha eṣa udīṣati; KS XI.10 yás somapīthás sá ūrdhvó 'patat). I would suggest that this asyā́(ḥ) was added in imitation of a nearly identical previous passage in MS I containing ud √īṣ, where the asyā́(ḥ) has clear reference to 'this (earth)':

> MS I.6.3 asyā́ evaínam ánabhimṛté 'dhyā́dhatte ráso vā́ eṣò 'syā́ údaiṣat . . . ū́rg vā́ eṣò 'syā́ údaiṣat
>
> He thus lays it (the fire) on an undefiled (part) of this (earth). Truly, the essence/nourishment went up from this (earth).

Thus asyā́(ḥ) in MS I.10.12 is an intrusive addition to the passage and has no obvious referent.

[86]See Sec. C.1.

soma-drink, the mongoose/gazelle (hariṇa) can consume it without ill effect, for he has a right to it (somapīthó hy ásyaiṣá 'for it was his soma-drink').[87]

B. The Yatis' Place on the Ritual Ground: The Uttaravedi

Let us now consider the possibility that the Yatis fulfilled their ritual objectives with their own deaths. To explore this requires determining what those objectives might have been, what ritual(s) the Yatis may have been engaged in. A clue can be found in the part of the ritual ground most closely associated with the Yatis. Two of the most dramatic presentations of the myth (TS VI.2.7.5, KS XXV.6) relate the eating of the Yatis at or on the Uttaravedi, the upper altar. Both the passages appear in sections devoted to the construction of the Uttaravedi and, especially, the purification of it and the ground south of it with water. Another striking passage, MS III.9.3, explains the use of rohītaka wood for the Yūpa, the post to which the sacrificial victim is tied, which lies directly east of the Uttaravedi. Hence, the Yatis' activity seems especially concentrated in this portion of the sacrificial ground, and it seems worthwhile to inquire into the function of the Uttaravedi (and the Yūpa). In what rituals is it used and for what purposes?

[87]In this connection a more exact identification of the svajá- becomes crucial. Its presumed derivation, from √svaj 'embrace', suggests 'constrictor' (or python), as Whitney consistently translates it in his AV (also Caland, with hestitation, in his translation of the passage given above). Its tendency to lurk in trees (tásmād rohītake-rohītake svajáḥ 'therefore there's a svaja in every rohītaka tree') may also fit this snake. But a serious problem with this identification for my interpretation of the passage is that constrictors are apparently nonpoisonous. Hence, I am inclined to accept the more usual rendering of svajá- as 'viper' (BR; Monier-Williams, both s.v.; Mayrhofer, *KEWA*, sub svájate; Keith, TS translation, etc.), or, perhaps better, to substitute 'cobra', the traditional enemy of the mongoose. The Vedic svajá- was not always arboreal: cf. AV V.14.10 svajá ivābhíṣṭhito daśa 'Bite like a svaja when *stepped on*'. If the svaja is a viper or a cobra, its derivation from √svaj 'embrace' may be simply because of the usual coiled position of snakes lying in wait or striking, rather than because of its method of killing its prey.

Of course, another possibility is that the ancient Indians simply did not know that the python's bite was nonvenomous. But they were keener-eyed observers of nature than we often allow, especially in matters that would literally mean life or death. Needless to say, Vedic knows a good many names for snakes, besides the generic ahi-. AV X.4 alone has more than ten such names.

1. The Uttaravedi: A Dangerous Place

In the simpler śrauta rituals, the three sacred fires are set up in a relatively restricted space, with an east-west axis. The Gārhapatya (householder's) fire is at the extreme west of the space, with the Dakṣināgni (southern fire) to the south and a bit to the east of it. The Āhavanīya (offering) fire is at the extreme east, with the Vedi (altar) just to its west, between it and the Gārhapatya. (See figure 1, Introduction.) However, for a number of the more elaborate rites the sacrificial ground is greatly expanded to the east, a Mahāvedi (great altar) is demarked, and at the extreme east of this the Uttaravedi (upper altar) is raised by piling up earth. On this somewhat elevated part of the Mahāvedi a new Āhavanīya fire is established, carried eastward from the original Āhavanīya (which now becomes the Gārhapatya).[88] (See figure 2.)

Though the Uttaravedi is not used in all the śrauta rituals, it is a standard fixture in the more elaborate ones, the soma sacrifices; it is also used in several non-soma sacrifices. In the Agnicayana (laying of the fire) the new fire altar is built on it (cf., e.g., KS XX.4; MS III.2.5). It is used in the Paśubandha, the animal sacrifice (the independent one as well as the one embedded in the soma sacrifice), in the Sautrāmaṇī, and in the Varuṇapraghāsa, the second of the Cāturmāsyāni (the 'four-monthly' or seasonal sacrifices), the only one of these seasonal sacrifices to use it. The usual offerings are poured into the Āhavanīya fire in these rites, but the Uttaravedi also has some particular uses in some rituals. In the Paśubandha, the Sautrāmaṇī, and the Varuṇapraghāsa, there is a complication, which provides some source for confusion. *Two* new altars are built to the east: a northern Vedi (uttarā- vedi-) and a southern Vedi (dakṣiṇā- vedi-). The Uttaravedi proper is then constructed on the *northern* Vedi. For example, regarding the Varuṇapraghāsa, a ŚS prescribes the construction:

> ĀpŚS VIII.5.21 uttarasyāṃ vedyāṃ paśubandhavad uttaravedim upavapati
>
> He builds (lit. strews) the Uttaravedi (upper altar) on the Uttarā Vedi (northern altar), as at the Paśubandha.

[88]On the creation of these altars, see, e.g., Eggeling's note to ŚB II.5.2.5.

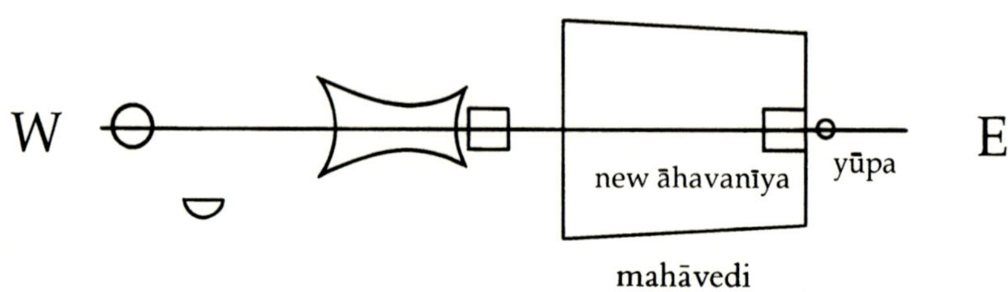

Figure 2. The Expanded Ritual Ground

Ideally then, the difference is signalled syntactically: the northern Vedi has an attributive adjective (fem. uttarā-), while the Uttaravedi proper is a compound. Unfortunately the ritual texts are not always grammatically punctilious in this matter. The problem arises, of course, because of the ambiguity of the term uttara-, which can mean both 'higher' and '(more) north'.[89]

So far this description of ritual geography may seem irrelevant and fussy, but both the Uttarā Vedi and the Uttaravedi have some surprising associations that one would not predict from the mere description of their positioning. The Uttarā Vedi (northern Vedi) is called 'the place/womb of the devourers', for example, in a passage concerning the Varuṇapraghāsa rite:

> MS I.10.13 (≅ KS XXXVI.7) yéyám úttarā védir *yā́ atrī́ḥ prajā́s* tā́sām eṣā́ yóniḥ

> The northern Vedi is the place/womb of *the devouring creatures*.

[89]Indeed, Dange (1980–81, p. 114) falls victim to this confusion and mistranslates uttaravedi- in KS XXV.6 as 'northern altar', a mistake that Bodewitz points out (1984, p. 66, n. 9).

It is contrasted with the southern Vedi (daksiṇā vedi), which is 'the place/womb of the creatures to be devoured' (yéyáṃ dákṣiṇā védir yā́ ādyā̀ḥ prajā́s tā́sām eṣā́ yóniḥ).

Moreover, when the Uttaravedi proper, the upper altar associated with the Yatis, is constructed, the mantras addressed to her (the noun vedi- is feminine in gender) include

> siṁhī́(r) asi 'Thou art a lioness'.
> [VS V.12, MS III.8.5, KS XXV.6, etc.]

This mantra will provide the final clue to link Indra/Salāvr̥kī with the Uttaravedi and the ritual activity taking place there.

2. *Some Fierce Transformations*

The mantra makes reference to a tale in which the Uttaravedi is transformed into a lioness and stands between the gods and the Asuras.

> TS VI.2.7.1 tébhya *uttaravedíḥ siṁhī́ rūpáṃ kr̥tvó*bháyān antarā́pa-krámyā́tiṣṭhat té devā́ amanyanta yatarā́n vā́ iyám upāvartsyáti tá idám bhaviṣyantī́ti
>
> *The Uttaravedi, having made herself a lioness in form,* having stridden away from them, stood between both (parties). The gods thought, "Whichever (party) she will turn to, they will thrive here."[90]

Needless to say, she goes over to the gods, in return for a share of the sacrifice, and the gods thrive.

Let us examine the position and form of the story. In both TS and MS this passage follows relatively soon after the winning of the world (and the Vedi) by the Salāvr̥kî (TS VI.2.4.4, MS III.8.3), and in fact it is a direct continuation of it. Though a few pages of text intervene in both TS and MS, the text in between contains no mythological material,[91] and in TS VI.2.7.1 the abrupt introductory pronoun tébhya(ḥ) 'from

[90]Cf. also MS III.8.5, KS XXV.6.

[91]At least in the TS. The MS contains a few parenthetical mythological remarks about different potential places for worship and a mythological etymology of the term uttaravedi-.

them' shows that the passage must be extracted from the middle of a myth, since there is no referent for this pronoun in the sentence.[92] Since different myths are often narrated in the same section of the text in order to bolster the same ritual point, the proximity of the two stories is most likely significant, not accidental.

First, consider again the passage concerning the Salāvr̥kī's winning of the world, noting especially the exact parallelism in language between Indra's transformation and the Uttaravedi's:

> TS VI.2.4.3–4 ásurāṇāṃ vā́ iyám ágra āsīd yā́vad ā́sīnaḥ parāpáśyati tā́vad devā́nāṃ té devā́ abruvann ástv evá no 'syām ápīti kíyad vo dāsyāma íti yā́vad iyáṁ salāvr̥kī́ tríḥ parikrā́mati tā́van no dattéti *sá índraḥ salāvr̥kī́ rūpáṃ kr̥tvé*mā́ṃ tríḥ sarvátaḥ páryakrāmat
>
> In the beginning this (earth) was the Asuras'. (Only) as much as one sees while sitting down, so much was the gods'. The gods said, "Let there be (a share) for us in this (earth) also." "How much shall we give you?" "As much as this Salāvr̥kī goes around three times, that much give us." *Indra, having made himself a Salāvr̥kī in form,* went around this (earth) completely three times.
>
> TS VI.2.7.1 *uttaravedíḥ siṁhī́ rūpáṃ kr̥tvā́ . . .*
>
> *The Uttaravedi, having made herself a lioness in form . . .*

Thus, both Indra and the Uttaravedi transform themselves into fierce female animals. The similarity between the stories was obviously clear to the composers of these texts, since they occur in close proximity.

There are further, covert parallels between the stories. Vedic texts tell of another transformation into a Salāvr̥kī besides the one Indra undergoes. In KS XXVIII.4/KapS XLIV.4 (cf. ĀpŚS XIII.7.12) a rejected Dakṣiṇā becomes a salāvr̥kī. (The original and prototypical Dakṣiṇā is a cow, hence the feminine gender of the word.) In the KS/KapS passage the Dakṣiṇā was given to the gods by the Asuras; taking it back, when the gods reject it, proves to be the Asuras' downfall.

[92]Pronominal forms of sá/tám are almost without exception anaphoric to a referent in the immediately preceding sentence. (Cf. Jamison, forthcoming, a; M. Hale, forthcoming; Hock 1982.) We must then assume that there *was* originally a preceding sentence in this myth.

KS XXVIII.4/KapS XLIV.4 asurā vai devebhyo dakṣiṇām anayaṁs tāṃ pratyanudanta . . . sā [dakṣiṇā] sālāvṛkī saṃbhūyāsurān prāviśat sainān niradahat tasmād dakṣiṇā pratinuttā na pratigṛhyā na goṣu cālayet [Kap cārayet] sālāvṛky evainaṃ bhūtvā praviśati sainaṃ nirdahati

The Asuras brought the gods a Dakṣiṇā. They rejected her. . . . She (the rejected Dakṣiṇā) having become a female hyena entered (the ranks of) the Asuras and burned them up. Therefore, a Dakṣiṇā, once rejected, is not to be accepted /taken back, nor allowed to wander among the (other) cows.[93] (If so,) having become a female hyena, she enters him and burns him up.

This story exists in several other versions (AB VI.35–36, ŚB III.5.1.18–25; cf. MS IV.8.3), with variants in the identity of the priests and Yajamāna, in the exact nature of the Dakṣiṇā, and in the creature she is transformed into. Though in the KS passage just cited, the Asuras give the Dakṣiṇā to the gods, in AB VI.35 and ŚB III.5.1.18 the Ādityas offer it to the Aṅgirases. KS does not specify what the Dakṣiṇā is, but in AB it is the earth, itself full of Dakṣiṇās, and in ŚB III.5.1.18 it is Vāc 'Speech'.

AB VI.35 te hādityān aṅgiraso 'yājayaṃs tebhya yājayadbhya imām pṛthivīm pūrṇāṃ dakṣiṇānām adadus tān iyam pratigṛhītātapat tāṃ nyavṛñjan

The Aṅgirases performed worship for the Ādityas. To them performing the worship (the Aṅgirases) they (the Ādityas) gave this earth,

[93]This apparent perception of the Sālāvṛka/ī as especially dangerous to the herd seems to remain a motif in the later, transformed versions of the Yati myth. In both the Bṛhaddevatā version and the MBh. version, the victim is a herdsman.

Bṛhaddev. III.132 tritaṃ gās tv anugacchantam . . .

Trita following the cows . . .

MBh. I.71.25–26 . . . kacam / /

gā rakṣantaṃ vane

Kaca guarding cows in the forest . . .

In the Bṛhaddev. the hyenas make off with all the cows (gāḥ sarvāḥ . . . apajahrire), but in the MBh. the cows get home without their master (I.71.27 tato gāvo nivṛttās tā agopāḥ svaṃ niveśanam) and reveal the murder.

The Indian subspecies of hyena does kill livestock. Cf. Rieger 1979, p. 87, with references.

full of Dakṣiṇās. Once accepted, she burned them (the Ādityas). They turned her back.

ŚB III.5.1.17–18 áṅgirasa ādityā́n ayājayan . . . / / tébhyo vā́caṃ dákṣiṇām ā́nayan tā́ṃ ná prátyagr̥hṇan

The Aṅgirases performed worship for the Ādityas. To them (Aṅgirases) they (Ādityas) brought Speech (as) a Dakṣiṇā. They did not accept her.

The transformations the Dakṣiṇā undergoes are likewise various. She is a lioness in both AB and ŚB, but a rejected Dakṣiṇā is called a tigress in MS, and a female hyena in ĀpŚS, as in the KS passage quoted above.

AB VI.35 (cont.) sā *siṃhī* bhūtvā . . .

She, having become *a lioness* . . .

ŚB III.5.1.21 tébhyo ha vā́k cukrodha . . . *siṁhī́* bhūtvā́ . . .

Speech was angry at them. . . . Having become *a lioness* . . .

MS IV.8.3 yā́ṃ pratinudáte sā́ *vyāghrī́* dákṣiṇā yát tā́ṃ púnaḥ pratigr̥hṇīyā́d vyāghry ènaṃ bhūtā́ právlinīyāt

A Dakṣiṇā that one rejects (becomes) *a tigress*. If (the giver) should accept her again, she, become a tigress, would crush him.

ĀpŚS XIII.7.12 yat pratinuttāṃ dakṣiṇāṃ goṣu cārayet prati vā gr̥hṇīyāt *salāvr̥ky* enaṃ bhūtvā pravlinīyāt

If he should allow a rejected Dakṣiṇā to go among his (other) cows or should accept her (again), she, having become a *female hyena,* would crush him.

Thus we have three very similar transformations into fierce female animals:

Uttaravedi ⇒ siṁhī- 'lioness' (TS VI.2.7.1, MS III.8.5, KS XXV.6)

rejected Dakṣiṇā ⇒ siṃhī- (AB VI.36, ŚB III.5.1.21)

⇒ salāvr̥kī = 'female hyena' (KS XXVIII.4, ĀpŚS XIII.7.12)
⇒ vyāghrī = 'tigress' (MS IV.8.3)

Indra ⇒ salāvr̥kī- (TS VI.2.4.4)

The parallelism is in itself suggestive: since the female creatures on the right side of the arrows are similar and superimposable, the terms on the left side may share some features as well. And in fact this possibility is borne out, at least for the first two transformations.

In the ŚB the *rejected Dakṣiṇā* story is told in the part of the text that concerns the construction of the *Uttaravedi* (III.5.1.12–36), and, quite surprisingly, the story of the Uttaravedi's transformation serves as the denouement of the rejected Dakṣiṇā story, told in the same phraseology as in the BYV versions. The angry rejected Dakṣiṇā, Vāc, becomes a lioness, as we saw above. This is so far parallel to the other rejected Dakṣiṇā tales. But having done so, she stands between the gods and the Asuras, harassing both.

> ŚBK IV.5.1.11 (≅ ŚBM III.5.1.21) sā́ ha siṁhī́ bhūtvā́ntarā́ devāsurā́nt sáṃyattān ādádānā kṣiṇatī́ cacāra tā́ṁ hobháya evá vidā́ṃ cakrur yatarā́n evá na iyám upāvartsyátī́ti té bhaviṣyánti
>
> Having become a lioness, she went about between the gods and Asuras (who were) in conflict, taking (their goods) and harming them. Both (sides) knew, "Whichever of us this one will turn to, they will thrive."

Note the exact parallelism in language to TS VI.2.7.1, the Uttaravedi story:

> TS VI.2.7.1 tébhya uttaravedíḥ siṁhī́ rūpáṃ kr̥tvóbháyān antarā́pakrámyā́tiṣṭhat *té devā́ amanyanta yatarā́n vā́ iyám upā́vartsyati tá idám bhaviṣyantī́ti*
>
> The Uttaravedi, having made herself a lioness in form, having stridden away from them, *stood between both (parties). The gods thought, "Whichever (party) she will turn to, they will thrive here."*

And the parallelism is carried through. She (our rejected Dakṣiṇā, Vāc 'Speech') extracts from the gods the same boon as the Uttaravedi does in TS VI.2.7.1, MS III.8.5, KS XXV.6, and turns to the gods, who then thrive, as in those texts. The identity of rejected Dakṣiṇā/Vāc = Uttaravedi is made explicit at the end of the story:

ŚBK IV.5.1.14 (≅ ŚBM III.5.1.23) vā́g vā́ uttaravedíḥ

Speech is really the Uttaravedi.

Now I am not entirely sure what to make of this. Most of our texts have two separate myths: the rejected Dakṣiṇā destroys her givers and the Uttaravedi yields to the gods, both involving a similar transformation. Only in the ŚB do they form two parts of a whole story. The ŚB version has the merit of providing a motive for the Uttaravedi's transformation into a lioness, an act that has no apparent reason in the other texts.[94] Given the isolation of the ŚB version and its lateness (vis-à-vis the BYV versions), it seems likely that the composers of the ŚB have combined two originally separate myths.[95] But, even so, this shows that the parallelism between the two stories was strongly sensed in Vedic times; the transformations that form the major point of contact between the two stories were viewed as essentially identical. Indra's transformation into a Salāvr̥kī fits the same pattern, as is demonstrated by the facts that he became the same animal (a Salāvr̥kī) as the Dakṣiṇā does in some versions and that his transformation is phrased in the same manner as that of the Uttarvedi.

3. *Why Is the Uttaravedi Dangerous?*

Given this parallelism, it makes sense that Indra as Salāvr̥kī should be localized at the Uttaravedi—the place in the ritual ground that seems most dangerous, since she is a devourer, a fierce lioness—and that violence, the slaughter of the Yatis, should be committed at just this spot. Indeed, the violent death of the Yatis there also has its analogue in the ritual.

What still eludes us is *why* the Uttaravedi should make this fierce transformation. The ŚB solves this problem by identifying the Uttaravedi with the rejected Dakṣiṇā, but this seems secondary. The clue to

[94]The likely reason we will investigate below.

[95]The awkward change in personnel suggests this, too. The Aṅgirases and Ādityas of the first half give way without warning to the gods and Asuras of the second.

the real reason for her transformation lies in the method used to construct the Uttaravedi. The Uttaravedi is made by piling up earth on the demarked Mahāvedi, and digging up the earth is always considered a cruel act, which must be appeased by some ritual action (usually sprinkling with water).

> MS IV.1.10 (≅ MS III.2.3, III.8.5, etc.) átho yád evā́syā udghnántaḥ krū́ram ákraṁs tád ákrūram akas tā́ñ śamayati
>
> Moreover, what cruel (act) they have done (in) 'smashing' up [note the violent verb √han 'smash'] (part) of this (earth), that he has made uncruel, that he appeases.

It is likely that the Uttaravedi becomes a lioness because of this assault on the earth; the Uttaravedi is necessarily created by an act of violence, and she remains a violent creature until she is appeased by sprinkling her with water. This is explicitly stated in the ŚB at the end of the section concerning the creation of the Uttaravedi.

> ŚB III.5.1.35 tā́m adbhír abhyùkṣati / sā́ yád evā́dáḥ siṁhī́ bhūtvā́śāntevā́carac chā́ntir ā́pas tā́m adbhíḥ śamayati
>
> He sprinkles her (= the Uttaravedi) with waters. Since she, having at the time become a lioness, went about unappeased, as it were—waters are appeasement—he (now) appeases her with the waters.

Though the digging of the earth is never stated as the *mythological* cause for the fierceness of the Uttaravedi (who becomes a wild beast), it is thus given here as the *ritual* cause (for the sprinkling of waters following the construction of the Uttaravedi).[96]

C. The Yatis' Ritual Successes

This treatment of the Uttaravedi and related myths of transformation has allowed us to understand why this portion of the ritual ground is associated with fierce female animals and therefore why Indra (as Salāvr̥kī) and the Sālāvr̥keyas should be located there. Now we must

[96]Note also that one MS statement about the cruelty of digging up the earth is in MS III.8.5, which contains the Uttaravedi transformation story.

understand why the Yatis find themselves there, and this requires us to examine some particular rituals that make use of the Uttaravedi.

1. *The Sautrāmaṇī*

The Sautrāmaṇī seems to be a healing or reinvigorating rite, and, curiously, involves the drinking of the intoxicant surā, otherwise forbidden to Brahmans.[97] This ritual is prescribed for people in a number of circumstances, but the common thread that connects them is loss of strength or vigor. Interestingly enough, one for whom it is required is a newly consecrated king. There are two forms of the Sautrāmaṇī, one independent (the Kaukilā form), one a part of the Rājasūya 'royal consecration' (the Carakā form). The process of royal consecration is clearly a dangerously weakening one, as is often stressed.

> MS II.4.1 rājasū́yenābhiṣiṣicānáṁ yājayed indriyéṇa vā́ eṣá vīryèṇa vyṛ̥dhyate yó rājasū́yenābhiṣiñcáte
>
> He should have one being consecrated by the Rājasūya to worship (with the Sautrāmaṇī). Truly he is deprived of strength and manliness who is consecrated with the Rājasūya.[98]

The motif of weakness strengthened by performance of the Sautrāmaṇī is expressed by two small details in the Sautrāmaṇī ritual itself. At the beginning of the ritual the necessary materials are bought from a eunuch, the very image of a lack of virile force.

> KS XII.11 klībāt sīsena tokmāni krīṇāti
>
> He buys the young shoots from a eunuch with lead.[99]

Then at the preparation of the cups of surā, hairs from fierce animals—wolf, tiger, and lion—are placed in each cup.

[97]Treatments of the Sautrāmaṇī in the ritual manuals include ĀpŚS XIX.1–10, BŚS XVII.31–38, MŚS V.2.4, and so on. Cf. also KS XII.9ff, MS II.3.8ff, ŚB V.5.4, XII.7.3.5–13. See also esp. Weber 1893, pp. 91–106; Heesterman 1957, pp. 109f.

[98]The Sautrāmaṇī is prescribed for the newly consecrated king also at ĀpŚS XIX.4, VārŚS III.2.7, MŚS V.2.4.1.

[99]Also MS II.4.2, VārŚS III.2.7.2, ĀpŚS XIX.1.1, BŚS XVII.31, etc. ŚB XII.7.2.12, however, expressly rejects the eunuch as seller.

ĀpŚS XIX.2.10 siṃhalomabhiś cāśvinaṃ śrīṇāti . . . śārdūlalomabhiś ca sārasvatam . . . vṛkalomabhiś caindram

He (the Pratiprasthātar) mixes (the surā-drink) for the Aśvins with lions' hairs, that for Sarasvatī with tigers' hairs, that for Indra with wolves' hairs.

This must be in order to secure their powerful qualities, as the ŚB makes clear.[100]

ŚB XII.7.2.8 āraṇyā́ṇāṃ paśūnā́ṃ lomā́ni bhavanty āraṇyā́ṇāṃ paśūnā́m ávaruddhyai vṛkalomā́ni bhavanty ójo evá jūtím āraṇyā́ṇāṃ paśūnā́m ávarunddhe vyāghralomā́ni bhavanti manyúm evá rājyám āraṇyā́ṇāṃ paśūnā́m ávarunddhe siṁhalomā́ni bhavanti sáha evéśā́m āraṇyā́ṇāṃ paśūnā́m ávarunddhe

There are hairs of wild beasts, for the attainment of (the qualities) of wild beasts. There are wolf hairs; thus he gains the strength and speed of wild beasts. There are tiger hairs; thus he gains the rage and sovereignty of wild beasts. There are lion hairs; thus he gains the might and lordship of wild beasts.

One might also note that consuming (a part of) a wild animal in this ritual is the mirror image of what happened to the Yatis: they were consumed by wild animals.[101]

One of the most common circumstances that requires the Sautrāmaṇī is the vomiting or otherwise purging (ati √pū) of soma. Some prescriptions for the Sautrāmaṇī:

ĀpŚS XIX.4.11 tayā somavāminaṃ somātipavitam . . . yājayet

One should cause someone to worship with this (Sautrāmaṇī ritual) who has vomited soma or been purged by soma.

ŚB XII.7.3.9, 10 sómātipūtasya . . . somavāmínaḥ

(The Sautrāmaṇī is) for one purged by soma or having vomited soma.

[100]Cf. also ŚB XII.7.3.20, V.5.4.18f.; MŚS V.2.11.16; BŚS XVII.34, etc.

[101]The preparation and offering of the surā takes place entirely on the Dakṣiṇā Vedi (southern altar). Only milk drinks are prepared at the Uttarā Vedi (northern altar), so that the wild animal hairs are not *directly* connected with the Uttaravedi, as we might wish.

MŚS V.2.11.2 te kāmāḥ somavāminaś ca

(It is offered for) these (aforementioned) wishes and for one who has vomited soma.

VārŚS III.2.7.1 sautrāmaṇīṁ somavāminaḥ somābhivyajanasya

(One should offer) the Sautrāmaṇī for one having vomited soma (or) having ?-ed[102] soma.

The soma vomiter is not just an afterthought in the list of those who should perform this ritual, for in the YV the discussion of the ritual is almost always introduced by the story of Indra's killing of Viśvarūpa and its aftermath[103]—the story we just examined in which Indra vomits soma and loses his strength. In other words, the soma vomiter is the very symbol of loss of power, of one in need of healing, and those who have lost strength in other ways are later assimilated to him.[104]

[102]The meaning and derivation of the second term, soma-abhivyajana, is not entirely clear. It may belong with later vyajana 'fan' (itself of unclear etymology: cf. Mayrhofer, *KEWA*, s.v.) or—semantically more likely—be formed from a lexeme abhi-vi + √aj 'drive through' (or the like), referring to the violent passage of soma through the body. In any case it seems to be equivalent to somātipūta-.

[103]ŚB XII.7, V.5.4; KS XII.10; MS II.4.1. On this story see Bloomfield 1893, pp. 150, 154f.; Oldenberg 1893, esp. p. 346; Hopkins 1909, p. 50.

[104]The one-day soma rite (ekāha) called the Tīvrasoma ('sharp' or 'bitter' soma) or Tīvrastut seems somewhat related to the Sautrāmaṇī, as Weber already noticed in 1893, p. 98. Its mythological justification is similar: Indra loses his strength after slaying Vr̥tra.

PB XVIII.5.2 indro vr̥tram ahan sa viṣvaṅ vīryeṇa vyārchat tasmai devāḥ prāyaścittim aichaṁs tan na kiñ canādhinot taṃ tīvrasoma evādhinot

Indra slew Vr̥tra. He went asunder in regard to his strength in every direction [so Caland]. The gods sought an expiation for him. Nothing satisfied him. But the Tīvrasoma (ritual) satisfied him.

And in PB XVIII.5.3, MŚS IX.3.4.22, LāṭyŚS VIII.10.7, and KātyŚS XXII.9.15 the ritual is prescribed for (among others) 'one who has purged soma' (somātipavita-), just as the Sautrāmaṇī is. (The somātipavita does not, however, appear in some other treatments of the Tīvrasoma [e.g., JB II.152, BŚS XVIII.29–30, ĀpŚS XXII.10.6–18]).

The special features of this ritual are (1) that for some portion of the ceremony the priests do not taste the soma, as is usual, but merely smell it (PB XVIII.5.15 etc.).

PB XVIII.5.15 tad abhakṣayanta r̥tvijaś camasān avajighranti

Then the priests, not partaking, (just) smell the cups.

Thus, because of their inadvertent soma vomiting the Yatis are in need of the expiatory and healing Sautrāmaṇī. Another detail of vocabulary also shows this. In the two passages in which they vomit, we find directly preceding the vomiting this passage:

KS XI.10 (≅ TS II.4.9.2) téṣāṁ śīrṣā́ṇi *párāpataṁs* té kharjū́rā abhavan

Their heads 'flew off' and became kharjūra (trees).[105]

The idiom párā √pat is relatively common in Vedic prose, and generally describes, as here, the violent or precipitous loss of a body part or bodily fluid, usually either the falling off of head or limb in a hostile encounter or sickness, or the unforeseen release of semen in forbidden sexual encounters such as incest.

KS XXIII.1 índro vaí vṛtrám ahaṁs tásya *cákṣuḥ párāpatat*

Indra smashed Vṛtra. His eye 'flew off'.

MS III.6.5 prajā́patir vaí svā́ṃ duhitáram ádhyaid uṣásaṃ tásya *rétaḥ párāpatat*

Prajāpati approached his own daughter, Dawn. His semen 'flew off'.

What unites these contexts is the loss of strength, of force, and these abstract nouns can also serve as subjects of párā √pat.

MS II.5.7 yád vaí tā́ñ śīrṣṇáś chinnā́t *téja indriyáṁ vīryàṃ parā́patat* . . .

---

and (2) that the two Adhvaryus and *all the Camasādhvaryus* (rather than the Pratiprasthātar alone, as is usual) make a particular response (to the Acchāvāka) (PB XVIII.3.14, JB II.152, ĀpŚS XXII.10.15, BŚS XVIII.29–30, MŚS IX.3.4.28). The avoidance of soma might be a ritualistic reference to the effect soma has on the somātipavita. The participation of the Camasādhvaryus reminds us of the mention of the Yatis' Camasādhvaryu in MS III.9.3. Since the Camasādhvaryu otherwise plays such a minor role in most rituals and is mentioned so rarely in the ritual manuals, one is tempted to see some special connection here between the Tīvrasoma and the Yati passage, but such a connection so far eludes me.

[105]The other two passages concerning the somapītha (MS I.10.12, KS XXXVI.7) also mention the transformation of the heads into kharjūra, but without the verb párāpatan.

When from his (Gāyatri's) split head the splendor, the Indriyan strength, the vigor 'flew off' . . .

Indeed, in one passage in the TS it is Indra's forces that párā √pat, and he is healed by the Sautrāmaṇī.

TS V.6.3.4 índrasya suṣuvāṇásya daśadh*éndriyáṃ vīryàṃ párāpatat* tád devā́ḥ sautrāmaṇyā́ sám abharan

Of Indra, having been consecrated (as king), the Indriyan strength and vigor 'flew forth' in ten parts. Then the gods (re)assembled (him) with the Sautrāmaṇī.

The Yatis may have experienced the same 'flying forth' of téjas- 'splendor', though our evidence is indirect. Consider again the KS passage concerning their smiling. The Yatis, having taken refuge on the Uttaravedi, seem temporarily safe from the Sālāvr̥keyas, but then one of them smiles:

KS XXV.6 (= KapS XXXIX.4) *teṣām eko 'smayata* tata enān abhyadhr̥ṣṇuvan . . . tasmān na moghahāsinā bhavyam

One of them (the Yatis) smiled. Then they (the Sālāvr̥keyas) dared against them. . . . Therefore, there is to be no foolish laughing.

In the MS 'unseasonable smiling' is identified as the cause of the 'flying forth' of tejas:

MS III.6.7 yád anr̥tú smáyeta *téjo 'sya parāpā́tukaṁ syāt* tásmān nā́nr̥tú smetavyàṃ *téjasó 'parāpātāya*

If (someone) should smile unseasonably, his splendor would be liable to 'fly forth'. Therefore there is to be no unseasonable smiling, for the 'non-flying-forth' of splendor.

We can perhaps assume that this same loss of tejas resulted from the Yati's fatal smile. And as we just saw in TS V.6.3.4 the ritual remedy for this precise situation is the Sautrāmaṇī.

Thus the apparently innocent lexemes found in two Yati passages (KS XI.10, TS II.4.9.2), párā √pat and ūrdhváḥ √pat, turn out to have quite specific uses in Vedic prose and to belong to a nexus of mythological narrative and ritual exegesis concerned with the loss of vital strength through both violent attack and soma vomiting. The use of this vocabulary sets up the Yatis as latter-day images of Indra when he became exhausted:[106] the mythological situation that relates the creation of the Sautrāmaṇī ritual, for the healing of Indra. The Yatis were attacked by the Sālāvr̥keyas and brutally dismembered; in the course of the attack the Yatis inadvertently committed ritual flaws, including the vomiting of soma. For both of these reasons they lose their power; it is the Sautrāmaṇī ritual that will restore it. And, providentially, they may have been performing the Sautrāmaṇī when they were attacked, as the employment of the Uttaravedi might suggest. In other words, I think it possible that in the condensed and dreamlike world of the myth, the necessary ritual was begun before the need for it arose.

I will now go further and suggest that several different rituals may be implied simultaneously in this one myth, that the ritual details apparently embedded so casually in the narrative can be related to other of the Yatis' concerns. Let us look in turn at the Paśubandha and the Varuṇapraghāsa.

2. *The Paśubandha*

When we examine the possible role of the Yatis in the Paśubandha, the animal sacrifice, their position on the ritual ground becomes crucial. Remember first that MS III.9.3 concerns the proper wood for the Yūpa or sacrificial post.

[106]The Yatis also parallel Indra in another passage: in KS XXV.6 the treatment of the Yatis is identical to that which befalls the young Indra in another KS passage; however, he is luckier than the Yatis and contrives an escape.

> KS XXV.6 yatīn vai sālāvr̥keyā ādaṁs *ta ādīyamānās saṃmr̥śyamānā* uttavediṁ samudakrāman
>
> The Sālāvr̥keyas ate the Yatis. *They, being taken, being seized,* went up upon the Uttaravedi.
>
> KS X.5. índraṃ vaí jātáṃ rákṣāṁsy asacanta *sá ādīyámāno rákṣobhis saṃmr̥śyámāno* 'gníṃ prā́viśat
>
> The demons followed the newborn Indra. *He, being taken by the demons, being seized,* entered a horse.

Notice that the escape is similar to that devised by the Yati Syūmaraśmi (KS VIII.5, discussed below), who also enters a horse.

MS III.9.3 sá yátra camasám̩ nyaùbjat táto rohítako 'jāyata tásmād raúhītakas tásmād rohī́take-rohītake svajáḥ.

Where he overturned the cup a rohītaka tree arose. Therefore (the Yūpa) is made of rohītaka (wood). Therefore, there's a viper in every rohītaka tree.

The Yūpa is not only adjacent to the Uttaravedi, as noted above; it is also the post to which the animal to be sacrificed is tethered.

The Yatis have even closer affinities to the sacrificial animal. The precise disposition of the animal, once dead, is laid out with great care in the ritual manuals. It is notable that the omentum, the first and perhaps most important of the parts of the victim to be ritually dealt with, is brought to the Uttaravedi after a preliminary warming, and cooked over the Āhavanīya fire on the Uttaravedi by the Pratiprasthātar (the chief assistant of the Adhvaryu), who is sitting *south* of the Uttaravedi; then it is placed on the southern part of the Uttaravedi on the strew.[107]

ĀpŚS VII.19.4 śāmitre vapāṃ pratitapya . . . abhipravrajati

Having heated the omentum on the 'appeaser's (fire)' [north of the Uttaravedi], he goes forth.

.8 āhavanīyasyāntame 'ṅgāre vapāṃ nikūḍyāntarā yūpam āhavanīyaṃ ca *dakṣiṇā*tihṛtya pratiprasthātre *prayacchati*

Having singed the omentum over the outermost coal of the Āhavanīya fire [i.e., the fire on the Uttaravedi], having carried it between the Yūpa and the Āhavanīya fire *toward the south, he hands it over* to the Pratiprasthātar.

.9 tāṃ *dakṣiṇata āsīnaḥ* pratiprasthāt*āhavanīye* śrapayati

The Pratiprasthātar, *sitting south* (of the Āhavanīya fire), cooks it *on the Āhavanīya.*

20.4 alohinīṃ suśṛtāṃ kṛtvā . . . *dakṣiṇasyāṃ vediśroṇyāṃ* barhiṣi plakṣaśākhāyām *āsādya*

107Cf. ĀpŚS VII.19.4–20.4; also ŚB III.8.2.18ff.; MŚS I.8.4.20–27; BŚS IV.7, etc.

Having made it well cooked and no (longer) blood red, *having set it on the southern*/right *hip of the Vedi,* on the barhis on a plakṣa branch . . .

Note the verb in sūtra 8: prayacchati describes the transfer of the Vapā (omentum) to the Pratiprasthātar sitting south of the Uttaravedi, who will cook the meat, make it into food. Prāyacchat is, of course, the verb in the initial sentence of our myth:[108]

índro vaí yátīnt sālāvr̥keyébhyaḥ *prā́yachat*

Indra *handed over* the Yatis to the hyenas.

The Yatis are handed over to the Sālāvr̥keyas, who are also south of the Uttaravedi and who treat the Yatis as food.

KS XXV.6 te . . . uttaravedim̐ samudakrāman . . . teṣām ekaikam āvarham ādan

They (the Yatis) went up to/upon the Uttaravedi. . . . Tearing them off one by one, they (the Sālāvr̥keyas) ate them.

TS VI.2.7.5 tā́n dakṣiṇatá uttaravedyā́ ādan

They ate them south of the Uttaravedi.

In other words, the orderly processes of the ritual animal sacrifice reproduce almost exactly the violent death of the Yatis, who were pulled off the Uttaravedi and eaten south of it. They became, albeit inadvertently, an animal sacrifice, and with their own bodies accomplish the rite they may have set out to perform.

So, once again, as with the Sautrāmaṇī ritual above, we see that a seemingly casual detail in the mythical fragments—the Uttaravedi—can relate the myth and the ritual. Since one of several rites that uses the Uttaravedi is the Paśubandha or animal sacrifice, the Yatis could have been performing a Paśubandha when attacked by the Sālāvr̥keyas, and as the parallelism between mythic and ritual action shows, the Yatis' death enacts an animal sacrifice, perhaps re-enacts the origin of the Paśubandha, just as they re-enacted the origin of the Sautrāmaṇī.

[108]Though perhaps one should not invest this agreement between these particular verbs with too much importance, given that pra √yam is quite a common verb in the meaning 'give'.

One further passage suggests that this speculation is correct. Consider again the passage in which the Yatis took refuge on the Uttaravedi, and the Sālāvṛkeyas did not 'dare against' them (abhyadhṛṣṇuvan).

> KS XXV.6 ta ādīyamānās saṃmṛśyamānā uttaravediṁ samudakrāmaṁs *tān nābhyadhṛsṇuvan*
>
> They (the Yatis) being taken, being seized, went up to/upon the Uttaravedi. They (the Sālāvṛkeyas) did not dare against them.

Almost exactly this phrase is found in a ŚB passage apparently alluding to the origin of the animal sacrifice and found in that section of the text.[109]

> ŚB III.7.4.2 ná vā́ *etám* ágre manuṣyò *'dhṛṣṇot*
>
> In the beginning man did not dare (against) him (the victim).

The Yati myth rationalizes the killing, makes the Yatis in part responsible, by their ritual error, for the Sālāvṛkeyas' courage to kill them, and thus makes the slaughter in the actual Paśubandha legitimate and without evil consequences for the ritual performers.

It is surely no accident that the animal victim is so disposed on the Uttaravedi, given the violent and ferocious nature of this part of the ritual ground. Indeed the vital link between the Uttaravedi and the Paśubandha is asserted in a curious passage in the Vādhūla Sūtra, which begins as the familiar story of the fetching of soma from heaven.

> VādhS no. 41[110] tṛtīyasyām ito divi soma āsīt taṃ gāyatry āharat tasya parṇam acchidyata tat parṇo 'bhavat . . . te devā 'brūvan ka etaṃ somāṃśum anveṣyati kasyaiṣa somapītho bhaviṣyatīti sottaravedir abravīd ahaṃ ca paśubandhaś ceti tau saṃvidānāv etaṃ somāṃśum anvaitāṃ tayor eṣa somapīthas tasmād yatra kva ca paśur ālabhyate tad eṣā nyupyata uttaravediḥ

[109]Abhi √dhṛṣ is elsewhere several times used of someone either daring or not daring to attack an enemy; for example, Indra at first did not 'dare against' Vṛtra (ánabhidhṛṣṇuvann atiṣṭhat MS I.10.14), but the Maruts give him the daring (tè 'bhyàdharṣayan MS I.10.16). Cf. also MS IV.5.9 (Indra against the demon Makha).

[110]Caland 1926b, p. 36.

Soma was in the third heaven from here. The Gāyatrī (meter) [as bird] fetched it. One of its feathers was cut and became the parṇa (tree). . . . The gods said, "Who will pursue this soma-stalk? Whose soma-drink will this be?" The Uttaravedi said, "I and the Paśubandha." They, in agreement, pursued this soma-stalk. It became the soma-drink of those two. Therefore whenever an animal is sacrificed, then the Uttaravedi is constructed.

3. The Varuṇapraghāsa and the Karīrī Iṣṭi

In another rite using the Uttaravedi, the Varuṇapraghāsa (lit. 'the devouring of Varuṇa' [subjective genitive]), we will see that the sacrifice of the Yatis not only did not have evil consequences, but had significant good ones. The Varuṇapraghāsa is the only one of the seasonal rites to employ the Uttaravedi. For us another important feature of the Varuṇapraghāsa is that it employs karīra fruits (or the meal made from them), along with śamī leaves, in an offering of curds.[111]

ŚB II.5.2.9 ubhayátra payasyè bhavataḥ . . .
.11 táyor ubháyor evá karī́rāṇi

On both (altars) there are offerings of curds. . . .
On both of these (he sprinkles) karīra (fruits).

Alternatively, VārŚS prescribes kharjūra meal for the same purpose.

VārŚS I.7.2.23 āmikṣayoḥ kharjūrasaktūn āvapataḥ

The two (priests) scatter kharjūra meal in the two (dishes of) curds.

Karīra and kharjūra are an important part of our myth. In four of the eight YV passages, both the heads and the somapītha of the Yatis are transformed into plants[112]—their heads into kharjūra plants (the wild

[111]Cf. also MŚS I.7.4.7, ĀpŚS VIII.6.13–14, BŚS I.5.5, KātyŚS V.5.11, etc.

[112]The faint MBh. echo of the myth may present a similar transformation of the victim into something akin to plants. The herdsman Kaca is made into pieces like sesame seeds before being fed to the hyenas:

MBh. I.71.26 hatvā śālāvr̥kebhyaś ca prāyacchaṃs tilaśaḥ kr̥tam

Having killed (him), they gave him, made into sesame-seed-sized pieces, to the hyenas.

date, *Phoenix sylvestris*) and the soma into karīra fruits (the caper bush, *Capparis aphylla*).[113]

MS I.10.12 téṣāṁ vā́ etā́ni śīrṣā́ṇi yát kharjū́rāḥ somapīthó vā́ eṣò 'syā́ údaiṣad yát karī́rāṇi

Their heads are (now) kharjūra (plants). The soma-drink that went up from this (earth?) is (now) karīra (fruits).

KS XI.10 téṣāṁ śīrṣā́ṇi párāpataṁs té kharjū́rā abhavan yás somapīthás sá ūrdhvó 'patat tā́ni karī́rāṇi

Their heads flew off and became kharjūra (plants). The soma-drink flew straight up. (It became) these karīra (fruits).

KS XXXVI.7 teṣām etāni śīrṣāṇi yat kharjūrās somapītha eṣa udīṣati yat karīrāṇi

Their heads are (now) kharjūra (plants). The soma-drink that goes up is the karīra (fruits).

TS II.4.9.2 yátīnām adyámānānāṁ śīrṣā́ṇi párāpatan té kharjū́rā abhavan téṣāṁ rása ūrdhvò 'patat tā́ni karī́rāṇy abhavan

Of the Yatis being eaten the heads flew away. They became these kharjūrā (plants). Their sap flew straight up. It became these karīra (fruits).

So, in the Varuṇapraghāsa ritual we have substances closely associated with the Yatis actually offered on the Uttaravedi, exactly where the myth places them.

The ritual makes abundantly clear what the karīra and kharjūra are doing in these passages: in Vedic ritual in general the primary use of karīra fruits is in a particular Kāmyā Iṣṭi 'special rite', called the Karīrī Iṣṭi, which is a rain charm. In this rite, balls made of karīra meal, along with various black objects (clearly sympathetic magic), are assembled

[113]Or such are the usual (though not universal) identifications of these plant names. Cf., e.g., BR s.vv.; Gonda 1980, p. 119; Meulenbeld 1974, pp. 538, 549. Needless to say, it is difficult to judge the accuracy of such identifications. For further discussion, see also Bhide 1972.

on a black antelope skin and variously manipulated to produce rain. Most of the Vedic texts mention only karīra meal.[114]

BŚS XIII.38 athāntarvedi kṛṣṇājine madhuṣā karīrasaktūn saṃyauti . . . tisraḥ piṇḍīḥ kṛtvā

Then within the Vedi on the black antelope (skin) he mixes karīra meal with honey; having made three balls . . .

But Āpastambha gives a choice of karīra or kharjūra, that is, the plant created from the Yatis' heads.

ĀpŚS XIX.26.1 tasmin *kharjūrasaktūn karīrasaktūn vā* . . . kṛṣṇamadhuṣā saṃyutya tisraḥ piṇḍīḥ kṛtvā

On it (the skin) having mixed together *kharjūra or karīra meal* with black honey, having made three balls . . .

The association of karīra fruits with rain is even clearer in another Vedic mythological episode also associated with rain. When Indra cuts the wings off the mountains to steady the earth, the sap/essence that flowed out became karīra fruits. This detail appears in both the MS and KS versions of this myth, which in both cases follows immediately on the Yati tale.

MS I.10.13 prajā́pater vā́ etáj jyeṣṭháṃ tokáṁ yát párvatās té pakṣíṇa āsaṁs té parāpātám āsata yátra-yatrā́kāmayantā́tha vā́ iyáṃ tárhi śithirā́sīt téṣām índraḥ pakṣā́n achinat taír imā́m adṛ̥ṁhad yé pakṣā́ ā́saṁs té jīmū́tā abhavan . . . eṣá táto yáḥ prathamó rásaḥ prā́kṣarat tā́ni karī́rāṇy abhavan . . . vṛ̥́ṣṭiṃ taíḥ sáṃtanoti

The mountains were the oldest progeny of Prajāpati. They had wings. They were continually flying forth wherever they liked. Now at this time this (earth) was shaky. Indra cut the wings off these (mountains). With these (wings) he steadied this (earth). The wings became these clouds. . . . The sap that first flowed forth thence became these karīra fruits. He extends rain with them.

[114]E.g., MS II.4.8; KS XI.10; MŚS V.2.6.3, 5; BŚS XIII.37–38. For another important connection between the Karīrī Iṣṭi and the Yati myth, see Chap. 4, A.3.

I assume that karīra and kharjūra fruits have certain characteristics that make them appropriate both as transformed soma-drinks and heads, respectively, and as symbols of rain, but I have so far not been able to identify those characteristics.[115] It is noteworthy, however, that the diet of striped hyenas consists not only of meat (scavenged or not) but also of plants; they are especially fond of fruit, and apparently pose some threat to the fruit crops of Israel, especially melons, also *dates*.[116]

The connection between the Karīrī Iṣṭi and the Varuṇapraghāsa is clear. The Varuṇapraghāsa is performed 'in the rainy season' (cf., e.g., ĀpŚS VIII.4.13); since karīra fruits are especially associated with rain, they are ordinarily employed in the Varuṇapraghāsa ceremony. Moreover, the Karīrī Iṣṭi, the 'rain-charm', was probably often performed in conjunction with the Varuṇapraghāsa, or at least in the same season. For even the dullest observers of nature, it makes little sense to perform a rain charm during the times of the year when rain never comes; one would perform such a ceremony directly before rain is expected, or, even more likely, during a period when it is expected but has not come—in other words a period potentially coinciding with the Varuṇapraghāsa. The position of our mythological passages supports this: KS XI.10 and TS II.4.9.2 are in special rites for rain, while MS I.10.12 and KS XXXVI.7 are in the Varuṇapraghāsa section, but in passages especially devoted to bringing rain. Immediately after the Yati story, the passage continues:

> MS I.10.12 yát karī́rāṇi bhávanti vṛ́ṣṭyā annā́dyasyā́varuddhyai
>
> In that there are karīra (fruits) [used at the Varuṇapraghāsa], it is for the gaining of rain and of food eating.

(Cf. also MS II.4.8.) The KS explicitly states the link between rain and the Varuṇapraghāsa:

> KS XXXVI.7 varuṇapraghāsair vr̥ṣṭim eva saṃtanoti tasmāt tarhi bhūyiṣṭhaṃ varṣati
>
> He extends rain with the Varuṇapraghāsa (rites). Therefore it rains best at this time.

[115] Dange (1980–81, p. 114) suggests that the Yatis' heads turn into kharjūra fruits (wild dates) because their heads were shaved. Needless to say, this rests on no textual evidence.

[116] Kruuk 1976, p. 10. In Israel: Ilani 1975, p. 13.

Again we see the Yatis fulfilling sacrificial objectives by their deaths. They are not merely performing a ritual to bring rain; they actually become the *ritual materials* that bring rain, that, by the principle of sympathetic magic, *are* rain. It is in this context that we can return to the difficult RVic passage we took up long ago.

RV X.72.7 yád devā yátayo yáthā, bhúvanāny ápinvata
átrā samudrá ā́ gūḷhám, ā́ sū́ryam ajabhartana

[Geldner:] Als ihr Götter *wie Zauberer* die Welten anschwelltet, da holtet ihr die im Meere versteckte Sonne.
[When, O Gods, like magicians you swelled the worlds, then you brought the sun hidden in the ocean.]

We are now in a position to understand how the Yatis' 'swelled the creatures', not as magicians, shamans performing a cosmic dance, but as ritual priests[117] whose slaughter transformed them into the plants that bring rain, into rain itself, the vital element that does indeed 'swell the world': the plants, the animals, the food that humans depend on.

The central connection between rain, food, and well-being hardly needs to be demonstrated, especially for India, but note passages such as these extracted from RV V.63:

RV V.63.1cd yám átra mitrāvaruṇā́vatho yuvám̥, tásmai vr̥ṣṭír
mádhumat pinvate diváḥ

O Mitra and Varuṇa, whom you aid here, for him rain from heaven swells sweetness [= food].

.2c vr̥ṣṭím̥ vām̥ rā́dho amr̥tatvám īmahe

We implore you two for rain—your gift, immortality.

.5d diváḥ samrājā páyasā na ukṣatam

O you two All-kings, sprinkle/increase[118] us with the 'milk' of heaven.

[117]Von Schroeder himself (1909, p. 14) recognized the Yatis' affinity with rain ("wenigstens werden ihre Überreste zu regenschaffenden Potenzen": "at least their remains came to have rain-creating power") and suggested they were something like 'Regendoktoren' (rain doctors), nonetheless still concluding that they were shamans.

[118]Ukṣatam can come either from √ukṣ 'sprinkle' or √vakṣ/ukṣ 'make grow', and in this case both meanings may be present.

Thus, the myth of Indra, the Yatis, and the Sālāvr̥keyas seems to represent a model Vedic sacrifice, perhaps recounting the origin of the animal sacrifice itself, and as such it can be reckoned among Indra's beneficial cosmogonic activities.

CHAPTER 4

The Episode of the Survivors

We have not as yet examined the other strain of the Yati story, that found primarily in the SV Brāhmaṇas. As noted above, the major narrative thrust of this version seems at first to be unrelated to the rest of the story and at best might seem to have been attached to the beginning of the Sālāvr̥keya tale because of thematic parallelism: the motif of Indra as adoptive parent. However, closer examination reveals that this version, at least in its broad outlines, must be part of the original mythic complex: the episode of the survivors.

Although almost all of the YV passages concerning the Yati myth[119] imply that the Yatis were entirely lost, in a curious KS passage one Yati makes an ingenious escape.

> KS VIII.5 indro vai yatīn sālāvr̥keyebhyaḥ prāyacchat teṣām adyamānānāṁ syūmaraśmir r̥ṣir aśvaṃ prāviśat

> Indra handed over the Yatis to the hyenas. Of them being eaten, the r̥ṣi (seer) Syūmaraśmi entered a horse.

This detail in the story, like so many others, has a fractured reflection in a later text. MBh. XII.260–262 presents a dialogue between the well-known ascetic Kapila and a certain Syūmaraśmi. It begins, in the Crit. Ed.,

[119] As well as shorter passages in PB XIV.11.28 (= XIX.4.7), XVIII.1.9; JB II.134; and elsewhere (AB VII.28).

MBh. XII.260.9 tāṃ gām *ṛsiḥ syūmaraśmir, praviśya yatim* abravīt

The *ṛsi Syūmaraśmi,* having *entered* the cow, said to the ascetic/*Yati* . . .

The situation and the vocabulary are exactly the same as in our KS passage, save for the identity of the invaded animal. Moreover, two manuscripts (T_1 G_2) have, instead of yatim, yatir, which I would be tempted to edit. Though Kapila, the addressee, can appropriately be called yati- 'ascetic'—he is frequently identified as a muṇi- 'id.' and sometimes as a yati-[120]—this passage so slavishly echoes KS VIII.5 that the stem yati- must originally have been introduced on its model. Thus the passage would begin 'The ṛṣi Syūmaraśmi, a Yati, having entered the cow. . . .' The content of the MBh. dialogue is not otherwise relevant to our passage.

The second sentence of the KS passage begins exactly as the long JB version does:

KS VIII.5 *teṣām adyamānānām̐* syūmaraśmir ṛṣir aśvaṃ prāviśat

Of them being eaten, the ṛṣi Syūmaraśmi entered a horse.

JB I.185 indro yatīn sālāvṛkebhyaḥ prāyacchat *teṣām adyamānānāṃ* trayaḥ kumārāḥ paryaśiṣyanta rāyovājaḥ pṛthuraśmir bṛhadgiriḥ

Indra handed over the Yatis to the hyenas. *Of them being eaten,* three boys were left: Rāyovāja, Pṛthuraśmi, Bṛhadgiri.

The PB version is simply a stripped down variant of this:

PB XIII.4.17 indro yatīn sālāvṛkebhyaḥ prāyacchat *teṣāṃ* traya udaśiṣyanta pṛthuraśmir bṛhadgirī rāyovājaḥ

Of them three were left: Pṛthuraśmi, Bṛhadgiri, Rāyovāja.

The agreement in phraseology here between KS VIII.5, on the one hand, and the JB/PB passages just cited is what leads me to believe that the episode, or its beginning, belongs to the pan-Vedic version of the myth and is not confined to the SVic texts. The parallelism between

[120]Cf. Sörensen 1904, sub Kapila.

the names Syūmaraśmi (KS) and Pṛthuraśmi (JB/PB) provides ad tional evidence for this connection.[121]

A. Syūmaraśmi and the Horse

1. *A Clever Escape and a Second Birth*

The KS passage continues, indeed concludes, very oddly indeed:

> KS VIII.5 tasmād aśvas svaṁ śakṛd upajighrati kaś cid [better reading KapS VII.1 kac cid) ṛṣiṃ cāgniṃ ca na nirāsthā3m
>
> Therefore a horse sniffs its own excrement (thinking), "Have I not expelled the/an ṛsi and Agni/the fire?"

Agni is here because the immediately preceding story in this passage concerns Agni's entering a horse; it begins agnir vā aśvaṃ prāviśat 'Agni entered a horse'.[122]

What are we to make of this bizarre twist? The clue, as usual, lies in the vocabulary, specifically the two verbs nirāsthā3m 'Have I expelled?' and upajighrati 'he sniffs'. Despite its unusual form, nirāsthā3m belongs to the root √as 'throw'.[123] The idiom nir √as is fairly common in Vedic texts, ordinarily meaning literally 'cast out', hence 'expel'. Once in the ŚB it is also used specifically of some type of elimination of quasi food from the body, either by vomiting or by excretion. In this passage the sun (= Indra) swallows the moon (= Vṛtra), sucks out his essence, and then expels him, to swell again.

[121]Syūmaraśmi/Pṛthuraśmi are the only figures with apparent existence outside this story. Syūmaraśmi is twice mentioned in the RV, though glancingly, in lists of mortals patronized by the Aśvins (I.112.16) or Indra (VIII.52.2 [= Vālakh]). Syūmaraśmi Bhārgava also appears in the Anukramaṇī as author of RV X.77–78.

Pṛthuraśmi's sāman (the Pārthuraśma) is mentioned not only directly in connection with this story, but also elsewhere (cf. TS V.4.12.2–3; ŚB XIII.3.3.5). Moreover, as we will see, in JB I.185 Pṛthuraśmi is identified with well-known Pṛthu Vainya (cf. Macdonell and Keith 1912, sub Pṛthi).

Bṛhadgiri occurs once in the RV, but as an epithet of the Maruts ('having lofty mountains', V.57.8), and not apparently elsewhere as a proper name. Rāyovāja seems similarly isolated.

[122]The entering (pra √viś) of animals and other objects is a common Vedic topos, whose dimensions we cannot explore here.

[123]On this aorist, see Hoffmann 1967, pp. 59f.; Hoffmann 1976, p. 566, n. 19.

> ŚB I.6.4.18 tád vā́ eṣá evéndraḥ / yá eṣá tápaty áthaiṣá evá vr̥tró yác candrámāḥ . . . úpaivá nyā́plavate sò 'sya vyā́ttam ā́padyate
> .19 táṃ grasitvā́ . . . (20) táṃ nirdhī́ya *nirasyati*
>
> The one that burns [= sun] is Indra, and the moon is Vr̥tra. . . . He (Vr̥tra) swims to (him = Indra) and falls into his opened mouth.
> (Indra), having swallowed him, . . . having sucked him out, *expels* him.

In another Vedic passage the verbal idiom describes the expulsion of an embryo, in the well-known story of the abortion of Mārtāṇḍa.[124]

> KS XI.6 *sā́ gárbham adhatta* sò 'ntár evá gárbho 'vadat tá ādityā́ amanyantāyáṃ ca vaí janiṣyáte sá evédáṃ bhaviṣyatī́ti táṃ níraghnan *sá nírasto* 'śayat
>
> She (Aditi) became pregnant (lit. put an embryo (in) herself). The embryo, (still) within (her), spoke. The Ādityas [= his brothers] thought, "If this one will be born, he will thrive here." They smashed him out [= aborted him]. *Expelled/aborted* he lay there.

Nir √as is thus not an unusual idiom for expressing either defecation or birth, the two events simultaneously described in KS VIII.5. We will return to this oddly produced newborn.

2. *The Sniff-Kiss*

The root √ghrā 'sniff' and its compounds are also common and even more telling. Sniffing, particularly sniffing by animals, serves particular purposes in Vedic ritual, mythology, and daily life, and this KS passage, besides simply describing a facet of equine behavior, alludes to these wider applications. As Hopkins long ago clearly (and indeed entertainingly) demonstrated, sniffing—what he calls the "sniff-kiss"—is an important physical gesture of affection in ancient India, particularly between parents and their children, as "a token of family love and chaste affection."[125] It is indeed prescribed by the Gr̥hya

[124]For more on this myth, see Chap. 7, C.2.

[125]Hopkins 1907, p. 131. Accepting Hopkins's evidence for the sniff-kiss does not require accepting his belief that the "mouth-kiss" did not exist at this time. Nonetheless, his statement of this underlying premise deserves wider circulation: "We may start with the assumption that there was a primeval barbarism to which kissing was unknown, for the reason . . . that if people had ever known so agreeable a practice they could never

Sūtras on various ceremonial occasions, particularly in the Jātakarman ceremony (rites for the newborn) and when a father returns from a journey. For example, in the Jātakarman:

ĀpGS VI.15.1 jātaṃ vātsapreṇābhimṛśyottareṇa yajuṣopastha ādhāyottarābhyām abhimantraṇaṃ *mūrdhany avaghrāṇaṃ* dakṣiṇe karṇe jāpaḥ

Having touched the newborn with (the accompaniment of) the Vātsapra (hymn), having put him on his lap with the next yajus, (there is) addressing (of the child) with the next two, *sniffing at his head,* (and) murmuring into his right ear.

KāṭhGS XXXIV.7 *mūrdhani nighrāpya* svastyayanaṃ vācayati

Making (him = the father) sniff at (the child's) head, he (the priest) asks the blessing.

JGS 1.8 *athāsya mūrdhānam upajighrati . . . paśūnāṃ tvā hiṃkārenābhijighrāmī*ty evam eva pravāsād etya putrāṇām upajighrati

Then he sniffs his head (saying), "*I sniff thee with the paśu's sound* 'him.'" Even so he sniffs (the heads) of his children on returning from a journey.

The gesture is clearly understood as modelled on the behavior of domestic animals, particularly cows.[126]

What Hopkins does not bring out is the apparent reason for this practice. The sniffing of the infant child by its father, as well as its analogue among the animals, is most clearly to establish breath (prāṇa), hence life, in the newborn. This power of animation ascribed to sniffing, especially horses' sniffing, is found in a mythological episode briefly told twice in PB. Prajāpati has created the creatures, but they do not thrive. Having become a horse, he sniffs at them, and the problem is solved.

PB XX.4.5 prajāpatiḥ prajā asṛjata *tā na prājāyanta[127] . . . *tā aśvo bhūtvābhyajighrat* tāḥ prājāyanta

---

have forgotten it, or, if this is not sufficient, the absence of the practice among savages and the cult of kissing among civilized people of the highest class may serve as an indication of the course of development" (p. 121).

[126]Cf. Hopkins 1907, and see esp. the JGS passage just quoted.

[127]Following Caland 1931, ad loc.

Prajāpati created the creatures, (but) they (themselves) did not reproduce. *Having become a horse, he sniffed at them.* They reproduced.

PB VII.10.15 prajāpatiḥ prajā asṛjata tāḥ sṛṣṭā aśocaṁs *tāḥ* śyaitena hummā ity *abhyajighrat* tato vai tāḥ samaidhanta

Prajāpati created the creatures. They, once created, suffered. With the Śyaita (Sāman) with 'hummā' [note the onomatopoetic animal noise] *he sniffed at them.* Thereupon they throve.

This same myth seems to be glancingly referred to in the TS explanation for the bovine equivalent of the Jātakarman rite:

TS VI.4.11.3–4 prajā́patir evá tát prajā́ abhíjighrati tásmād vatsáṃ jātáṃ gaúr abhíjighrati

Prajāpati then sniffs the creatures. Therefore a cow sniffs (her) calf, just born.

The connection between this sniffing and breath is made explicit in the ritual application of this concept. In the Agnicayana, when the svayamātṛṇṇā (self-perforated) brick is laid, a horse is made to sniff it, to establish breath in it:

TS V.2.8.1 (= .3.2.1; .3.7.4) svayamātṛṇṇā́m úpadadhāti . . . áśvam úpaghrāpayati prāṇám evā́syāṃ dadhāti

He puts on the 'self-perforated' (brick). . . . He makes the horse sniff it. Thus he puts breath in it.

MS III.2.6. áthaiṣā́ svayamātṛṇṇā́ . . . áśvam upaghrā́yya[128] sādáyati . . . átho prāṇā́nām útsṛṣṭyai

Then (there is) the 'self-perforated' (brick). . . . Having made the horse sniff (it), he sets (it) down. . . . Moreover (this is) for the creation of breaths.

[128]If the text is correct (there are no variants reported), upaghrā́y-ya must be a gerund to a causative stem *ghrāyáyati, parallel to ghrāpayati found in the TS passage (V.2.8.1). Whitney (*Roots*) does not record such a stem, but it could have easily been formed in the same manner as pāyáyati 'makes drink', pyāyáyati 'makes swell'. However, Stanley Insler (pers. comm.) prefers to consider this a false reading for *upa-ghrā́-ya, since -āyáyati causatives are avoided in Vedic. See Insler 1987, esp. pp. 64f.

Similarly, in the Pravargya rite,[129] the priest animates the clay used to make the ritual pots by causing a horse to sniff it:

> MŚS IV.1.1.14 piṇḍaṁ samavadānīkṛtvāyur dhehīty aśvenopaghrāpya . . .
>
> Having broken off a lump (of clay), having made a horse sniff it (with the words) "Establish life" . . .

There are several other reasons for sniffing. One, especially among animals, is for recognition or knowledge. This belief is succinctly expressed in the MBh. dictum (V.34.32) gandhena gāvaḥ paśyanti 'cows see by smell'. A ŚB passage explains why paśus ([domestic] animals) use smell to learn things:

> ŚB XI.8.3.10 cákṣur evá paśūnā́m ā́datta / tásmād eté cākaśyámānā ivaivá ná jānanty átha yádaivópajighranty átha jānanti
>
> (The sun) took the paśus' eye. Therefore they, though looking about very hard, don't recognize/know (anything). But when they sniff at (it), then they recognize/know (it).[130]

Similarly, in the ritual, smell gives recognition:

> ŚB IV.5.8.5 tā́m . . . droṇakalaśám ávaghrāpayati yajñó vaí droṇakalaśó yajñám evaínām etád darśayati
>
> He makes her (the cow) sniff the wooden tub. The wooden tub is the worship. Thus he makes her see [= recognize] the worship.

It is worth noting that elsewhere the droṇakalaśá 'wooden tub' is identified with the head 'mūrdhán-' (cf., e.g., MS IV.5.9), so that the cow

[129]The Pravargya ceremony is a rite associated with the soma sacrifice. The principal action in it is the preparation of a hot milk drink in a large clay pot known as the Mahāvīra.

[130]A personal note might lend support to the superiority of smell for recognition in animals. Our frightened and angry cat was prepared to attack us as we were trying to take him from a veterinarian's cage, though he could see and hear us. But when my husband breathed on him, he became immediately calm.

The famous dog trainer Barbara Woodhouse apparently also used this method. "Her way of getting to know an animal was to breathe into its nose" (obit., *New York Times*, July 11, 1988).

in this passage is sniffing the 'head', just as in the Jātakarman rites. She is, as it were, recognizing her own offspring.

The last reason for sniffing relevant to our passage is purification. In early Vedic this seems to appear only obliquely, in an MS story. Rathaprota Dārbhya is accused. He is told to go and sit silently in the forest, whatever happens. And then:

> MS II.1.3 tám̐ ha sma vaí vyāghrā́ upaghrā́yaṃ tūṣṇī́m evā́pakrāmanti
>
> Then tigers, having sniffed him, went away silently.

This, along with the appropriate worship, effects his purification.

> MS II.1.3 taú vaí tátraivá śvó bhūté yajñāyudhaír anvétyāgníṃ mathitv*ā́gnáye surabhimáte* 'ṣṭā́kapālaṃ nír avapatāṃ táto vā́ enaṃ ná páryavr̥ñjan
>
> Then on the next day the two (r̥ṣis), having followed (him) with the sacrificial vessels, having churned the fire, offered to *Agni the Fragrant* on eight dishes. Thenceforth (people) did not avoid him.

Since accused people smell bad (MS II.1.3 durabhí vā́ etám ā́rad yám abhiśám̐santi: 'a bad smell has reached him whom (people) accuse'), it was presumably the sniffing of the tigers that removed the smell and brought about the cure.

3. What the Horse Did

In KS VIII.5, with which we began, I would claim that all three of these factors are at play in this apparently straightforward description of animal behavior.

> KS VIII.5 indro vai yatīn sālāvr̥keyebhyaḥ prāyacchat teṣām adyamānānām̐ syūmaraśmir r̥ṣir aśvaṃ prāviśat tasmād aśvas svam̐ śakr̥d upajighrati kaś cid [better reading KapS VII.1 kac cid] r̥ṣiṃ cāgniṃ ca na nirāsthā3m iti
>
> Indra handed over the Yatis to the hyenas. Of them being eaten, the rṣi Syūmaraśmi entered a horse. Therefore a horse sniffs its own excrement (thinking), "Have I not expelled the/an r̥ṣi and Agni/the fire?"

The image of the horse sniffing at the two beings it has just excreted/aborted seems precisely designed to evoke the picture of the ritual sniffing of the newborn at the Jātakarman, and more particularly of Prajāpati as (primal?) horse infusing the creatures with breath in the mythological model of the Jātakarman. In other words, the horse in the KS passage is animating, by prescribed ritual means, the creatures he has just in some sense given birth to. One of these creatures is our leftover Yati Syūmaraśmi. The horse is at the same time recognizing them as his progeny—hence the semirhetorical question kaccid r̥ṣiṃ cāgniṃ ca nirāsthā3m 'have I not just expelled a/the seer and a/the fire?'

And I think we can see this action as a sort of purification, too. As we have seen, part of the Yati myth concerns the expiation of the impurity incurred by vomiting or otherwise purging of soma. This birth of Agni and Syūmaraśmi in excrement seems parallel and would require parallel purificatory procedures: the horse's sniffing removes this impurity.

Burning horse dung is used for purification, for example, in the Pravargya ceremony. The pots, once fashioned, are themselves called horse dung and fumigated with horse dung:

> MŚS IV.1.1.21 athainān udīco 'ṅgārān upohya vr̥ṣṇo aśvasya niṣpad asi vr̥ṣṇas tvāśvasya niṣpadā dhūpayāmasīty aśvaśakena kharadeśe dhūpayati
>
> Then having pushed these (pots) northward onto the coals, he smokes/fumigates them with horse dung on the mound (with the words), "You are the excrement of a virile horse. We smoke/fumigate you with the excrement of a virile horse."[131]

This ritual detail precisely recreates our mythic scene. The pots in the Pravargya ceremony are symbolically born as excrement of a stallion, given life by the horse's sniffing of this symbolic excrement, and then purified by the smoke of horse's excrement.

The birth of Śyūmaraśmi and Agni also has a precise ritual application in another sphere. This KS passage is found in the Agnyādhāna section, the initial establishment of the śrauta ritual fires by a householder. The passage continues by chronicling the difficulties the gods

[131] For the mantra, see MS IV.9.1.

face in doing so, particularly in 'dividing' the fire into the three fires necessary for the śrauta ritual. The horse enables them to do so.

> KS VIII.5 agniṃ vai vibhājaṃ nāśaknuvaṁs tam aśvena vyabhajan . . . yau vāva tā ṛṣiś cāgniś ca te evainaṃ tad devate vibhajataḥ.
>
> (The gods) were not able to divide the fire. They divided it with the horse. . . . These two divinities, which are the Seer and the Fire, thus divide it in this way.[132]

Elsewhere a similar dilemma is posed in the area of ritual utterance by the refusal of speech to divide.

> KS XXVII.3 (≅ MS IV.5.8) vāk sṛṣṭā na vyāvartatādhvanad eva sa indro 'bravīn mahyam atrāpigṛhyatām aham etāṃ vyāvartayiṣyāmīti
>
> Speech, (just) created, did not become separated; she just sounded. Indra said, "Let (a soma cup) be drawn for me here. I will separate her."

The MS parallel makes the unity of Speech even clearer:

> MS IV.5.8 sā́ vaí vā́g ekadhā́vadad yā́vad ávyāvṛttā́sīt
>
> Speech spoke only in a single way as long as she was unseparated.

Now there are many stories of the division of speech,[133] but in this case what is at issue is the various formal types of ritual utterance necessary for the performance of the ritual. Just as three fires must be produced from the undifferentiated fire, so must the ṛc, the sāman, and the yajus become distinguished from the unity of speech (and set off from nonreligious speech).

> MS IV.4.9 bráhma vaí yád ágre vyábhavad ṛ́k sā́ma yájuḥ
>
> When the formulation divided in the beginning, the ṛc, the sāman, and the yajus (resulted).

To return to KS VIII.5, the horse, by 'giving birth' to the fire and the seer and breathing life into them, produces the archetypal ritual, the

[132] I still do not understand this last statement.
[133] See below, Chap. 9, C.3, for further discussion.

basic necessities for ritual performance, namely, the fire, the center of ritual *activity*, and the seer (ṛṣi), the fashioner of ritual *speech*. This can be seen as the primal Ādhāna, establishment of the ritual. Just as in the main version of the myth the Yatis reenact the origins of the ritual, so in this brief passage one of the Yatis is (re)born as prototype ritual participant.

There is a further, more precise ritual reminiscence in this KS passage as well. Recall the Karīrī Iṣṭi, the rain charm, in which karīra (and kharjūra), that is, plant material made from the Yatis' bodies, forms an important part of the ritual. This ritual also contains another transformed (albeit disguised) Yati, as sign of impending rain. A black horse is tethered near or in the ritual ground, then frightened by a flapping cloak. If the horse shakes itself or urinates or defecates, it will rain.

> BŚS XIII.38 athaitam aśvaṁ saṃdānāt pramucyottaravargyeṇābhivikṣipaty abhikranda stanaya garbham ādhā iti sa yadi vidhūnute yadi mehati *yadi śakṛt karoti* varṣiṣyatīti eva veda

> Then having released the horse from the fetter, he shakes at (it) with the upper garment, (saying), "Roar; thunder; get an embryo [= become pregnant]." If it shakes itself, if it urinates, *if it makes excrement,* he (the priest) knows "it will rain."[134]

Note especially the mantra (= TS III.1.11.6 etc.: abhikranda stanaya garbham ādhā iti 'Roar; thunder; get an embryo'), in which the horse is enjoined to become pregnant, using the same phrase, garbham ā √dhā, as in the Aditi passage above (KS XI.6). The horse becomes pregnant with rain and then gives birth to it as urine and excrement, just as Syūmaraśmi is reborn as excrement in KS VIII.5. Once again, the Yatis (or, here, one Yati) become rain after their violent death.

B. Indra as Father

What possible relation to the KS passage can the JB/PB passages have, beyond the existence of survivor(s)? Our investigation of the sniffing horse has given us the clue. The horse sniffing its own excrement can serve as an image of a father breathing life into, and giving

[134]Cf. ĀpŚS XIX.25.20–22 and Caland's comments there and in 1908, no. 180, p. 130.

recognition to, his newborn child. This is precisely the episode described in the JB/PB versions. The major difference is that rather than having the horse represent the primal father Prajāpati, we instead have as the father Indra, transformed from tormentor to nurturer of the Yatis. Here the Yati survivors seek a father, and Indra adopts them. Like the horse in KS VIII.5, he gives them a new life, and he acknowledges them as his sons.

> PB XIII.4.17 te 'bruvan ko na imān putrān bhariṣyatīty aham itīndro 'bravīt tān adhinidhāya paricāryācarad vardhayan
>
> They said, "Who will bear us (as) sons?" "I," said Indra. Having put (them) (on his back?), having served them, he set about raising (them).

The boys may in fact be using a verbal formula to compel Indra to acknowledge and take responsibility for them. A ŚB passage describes how a dependent can force a reluctant or forgetful master to take up his duties:

> ŚB II.3.4.7 utó bhartā́ bhāryàṃ nā́nubudhyate sá yádaivā́ha bhāryò vaí te 'smi *bibhṛhí mé*ty áthainaṃ vedā́thainaṃ bhāryàṃ manyate
>
> And (in the case) a supporter does not recognize (a person as one) to be supported: when he (the dependent) says, "I am to be supported by you. *Support me,*" then he knows him and realizes he is to be supported.

The command bibhṛhí mā 'support me' is precisely that found in JB I.186 when the boys praise Indra and then order him bibhṛhy eva naḥ 'support us'.[135] This simple formula may, under the circumstances, have coercive power.

The parallelism between the KS and JB/PB versions is underscored by the likelihood that parental Indra in JB/PB is now in one of his more familiar guises, that of bull. In JB/PB Indra is called trikakubh (and the JB/PB passages are in explanation of the Traikakubha Sāman):

> PB VIII.1.4 tāṁs trikakub adhinidhāyācarat
>
> The Trikakubh, having put (them) on (his back), went along.

[135]See also the words of the little fish in the story of Manu and the flood below (Chap. 8, D.3).

And in the JB Indra puts the three boys between his shoulders, where they hang from his three kakubhs (humps?):

> JB I.185 tān antarāṃsayor adhyāsyata tā asya tisraḥ kakubho 'lambanta
>
> He threw them between his two shoulders. They hung on his three kakubhs.

Indra is called trikakúbh- also at RV I.121.4, where he is giving aid and direction to cows, and Geldner there and Caland (ad PB VIII.1.4) plausibly suggest that trikakúbh- refers to a bull or three-humped bull.[136]

> RV I.121.4 asyá máde svaryàṃ dā r̥tā́yā́pīvr̥tam usríyāṇām ánīkam
> yád dha prasárge trikakúm nivártat . . .
>
> In the exhilaration of this (soma) you gave the confined, bellowing rank
> of cows to the truth [i.e., freed them]
> When the Trikakubh brought (them) down in (their) streaming . . .

The bull-father would then fill the same slot as the horse-father in KS VIII.5.

The remainder of the stories diverge. The JB/PB version concludes,[137] as I mentioned above, with a trifunctional twist (unnoticed by Dumézil or his followers, as far as I can tell). Having raised them, Indra offers the three boys boons, and they choose, especially in the PB, a neatly trifunctional set of gifts.[138] Pr̥thuraśmi desires kṣatra- 'might, dominion' (second function), Br̥hadgiri brahmavarcasa- 'brahmaṇic glory' (first function), and Rāyovāja paśu- 'cattle' (third function).

[136] Cf. also Gonda 1976, p. 106; Bodewitz 1984, p. 68, n. 11; with a slightly different interpretation, Lüders 1951, p. 85.

[137] Note that Bodewitz's article (1984), which deals at length with the JB version of this myth, does not mention the dénouement; it treats only the portion of the story contained in JB 1.185.

[138] Except in PB VIII.1.5, where Indra simply gives them all cattle:

> PB VIII.1.5 sa etena ca pragāthenaitena [ca] sāmnā sahasraṃ paśūn asr̥jata tān ebhyo prāyacchat te pratyatiṣṭhan
>
> With this pragātha [just quoted] and this sāman, he created a thousand cattle. He gave these to them (the boys). They (thus) got firm standing.

PB XIII.4.17 tān vardhayitvābravīt kumārakā varān vṛṇīdhvam iti kṣatraṃ mahyam ity abravīt pṛthuraśmis tasmā etena pārthuraśmena kṣatraṃ prāyacchat . . . brahmavarcasaṃ mahyam ity abravīd bṛhadgiris tasmā etena bārhadgireṇa brahmavarcasaṃ prāyacchat . . . paśūn mahyam ity abravīd rāyovājas tasmā etena rāyovājīyena paśūn prāyacchat

Having raised them he said, "Boys, choose yourself boons." "(Give) me dominion," said Pṛthuraśmi. He gave him dominion with this Pārthuraśma (Sāman). . . . "(Give) me brahmaṇic glory," said Bṛhadgiri. He gave him brahmaṇic glory with this Bārhadgira (Sāman). . . . "(Give) me cattle," said Rāyovāja. He gave him cattle with this Rāyovājīya (Sāman).

The functionality was recognized by the composers of the texts themselves. In PB XIII.4.18 they recommend the Pārthuraśma Sāman for a rājanya- 'warrior', the Bārhadgira Sāman for a brahman, and the Rāyovājīya Sāman for a vaiśya- 'clansman, villager', concluding

PB XIII.4.18 svenaivaināṁs tad rūpeṇa samardhayati stomaḥ

By means of each one's own characteristic the stoma thereby makes them (/him?) prosper.

The JB is somewhat less orthodox, at least superficially, and the distribution of boys and boons somewhat different. Rāyovāja asks for cattle (paśu) as in PB and is given iḷā, the refreshing ritual drink often identified with paśu. Pṛthuraśmi asks for and gets kṣatra- 'might, dominion'. Bṛhadgiri asks for annādyam 'food/the possession of food' and is given his wish (kāman).[139]

JB I.186 tān abravīt kiṃkāmo vā ekaḥ kiṃkāma ekaḥ kiṃkāma eka iti / so 'bravīd rāyovajaḥ paśukāmo 'ham asmīti / tasmā iḷāṃ prāyacchat / paśavo vā iḷā / athābravīt pṛthuraśmiḥ kṣatrakāmo 'ham asmīti / tasmai kṣatraṃ prāyacchat / sa eva pṛthur vainyaḥ / athābravīd bṛhadgirir annādyakāmo 'ham asmīti / tasmā athakāraṃ [?] prāyacchat / annaṃ vā athakāraḥ

[139]Perhaps. As discussed in n. 4, this is Oertel's interpretation (1898, p. 124), but the text is disturbed.

> He said to them, "What wish does this one have? What wish this one? What wish this one?" Rāyovāja said, "I want cattle." He (Indra) gave[140] him iḷā. The iḷā is really cattle. Then Pṛthuraśmi said, "I want dominion." To him he gave dominion. He thus (became) Pṛthu Vainya. Then Bṛhadgiri said, "I want food/the eating of food." To him he gave ______ (?). For ______ is food.

Neither Rāyovāja nor Bṛhadgiri seems adequately to represent the first function here, though one could press Rāyovāja into it on account of the iḷā.

This conclusion, with its distribution of boons, may be, as I suggested above, a folktale grafted onto the episode of the survivors, which may originally have ended with Indra's adoption of the boys. It may, however, also reflect dimly the same concerns as the KS passage. The Yajur Veda (to which the KS belongs) is often preoccupied with the proper establishment and maintenance of the ritual, both now in the human sphere and in its original form among the gods. It is fitting that the KS passage should ultimately concern the initial establishment of the ritual. But the Sāma Veda Brāhmaṇas are less concerned with the ritual per se (as opposed to the sāmans in it); the equivalent to the establishment of the primal ritual in the KS passage might be the establishment of the prototype Vedic society in the SV Brāhmaṇas, with the three surviving Yatis each representing one of the three twice-born classes. This would be comparable to the 'division' of the fires in KS VIII.5. In each case a central social institution will have arisen from the terror and disorder of the Indra-impelled attack by the hyenas.

Thus, careful examination of the context and vocabulary of the mythic fragments concerning Indra and the Yatis has created a far different picture from the one that results from a superficial scanning of the story. The Yatis, far from being enemies or victims of Indra, are his righteously sacrificing devotees. When Indra delivers them to the hyenas, he is not committing a callous act of violence, but is acting benevolently toward both the Yatis and the hyenas and furthering the proper functioning of both cosmos (macrocosm) and ritual (microcosm).

[140]Note that the same verb (prāyacchat) is used for Indra's granting boons to the surviving Yatis (in JB I.186 and PB VIII.1.5, XIII.4.17; cf. also PB XVIII.1.9, with Prajāpati and Indra) as for his handing over their hapless brethren to the hyenas.

It is Indra transformed into a female hyena (Salāvṛkī) who hands over the Yatis as food to her young hyenas (Sālāvṛkeya). She/he is rather nurturing her young than murdering the Yatis. The Yatis, on the one hand, "deserve" their death because of certain ritual flaws committed when under attack. On the other hand, in death they fulfill their ritual objectives. These objectives are various, but they all center around the portion of the ritual ground known as the Uttaravedi. It is in the vicinity of the Uttaravedi that animal sacrifices are performed, and the animal-sacrificing Yatis, by a sort of ritual symmetry, become sacrifices to animals. The Uttaravedi is also used in the Varuṇapraghāsa ceremony and its associated rain-making rituals, and the plants into which the Yatis are transformed are precisely those used to bring the rain that ensures life on earth.

In several versions of the myth certain Yatis survive, are in fact reborn by acquiring a new father: a horse or Indra in the guise of three-humped bull. In these versions the reborn Yati(s) appear to take roles as archetypal figures in Vedic society, as the priest in the primal establishment of the ritual (KS) or as representatives of the three twice-born classes (JB/PB). However each myth fragment ends, they all convey the message that from disruptive yet ritualized violence comes a new and fructifying order.

APPENDIX
On Two Recent Treatments of the Yati Myth

After many decades of neglect, the Yati myth has formed the subject of two recent articles, by S. A. Dange and H. W. Bodewitz.[141]

Dange presents a most remarkable interpretation. By a series of inferences of what one can only deem breathtaking creativity and independence from the texts, he has concluded that the ascetic Yatis came to a place frequented by wolves to offer themselves to the animals in ritual suicide (see esp. p. 116): "The Yatis, who have been known even to the Rigvedic seers as wandering ascetics, came to a particular place, when completely emaciated, as the last resort and with a determined mind to meet their last fate. The wolves (or dogs . . .) might be knowing the

[141] Dange 1980–81; Bodewitz 1984. As it happens, I did not come upon either article until my treatment of the myth was more or less complete.

place by habit." Note details such as "completely emaciated," which are completely invented.

He further suggests that this act "was customary for the Yatis themselves." And, as noted above (n. 9), he considers Indra a secondary intrusion in the text, with little justification. He offers no further textual support for his hypothesis, beyond the suggestion that the "smile" in KS XXV.6 is a sign of the Yatis' "complacency" (p. 115), indicating that the Yatis want to be eaten.

Bodewitz (pp. 66–67) rightly rejects this theory of Dange's—both the notion that the Yatis committed suicide and that Indra had no part in the killing. Most of the rest of Bodewitz's article concerns the JB version of the myth. However, I should comment here on some of his assumptions about the myth in general that in certain cases lead him to what seem to me erroneous conclusions.

Some minor points:

(1) He suggests that the expression "to surrender people to the sālāvr̥kas" may originally simply have meant "to kill people and leave them uncremated or unburied" (p. 67). But in Vedic this "expression" occurs only in our myth, with Indra as subject and the Yatis as object. There is no evidence for a general expression of this form.

(2) He states that "in every passage where the Yatis and the sālāvr̥kas occur together . . . some of them are alive and escape from these wolves and hyaenas" (p. 69). While it is undoubtedly true (and the point of the story in a way) that all the Yatis are alive *when attacked,* individuals escape only rarely—in the JB (I.185) and PB (XIII.4.17) versions and in KS VIII.5, where Syūmaraśmi enters the horse. The other passages give us no reason to believe that any Yatis escaped.

(3) He seems to consider the Uttaravedi only as a "refuge" (p. 70, n. 15), an "asylum" (p. 71), without recognizing its dangerous aspects. He sees it as representing "the cosmic hill, the axis mundi, the centre of the world" (p. 70, n. 15). But, as the textual evidence assembled above demonstrates, the Uttaravedi evokes far more ambivalent feelings.

More important is the last point:

(4) He believes that "the Yatis of these Vedic myths can hardly be disconnected from the ascetics who are (later) denoted by this term" (p. 70) and goes so far as to call them "*non-sacrificing* ascetics" (my italics, p. 71). Their association with the Bhr̥gus (duly recognized in n. 16) he explains by assuming (from ŚB and JB evidence) that the Bhr̥gus were late converts to ritualism: "The Bhr̥gus as well as the Yatis were on the fringe of Vedic orthodoxy." But the *earlier,* RVic evidence never calls

the orthodoxy of the Bhṛgus into question, and, for the Yatis, the passages collected above detailing their participation in the ritual should decisively refute this assumption about the Yatis' heterodox practices.

By assuming that the Yatis were nonritualists, Bodewitz can then explain the rescue of some of the Yatis by attributing to them a deathbed conversion to ritualism, as it were. Indra saves the survivors because they have just acknowledged the proper religion. They praise Indra; they climb on the Uttaravedi: this "implies an exaltation of the power of Vedic ritualism" and "may also indicate that under pressure of the circumstances the Yatis came to acknowledge the efficacy of the Vedic religion (especially its ritual)" (p. 70). This textually unsupported, albeit dramatic picture of religious change of heart muddies the waters and prevents us from seeing what is really going on.

PART II

SVARBHĀNU AND THE WOUNDED SUN

CHAPTER 5

The Texts and the Myth

The myth of Svarbhānu and the sun is related, in full or in part, no fewer than twenty times in Vedic prose, in texts belonging to all four Vedas (though the AB is surprisingly absent); the Rig Veda also treats it in V.40.5–9 with an amplitude and coherence rare for that text, although unfortunately not quite coherently enough.

A. The Texts

MS II.1.5 svàrbhānur vā́ āsuráḥ sū́ryaṃ támasāvidhyat táṁ sómārudrā́ abhiṣajyatāṃ tásya vā́ eténaivá śámalam apā́hatām eténāsmiṁs téjo 'dhattām

Svarbhānu Āsura pierced the sun with darkness. Soma and Rudra healed him. With this (worship?) they smashed away his blemish. With this (worship?) they placed splendor in him.

MS II.5.2 svàrbhānur vā́ āsuráḥ sū́ryaṃ támasāvidhyat tásya devā́s támó 'pāghnan yát prathamáṃ támo 'pā́ghnant sā́viḥ kr̥ṣṇā́bhavad yád dvitī́yaṁ sā́ lóhinī yát tr̥tī́yaṁ sā́ balakṣī́ yád adhyastā́d apā́kr̥ntat [→ *apā́kr̥ntant?] sā́vir vaśā́bhavat tè 'bruvan devapaśúm imáṃ kā́māyā́labhāmahā íty átha vā́ iyáṃ tárhy r̥kṣā́sīd alómikā tè 'bruvaṁs tásmai kā́māyā́labhāmahai yáthāsyā́m óṣadhayaś ca vánaspátayaś ca jā́yantā íti tā́ṁ vaí tásmai kā́māyā́labhanta táto 'syā́m óṣadhayaś ca vánaspátayaś cājāyanta

Svarbhānu Āsura pierced the sun with darkness. The gods smashed away his darkness. The first darkness they smashed away became a black ewe. The second a reddish one. The third a white one. What he [→ *they] cut off from the ______[1] became a vaśā ewe. They said, "Let us seize [= sacrifice] this divine beast for (some) wish." Now at this time this (earth) was bald and hairless. They said, "Let us seize (her) for *this* wish, that plants and trees shall arise on this (earth)." They seized her for this wish. Thereupon plants and trees arose on this (earth).

MS IV.5.7 svàrbhānur vā́ āsuráḥ sū́ryaṃ támasāvidhyat tásya devā́s támó 'pāghnan yát prathamáṃ támo 'pā́ghnant sā́viḥ kr̥ṣṇā́bhavad yád dvitī́yam̐ sā́ lóhinī yát tr̥tī́yam̐ sā́ balakṣī́ sá svéna rūpéṇa niramucyata

Svarbhānu Āsura pierced the sun with darkness. The gods smashed away his darkness. The first darkness they smashed away became a black ewe. The second a reddish one. The third a white one. He (the sun) was released with his own form/color.

MS IV.8.3 svàrbhānur vā́ āsuráḥ sū́ryaṃ támasāvidhyat tám átrir ánvapaśyat

Svarbhānu Āsura pierced the sun with darkness. Atri saw him.

KS XI.5 svàrbhānur vā́ āsurás sū́ryaṃ támasāvidhyat sá ná vyàrocata tásmai devā́ḥ prā́yaścittim aicham̐s tám etáyéṣṭyāyājayam̐s táyāsmāt támó 'pāghnan

Svarbhānu Āsura pierced the sun with darkness. He did not shine forth. The gods sought an expiation for him. They had him worship with this Iṣṭi. With it they smashed the darkness from him.

KS XII.13 svàrbhānur vā́ āsurás sū́ryaṃ támasāvidhyat sá ná vyàrocyata tásmād devā́s támó 'pālumpan yát prathamám apā́lumpan sā́viṣ kr̥ṣṇā́bhavad yád dvitī́yam̐ sā́ phalgúr yát tr̥tī́yam̐ sā́ balakṣī́ yád adhyasthā́d apā́lumpan sā́vir vaśā́bhavad átha vā́ iyáṃ tárhy r̥kṣā́lomákāsīt tā́ṃ devā́ ádityai kā́māyā́labhanta táyāsyā́ṃ lómāny arohayam̐s táto vā́ iyáṃ lómāny agr̥hṇāt

Svarbhānu Āsura pierced the sun with darkness. He did not shine forth. The gods stripped off the darkness from him. The first darkness

[1]For this and the equivalent phrases in KS XII.13, TS II.1.2.2–3, see below, Chap. 7, B.3.

they stripped off became a black ewe. The second a reddish one. The third a white one. What they stripped off from the ______ became a vaśā ewe. Now at this time this (earth) was bald and without hair. The gods seized [= sacrificed] this (ewe) to Aditi for this wish. With her they made hair grow on this (earth). Thereupon this (earth) got hair.

KS XXVII.2 svarbhānur vā āsuras sūryaṃ tamasāvidhyat sa na vyarocyata tasmād devās tamo 'pālumpan yat prathamam apālumpan sāviṣ kṛṣṇābhavad yad dvitīyaṁ sā phalgur yat tṛtīyaṁ sā balakṣī

Svarbhānu Āsura pierced the sun with darkness. He did not shine forth. The gods stripped off the darkness from him. The first darkness they stripped off became a black ewe. The second a reddish one. The third a white one.

KS XXVIII.4 svarbhānur vā āsuras sūryaṃ tamasāvidhyat tam atrir evāgre 'nvavindat

Svarbhānu Āsura pierced the sun with darkness. Atri found him at first.

TS II.1.2.2–3 súvarbhānur āsuráḥ sū́ryaṃ támasāvidhyat tásmai devā́ḥ prā́yaścittim aichan tásya yát prathamáṃ támo 'pā́ghnant sā́ kṛṣṇā́vir abhavad yád dvitī́yaṁ sā́ phálgunī yát tṛtī́yaṁ sā́ balakṣī́ yád adhyasthā́d apā́kṛntant sā́vir vaśā́ // sám abhavat té devā́ abruvan devapaśúr vā́ ayáṁ sám abhūt kásmā imám ā́lapsyāmaha íti átha vaí tárhy álpā pṛthivyā́sīd ájātā óṣadhayas tā́m áviṃ vaśā́m ādityébhyaḥ kā́māyā́labhanta táto vā́ áprathata pṛthivy ájāyantaúṣadhayaḥ

Svarbhānu Āsura pierced the sun with darkness. The gods sought an expiation for him. The first darkness they smashed off became a black ewe. The second a reddish one. The third a white one. What they cut off from the ______ became a vaśā ewe. The gods said, "A divine beast has come into being. For what/to whom shall we offer it?" Now at this time the earth was small and plants had not arisen. They seized [= sacrificed] this vaśā ewe to the Ādityas for this wish. Thereupon the earth spread out and plants arose.

ŚB V.3.2.2 (≅ ŚBK VII.2.1.1) svàrbhānur ha vā́ āsuráḥ / sū́ryaṃ támasā vivyādha sá támasā viddhó ná vyàrocata tásya somārudrā́v evaítát támó 'pāhatām

Svarbhānu Āsura pierced the sun with darkness. Pierced with darkness, he did not shine forth. Soma and Rudra smashed away his darkness.

PB IV.5.2 svarbhānur vā āsura ādityaṃ tamasāvidhyat taṃ devāḥ svarair aspr̥ṇvan

Svarbhānu Āsura pierced the Āditya [= sun] with darkness. The gods won him with the Svara (Sāmans).

PB IV.6.13 svarbhānur vā āsura ādityaṃ tamasāvidhyat tasya devā divākīrtyais tamo 'pāghnan

Svarbhānu Āsura pierced the Āditya [= sun] with darkness. The gods smashed away his darkness with the Divākīrtya (Sāmans).

PB VI.6.8 svarbhānur vā āsura ādityaṃ tamasāvidhyat taṃ devā na vyajānaṁs te 'trim upādhāvaṁs tasyātrir bhāsena tamo 'pāhan yat prathamam apāhan sā kr̥ṣṇāvir abhavad yad dvitīyaṁ sā rajatā yat tr̥tīyaṁ sā lohinī yayā varṇam abhyatr̥ṇat sā śuklāsīt

Svarbhānu Āsura pierced the Āditya [= sun] with darkness. The gods did not discern him. They resorted to Atri. Atri smashed away his darkness with the Bhāsa (Sāman). The first (darkness) he smashed away became a black ewe. The second a silvery one. The third a reddish one. With which ______ he bored through to (his) color, that became a bright/white one.

PB XIV.11.14 svarbhānur vā āsura ādityaṃ tamasāvidhyat sa na vyarocata tasyātrir bhāsena tamo 'pāhan sa vyarocata

Svarbhānu Āsura pierced the Āditya [= sun] with darkness. He did not shine forth. Atri smashed away his darkness with the Bhāsa (Sāman). He shone forth.

PB XXIII.16.2 svarbhānur vā āsuraḥ sūryaṃ tamasāvidhyat tasmai devāḥ prāyaścittim aichaṁs te etā avindaṁs tābhir asmāt tamo 'pāghnan

Svarbhānu Āsura pierced the sun with darkness. The gods sought an expiation for him. They found these (observances). With them they smashed away the darkness from him.

JB I.80–81 svarbhānur vā āsura ādityaṃ tamasāvidhyat / taṃ devāś carṣayaś cābhiṣajyan / te 'trim abruvann ṛṣe tvam idam apajahīti / tatheti / tad atrir apāhan / . . .

sa yat prathamam apāhan sā kṛṣṇāvir abhavat / yad dvitīyam apāhan sā dhūmrāvir abhavat / yat tṛtīyam apāhan sā phālguny avir abhavat

Svarbhānu Āsura pierced the Āditya [= sun] with darkness. The gods and seers healed him. They said to Atri, "Seer, smash this (darkness) away." (Saying) yes, Atri smashed it away. . . .
The first (darkness) he smashed away became a black ewe. The second he smashed away became a smoke-colored ewe. The third he smashed away became a reddish ewe.

JB II.386 svarbhānur vā āsura ādityaṃ tamasāvidhyat / taṃ devāś carṣayaś cābhiṣajyan / ta etāni svarāṇy apaśyan / tair etam aspṛṇvan

Svarbhānu Āsura pierced the Āditya [= sun] with darkness. The gods and seers healed him. They saw these Svara (Sāmans). With them they won him.

JB II.390 svarbhānur vā āsura ādityaṃ tamasāvidhyat / taṃ devāś carṣayaś cābhiṣajyan / ta etāni divākīrtyāni sāmāny apaśyan / tair asya tamo 'pāghnan

Svarbhānu Āsura pierced the Āditya [= sun] with darkness. The gods and seers healed him. They saw these Divākīrtya Sāmans. With them they smashed away his darkness.

KB XXIV.3 svarbhānur ha vā āsura ādityaṃ tamasāvidhyat / tasyātrayas tamo 'pajighāṃsanta etam saptadaśastomaṃ tryaham purastād viṣuvata upāyan / tasya purastāt tamo 'pajaghnuḥ / tat purastād [Keith, ad loc. → *parastād] asīdat ta etam eva tryaham upariṣṭād viṣuvata upāyan tasyopariṣṭāt tamo 'pajaghnuḥ / tat parastād asīdat tān vai svarasāmāna iti ācakṣate / etair ha vā atraya ādityaṃ tamaso 'spṛṇvata

Svarbhānu Āsura pierced the Āditya [= sun] with darkness. The Atris wished to smash away his darkness. Before the Viṣuvant (Day) they performed this three-day (rite) with the Saptadaśa Stoma. They smashed away the darkness from in front of him. It settled beyond. They performed this three-day (rite) after the Viṣuvant (Day). They smashed away the darkness from behind him. It settled beyond. These they call

"the Svarasāman (Days)." With them the Atris won the Āditya from darkness.

GB II.3.19 svarbhānur vā āsuriḥ [*sic*] sūryan tamasāvidhyat / tad atrir apanunoda / tad atrir anvapaśyat

Svarbhānu Āsura pierced the sun with darkness. Atri pushed it away. Then Atri saw (the sun).

RV V.40.5 yát tvā sūrya svàrbhānus, támasā́vidhyad āsuráḥ
ákṣetravid yáthā mugdhó, bhúvanāny adīdhayuḥ
.6 svàrbhānor ádha yád indra māyā́, avó divó vártamānā avā́han
gūḷhám̐ sū́ryam̐ támasā́pavratena, turī́yeṇa bráhmaṇāvindad átriḥ
.7 mā́ mā́m imám̐ táva sántam atra, irasyā́ drugdhó bhiyásā ní gārīt
tvám mitró asi satyárādhās, taú mehā́vatam̐ váruṇaś ca rā́jā
.8 grā́vṇo brahmā́ yuyujānáḥ saparyán, kīríṇā devā́n námasopaśíkṣan
átriḥ sū́ryasya diví cákṣur ā́dhāt, svàrbhānor ápa māyā́ aghukṣat
.9 yám̐ vaí sū́ryam̐ svàrbhānus, támasā́vidhyad āsuráḥ
átrayas tám ánv avindan, nahy ànyé áśaknuvan

.5 When, O sun, Svarbhānu Āsura pierced you with darkness, the creatures perceived like a bewildered one, not knowing the territory.
.6 Then, O Indra, when you smashed down from heaven the circling magic spells of Svarbhānu, Atri with the fourth formulation found the sun, hidden by darkness because of (an act) contrary to commandment.
.7 [The sun:] "O Atri, let him not, deceived by jealousy and fear, swallow me, being this one of yours. You are an ally, whose gifts are true; do you and King Varuṇa help me here."
.8 The Brahman (Atri), yoking the pressing stones, serving the gods with plain/mere reverence, seeking to win (the sun), Atri placed the eye of the sun in heaven. He hid away the magic spells of Svarbhānu.
.9 Which sun Svarbhānu Āsura pierced with darkness, that one the Atris found, for no others were able.

The Mahābhārata also contains a rather garbled version of the story:

MBh. XIII.141.1 śṛṇu me haihayaśreṣṭha, karmātreḥ sumahātmanaḥ
.2 ghore tamasy ayudhyanta, sahitā devadānavaḥ
avidhyata śarais tatra, svarbhānuḥ somabhāskarau
.3 atha te tamasā grastā, nihanyante sma dānavaiḥ

devā nṛpatiśārdūla, sahaiva balibhis tadā
.4 asurair vadhyamānās te, kṣīnaprāṇā divaukasaḥ
apaśyanta tapasyantam, atriṃ vipraṃ mahāvane
.5 athainam abruvan devāḥ, śāntakrodhaṃ jitendriyam
asurair iṣubhir viddhau, candrādityāv imāv ubhau
.6 vayaṃ vadhyāmahe cāpi, śatrubhis tamasāvṛte
nādhigacchāma śāntiṃ ca, bhayāt trāyasva naḥ prabho
.7 kathaṃ rakṣāmi bhavatas, te 'bruvaṃś candramā bhava
timiraghnaś ca savitā, dasyuhā caiva no bhava
.8 evam uktas tadātris tu, tamonud abhavac chaśī
apaśyat saumabhāvaṃ ca, sūryasya pratidarśanam
.9 dṛṣṭvā nātiprabhaṃ somaṃ, tathā sūryaṃ ca pārthiva
prakāśam akarod atris, tapasā svena saṃyuge
.10 jagad vitimiraṃ cāpi, pradīptam akarot tadā
vyajayac chatrusaṃghāṃś ca, devānāṃ svena tejasā
.11 atriṇā dahyamānāṃs tān, dṛṣṭvā devā mahāsurān
parākramais te 'pi tadā, vyatyaghnann atrirakṣitāḥ
.12 udbhāsitaś ca savitā, devās trātā hatāsurāḥ
atriṇā tv atha somatvaṃ, kṛtam uttamatejasā
.13 advitīyena muninā, japatā carmavāsasā
phalabhakṣeṇa rājarṣe, paśya karmātriṇā kṛtam

.1 Hear from me, O best of the Haihayas, the deed of great-souled Atri:
.2 In terrible darkness the gods and the Dānavas were jointly contending. At that time Svarbhānu pierced the moon and sun with arrows.
.3 Then swallowed by darkness, the gods, along with their mighty (weapons), were smashed down by the Dānavas, O tiger of rulers.
.4 The heaven dwellers, being slain by the Asuras, with breath destroyed, saw the poet Atri practicing austerities in a great forest.
.5 Then the gods said to him, who had appeased anger and conquered senses, "Both these two, the moon and the sun, were pierced by the Asuras with arrows.
.6 "And we are also being slain by our enemies under cover of darkness. And we cannot reach peace. Rescue us from fear, O lord."

.7 [Atri said,] "How shall I protect your graces?"
They said, "Become the moon. And
(become) Savitar [= the sun], smasher of
the dark, and become the smasher of
Dasyus for us."
.8 Thus addressed, Atri became the moon, banisher
of darkness. He saw the lunar condition and
the appearance of the sun.
.9 Having seen that the moon and the sun were not
at all bright, Atri made (each) visible by use
of his own austerity.
.10 And he also made the world free from darkness,
blazing. And he vanquished the host of
enemies of the gods by his own splendor.
.11 Seeing the great Asuras being burned by Atri, the
gods, protected by Atri, with bold attacks
struck back at them, too.
.12 Savitar [= the sun] was (re)illuminated and, with
the Asuras smashed, the gods were saved,
and the moon's condition was restored—
(all) by Atri, possessing highest splendor.
.13 Behold, O royal seer, the deed done by the
incomparable ascetic, muttering (prayers),
dressed (only) in skins, eating (only) fruit—
by Atri.

B. Overview of the Myth

The prose version of this myth invariably begins

svàrbhānur vā́ āsuráḥ sū́ryaṃ támasāvidhyat (e.g., MS II.1.5)

Svarbhānu Āsura pierced/wounded the sun with darkness.

(Thus also three other passages in MS, five in PB, four in KS, three in JB, and one each in TS, ŚB, KB, GB, with minor differences in sandhi and particle choice, and substitution in PB, JB, and KB of ādityam for sū́ryam.)

The RV passage begins and ends with what used to be called transformational variants of this sentence:

RV V.40.5ab yát tvā sūrya svàrbhānus, támasā́vidhyad āsuráḥ

When, O sun, Svarbhānu Āsura pierced you with darkness . . .

.9ab yám̐ vaí sū́ryam̐ svàrbhānus, támasā́vidhyad āsuráḥ

Which sun Svarbhānu Āsura pierced with darkness . . .

Notice that like the RVic passages the prose version can also fall into two orthodox eight-syllable lines.[2] This might suggest that both the prose versions and the extant RVic version are based on an older, syntactically straightfoward account in verse.[3]

The rest of the myth is more fluid, like a number of other Vedic myths, including that of Indra and the Yatis, with a fixed first sentence, presumably of some age, thematically encapsulating the myth, and a freer treatment of what follows. In Svarbhānu what follows generally involves some sort of remedy for this disaster: in fullest form, it is usually the seer Atri, sometimes in conjunction with, or at the behest of, the gods, who finds the sun or removes the darkness by some ritual expedient.

Before looking more closely at some versions of this remedy, I will consider the usual interpretation of the myth, for this myth has a long agreed upon, standard interpretation. It is said to describe or be about

[2]Reading sú*v*arbhānur vā́ āsuráḥ and either sū́r*i*yam̐ támasāvidhyat or sū́ryam̐ támas*ā* *a*vidhyat. (I would favor the former possibility.) Note that RV V.40.5, 9 does not allow or require distraction in either sū́ryam or támas*ā*vidhyat. We should note that Lanman (1893, p. 187) considers these verses (V.40.5, 9) to be "of distinctly later origin" than 6–8.

[3]In fact Stanley Insler (pers. comm.) has produced a tentative, balladlike versification of the first half of the BYV version, in eight-syllable lines:

svàrbhānur vā́ āsuráḥ / sū́ryam̐ támasāvidhyat
sá ná vyàrocata *tásmād [*tádā?] / devā́ḥ prā́yaścittim aichaṁs
tám etáyéṣṭyāyājayaṁs / *táyā támo 'smād ápāghnan
[or] tásya devā́s támó 'pāghnan
yát prathamám̐ támo 'pā́ghnant / sā́vis *tátaḥ kr̥ṣṇā́bhavad
yád dvitī́yaṁ sā́ lóhinī / yát tr̥tī́yaṁ sā́ balakṣī́
yád adhyastā́d apā́kr̥ntant / sā́vir vaśā́ sám abhavat

with a possible ending:

táto 'prathata pr̥thivy / ájāyanta caúṣadhayaḥ
[or] iyám̐ lómāny agr̥hṇāt

The point of this exercise was not to construct a Schleicherian fable but to show with how little alteration or adaptation the prose version falls into verse lines.

an eclipse, and Svarbhānu is said to be the "Eclipse Demon," equivalent to later Rāhu.[4] Now, leaving aside the larger question of what it would mean for a myth simply to "be about" an eclipse, let us see if this interpretation makes any sense for the myth. In a general way, of course, it might. The darkness of the sun in the myth could have been suggested by the natural phenomenon. In other words, the sun does sometimes unaccountably get dark; since this is a possible natural situation, it is also a possible mythological situation. Indeed, the later[5] Rāhu myth does make sense in its detail as mirroring an eclipse: Rāhu *swallows* the sun, a reasonable metaphor of what one sees during an eclipse.

> MBh. I.17.8 tato vairavinirbandhaḥ, kr̥to rāhumukhena vai
> śāśvataś candrasūryābhyāṃ, grasaty adyāpi caiva tau
>
> Then an eternal quarrel was created between the head of Rāhu and the Moon and Sun. Even today he swallows them both.

However, the actions described in the Svarbhānu myth are quite different.[6] Svarbhānu 'pierces' or 'wounds' the sun with darkness. The action of the root √vyadh is often accomplished by a sharp object or

[4]Cf., e.g., Lanman 1893, pp. 187–90; Hopkins 1909, p. 35; Macdonell and Keith 1912, sub Sūrya, Svarbhānu; Macdonell 1897, p. 160; Keith 1925, p. 235; O'Flaherty 1981, p. 187.

[5]The name Rāhu is entirely absent from Vedic, except for one possible occurrence in the AVŚ, where the reading is disturbed; indeed rāhu- fails to appear in most of the manuscripts. (See Whitney, AV, ad loc.) [This hymn does not appear in AVP.] Even if Rāhu is to be read here, the passage contributes nothing to our understanding of the Svarbhānu myth:

> AV XIX.9.10ab śáṃ no gráhāś cāndramasā́ḥ, śáṃ ādityā́ś ca rāhúṇā (?)
>
> [Whitney:] Weal for us be the planets belonging to the moon, and weal the sun (āditya [Whitney here follows the commentator's reading, sg. ādityaś]) with Rāhu.

Most manuscripts have śarāhuṇā here, and I would suggest that the rāhuṇā of a few manuscripts and of the commentary is an emendation attempting to make sense of this difficult reading, based on knowledge of the later connection between the sun and Rāhu. Unfortunately I do not understand the original sense of the passage.

Caland (1926c) claims to have identified the Rāhu *story* (without the name Rāhu) in a different Vedic myth involving Vr̥tra (as the Rāhu figure), Agni, and Soma (TS II.4.12, II.5.2; MS II.4.3), which he considers closer to the later Rāhu myth than the Svarbhānu myth usually cited.

[6]The apparent reference to swallowing in the RVic version of this myth (V.40.7 mā́ mā́m . . . ní gārīt 'Let him not swallow me down') will be discussed below, Chap. 10, D.

something so conceived; it implies an abrupt attack on the center, the bull's-eye as it were, of the sun, not a gradual swallowing from the edge. Moreover, the remedy for the darkening of the sun in this myth is generally to 'smash off' (apa √han) or 'strip off' (apa √lup) the darkness, often in a series of three or four swipes. Again, this is not a particularly convincing way of describing the end of an eclipse, as far as I know. In other words, if this is a myth about an eclipse, it is a singularly incompetent one, revealing a dullard's powers of observation. In addition, the interpretation of this myth as describing an eclipse is an inert hypothesis, without resonance. It fails to explain the details of the myth itself or to relate them to anything external. It simply affixes a label to the whole complex and dismisses it.

In the post-Vedic period, Svarbhānu does become at least partially assimilated to Rāhu. In several brief mentions of the story in the Mahābhārata, the actions ascribed to Svarbhānu seem more appropriate to the Rāhu myth.

MBh. V.183.22 arkaṃ ca sahasā dīptaṃ, svarbhānur abhisaṃvr̥ṇot[7]

Svarbhānu suddenly covered the blazing sun.

Especially clear is a passage not included in the Crit. Ed. proper, though retained in an appendix to MBh. XII:

App. I, no. 28, 363f. praviśya vadanaṃ rāhor, yaḥ somaṃ pibate niśi
grasaty arkaṃ ca svarbhānur, bhūtvā māṃ so 'bhirakṣatu

(Śiva), who, having entered the mouth of *Rāhu,* drinks soma/the moon at night
And swallows the sun, having become *Svarbhānu*—let him protect me.

But it is noteworthy that in the extensive retelling of the Atri/Svarbhānu story in MBh. XIII.141 (quoted above), the assimilation of Rāhu is incomplete, indeed almost invisible. This story maintains some of the distinctive elements of the Vedic versions, though much has also been changed. Note first that the signature verb, √vyadh 'pierce', remains, though in the middle voice (avidhyata). The weapon is no

[7]Note the injunctive verb form, rather than the expected (but metrically impossible) imperfect *abhisamavr̥ṇot.

longer darkness, but it is sharp—'arrows' (śaraiḥ), and 'darkness' (tamas) surrounds the first mention of the wound.

MBh. XIII.141.2 ghore *tamasy* ayudhyanta, sahitā devadānavaḥ
avidhyata śarais tatra, *svarbhānuḥ* somabhāskarau
.3 atha te *tamasā* grastā, nihanyante sma dānavaiḥ
devāḥ . . .

.2 In terrible darkness the gods and the Dānavas were jointly contending. At that time Svarbhānu pierced the moon and sun with arrows.
.3 Then swallowed *by darkness,* the gods . . .

also vs.5

.5 asurair *iṣubhir viddhau,* candrādityāv imāv ubhau

.5 Both these two, the moon and the sun, were *pierced* by the Asuras *with arrows*.

Moreover, Atri is emphatically the restorer of the sun here, mentioned by name in vss. 1, 4, 8, 9, 11, 12, 13; he does not figure in the ordinary Rāhu myth. The only clear sign of the influence of the Rāhu story is the phrase tamasā grastāḥ '*swallowed* by darkness', but this is said of the gods, not the sun.

The rest of the story diverges from the Vedic material. Both sun and moon are wounded (as also in the Rāhu myth), not the sun alone, as in the Vedic Svarbhānu myth. The gods are themselves attacked; they do not simply seek a solution. And, most important, the remedy devised by Atri—to become the sun and the moon—not only differs entirely from his Vedic remedy but does not make much sense in its own terms.

Nonetheless, the kernel of the story remains: the three major participants, Svarbhānu, the sun, and Atri, and the two major actions, the wounding (√vyadh) of the sun by Svarbhānu and the rescue of the sun by Atri at the request of the gods. This configuration bears little resemblance to that of the Rāhu myth.

In order to understand this myth, we need to allow the myth itself to provide its own interpretation, not to impose one from outside. As in the case of the Yati myth, the versions of Svarbhānu are truncated and cryptic. As in the case of the Yatis, the best strategy for interpreting the myth is to focus on its different parts and details, on each of the participants and their actions in turn, and follow out any verbal or thematic clues we can unearth. Only after disassembling it in this way can we see how the parts fit together *and* connect with a tissue of other myths and their ritual encapsulations.

We will begin by looking at the end of the myth, its solution—the healing of the sun—and only later will we return to the problem—the wounding of the sun—and what caused it. In Chapter 6 we will examine the fullest treatment of the healing of the sun and identify its thematic constituents. We can then identify this same thematic complex in several apparently unrelated places in Vedic: in a superficially simple folktale about a girl's coming of age, in a ritual for attaining distinction, and in a magical charm against bad skin. In fact, the surprising concern that unites all these with our Svarbhānu myth is the theme of skin diseases and their cures.

In Chapter 7 we will look even more closely at the way the sun is healed. Verbal cues here lead us to identify another thematic complex, that of successful—and unsuccessful—birth. This preoccupation runs through a number of myths about the sun.

Next we focus on the rescuer of the sun, the (mortal) seer Atri (Chapter 8). Why does he succeed when the gods fail? The various mythic and ritual strains connected with this figure will give us the answer: his mythology shares crucial features with that of the sun. Chapter 9 continues with Atri, concentrating on the means he uses to rescue the sun and why they are appropriate both for Atri and for the sun.

With the remedy, the healing of the sun, thus understood, we can return in Chapter 10 to the beginning of the myth and the problems raised there. First we must ask who the wounder of the sun is—who is Svarbhānu? What exactly did he do to the sun—how is this manifested in the physical realm? And finally we want to know why. Why did Svarbhānu wound the sun? The answer is both surprising and surprisingly easy to find, with the information we will have acquired.

CHAPTER 6

The Remedies—Skin Diseases, Hair, and Fertility

The simplest statement of the remedy is that someone, god or gods, ṛṣi or ṛṣis, saw it (anu √paś, e.g., MS IV.8.3 tám átrir ánvapaśyat 'Atri saw him') or won it (√spṛ, e.g., PB IV.5.2 taṃ devāḥ svarair aspṛṇvan 'The gods won him with the Svara (Sāmans)') or found it (anu √vid, KS XXVIII.4 tam atrir evāgre 'nvavindat 'Atri found him at first') or 'smashed off its darkness' (tamo √han). This last phrase is, in fact, the most usual way of presenting the remedy, in both simple and elaborated versions.

tásya devā́s *támó 'pāghnan*	*MS II.5.2, IV.5.7*
táyāsmāt *támo 'pāghnan*	*KS XI.5*
tásya yát prathamáṃ *támo 'pā́ghnan*	*TS II.1.2.2*
tásya somārudrā́v evaítát *támó 'pāhatām*	*ŚB V.3.2.2*
tásya somārudraú tát *támó 'pajaghnatuḥ*	*ŚBK VII.2.1.1*
tasya devā divākīrtyais *tamo 'pāghnan*	*PB IV.6.13*
tasyātrir bhāsena *tamo 'pāhan*	*PB VI.6.8, XIV.11.14*
tābhir asmāt *tamo 'pāghnan*	*PB XXIII.16.2*
tad atrir *apāhan*	*JB I.80*
tair asya *tamo 'pāghnan*	*JB II.390*
tasyātrayas *tamo 'pajighāṃsanta*	*KB XXIV.3*
tasya purastāt *tamo 'pajaghnuḥ*	*KB XXIV.3*

Notice that no matter what the subject is, what the instrument is, how the pronoun referring to Sūrya is expressed, and what tense/aspect of √han is used, the verb phrase is invariant: tamo 'pa √han (except for JB I.80).

The minimalist statements of the myth just referred to, containing only problem plus solution, seem not to be meant as actual narrations of the myth; they often are found in texts that also have fuller versions (e.g., MS IV.8.3 vs. II.5.2 etc.). Instead they seem intended as rapid capsule summaries preliminary to the real issue, the ritual application of the myth in that particular context.

In the Brāhmaṇas of the SV and in the KB of the RV, there are slightly elaborated versions of the remedy: someone 'sees' a set of sāmans and wins the sun with them.

> JB II.390 svarbhānur vā āsura ādityaṃ tamasāvidhyat / taṃ devāś cārṣayaś cābhiṣajyan / ta etāni divākīrtyāni sāmāny apaśyan / tair asya tamo 'pāghnan

> Svarbhānu Āsura pierced the sun with darkness. The gods and seers healed him. They saw these Divākīrtya Sāmans. With them they smashed away his darkness.[8]

This solution is quite typical of mythology in the Sāmaveda and Rigveda Brāhmaṇas. All too frustratingly often the presentation of the remedy or denouement to a myth is short-circuited by the universal expedient of seeing a sāman or an ṛc or a rite; it is often only in Yajurveda prose that a narrative is allowed to proceed to anything resembling its natural conclusion. This difference in narrative strategy, of course, reflects the different ritual purpose of the separate Vedas and their Brāhmaṇas.

A fuller form of the remedy appears in at least some versions of the MS, KS, TS, PB, and JB. In these passages either the gods (the YV texts) or the seer Atri (the SV texts) strikes off the darkness three or four times. Each cast of the darkness becomes a different colored sheep. Compare two versions of this:[9]

> MS II.5.2 svàrbhānur vā́ āsuráḥ sū́ryaṃ támasāvidhyat tásya devā́s támó 'pāghnan yát prathamáṃ támo 'pā́ghnant sā́viḥ kṛṣṇā́bhavad yád dvitī́yaṁ sā́ lóhinī yát tṛtī́yaṁ sā́ balakṣī́ yád adhyastā́d apā́kṛntat [→ *apākṛntant?] sā́vir vaśā́bhavat

> Svarbhānu Āsura pierced the sun with darkness. The gods smashed away his darkness. The first darkness they smashed away became a black

[8]Cf. PB IV.5.2, IV.6.13, XXIII.16.2; JB II.386; KB XXIV.3.
[9]Also MS IV.5.7; KS XII.13, XXVII.2; TS II.1.2.2–3; JB I.80–81.

ewe. The second a reddish one. The third a white one. What he [→ *they] cut out from __?__ became a vaśā ewe.

PB VI.6.8 svarbhānur vā āsura ādityaṃ tamasāvidhyat taṃ devā na vyajānaṁs te 'trim upādhāvaṁs tasyātrir bhāsena tamo 'pāhan yat prathamam apāhan sā kṛṣṇāvir abhavad yad dvitīyaṁ sā rajatā yat tṛtīyaṁ sā lohinī yayā varṇam abhyatṛṇat sā śuklāsīt

Svarbhānu Āsura pierced the sun with darkness. The gods did not discern him. They resorted to Atri. Atri smashed away his darkness with the Bhāsa (Sāman). The first (darkness) he smashed away became a black ewe. The second a silvery one. The third a reddish one. With which ______ he bored through to (his) color, that became a bright/white one.

Now this elaborated remedy can end here, or with an upbeat summary, as in MS IV.5.7 sá svéna rūpéṇa niramucyata '(Thus) he was released with his own form/color'. But the BYV versions more often continue with a coda that at first seems to have only a tenuous, free-associative connection with the story of the sun. The earth was at that time hairless, without plants; the gods seize one of the recently created animals and offer it. The earth then grows plants. MS II.5.2 continues:[10]

MS II.5.2 tè 'bruvan devapaśúm imáṃ kā́māyā́labhāmahā íty átha vā́ iyáṃ tárhy ṛkṣā́sīd alómikā tè 'bruvaṁs tásmai kā́māyā́labhāmahai yáthāsyā́m óṣadhayaś ca vánaspátayaś ca jā́yantā íti tā́ṁ vaí tásmai kā́māyā́labhanta táto 'syā́m óṣadhayaś ca vánaspátayaś cājāyanta

They (the gods) said, "Let us seize (for sacrifice) this divine beast for (some) wish." Now at this time this (earth) was bald and hairless. They said, "Let us seize (her) for *this* wish that plants and trees shall arise on this (earth)." They seized her for this wish. Thereupon plants and trees arose on this (earth).

It is this apparently awkward pendant to the body of the myth that I consider the real key to the whole. The growth of vegetation on the earth is integrally linked to the healing of the sun, the removal of its affliction; and this affliction, which has been on the one hand so disastrous, turns out to be a positive boon. The darkness that ill becomes the sun is transformed in the proper context into something desirable: vegetation, the earth's 'hair'.[11]

[10]Cf. also KS XII.13, TS II.1.2.2–3.

[11]The metaphorical identification of plants and hair is a common one. Note, e.g., Tracy Kidder, *House* (1985), p. 5: "The first pass the machine [a bulldozer] makes over the ground, ripping the hair off the earth, looks like an act of great violence."

A. Apālā: A Parallel to Svarbhānu

1. Apālā's Story

The connection between hair, vegetation, and a superficial affliction reminds us immediately of another striking Vedic story, that of Apālā (RV VIII.91, JB I.220–21), which recently has been so ingeniously and convincingly treated by H.-P. Schmidt.[12] In the relevant part of this tale, the maiden Apālā, having laboriously pressed soma for Indra with her teeth, begs him to make hair grow 'in the fields, on her papa's head, and on her belly' (RV VIII.91.5). Indra, purifying her three times, does so; he also makes her 'sun-skinned' (sū́rya-tvac-). A detailed examination of this story will shed much light on the puzzles in Svarbhānu.

RV VIII.91.1 kanyā̀ vā́r avāyatī́, sómam ápi srutā́vidat
ástam bháranty abravīd, índrāya sunavai tvā, śakrā́ya
sunavai tvā
.2 asaú yá éṣi vīrakó, gr̥háṃ-gr̥haṃ vicā́kaśad
imā́ṃ jámbhasutam piba, dhānā́vantaṃ karambhíṇam,
apūpávantam ukthínam
.3 ā́ caná tvā cikitsāmó, 'dhi caná tvā némasi
śánair iva śanakaír ivéndrāyendo pári srava
.4 kuvíc chákat kuvít kárat, kuvín no vásyasas kárat
kuvít patidvíṣo yatī́r, índreṇa saṃgámāmahai
.5 imā́ni trī́ṇi viṣṭápā, tā́nīndra ví rohaya
śíras tatásyorvárām, ā́d idám ma úpodáre
.6 asaú ca yā́ na urvárā́d imā́ṃ tanvàm máma
átho tatásya yác chíraḥ, sárvā tā́ romaśā́ kr̥dhi
.7 khé ráthasya khé 'nasaḥ, khé yugásya śatakrato
apālā́m indra tríṣ pūtvy, ákr̥ṇoḥ sū́ryatvacam

.1 A maiden going down to the water found soma along
the way/at the stream.
Bringing it home she said, "I will press you for Indra; I
will press you for the able one.
.2 "Yonder (Indra), the 'little man,' you who go earnestly
looking from house to house,

[12] Schmidt 1987, Chap. 1, "The Affliction of Apālā," pp. 1–29. Cf. also the older literature cited and discussed by Schmidt, esp. von Schroeder 1908, pp. 223–44; von Schroeder 1909b, pp. 270–72. In my translations of the RV and JB passages and in the related discussion I am deeply indebted to Schmidt's interpretation. Particular points of agreement and disagreement will be treated as they arise. All references to Schmidt in the chapter are to Schmidt 1987, unless otherwise noted.

Drink this (soma), pressed by the jaws—(soma) accompanied by grain, by gruel, by cakes, by hymns.

.3 "We wish to comprehend you; we will not 'recite' you aloud.

O drop, flow around quietly, very quietly for Indra.

.4 "Will he be able? Will he do (it)? Will he make us better off?

Shall we, (though) coming as husband-haters, unite with Indra?

.5 "O Indra, make these three surfaces grow forth—the head of my Papa, the field, and this on my belly.

.6 "That field of ours, this body of mine, and my Papa's head—make all these hairy."

.7 In the nave of a chariot, in the nave of a wagon, in the nave of a yoke, O hundred-powered one,

Apālā, O Indra—having purified (her), you made (her) sun-skinned.

This story is also told in the JB apropos of this Vedic hymn and of the so-called Apālā Sāman. In this version some details are made clearer or are elaborated (perhaps anachronistically):

JB I.220 apālā ha vā ātreyī tilakā vā rucchvasā vāpy[13] āsa / sākāmayatāpa pāpaṃ varṇaṃ hanīyeti / saitat sāmāpaśyat / tenāstuta / sā tīrtham abhyavayatī somāṃśum avindat[14] / taṃ samakhādat / tasyai ha grāvāṇa iva dantā ūduḥ / sa indra ādravad grāvāṇo vai vadantīti / sābhivyāharat

[RV VIII.91.1] *kanyā . . . tvā* iti /

/ asyai vā idaṃ grāvāṇa iva dantā vadantīti viditvendraḥ parāṅ āvartata / tam abravīt

[RV VIII.91.2] *asau . . . ukthinam / /*

iti / anādriyamāṇaivaitam abravīt

[RV VIII.91.3ab] *ā . . . nemasi /*

iti / purā mā sarvayarcāpālā stautīty apaparyāvartata /

[RV VIII.93.3cd] *śanaiḥ . . . srava /*

/ ity evāsyai mukhāt somaṃ niradhayat / somapītha iva ha vā asya sa bhavati ya evaṃ vidvāṃs striyai mukham upājighrati

JB I.221 tām abravīd apāle kiṃkāmāsīti / sābravīt

[RV VIII.91.5, 6d] .5 *imāni . . . upodare / /*

[13]Quoted after Schmidt, p. 6. Crit. Ed. prints ruchvasāpy āsa.
[14]Crit. Ed. has avidant, a clear error.

.6d *sarvā tā romaśā kr̥dhi* / /

iti / khalatir hāsyai pitāsa / taṃ hākhalatiṃ cakāra / urvarā hāsya na jajñe / so ha jajñe / upasthe hāsyai romāṇi nāsuḥ / tāny u ha jajñire / tāṃ khe rathasyātyabr̥hat / sā godhābhavat / tāṃ khe 'naso 'tyabr̥hat / sā kr̥kalāsy abhavat / tāṃ khe yugasyātyabr̥hat / sā saṃśliṣṭikābhavat / tad eṣābhyanūcyate

[RV VIII.91.7] *khe . . . sūryatvacam* / /

iti / tasyai ha yat kalyāṇatamaṃ rūpāṇāṃ tad rūpam āsa

Apālā Ātreyī had tilaka (skin affliction) or rucchvasa (skin affliction).[15] She wished, "Might I smash off (my) bad color." She saw this sāman. She praised with it. She went down to the ford and found a soma-stalk. She chewed it. Her teeth spoke like pressing stones. Indra ran up (thinking), "The pressing stones are speaking." She said to him,

[RV VIII.91.1] "A maiden going down to the water found soma
along the way/at the stream.
Bringing it home she said, 'I will press you for
Indra; I will press you for the able one.'"

When he found out "It's (only) the teeth of that (girl) that are speaking [= sounding] here like pressing stones," Indra turned away.[16] She said to him,

[vs. 2] "Yonder (Indra), the 'little man,' you who go earnestly
looking from house to house,
Drink this (soma), pressed by the jaws—(soma) accompanied
by grain, by gruel, by cakes, by hymns."

Without heeding[17] she said to him,

[vs. 3ab] "We wish to comprehend you; we will not 'recite' you aloud."

15On these terms for skin diseases see Schmidt, pp. 6f. Tilaka seems to mean "having dark spots like a sesame corn." The reading rucchvasā is disturbed; see Schmidt, pp. 6f., for suggested readings. In any case it must also refer to some undesirable skin condition.

16In other words, Indra was hoping for soma and found that the sound of her teeth had misled him.

17Schmidt translates anādriyamānā as 'still not being heeded', but medial ādriyate, common in the Brāhmaṇas, is transitive, as in

JB I.154 atha ha kalayo gandharvā antasthāṃ cerur *netarān netarān ādriyamāṇāḥ*

The Kali-Gandharvas stayed in the middle, *heeding neither the ones nor the others.*

(Later in this same passage, *an*ādriyamāna- is used in the same sense.) The point is probably that Apālā does not pay attention to Indra's imminent departure, but keeps on reciting.

(Indra, thinking,) "Before long Apālā will praise me with the/an entire ṛc,"[18] turned back again. (She said,)

[vs. 3cd] "O drop, flow around quietly, very quietly for Indra."

He sucked the soma out of her mouth. Whoever knows thus, when he kisses[19] the mouth of a woman it becomes a soma-drink[20] for him.

He said to her, "Apālā, what is your wish?" She said,

[vss. 5, 6d] "O Indra, make these three surfaces grow forth—the head of my Papa, the field, and this on my belly—make all these hairy."

Her father was bald: he made him not bald. His field did not produce: it produced. There was no hair on her lap: it grew. He pulled her through the nave of a chariot. (She/the skin?) became a lizard. He pulled her through the nave of a wagon. She/it became a chameleon. He pulled her through the nave of a yoke. She became embraceable (?).[21] Even so is it said:

[vs. 7] "In the nave of a chariot, in the nave of a wagon, in the nave of a yoke, O hundred-powered one,
Apālā, O Indra—having purified (her), you made (her) sun-skinned."

Her form became the most beautiful of forms.

The standard older interpretation (both ancient and modern)[22] is that Apālā is a woman with a skin disease causing hair loss, and this interpretation is followed by most modern interpreters. But Schmidt has suggested rather that Apālā is simply a pubescent girl possessing an undesired sign of puberty (acne) and longing for a desirable one (pubic hair): "a young girl, on the verge of puberty, troubled by bad skin, which frequently goes with pubescence, and by the fact that her pubic hair has not yet appeared" (p. 22). Apālā makes a private soma offering to Indra, who in turn has intercourse with her and "makes her a woman," as it were, by causing her pubic hair to grow and curing her

[18]This is a very conjectural interpretation. I take purā + present stauti according to Pāṇini III.3.4; cf. Speijer 1886, p. 243: purā as an adverb meaning 'erelong' with a present-tense verb in future value. However, Speyer (= Speijer) himself in 1896, p. 86, does not consider this construction Vedic. Schmidt takes it as a present in past value: "Indra turned back thinking that Apālā had already praised him with one whole ṛc." The difference is actually of little importance for the rest of the passage, but the fact that Indra's thought comes in the *middle* of the RVic ṛc (vs. 3) might lend credence to my interpretation.

[19]Literally, 'sniffs'. See the discussion of the 'sniff-kiss' above, Chap. 4, A.2.

[20]On the important word somapītha, see above, Chap. 3, A.

[21]On this interpretation of saṃśliṣṭikā, see Schmidt, pp. 7–8.

[22]From the Indian commentaries (cf. Schmidt, pp. 9f.) to, for example, Geldner (cf. Schmidt, p. 15).

acne. She becomes sexually mature, fertile, and marriageable. The sprouting of plants in the field represents fertility parallel to Apālā's, as does the growing of hair on her father's head.[23]

2. *Apālā, Akūpārā, and Svarbhānu*

The parallels between the Apālā and Svarbhānu seem obvious. I do not exactly want to say that the Svarbhānu myth concerns an adolescent sun with pimples, but rather that the Svarbhānu myth presents a generalized cosmic pattern to which the human experience particularized in Apālā can be compared. The surface of the sun as it normally is represents the ideal skin surface (hence the adjective sū́rya-tvac- 'sun-skinned' at the very end of the Apālā hymn).[24] When the sun is pierced with darkness, its surface becomes flawed, imperfect as with a skin disease, and the blemish on the sun is all the more shocking because of the usual perfection of the sun's surface. But this disease, this śamala (blemish, affliction), as it is once called in the Svarbhānu myth (MS II.1.5), when removed, can be transformed into the vital vegetation or hair of the earth.

Since adolescent acne is associated with similar hair growth, by a sort of mythic wishful thinking one could hope to transform the dark and disfiguring spots on the skin into the desirable dark marks of hair, as in the cosmic version of this process. The blemishes, the pimples, would actually become the hair. An undesirable affliction of the skin is removed and changed into hair, which represents fertility and sexual maturity.

It is not hard to demonstrate that hairlessness in ancient Indian thought is equivalent to sterility and lack of living things. Of many, similar passages, consider, for example,

[23]Schmidt (p. 18) believes that the father's baldness is not permanent, but a temporary result of the ritual head-shaving in the seasonal (Cāturmāsyāni) rites, an act that is meant to ensure growth in the fields. This is certainly possible, but not altogether necessary. If hairlessness of any sort represents infertility, permanent baldness would obviously be undesirable. For more on the connection between hair/haircutting and fertility, see Heesterman 1957, pp. 215ff., and on the relation between hair and plants, in an Indo-European context, see Lincoln 1986, Chap. 4, "Cures for Baldness, Disposal of Hair," pp. 87–98, also n. 17 to chap. 3.

[24]Similarly, the surface of gold, especially of a golden disc, represents both the sun and the ideal skin in earthly terms (cf. the adj. hiraṇya-tvac- 'having golden skin'). We will have occasion to note this later.

KS XXV.2 yad ṛkṣam alomakaṃ tasmin yājayed yaṃ dviṣyād vyṛddhaṃ vā etad oṣadhibhir yad ṛkṣam alomakam oṣadhayaḥ paśavaḥ paśubhir evainaṃ vyardhayati

He should perform a worship for someone he hates in a (place) that is bald and hairless. A bald and hairless (place) is devoid of plants. Plants are cattle. Thus he deprives him of cattle.

Also the oft-repeated ṛkṣáṁ vā́ amedhyám 'a bald (thing/place) is unfit for (contact with) worship'.[25]

But it is worth noting that the matter is not so simple; the paradox is that the actual place of generation and gestation, the womb (yóni), is hairless.

ŚB XIV.4.2.11 (= BĀU I.4.6) alómakā hí yónir antaratáḥ

For the womb is hairless within.

This statement is introduced as explanation for the hairlessness of the inside of the mouth and the palms of the hands; since in the mythical creation of fire these places served as yoni, they too lack hair:

ŚB XIV.4.2.11 sá múkhāc ca yóner hástābhyāṃ cāgním asṛjata tásmād etád ubháyam alómakam antaratò ('lómakā hí yónir antaratáḥ)

He created fire from his mouth and his two hands as womb. Therefore they are both hairless inside. (For the womb is hairless inside.)[26]

The hair must be in the right places, and only in the right places, for it to symbolize fertility. In the wrong places it represents blemish for both Sūrya and Apālā.

The parallelism between Svarbhānu and Apālā is especially underscored by the emphatic finale with sū́rya-tvac- 'sun-skinned', the very last word of the Apālā hymn.

RV VIII.91.7cd apālā́m indra tríṣ pūtvy, ákṛṇoḥ *sū́ryatvacam*

Apālā—O Indra, having purified (her) three times, you made (her) *sun-skinned*.

[25] MS III.8.6, III.8.9; cf. TS II.6.5.1; KS XXV.9. On amedhyá- see above, Chap. 2, A.3.

[26] Cf. ŚB II.2.4.4

Note especially here the distracted object phrase, with apālā́m at the very beginning of the half line and her adjective sū́ryatvacam at the very end. The poet is deliberately signalling the importance of this phrase.

Let us examine a few more similarities between Svarbhānu and A-pālā, in both diction and detail, in one parallel and one later version of the Apālā story. The parallel story, briefly told in the PB, is that of an Aṅgiras known as Akūpārā, a name with some phonological resemblance to Apālā. The agreement between the Apālā and Akūpārā tales has long been recognized.[27] Indeed Schmidt believes that the Akūpārā story is simply "an imitation" of the JB Apālā story,[28] with the name Akūpārā semantically and morphologically modelled on A-pālā:

A-pālā	'who has no yonder shore, boundless'
A-kū-pārā[29]	'whose yonder shore is not small'

In the brief PB narration note especially the telltale adjective sūrya-tvacas- 'sun-skinned'.

> PB IX.2.14 akūpārāṅgirasy āsīt tasyā yathā godhāyās tvag evaṃ tvag āsīt tām etena triḥ sāmnendraḥ pūtvā sūryatvacasam akarot tad vāva sā tarhy akāmayata

> There was a female Aṅgiras (named) Akūpārā. Her skin was like the skin of a lizard. Indra, having purified her three times with this sāman, made her sun-skinned. This was what she wished then.

That the sāman with which Akūpārā is purified is the same as that referred to in the JB Apālā story[30] makes the underlying identity of these stories even more likely.

The later Bṛhaddevatā[31] also contains a lengthy (and somewhat fanciful) account of Apālā (VI.99–107), excerpts of which follow.

[27]Cf. Oertel 1897, pp. 26ff.

[28]Cf. Schmidt 1984, p. 48; also Schmidt 1987, pp. 20–21.

[29]The name Akūpāra- is otherwise only masculine and refers to a tortoise (kaśyapa) that took up residence in the sea (JB III.273) or a lake (MBh. III.191). The JB story concerning this tortoise displays some remarkable parallels to the Svarbhānu myth, and the MBh. story may also be connected, as we will see in n. 36.

[30]Schmidt 1987, p. 6, n. 1.

[31]Schmidt (1987, p. 8) puts the date of this text c. early fourth century B.C.

Bṛhaddev. VI.99 apālātrisutā tv āsīt, kanyā tvagdoṣiṇī purā
tām indraś cakame dṛṣṭvā, vijane pitur āśrame
.100 tapasā bubudhe sā tu, sarvam indracikīrṣitam
udakumbhaṃ samādāya, apām arthe jagāma sā
.101 daṣṭvā somam apām ante . . .
.102 sā suṣāva mukhe somam . . . papāv indraś ca tan mukhāt
.103 apūpāṃś caiva saktūṃś ca, bhakṣayitvā sa tad gṛhāt . . .
.104 sulomām anavadyāṅgīṃ, kuru māṃ śakra sutvacam . . .
.105 rathachidreṇa tām indraḥ, śakaṭasya yugasya ca
prakṣipya niścakarṣa triḥ, sutvak sā tu tato 'bhavat
.106 tasyās tvag apahatā yā, pūrvā sā śalyako 'bhavat
uttarā tv abhavad godhā, kṛkalāsas tvag uttamā

.99 Apālā, Atri's daughter, was previously a maiden with a skin disease.
Indra, having seen her in the unpeopled hermitage of her father, desired her.
.100 By asceticism she became aware of all Indra desired to do.
Taking a water pot, she went in search of water.
.101 Having bitten soma at the edge of the water . . .
.102 She pressed soma in her mouth.
Indra drank it from her mouth,
.103 having also eaten cakes and meal from her house.
.104 [She said] "Make me of good hair, of faultless limbs, of good skin, O able one."
.105 Having pressed her through the hole of the chariot, of the cart, and of the yoke three times,
Indra dragged her out. She thereupon became of good skin.
.106 The skin that was smashed off from her first became a hedgehog;
The next became a lizard; the last skin a chameleon.[32]

Note first an agreement in diction between Svarbhānu and Apālā. In the JB version, Apālā wishes to apa √han her skin affliction; the same lexeme is used of the sloughed off skin in the Bṛhaddev.

[32]On these animals, see Schmidt 1987, p. 7, with n. 3.

JB I.220 apālā ha vā ātreyī tilakā vā rucchvasā vāpi āsa / sākāmayat*āpa* pāpaṃ varṇaṃ *hanīye*ti

Apālā Ātreyī had tilaka (skin affliction) or rucchvasa (skin affliction). She wished, "Might I *smash off* (my) bad color."

Bṛhaddev. VI.106 tasyās tvag *apahatā* yā, pūrvā sā śalyako 'bhavat

The skin that was *smashed off* from her first became a hedgehog.

As we saw above, this is the precise idiom most generally used in the Svarbhānu myth for the removal of darkness from the sun, for example (of the many examples):

TS II.1.2.2 tásya yát prathamáṃ *támo 'pā́ghnan*

What darkness of his they *smashed off* first . . .

The threefold purification of Apālā/Akūpāra found in all three of the versions we have examined resembles the three times that the darkness is smashed or wiped off the sun in Svarbhānu.[33] Indeed, in the JB and Bṛhaddev. versions of the Apālā myth, the purifications result in animals, just as do the three removals of darkness from the sun.[34]

JB I.221 tāṃ khe rathasyātyabṛhat / sā godhābhavat / tāṃ khe 'naso 'tyabṛhat / sā kṛkalāsy abhavat

He pulled her through the nave of a chariot. (She/the skin?) became a lizard. He pulled her through the nave of a wagon. She/it became a chameleon.

Bṛhaddev. VI.106 tasyās tvag apahatā yā, pūrvā sā śalyako 'bhavat
uttarā tv abhavad godhā, kṛkalāsas tvag uttamā

[33]Though in some versions of Svarbhānu there are four actions of purification and four sheep produced (MS II.5.2, KS XII.13, TS II.1.2.2–3 [KS XXVII.2 and JB I.80–81 have only the three]), the *sun* is actually touched only three times. The fourth ewe comes from some substance other than the sun. See Chap. 7, B.3.

[34]It is true that the animal transformations do not appear in the RV Apālā hymn, and Oertel for one (1897, p. 31) thinks that they are a late addition to the story. But even if so, it might be that a perceived parallelism between the stories of Svarbhānu and Apālā suggested that her discarded skin (like the discarded darkness of the sun) might have turned into animals.

The skin that was smashed off from her first became a hedgehog;
The next became a lizard; the last skin a chameleon.

Similarly, the skin of Akūpārā is like that of a lizard (godhā), as is Apālā's in both JB and Bṛhaddev.:

PB IX.2.14 tasyā yathā godhāyās tvag evaṃ tvag āsīt

Her (Akūpārā's) skin was like the skin of a lizard.

A Svarbhānu parallel containing the animal transformations:

KS XXVII.2 svarbhānur vā āsuras sūryaṃ tamasāvidhyat sa na vyarocyata tasmād devās tamo 'pālumpan yat prathamam apālumpan sāviṣ kṛṣṇābhavad yad dvitīyaṁ sā phalgur yat tṛtīyaṁ sā balakṣī

Svarbhānu Āsura pierced the sun with darkness. He did not shine forth. The gods stripped off the darkness from him. The first darkness they stripped off became a black ewe. The second a reddish one. The third a white one.

The animals in the Apālā story and in the Svarbhānu myth are practically mirror images of each other: in Svarbhānu sheep are produced—the very embodiment of the hairy animal; it is no wonder that the sacrifice of one of them should give rise to hair on the earth. In Apālā they are all hairless animals, though their skins are rough and have unattractive excrescences.[35]

It is also a mere grammatical fact that the earth, on which 'hair' was made to grow in Svarbhānu, is a feminine noun, also typed frequently as semantically female, just like Apālā. Examining the Svarbhānu myth in the context afforded by Apālā, one can see the hairless earth as a girl before puberty, and the earth with hair made to grow on her as a girl reaching sexual maturity.

Moreover and perhaps most important, Apālā is said to be Atri's daughter in the JB (I.220 Apālā Ātreyī) and Bṛhaddev. (VI.99 apālā

[35]It may also be that the three khá- 'wheel naves', through which Apālā is pulled and by which her skins are removed and become animals, are meant to evoke the circular disc of the sun, but both etymology and usage make this suggestion unlikely. Khá- is derived from √khan 'dig' and often refers to apertures, canals, or pipes, which have been drilled or otherwise opened (cf., e.g., RV II.15.3 vájreṇa khā́ny atṛṇan nadī́nām 'with a cudgel he drilled openings/canals for the rivers'). The relevant semantic feature of the khá- of a wheel seems to be its opening, not its circularity.

atrisutī), and the RV Anukramaṇī gives Apālā Ātreyī as author of VIII.91. Although Schmidt considers this patronymic perhaps secondary and accidental, dependent "on the fact that the hymn was composed by a member of the Atri family" (p. 21), I think there are good reasons for it. Atri is, as rescuer of the sun in the Svarbhānu myth, associated with skin diseases and their cures. He is famous for having removed the spots from the sun's skin, just as Apālā wishes her blemishes to disappear and her face to become 'sun-skinned'. Other reasons for the association between Apālā Ātreyī and the Atri of the Svarbhānu myth we will examine shortly.

3. The Tortoise Akūpāra

There is also indirect evidence for the link between Atri of the Svarbhānu myth and Apālā/Akūpārā, in the tale concerning the tortoise named Akūpāra, whose name so closely resembles the young women with bad skin.

In JB III.203 the seers (ṛṣis) wish to see this tortoise Akūpāra, who lives in the sea. He does not appear, so they ask Atri for help. Since Indra is master of Akūpāra, the ṛṣis command Atri to praise Indra, in hopes that he will make the tortoise appear. Indra finally understands what they are after and obliges. Here is an excerpted version:

> JB III.203 akūpāro vā ayaṃ kaśyapas samudre 'ntaḥ . . . / eta taṃ paśyāmeti / . . . tebhyo ha nāvir āsa / te hocur etendram eva stavāma sa vāvāsyeśe / sa eva na imaṃ darśayiṣyatīti / te 'trim abruvann ṛṣe tvaṃ stutād iti / sa etam atris tṛcam apaśyat / . . . / sa hājajñāv akūpāraṃ vai didṛkṣanta iti / taṃ ha padodasyann uvāca . . . tam apaśyan

> (There was) this tortoise Akūpāra in the ocean. . . . [The seers said] "Come on. Let's see him." . . . (But) he was not visible to them. They said, "Come on. Let's praise Indra. He is master of him. He will show him to us." They said to Atri, "Ṛṣi, praise!" Atri saw this tṛca (and praised Indra) . . . (Indra) realized, "They want to see Akūpāra." Tossing him up with his foot, he spoke. . . . They (the ṛṣis) saw him (Akūpāra).

This curious little story is notable because it shows the same thematic configuration as the great rescue of the sun in Svarbhānu, especially in the RVic version. Just as here, *Atri,* along with *Indra,* makes (the sun) *visible* again, and as here, Atri's means in the RV are *praise* and acts of worship.

RV V.40.6 svàrbhānor ádha yád *indra* māyā́, avó divó vártamānā avā́han
gūḷhám̐ sū́ryam̐ támasā́pavratena, turī́yeṇa bráhmaṇā*vindad átrih . . .*
.8 grā́vṇo brahmā́ yuyujānáḥ saparyán, kīríṇā devā́n námasopaśíkṣan
átriḥ sū́ryasya diví cákṣur ā́dhāt

.6 Then, O *Indra,* when you smashed down from heaven the circling magic spells of Svarbhānu, *Atri* with the fourth formulation *found the sun, hidden by darkness* because of (an act) contrary to commandment.
.8 The Brahman, yoking the pressing stones, serving the gods with mere (?) reverence, seeking to win (the sun), Atri placed the eye of the sun in heaven.

Moreover, the abrupt order issued to Atri in the Akūpāra story has its exact analogue in a Svarbhānu passage in the JB, when the gods and ṛṣis together ask for Atri's help.

JB III.203[the Akūpāra passage] te 'trim abruvann ṛṣe tvaṃ stutād iti

They said to Atri, "Ṛṣi, praise!"

JB I.80 svarbhānur vā āsura ādityaṃ tamasāvidhyat / taṃ devāś carṣayaś cābhiṣajyan / *te 'trim abruvann ṛṣe tvam idam apajahīti*

Svarbhānu Āsura pierced the sun with darkness. The gods and seers healed him. *They said to Atri, "Seer, smash this (darkness) away!"*

So, the thematic shape of this passage is that of Svarbhānu, but the name Akūpāra connects it with the Apālā/Akūpārā story.[36]

[36]A later story involving the tortoise Akūpāra (MBh. III.191) may faintly echo this thematic complex. The royal seer Indradyumna (lit. 'having the radiance of Indra'—a name that connects him explicitly with Indra and semantically with the sun) falls from heaven because he is no longer remembered. After fruitlessly asking several animals if they remember him, he makes Akūpāra emerge from his lake. The long-lived tortoise recognizes Indradyumna, who as a result is restored to heaven. Here *remembering* Indradyumna may be equivalent to making him *visible,* but the tortoise is agent rather than object of this action. He makes Indradyumna visible/radiant again, whereas in the other Akūpāra story he himself was rendered visible (by Indra). I do not wish to push this parallelism too far, however, and do not insist that the stories are connected, much less mirror images.

4. Apālā as Ritualist

Let us now direct our attention to Apālā alone, to see how she sets about accomplishing her objectives (and, to some extent, what these objectives are). Though this investigation has no direct relevance to Svarbhānu, it will demonstrate how intimately entwined ritual and myth are, even in the Rig Veda, and this will help us when we come to inquire into what means Atri used to release the sun in the Svarbhānu myth.

It is, of course, clear that the Apālā tale has a ritual remedy: the mainspring of the action, which brings Indra and ultimately the fulfillment of Apālā's wish, is the pressing of soma, the quintessential Vedic ritual activity. But treatments of the hymn do not always make clear how precise this ritual focus is. As the tale is often paraphrased, Apālā finds soma as if by accident and presses it with the only means she has available—her teeth—almost as a lark. She is surprised when Indra arrives, but offers the soma to him. In exchange he grants her a wish, and things move on from there. It is the act of an ingenue; it is almost cute. Compare Schmidt's presentation of these events:

> By the river she once *happened* to find soma, and this *gave her the idea* to offer it to Indra. . . . Since she *had not the proper equipment* for pressing soma, she chewed the stalks and offered the juice to the god from her mouth, *supplementing* the offering with fried grain, gruel, cake and song.[37]

The way the RV presents the action is quite different. The first two verses of RV VIII.91 present a precisely definable ritual situation, one in which Apālā seems to know exactly what she is doing.

Let us look first at the most obvious aspect of this. When Apālā offers the soma to Indra, she does it with the words:

> RV VIII.91.2c–e imáṃ jámbhasutam piba, dhānā́vantaṃ
> karambhíṇam, apūpávantam ukthínam

> "Drink this (soma), pressed by the jaws—(soma) accompanied by
> grain, by gruel, by cakes, by hymns."

To say the least, this is not an artless and spontaneous invitation. Though Schmidt's words "supplementing the offering" seem to im-

[37]Schmidt 1987, p. 22; my italics.

ply[38] that she is trying to eke out a meagre amount of soma with an assortment of food from the pantry, these accompaniments are anything but an impromptu spread; they are orthodox side dishes at a particular ritual offering. The last two pādas then are the words of someone who knows her ritual. They seem almost pedantically priestly, on the lips of a prepubescent girl. Indeed the identical two pādas are found in RV III.52.1, a hymn that is little more than a versified menu of the dishes offered at the three soma pressings.

RV III.52.1 dhānā́vantaṃ karambhíṇam, apūpávantam ukthínam
índra prātár juṣasva naḥ

O Indra, early in the morning enjoy (this soma) of ours accompanied by grain, by gruel, by cakes, by hymns.

The precise ritual offering meant is easy to define. The context of III.52.1 suggests (through prātár 'early morning') the first or early-morning soma pressing (*Prātaḥ*savana), and in fact there is an offering at this ceremony that involves the substances named, the offering known as the Savanīya-puroḍāśa 'the pressing cakes.'[39] It involves a set of five offerings made of dhānā́ḥ karambháḥ parivāpáḥ puroḍāśáḥ payasyā̀ 'roasted grains, gruel, rice grains, an offering cake, and clotted milk'.[40] Here we have the major elements of Apālā's offering: dhānā́ḥ 'grains', karambháḥ 'gruel', and apūpáḥ 'cake', for the last of which the ritual texts substitute the roughly equivalent word puroḍāśa-.[41]

All these substances are offered to Indra (cf., e.g., ŚB IV.2.5.17 sárva aindrā́ bhavanti), but Indra in conjunction with other beings, as the mantras of dedication show.

[38]However, I am not at all certain he means his statement to be taken this way.

[39]This offering, sometimes distributed on a different number of dishes, also takes place at the other pressings.

[40]Cf. TS VI.5.11.4, MS III.10.5, AB II.23.

[41]I am not certain what, if any, difference there is between an apūpá cake and a puroḍāśá cake.

Other texts, especially the ritual sūtras, make further terminological substitutions. For example, already the ŚB lists the elements of the Savanīya-puroḍāśa as (IV.2.5.18) puroḍā́śaḥ dhānā́ḥ karambhó dádhy āmikṣā́, with dádhi 'sour curds' and āmikṣā́ 'clotted curds' substituting for parivāpá- 'rice grains' and payasyā̀- 'clotted milk', respectively. But in discussing this offering immediately afterwards, the text substitutes apūpá- for puroḍāśá- in IV.2.5.19, and payasyā̀ for āmikṣā́ in .22. Clearly the designations of the ingredients were somewhat flexible, while the actual foods fall within a basically fixed paradigm.

KS XXIX.1(≅ MS III.10.6, AB II.24, etc.) harivāṁ indro *dhānā* attu . . . pūṣaṇvān *karambham* . . . sarasvatīvān bhāratīvān *parivāpaḥ* . . . indrasy*āpūpaḥ* . . . mitrāvaruṇayoḥ *payasyā*

Let Indra accompanied by his bay steeds eat the roasted grain. . . . Accompanied by Pūṣan (let him eat) the gruel. . . . With Sarasvatī and Bhāratī the rice grains. . . . The cake is Indra's. . . . The curds are Mitra and Varuṇa's.

The prescription concerning Pūṣan is especially apposite, since gruel eating is one of Pūṣan's characteristics already in the RV, so characteristic that Pūṣan answers to the epithet karambhā́d- 'Gruel-eater'.

RV VI.56.1 yá enam ādídeśati, karambhā́d íti pūṣáṇam
ná téna devá ādíśe

Who points out/calls on him, Pūṣan, as "Gruel-eater," by him the god need not be pointed out/called on (again).

Indeed this ritual complex, including the particular offerings and their designated recipients, is clearly known in some form already in the RV, as shown by a verse found in the menu hymn cited above:

RV III.52.7 pūṣaṇváte te cakṛmā *karambháṃ,* hárivate háryaśvāya *dhānā́ḥ*
apūpám addhi ságaṇo marúdbhiḥ, sómam piba vṛtrahā́ śūra vidvā́n

We have made gruel for thee (Indra), accompanied by Pūṣan; roasted grain for (thee), accompanied by bay horses, possessor of bay horses.
Eat the cake in company with the Maruts. Drink the soma (as) knowing Vṛtra-smasher, O Hero.

Here all and only the substances mentioned in Apālā's offering in VIII.91.2 appear. Thus, Apālā is inviting Indra to partake of a particular ritual offering, not a chance collection of snacks.

Even the words with which Apālā introduces this offering (vs. 2c imáṃ *jámbhasutam* piba 'Drink this (soma) *pressed by the jaws*') are less of an innocent makeshift than they appear, for at least in Vedic prose the two parts of the handpress for pressing soma are identified with the jaws (hánū) and the pressing stones with the teeth.

MS IV.5.9 hánū adhiṣávane . . . grā́vāṇo dántāḥ

The two (parts of the) handpress are the two jaws; . . . the teeth are the pressing stones.

In calling the soma jámbha-suta- Apālā might be simply indulging in metaphor: soma pressed by the "jaws" of the handpress. Even if she has literally pressed the soma with her own teeth (the alternative I prefer, on literary grounds), she is utilizing instruments (her own jaws) that ritual exegesis teaches are equivalent to the proper equipment (the handpress).

The second half of vs. 3, in which Apālā again offers Indra the soma, also mirrors the ritual directly.

RV VIII.91.3cd śánair iva śanakaír ivéndrāyendo pári srava

O drop, flow around quietly, very quietly for Indra.

The first pāda, 'softly, very softly', no doubt reflects the "domestic or even private character of the ceremony," indeed its "secretiveness."[42] Apālā's ritual activity and Indra's visitation are not to be revealed, as pāda 3b seems also to indicate:

RV VIII.91.3ab ā́ caná tvā cikitsāmó, *'dhi caná tvā némasi*

"We wish to comprehend you; *we will not 'recite' you (aloud)*."[43]

[42]As Schmidt suggests (p. 14), though śánaiḥ 'softly' need not always imply secrecy and privacy. The only other instance of śánaiḥ in the RV applies the word to an ordinary, presumably public offering of soma to Indra: in VIII.45.11 the soma drops are described as śánaiś cid yántaḥ 'going (even though?) softly'.

[43]This translation of ádhi . . . imasi 'proclaim, announce, reveal' was suggested to me by Stanley Insler. Others take the idiom as more or less equivalent to ā́ . . . cikitsamaḥ: e.g., Schmidt: "We want to comprehend you, (but) we do not understand you." Such an interpretation is difficult to fit into the rest of the hymn, though Schmidt does a commendable job.

The idiom adhi √i elsewhere is a part of pedagogical vocabulary; in later Vedic (e.g., ŚB XI.5.6.3–9) it clearly means 'study (a text)'. In an oral culture like Vedic India, studying a text requires *reciting aloud*. Though there are no unambiguous examples of such a meaning for adhi √i in the RV, passages like the following, with specific verses as object of the verb, invite or allow such an interpretation:

RV IX.67.31 (≅32) yáḥ *pāvamānī́r adhyéty,* ṛ́ṣibhiḥ sáṃbhṛtaṃ rásam
sárvaṃ sá pūtám aśnāti, svaditám mātaríśvanā

Who(ever) *studies/recites the Pāvamānī(-verses),* the sap assembled by the seers,
He attains everything, purified (and) sweetened by Mātariśvan.

The last pāda (3d), on the other hand, is a blatant quotation of a ritual cliché. The phrase índrāyendo pári srava 'O drop, flow around for Indra' is a common refrain in the soma hymns of the late IXth Maṇḍala, occurring in IX.106.4, IX.112.1–4, IX.113.1–11, IX.114.1–4. Thus, the identical line is found twenty times in the RV alone, making it almost the unmarked envoi for the soma drop. Just as Apālā's ritual actions and accoutrements slavishly follow the prescribed ritual pattern, so she also takes no chances on novelty in ritual utterance, but adopts the precise phraseology of the public rite.

In other words, vss. 2 and 3 of the Apālā hymn show us a girl taking a conscious part in an early-morning soma ritual, a ritual that is as orthodox as she can make it. The orthodoxy is also to be seen in vs. 1, though in more disguised form.

RV VIII.91.1 kanyā̀ vā́r avāyatī́, sómam ápi srutā́vidat
ástam bháranty abravīd, índrāya sunavai tvā, śakrā́ya
sunavai tvā

A maiden going down to the water found soma along the way/at the
stream.
Bringing it home she said, "I will press you for Indra; I will press
you for the able one."

Even the apparently innocent journey she takes in this verse also has a precise ritual equivalent, already spelled out in RV V.37, a hymn to Indra (note especially the text not in brackets):

RV V.37.1 [sám bhānúnā yatate sū́ryasyājúhvāno ghṛtápṛṣṭhaḥ
sváñcāḥ
tásmā ámṛdhrā uṣáso vy ùchān,] *yá índrāya sunávāméty ā́ha*
.2 [sámiddhāgnir vanavat stīrṇábarhir, yuktágrāvā sutásomo
jarāte]
grā́vāṇo yásyeṣirám vádanty, áyad adhvaryúr havíṣā́va síndhum

---

From the notion of reciting aloud follows that of announcing something/someone publicly, which seems to be the purport of ádhi . . . imasi in VIII.91.3b. Apālā wants to keep the presence of Indra to herself; she wants to perceive and understand him inwardly and privately (ā́ . . .cikitsāmaḥ), but not to reveal ('recite') that knowledge or its source to others. The words sánair iva śanakaír iva 'softly, very softly' beginning the next pāda emphatically carry on this theme.

Both idioms (ā́ √cit and adhi √i) are adapted from the pedagogical context appropriate to the adolescent that Apālā is. (Though regular schooling of girls was no doubt nonexistent at the time, Apālā was clearly exceptional, as her uncanny knowledge of śrauta ritual shows.)

.1 [(Agni) takes his place with the brilliance of the sun,[44]
(Agni) bepoured (with ghee), with ghee on his back, agile.
Unfailing dawns will shine forth for him,] *who says, "We will press (soma) for Indra."*

.2 [He with a kindled fire and strewn barhis will win; he with yoked pressing stones and pressed soma will sing.]
Whose pressing stones speak eagerly, (his) Adhvaryu will go down to the river with an oblation.

This opening of this hymn describes in some detail the preparations for the morning pressing: as the sun rises, libations are poured into the kindled fire (1ab), the barhis (grass) is strewn, and the pressing stones are prepared to press the soma (2a–c); the recitations and the hymns are begun (2b). And the Adhvaryu goes down to the nearest river to fetch water.

Notice how closely the beginning of the Apālā hymn parallels this activity. As in V.37.1, she presses the soma (though with her teeth), announcing,

RV VIII.91.1d índrāya sunavai tvā, śakrā́ya sunavai tvā

"I will press you for Indra; I will press you for the able one."

in almost the same words as V.37.1d: índrāya sunávāma '"We will press (soma) for Indra".' The sound of the pressing stones is loud in V.37.2c; it is this same supposed sound that attracts Indra in the Apālā story. The parallelism is even clearer in the JB version:

JB I.220 [taṃ samakhādat / tasyai ha grāvāṇa iva dantā ūduḥ] / sa indra ādravad *grāvāṇo vai vadantī*ti

[She chewed it. Her teeth spoke like pressing stones.] Indra ran up (thinking), "*The pressing stones are speaking.*"

The last phrase, grāvāṇo vai vadanti, is found almost exactly in V.37.2c *grā́vāṇo* yásyeṣirā́ṃ *vádanti* 'whose *pressing stones speak* eagerly'.

[44]Note in passing the phrase bhānúnā . . . sū́ryasya 'with the brilliance of the sun' in conjunction with Agni. See below, Chap. 10, A.

Indra's house-to-house canvass in the Apālā hymn (2ab) also fits in this ritual scenario. In the early morning Indra goes seeking a soma presser, as we see in a hymn nearby the one just cited:

RV V.31.12 ā́yáṃ janā abhicákṣe jagāméndraḥ sákhāyaṃ sutásomam ichán

This Indra, O people, has come hither to look, seeking a friend who has pressed soma.

This recalls the search in the Apālā hymn:

RV VIII.91.2ab asaú yá éṣi vīrakó, gṛháṃ-gṛhaṃ vicā́kaśat . . .

Yonder (Indra), the little man (?), you who go earnestly looking from house to house . . .

just before Apālā offers him soma. Though Schmidt believes Indra here "is in search of maidens on the brink of puberty" (p. 13), the emphasis on ritualistic details in these verses suggests rather that the soma of the early-morning pressing is his object here too.

But the most remarkable parallel is between V.37.2d and the opening of the Apālā hymn, VIII.91.1a:

RV V.37.2d áyad adhvaryúr háviṣā́va síndhum

(His) Adhvaryu will go down to the river with an oblation.

RV VIII.91.1a kanyā̀ vā́r avāyatī́ . . .

A girl going down to the water . . .

The latter is seemingly casual in its own context; indeed Schmidt is uncertain of the purpose of Apālā's journey and suggests it is either to fetch water or to take a bath (pp. 11, 22). But in ritual context it begins to seem purposeful. One of the first acts of the morning pressing is to fetch water, and V.37.2d, which expresses this in ritual context, even contains the same preverb-verb combination (ava + √i, a rare combination in the RV) as is used of Apālā's journey.[45]

[45]VIII.91.1 of course reads avā́yatī́, with the apparent sequence of preverbs ava-ā, but the Pp has ava-yatī́, which Oldenberg suggests is the proper interpretation. Cf. Oldenberg, *Noten,* ad loc.; Oldenberg 1906, p. 151, n. 3.

The ritual act of fetching water for the morning pressing is specified already in early Vedic prose.

> MS IV.5.2 yátra hótuḥ prātaranuvākám anubruvatá upaśr̥̄ṇuyā́t tád apò 'dhvaryúr gr̥̄hṇīyāt
>
> When he should hear the Hotar reciting the Prātaranuvāka (early-morning recitation), then the Adhvaryu should get water.

This water is more clearly specified as 'flowing water' (i.e., from a river or stream) in the ritual sūtras.

> MŚS II.3.2.14 (≅ ĀpŚS XII.5.5) yatra hotuḥ prātaranuvākam anubruvata upaśr̥̄ṇuyāt tad apo 'dhvaryur *vahatīnāṃ* gr̥̄hṇīyāt
>
> When he should hear the Hotar reciting the Prātaranuvāka (early-morning recitation), then the Adhvaryu should get water *of flowing* (streams/rivers).

5. *Apālā's Objectives*

What makes this parallel more remarkable still is the verse that follows the trip to the river in RV V.37, the hymn describing the early-morning pressing. So far this hymn has done little more than establish a ritual mise-en-scène, but in vs. 3 we move abruptly into the realm of metaphor.

> RV V.37.3ab vadhū́r iyám pátim ichánty eti, yá īṃ váhāte máhiṣīm iṣirā́m
>
> This bride goes seeking a husband who will convey (her) [= marry her], the eager one, (as) chief wife.

It is not entirely clear to me to whom this half verse refers. It may well be, as Geldner suggests, Speech as "Lieblingsfrau des Indra," or dawn, or the cow('s) milk going in search of soma, with which she is mixed for the manthin- or 'stirred' oblation, which follows later in the ceremony (cf., e.g., MŚS II.3.5.6). All of these are common and applicable female metaphorical figures in the RV. It may not really matter who the referent is; what is important is that a female figure much like Apālā goes forth in search of a husband at precisely this moment in the ritual—the moment that Apālā seems to have reached in her own ritual observance.

What I am suggesting, somewhat tentatively, is that at this point in the morning pressing it seems appropriate (at least in RV V.37) to evoke the image of a young woman in search of a husband. This might suggest that there is some association between the search and this part of the ritual *and* that a girl desiring marriage might thereby benefit from performing the ritual. We might then infer that Apālā is acting as she does to achieve marriage. The chain of reasoning that leads from RV V.37.3 to this conclusion is, I realize, long and slender. Fortunately we have other evidence that Apālā has a further objective than just the immediate one of curing her pimples and acquiring pubic hair.

Given her desire also for growth of plants in the field, it is obvious that her request is not merely for beauty but for fertility. Her desire for pubic hair has the same point, for the importance of (pubic) hair as a sign of sexual maturity and indeed of marriageability is clear from later texts. In the law code of Manu marriage is forbidden with 'a hairless maiden' (MDŚ III.8 nodvahet . . . kanyām . . . alomikām 'one should not marry a maiden without hair'). Zysk[46] interprets this as showing that "hair-loss was a definite mark of inauspiciousness," but there is no reference to hair-*loss* here, and the word kanyā 'maiden' suggests a girl before puberty. The Gr̥hya Sūtras are even more explicit, forbidding "sport" with a female whose hair has not grown (ajāta-lomnī-).

> GobhGS III.5.3 nājātalomnyopahāsam icchet
>
> One should not seek "sport" with a female whose hair has not (yet) grown.[47]

Several terms used to define marriageable age also refer to this condition: nagnikā- (prepubescent girl, 'naked' of [pubic] hair) and a-nagnikā- ('not naked' of [pubic] hair), as Thieme has shown.[48]

Thus it seems that Apālā is concerned specifically with marriage, that this hymn is ultimately a spell to obtain a husband or the first step on the way to one. Indeed, the last verse of the hymn appears (as vs. 41) in a hymn of marriage verses in the AV (XIV.1), and von

[46]Zysk 1985, p. 88.

[47]Cf. also PāraskGS II.7.9. Oldenberg (1886, 1892, ad locc.) delicately leaves these passages untranslated. Schmidt (1987, p. 15) dissociates the GobhGS passage from the MDŚ one and suggests that the latter does refer to "permanent hairlessness," since marriage with one having too much hair (atiloman-) is also forbidden. But the mention of hair could simply have suggested the other provision, and I am inclined to think that sexual maturity is at issue in the alomikā provision.

[48]Treated by Thieme 1963, pp. 170–80, esp. 178 (1984, pp. 435–45, esp. 443).

Schroeder[49] suggests that the hymn refers to ritual purification before sexual and marital union, a puberty spell. Schmidt perceptively points out that the hymn presents "an ideal situation which is rarely met in reality," when the time of attaining puberty coincides with the moment of marriage and sexual union (p. 22) and thinks that the Apālā hymn reflects a combined female puberty rite and marriage ritual (p. 28). "The hymn telescopes the slow process of incipient pubescence to full maturity."

In this context the adjective pati-dvíṣ- takes on a special poignancy.

RV VIII.91.4 kuvít patidvíṣo yatī́r, índreṇa saṃgámāmahai

Shall we, (though) coming as husband-haters, unite with Indra?

As has long been recognized, this word is grammatically incapable of meaning 'hated by her husband',[50] as the Indian tradition would have it, a tradition maintained, in the face of the grammatical evidence, by, for example, Geldner and O'Flaherty. A compound with the meaning 'hated by her husband' should have had the form *páti-dviṣṭa-. Not only could this have been easily formed (cf. RV índra-dviṣṭa- 'hated by Indra'), but it would also fill almost the same metrical slot as pati-dvíṣaḥ in this verse, merely changing the quantity of one syllable (*pátidviṣṭā yatī́ḥ# with long third syllable rather than the short of patidvíṣo yatī́ḥ). In other words, if the poet had meant to say this, he would have.

Rather, in a compound of the shape we have here, with accented root noun as final compound member, the final member should govern the first, as in parallel forms like anr̥ta-dvíṣ- 'hating untruth', r̥ṣi-dvíṣ- 'hating the seer'. Schmidt has interpreted, I think rightly, this compound as capturing the fearful reluctance of the girl who dreams, perhaps for the first time, of love in an abstract and idealized way but shies away from actual experience: "The author wanted to convey the idea that pubescent girls, for all their yearning for sexual maturation, hate the idea of marriage and sexual intercourse, be it instinctively or on account of socially imposed attitudes" (p. 16). The hymn provides "a glimpse into the girl's private worries and fantasies while she is preparing herself for the event she is half dreading, half yearning for: to be a woman and a wife" (p. 29). So, though she has, with purpose,

[49] Von Schroeder 1908, pp. 229f.

[50] Cf. Oldenberg 1885, p. 76; Oldenberg, *Noten*, ad loc.; Wackernagel-Debrunner, *AIG*, vol. 2.2, pp. 5, 10; and see esp. Schmidt 1987, p. 15.

embarked on a ritual to obtain physical maturity and ultimately a husband, she is still pati-dvíṣ- 'hating husbands'.[51]

But—what better way to attain her first sexual experience than with a god; this *is* an abstract and idealized experience. Hence one can translate VIII.91.4cd kuvít patidvíṣo yatī́r, índreṇa saṃgámāmahai 'shall we, *though* coming as husband-haters, unite with Indra?' But even this seems to produce ambivalence, as her wavering words in 4ab suggest.

.4ab kuvíc chákat kuvít kárat, kuvín no vásyasas[52] kárat

Will he be able? Will he do (it)? Will he make us better off?

Perhaps Indra serves rather the same function here as the variety of nonmortal lovers do in the wedding hymn, in which, before the mortal man marries the woman, Soma, a Gandharva, and Agni have been her husbands.

RV X.85.40 sómaḥ prathamó vivide, gandharvó vivida úttaraḥ
tr̥tī́yo agníṣ ṭe pátis, turī́yas te manuṣyajā́ḥ

Soma first acquired (you = the bride). The Gandharva acquired (you) next. Agni (was) your third husband. The fourth is born of man.

Schmidt (pp. 21–22) believes that Apālā is actually Indra's own wife (-to-be), but I think that a human Apālā, using Indra as a surrogate and practice husband, fits the tone of the hymn much better.[53]

[51]Or perhaps, since páti- usually means 'master', pati-dvíṣ- can mean 'hating masters, hating (the idea of) mastery', as Stanley Insler has suggested to me. She is, after all, a very spunky girl.

[52]Pāda b presents a slight grammatical problem. If the referent of nas 'us' is the same as the other first plural referents (vs. 3, vs. 4cd), it should be feminine, and the adjective vásyasas should agree in gender (expect *vásyasīs, not masc. vásyasas). However, the idiom √kr̥ vásyaso naḥ 'make us better off' is widespread in the RV (II.17.8, IV.2.20, VIII.48.6, IX.4.1–10), and its formulaic nature would probably override gender agreement in this passage. Indeed it is possible that a "correct" *vásyasīs kárat was formulaically normalized (which would be possible without metrical disturbance), as the correct interpretation of the verse became unclear. That the verse was already difficult to understand in Vedic times seems likely from the fact that it alone is omitted from the JB retelling of the story.

[53]Though given Indra's fierce and supervirile character, I would think he would be an alarming first sexual partner.

6. *Indra, Pūṣan, and Marriage?*

Thus, in the Apālā hymn we see a maiden performing a carefully orthodox morning soma pressing in hopes of achieving both sexual maturity and the marriage that should follow quickly thereafter. Something about this particular part of the ritual seems appropriate to these desires, but *what?* I do not have a certain answer here, merely a tentative suggestion. Remember that Apālā in vs. 2 offers Indra a Savanīya-puroḍāśa or rather a portion of one, containing roasted grain (for Indra and his bay horses), gruel (for Indra and Pūṣan), and a cake (for Indra alone). Compare the Apālā passage again with the relevant parts of the ritual prescriptions:

RV VIII.91.2 imáṃ jámbhasutam piba, dhānā́vantaṃ karambhíṇam, apūpávantam ukthínam

Drink this (soma), pressed by the jaws—(soma) accompanied by grain, by gruel, by cakes, by hymns.

KS XXIX.1 (≅ MS III.10.6, AB II.24, etc.) *harivā̆m̐* indro *dhānā* attu . . . *pūṣaṇvān karambham* . . . indrasy*āpūpaḥ* . . .

Let Indra accompanied by his bay steeds eat the roasted grain. . . . Accompanied by Pūṣan (let him eat) the gruel. . . . The cake is Indra's. . . .

This set of figures, Indra, Pūṣan, and the bay horses, along with another figure, Indra's wife, seems to correspond to a mythic fragment, which is suggestive, though too slight to be fully comprehensible.

RV I.82.6 yunájmi te bráhmaṇā keśínā *hárī,* úpa prá yāhi dadhiṣé gábhastyoḥ
út tvā sutā́so rabhasā́ amandiṣuḥ, *pūṣaṇvā́n* vajrin sám u *pátnyā*madaḥ

With a formulation I yoke the two maned *bay steeds* for you (Indra). Drive hither; you hold (the reins) in your hands.
The strong pressings have intoxicated you. *Accompanied by Pūṣan,* you became intoxicated along *with your wife,* O cudgel-possessor.

The presence of Indra's wife along with Pūṣan reminds us of a fact about the latter god. Pūṣan appears as a leader of the bride in the wedding hymn:

RV X.85.26 pūṣā́ tvetó nayatu hastagŕ̥hya

Let Pūṣan lead thee (the bride) from here, having grasped (thee) by the hand.

More tellingly, in the same hymn he rouses her for an explicitly sexual connection, presumably her first. This is the most crudely sexual verse in the entire hymn:

RV X.85.37 tā́m pūṣañ chivátamām érayasva, yásyām bī́jam manuṣyā̀ vápanti
yā́ na ūrū́ uśatī́ viśrā́yāte, yásyām uśántaḥ prahárāma śépam

O Pūṣan, bring hither this most auspicious (female) one, in which men plant seed,
(She) who will willingly spread her thighs for us, in whom willingly we will put our penis.

It may be that Pūṣan's participation in the Savanīya-puroḍāśa makes this part of the morning pressing seem especially connected with puberty and marriage rites, since it evokes both the shadowy myth (of RV I.82.6) involving Pūṣan, Indra, and Indra's wife *and* Pūṣan's functions at the wedding. But in the absence of stronger evidence, I present this only as a conjecture.

B. Ritual and Magic Reflections of the Myth

We have so far looked at two myths of superficially very different type, which nonetheless share important thematic elements and patterns. In the cosmic myth of Svarbhānu, the surface of the sun is marred by darkness. This darkness, when removed, becomes vegetation, specifically identified as the earth's hair. In the human realm, in the story of Apālā, the skin of this young girl is marred by a skin affliction (acne). This affliction is removed, and at the same time she grows (pubic) hair, her father's head grows hair, and her father's field vegetation. Apālā becomes 'sun-skinned'. If we accept that the two stories are parallel, then the darkness on the sun's surface must be equivalent to a skin disease. We have not so far established this equivalence directly, but only indirectly through the hints of the Apālā story. But there is, in fact, a good deal of evidence connecting the sun, especially the wounded sun in Svarbhānu, with skin diseases—and their cures. Just as in Apālā, however, these skin afflictions have moral and symbolic dimensions.

1. Skin Diseases and the Sun: Śamala

We can begin with the word once used of the sun's affliction in a Svarbhānu passage: śámala- 'blemish'.[54]

> MS II.1.5 svàrbhānur vā́ āsuráḥ sū́ryaṃ támasāvidhyat tám̐ sómārudrā́ abhiṣajyatāṃ tásya vā́ eténaivá *śámalam apā́hatām* eténāsmim̐s téjo 'dhattām

> Svarbhānu Āsura pierced the sun with darkness. Soma and Rudra healed him. With this (worship?) they *smashed away his blemish*. With this (worship?) they placed splendor in him.

Śámala- seems a carefully chosen word here, for rather like English 'blemish' it has both a physical and a moral dimension. It often serves as a kind of cover term for all the impurities that one must cleanse away physically before being consecrated.

> MS III.6.2 keśaśmaśrú vapate dató dhāvate nakhā́n níkr̥ntate snā́ti mr̥tā́ vā́ eṣā́ tvág amedhyám̐ vā́ asyaitád ātmáni *śámalaṃ* tád *evā́pahate*[55]

> He shaves hair and beard; he rinses his teeth; he cuts his nails; he bathes. Skin is dead. This impurity of his, the *blemish* on himself—this he thus '*smashes off*'.

Note the disdainful reference to skin, and the verb apa √han 'smash off', our usual remedy for darkness in Svarbhānu. Other than apa √han, the ordinary means of removing śamala are washing with water or wiping.[56]

But though these are all physical means of removal, the cause of the śamala is more often a moral breach. In the AV śamala- is several times conjoined with duṣkr̥tá- '(something) ill-done',[57] and śamala is something you can do/commit (√kr̥).

[54] A word that we will also discuss in another connection, Chap. 7, B.3.

[55] Cf. also MS III.8.7, 9.6.

[56] Washing with water: MS III.8.7 prā́ṇenijati 'they wash'; TS VI.4.3.4 ápa plāvayati 'he makes float away'; AV XII.2.40 ā́po mā tásmāc chumbhantu 'let the waters cleanse me from that (impurity)'. Wiping: (ápa) √mr̥j, cf. AV VII.65.2, XIII.1.58, XIV.2.66.

[57] AV IV.9.6, VII.65.2, XII.2.40, XIV.2.66.

AV XII.2.40 yád ripráṃ śámalaṃ cakr̥má yác ca duṣkr̥tám . . .

What defilement, blemish we have done, and what ill-done (deed) . . .

In later texts one is 'seized by' śamala (śámala-gr̥hītá-) if he is ill-spoken of (duruktoktaḥ AB II.17) or if 'an ugly[58] report reaches him' (śamalaṃ vā etam r̥cchati yam aślīlā vāg r̥cchati PB II.17.4), and śamala is suspected if one does not achieve the glory one deserves.

KS X.4 śamalagr̥hīto vā eṣa yo 'laṃ brahmavarcasāya san na brahmavarcasī bhavati

Seized by blemish is he who, though fit for brahmaṇic splendor, does not have it.

Śamala is on several occasions compared with silver (KS VIII.5, X.4), a metal despised in comparison to gold; the connection between śamala and silver is presumably that the latter tarnishes, producing a superficial blemish.

KS X.4 yad rajataṃ tat saha bhasmanāpohati . . . śamalam evāsmād apahanti

The silver he sweeps away together with the ashes. . . . Thus he smashes away blemish from him.

More surprising, but more relevant, is the fact that gold, specifically a golden disk or ornament (niṣka-), can also have a śamala. This we learn when its blemish is compared with that of a person who has failed to become distinguished:

JB II.136 sa yo 'nūcānas san na viroceta sa etena yajeteti / yathā ha vai niṣkaś śamalagr̥hīta evaṃ sa yo 'nūcānas san na virocate / . . . yathā niṣkaṃ śamalagr̥hītam agnau prāsya tasyāyoghanena sarvaṃ śamalaṃ nirhanyād evaṃ haivāsya sarvaṃ pāpmānaṃ nirghnanti

Someone who, though being learned, has not 'shone forth' [= reached distinction], should worship in this way. Someone, who, though being learned, does not 'shine forth', is like a gold plate seized by blemish. Just as you throw a gold plate with a blemish (lit. seized by blemish) into the fire and (then) beat out all of its blemish with a metal hammer, so they beat out all of his evil in this way.

58 On aślīlā vāc (ugly speech/report), see above, Chap. 2, A.3.

This entire passage evokes the image of the blemished sun, after receiving Svarbhānu's wound. Notice first the verb used of the unsuccessful performer of the worship: he does not 'shine forth' (ví √ruc), just like Sūrya after his wounding.

> KS XI.5 svàrbhānur vā́ āsurás sū́ryaṃ támasāvidhyat sá *ná vyàrocata*[59]
>
> Svarbhānu Āsura pierced the sun with darkness. He *did not shine forth*.

Moreover, gold, especially a golden disk, represents both the sun and the ideal skin surface. A golden disk often represents the sun in ritual contexts. In JB II.136, just cited, the blemished niṣka or 'golden disk'[60] is also clearly an image of the sun, and its restoration to brightness is accomplished in much the same way as Sūrya's is, after his wound, by striking it out (nír √han, similar to ápa √han, the usual verb).

In other words, the remedy for the worshipper who is śamalagr̥hīta- 'seized with blemish' is the same as that for Sūrya, when wounded by Svarbhānu and afflicted with a śamala, and this remedy is physically acted out in the removal of blemish from the golden disk. The removal of darkness from the sun/gold disk serves as model for the removal of the worshipper's blemish. This connection is more explicit in the texts than I have so far revealed, for on several occasions the Svarbhānu myth is told in a rite on behalf of someone who is in need of this removal.

2. *The Rite for Splendor*

In MS II.1.5 and KS XI.5 the Svarbhānu myth is embedded in an Iṣṭi (special rite) for one desiring brahmavarcasa- (priestly luster/brahmaṇic splendor); an explicit statement of this is found in the MS passage:

[59]Cf. KS XII.13, XXVII.2; ŚB V.3.2.2; PB XIV.11.14.

[60]That the niṣka is regularly made of gold is clear from passages like the following:

> ŚB XIII.4.1.11 átha yò 'sya *niṣkáḥ* prátimukto bhávati / tám adhvaryáve dadāty adhvaryáve dádad amṛ̥́tam ā́yur ātmán dhatte 'mṛ̥taṁ hy ā́yur *híraṇyam*
>
> Then the *niṣka* attached to him he gives to the Adhvaryu. Giving it to the Adhvaryu, he establishes in himself immortal life. For *gold* is immortal life.

MS II.1.5 saumāraudrā́ṃ ghr̥té carúṃ nírvapeñ śuklā́nāṁ vrīhīṇā́ṃ brahmavarcasákāmaḥ svàrbhānur vā́ āsuráḥ sū́ryaṃ támasāvidhyat táṁ sómārudrā́ abhiṣajyatāṃ tásya vā́ eténaivá śámalam apā́hatām eténāsmiṁs téjo 'dhattāṁ yó brahmavarcasákāmaḥ syā́t tám etáyā yājayeñ śámalam evā́syāpahánti téjo 'smin dadhāti

One desiring brahmaṇic splendor should offer a caru of white rice in ghee to Soma and Rudra. Svarbhānu Āsura pierced the sun with darkness. Soma and Rudra healed him. With this (worship?) they smashed away his blemish. With this (worship?) they placed splendor in him. Whoever should be desirous of brahmaṇic splendor, him should (the priest) cause to worship with this (Iṣṭi). Thus he smashes off his blemish. He puts splendor in him.

The connection between the Svarbhānu myth and brahmavarcasa is also made in other texts, though not quite as straightforwardly as in MS II.1.5 and KS XI.5. PB XXIII.16.2, another token of the Svarbhānu myth, is a passage directly dependent on these two BYV passages.[61] Though this PB passage is in a section concerning the second twenty-one-day Sattra, which surrounds the summer solstice, it also concerns the desire for brahmavarcasa, like the MS/KS parallels, as is indicated by a statement immediately before the telling of the myth:

PB XXIII.16.1 brahmavarcasakāmā upeyuḥ

Those who are desirous of brahmaṇic splendor should undertake (this rite).

The TS parallel to this brahmavarcasa Iṣṭi does not refer to Svarbhānu by name, but it also begins with the darkened sun:

TS II.2.10.1 asā́v ādityó ná vyàrocata tásmai devā́ḥ prā́yaścittim aichan

Yonder Āditya [= the sun] did not shine forth. The gods sought an expiation for it.

[61] As Caland pointed out (1931), ad PB XXIII.16.12. According to Caland, the entire section PB XXIII.16 depends on the MS/KS passages. Especially telling evidence is the opening sentence in PB XXIII.16.2. The object of avidhyat 'he pierced', the sun, is expressed by the word sūryam, as in the Black Yajur Veda. All other PB variants of the myth use the epithet ādityam '(yonder) Āditya' instead. For more on PB XXIII.16, see Chap. 10, C.2.

This is almost exactly identical to KS XI.5 and clearly refers to the Svarbhānu myth. Note especially the phrase ná vyàrocata 'did not shine forth', which occurs in the second sentence of the Svarbhānu passages KS XI.5, XII.13, XXVII.2, PB XIV.11.14.

Thus, the Svarbhānu story is clearly the appropriate mythical introduction to this Iṣṭi for brahmavarcasa. In fact, this little Iṣṭi combines, albeit in slightly confused fashion, all the fundamental elements of the Svarbhānu (and Apālā) myth(s): the sun, hair, and skin disease. Skin affliction is actually encoded twice.

The first encoding of skin disease is indirect, in the word śamala. This word can be used for the blemish to be removed from the surface of the sun (at MS II.1.5), and hence is equivalent to 'skin blemish'. As we just saw (KS X.4), the failure to obtain brahmavarcasa 'brahmaṇic splendor' is due to a śamala 'blemish'. Indeed MS II.1.5 goes on to promise that performing this Iṣṭi will remove the śamala from the worshipper hoping for brahmavarcasa. Thus, one must undertake the Iṣṭi to obtain brahmaṇic splendor because one's skin is metaphorically blemished, and the successful result is the removal of that blemish.

The sun is involved in this Iṣṭi not only as its mythical model (as the blemished being in need of healing), explicit in the telling of the Svarbhānu myth at this time, but also in the performance of the ritual. The ritual takes place at sunrise in the BYV:

> KS XI.5 (cf. MS II.1.5) sākáṃ raśmíbhiḥ prácaranty asā́ evā́smād ādityá udyáṁs támó 'pahanti
>
> They proceed (with the ritual) 'with the rays' [i.e., at the appearance of the first rays of the sun]. Thus yonder Āditya, rising, smashes darkness off from him.

Or, in PB XXIII.16.8–9, at the time of the hottest sun:

> .8 naidāghīya upeyuḥ
>
> They should undertake (this rite) in summer.
>
> .9 tad dhy eṣa pratitejiṣṭhaṃ tapati
>
> For at that time this (sun) heats most sharply.

The second encoding of skin disease in this Iṣṭi is more explicit, if more curious: performing the ritual puts the worshipper in jeopardy of contracting such a disease. There is danger in the very power of the sun to bestow brahmaṇic splendor, for it may release too much heat on the worshipper: it may give him leprosy or some other skin disease. All four texts mention this possibility.

MS II.1.5 (≅ PB XXIII.16.10; cf. also PB II.17.3) kilāsatvā́d vā́ etásya bhayám áti hy àpahánti[62]

(But) there is fear of kilāsa (leprosy/leukoderma?). For (the sun) smashes away too much (darkness).

KS XI.5 īśvaró duścármā bhávitor yá etáyā yájaté 'tīva hy àsmād apahánti

(But) anyone who worships with this (rite) is liable to get bad skin. For (the sun) smashes away too much (darkness) from him.

TS II.2.10.2 áti brahmavarcasáṃ kriyata íty āhur īśvaró duścármā bhávitor íti

Some say, "Too much brahmaṇic splendor is created. He is likely to get bad skin."

Though on the practical side, this may be a warning against severe sunburn, on the mythic level it seems to treat, in a slightly incoherent fashion, a possible undesirable transfer of the sun's skin blemishes to the worshipper. Recall that the sheep produced from the darkness removed from the sun became progressively brighter. The very brightest may be too bright for the merely mortal worshipper, and aspiring to the dim human equivalent of the sun's brilliance, namely brahmavarcasa, he may go too far. ←

So it seems to have happened to one Ugradeva Rājani, who undertook the rite—a cautionary instance offered in PB.[63]

PB XXIII.16.11 etā vā ugradevo rājanir upait sakilāso 'bhavat

These (observances) Ugradeva Rājani undertook. He became afflicted with kilāsa.

[62]Von Schroeder's edition reads (with no variants noted): kilāsatvā́d vā́ etásya bhayámati hy àpahánti, but given the parallel passages (which both contain áti) and the syntax, it seems better to accent áti and interpret it as a separate word.

[63]Cf. also the version in JB II.342 and Caland 1931, ad PB XXIII.16.12.

Note the word used of the skin condition resulting from the sun's overbrightness in MS/PB: kilā́sa. The word is usually translated as 'leprosy', but has recently been taken by Zysk as 'leukoderma', "a condition of defective pigmentation of the skin," characterized by "cutaneous white marks or spots."[64] The last bright spots removed from the sun (as sheep) in the Svarbhānu cure may end up disfiguring the hubristic human worshipper who undertakes too much.

The susceptibility to skin affliction described in these passages connects with another part of the mythic complex: the desirability of hair, albeit indirectly. Human skin is vulnerable (to damage from the sun, among other things), as opposed to that of animals, which is protected by hair or fur. This is expressed in a passage like the following:

> AV XII.3.51 eṣā́ tvacā́ṃ púruṣe sáṃ babhūvā́nagnāḥ sárve paśávo yé anyé
>
> This (kind) of skin came into being on man (alone); all the other animals are not naked.

The word á-nagna- 'not naked' must refer to the fact that animals have hair/fur covering their skin, rather than having the bare skin of humans. The term itself immediately reminds us of the terms nagnikā- and a-nagnikā- (lit. 'naked' [fem.] and 'not naked' [fem.]) referring to pre- and post-pubescent girls, respectively. As we saw above, Thieme has explained these terms as meaning 'not having (pubic) hair' and 'having (pubic) hair'. That this 'nakedness' consists in not having hair is supported by this AV passage.

And animal hair may be the ultimate protection in this rite against the danger of skin disease. In all four of these texts an offering is made to (Soma and) Pūṣan to protect against the danger. In the PB (XXIII.16.4) this offering is an animal victim. In the other texts it is only a vegetative offering (a caru), but Pūṣan is mentioned explicitly as connected with animals (paśu). In all four texts the worshipper by this offering is said to 'make a skin for himself' (or similar)—presumably a symbolic hairy animal skin to ward off the potentially bad effects of the too-brilliant sun.

> TS II.2.10.3 sváyaivā́smai devátayā paśúbhis tvácaṃ karoti ná dúś-cármā bhavati

[64]'Leprosy': e.g., Bloomfield (1897, ad I.24.1); 'Leprous spot': Whitney (ad AV I.24.1); 'White leprosy': e.g., Monier-Williams; Macdonell and Keith 1912, both s.v.; 'Leukoderma': Zysk 1985, p. 81.

With his own deity and with animals he makes him a skin. He does not become one with bad skin.

KS XI.5 (≅ MS II.1.5, PB XXIII.16.5) tvácam evá kurute

Thus he makes himself a skin.

Thus, in this little Iṣṭi we see combined again, if slightly garbled, the sun, a skin disease, and hair, as in Svarbhānu and Apālā.

3. A Charm against Skin Disease

An even more remarkable example of this same nexus is found in an AV charm against the same skin disease, kilāsa, that threatens the worshipper in the Iṣṭi just described. But here the sun, rather than causing kilāsa, provides a cure for it. The passage is somewhat obscure, but is not the less striking thereby.

AV I.24.1 suparṇó jātáḥ prathamás, tásya tváṃ pittám āsitha
tád āsurī́ yudhā́ jitā́, rūpáṃ cakre vánaspátīn

Much in this passage remains puzzling, but for our purposes let us concentrate on pāda a. Suparṇáḥ here is usually translated as 'eagle', but Weber's old rendering as 'sun' seems equally possible.[65] Suparṇá- is often a riddling name for the sun in both the RV and the AV, and indeed when the word in the RV occurs in a collocation like our jātáḥ prathamáḥ, it refers to Garutmant, Savitar's bird, quite possibly a name for the sun.[66]

This gives us an interpretation of AV I.24.1:

The 'well-winged' (sun) was born first; of it thou wast the gall. This the Āsurī, conquered in battle(?), gave form to as trees.

As in the Svarbhānu myth a possibly dark, possibly unpleasant substance (in this case 'gall') removed from the sun is transformed into trees (the earth's hair, as we know) and, as the next verse shows, into the plant that cures the skin disease.

AV I.24.2 āsurī́ cakre prathamédáṃ kilāsabheṣajám idáṃ kilāsanā́śanam

[65]'Eagle': e.g., Bloomfield; Whitney (both AV I.24.1); Zysk 1985, p. 82. 'Sun': Weber 1858, p. 418.

[66]Cf. Geldner, ad RV X.149.3 suparṇó aṅgá savitúr garútmān, pū́rvo jātáḥ . . . 'Well-winged Garutmant of Savitar, born previously . . .'.

ánīnaśat kilā́saṃ sárūpām akarat tvácam

The Āsurī first made this a cure for kilāsa, a destroyer of kilāsa.
She destroyed the kilāsa (and) made the skin of even color/form.

The result is similar to what happens both to Apālā (who becomes sū́ryatvac- 'sun-skinned') and to the sun himself (remember sá *svéna rūpéṇa* niramucyata 'he was released *with his own form*' of MS IV.5.7): the second verse ends sárūpam akarat tvácam 'she (the Āsurī) has made the skin of even color/form'.

This brief tale easily fits into the paradigm established in the other episodes we have treated: something removed from the sun (blemish/gall) becomes trees/hair. This in turn cures or protects against skin disease (specifically kilāsa).

Two questions remain, which we must postpone for awhile—who is the Āsurī and why, if she was conquered in battle, does she have the power to make this remedy? The second question is troubling enough that commentators have been tempted to ignore or emend the clear past passive participle jitā́ in favor of an interpretation that allows the āsurī to *conquer* the pittám (gall).[67] However, there is a possible solution that leaves the text alone.

To summarize, a dark substance obtained from the sun both causes the growth of vegetation (and, by a commonplace metaphorical transference, hair) and cures skin disease. This nexus of ideas can be seen on the cosmic level in the myth of Svarbhānu and the sun, on the magico-ritualistic level in the brahmavarcasa Iṣṭi and the AV charm, and in the realm of human mythology in the tale of Apālā. In the last the role of the sun is less evident—only in the state to which she attains, sun-skinnedness, and perhaps in the fact that her three purifications occur 'in the nave of a chariot, in the nave of a wagon, in the nave of a yoke' (RV VIII.91.7ab khé ráthasya khé 'nasaḥ khé yugásya . . .), where the nave (khá-) may be an oblique reference to the circular disc of the sun.[68] But Apālā has further, more covert connections with the Svarbhānu myth, through her father Atri, as we will see below.

[67]Sāyaṇa glosses jitā́ (lit. 'having been conquered') with jitavatī 'having conquered', and Bloomfield favors an emendation to jitvā́ 'having conquered' (or Ludwig's to jitám) (cf. Bloomfield 1897, ad loc.). Bloomfield suggests that an earlier emendation of his *jitvā́ to jitā́ may have been made by "a later transcriber, shocked by the imputation that the Asurī was victorious." The solution to this puzzle will be presented below, Chap. 10, B.3.

[68]Though cf. n. 35 above.

CHAPTER 7

Rescuing the Sun— Failed Birth and Rebirth

We have seen the cosmic good effects brought about by the sun's release from darkness. We now need to inquire how this release was effected, who did it, and why. And this requires looking at the sun's afflictions from a slightly different viewpoint. But let us turn first to the rescuers of the sun.

A. Atri and Company: The Rescuers of the Sun

The remedy for Sūrya's wounding is generally the same in the various versions of the myth. Except when the solution is given in barest summary, the remedy is to 'smash away' (apa √han) or 'strip away' (apa √lup) the darkness. However, the effector of this remedy differs from text to text. Often it is simply 'the gods'.

MS II.5.2 tásya devā́s támó 'pāghnan

The gods smashed away his darkness.[69]

Or the gods and the r̥ṣis, in the JB:

JB II.390 taṃ devāś carṣayaś cābhiṣajyan / ta etāni divākīrtyāni sāmāny apaśyan / tair asya tamo 'pāghnan

[69]= MS IV.5.7; ≅ KS XI.5, XII.13, XXVII.2; TS II.1.2.2; PB IV.5.2, IV.6.13, XXIII.16.2.

The gods and seers healed him. They saw these Divākīrtya Sāmans. With them they smashed away his darkness.

And a few texts name two specific gods, Soma and Rudra:

ŚB V.3.2.2 tásya somārudrā̃v evaítát támó 'pāhatām

Soma and Rudra smashed away his darkness.[70]

But by far the most commonly *named* rescuer of the sun is the seer Atri. On several occasions the gods go to him to ask for his aid.

PB VI.6.8 svarbhānur vā āsura ādityaṃ tamasāvidhyat taṃ devā na vyajānaṁs te 'trim upādhāvaṁs tasyātrir bhāsena tamo 'pāhan

Svarbhānu Āsura pierced the Āditya [= sun] with darkness. The gods did not discern him. They resorted to Atri. Atri smashed away his darkness with the Bhāsa (Light) (Sāman).

The JB more vividly:

JB I.80 taṃ devāś carṣayaś cābhiṣajyan / te 'trim abruvann ṛṣe tvam idam apajahīti / tatheti / tad atrir apāhan

The gods and seers healed him. They said to Atri, "Seer, smash this (darkness) away." (Saying) yes, Atri smashed it away.

Atri also heals the sun without the gods' explicit request:

MS IV.8.3 (cf. GB II.3.19) tám átrir ánvapaśyat

Atri saw him.

KS XXVIII.4 tam atrir evāgre 'nvavindat

Atri found him in the beginning.

PB XIV.11.14 tasyātrir bhāsena tamo 'pāhan

Atri smashed away its darkness with the Bhāsa (Sāman).

[70]Cf. ŚBK VII.2.1.1; MS II.1.5.

In the KB it is the Atris, plural, who perform the same deed:

> KB XXIV.3 tasyātrayas tamo 'pajighāṃsanta . . . etair ha vā atraya ādityaṃ tamaso 'spr̥ṇvata
>
> The Atris wished to smash away his darkness. . . . With them the Atris won the Āditya from darkness.

In addition to these passages explicitly concerned with Svarbhānu, we find in the ŚB a ritually adapted variant of Atri's sun-healing exploit, in which the gods ask Atri to banish darkness from a portion of the ritual enclosure. The story is told in connection with a minor part of the soma ritual, namely, the giving of gold to an Ātreya.[71] The Ātreya (lit. 'descendant of Atri') is a nonofficiating priest, a Brahman who attends or oversees the ritual in the Sadas (shed), that is, a so-called Prasarpaka.[72] His major function in this ritual (the midday pressing at the Agniṣṭoma) is to receive a Dakṣiṇā of gold. He "does not officiate as a priest, and . . . is seated in front of the Sadas".[73] This receiving of gold is well noted in the ritual sūtras.[74]

In the ŚB this presentation of gold to 'Atri's descendant' recalls the story of Atri's feat, but the Atri story there presented seems to have been altered from Atri's usual rescue of the sun to fit the particular facts of the Ātreya's ritual function, specifically, his place in the Sadas and his receiving of gold, which represents the sun. The ŚBK version is clearer in some regards than that of ŚBM (IV.3.4.21), so that it is worthwhile quoting them both.

> ŚBK V.4.1.16–17 áthātreyám abhyaíti ká ātreyáṃ ká ātreyáṃ ká ātreyám íti tásmā upasádya híraṇyaṃ dadāti . . . átrir hí vā́ ŕ̥ṣīṇām̐ hótāsa yatró ha vā́ adá ā́sīnaḥ prātaranuvākám anvā́ha tád dha smaitát purā́sīno hótā śam̐saty átha paścā́t támaḥ sádo 'bhípupluve // té hocus támo vā́ idám̐ sádó 'bhyaproṣṭéti pratyáṅ préhī́ti sá pratyáṅ praít sá tát támó 'pāhan

[71]We will treat this episode in greater detail in Chap. 9, C.1.

[72]Renou 1954: "ceux qui à coté des officiants et des servants ont été admis à entrer comme spectateurs" (those who along with the officiants and the servants have been allowed to enter as spectators); cf. MŚS II.4.5.15.

[73]Eggeling, SB IV.3.4.21, n.2.

[74]E.g., ĀpŚS XIII.6.12, BŚS VIII.6, MŚS II.4.5.15. The other place in the ritual where the Ātreya appears is a curious portion of the Aśvamedha (horse sacrifice), which will be treated later, Chap. 8, C.

Then he (the Adhvaryu[75]) goes up to the Ātreya (and says), "Who (sees?)[76] the Ātreya? Who (sees) the Ātreya? Who (sees) the Ātreya?" Approacing reverently, he (the Yajamāna?) gives him (the Ātreya) gold. . . . For Atri was the Hotar of the ṛṣis. In the place where now one sits to recite the Prātaranuvāka (morning recitation), the Hotar (Atri) once sat reciting. Then darkness floated into the Sadas behind (him). They said, "Darkness has just floated into this shed. Come back here." He came back and smashed away this darkness.

ŚBM IV.3.4.21 áthaivám evópasádya / ātreyā́ya híraṇyaṃ dadāti yátra vā́ adáḥ prātaranuvākám anvāhús tád dha smaitát purā́ śaṁsanty átrir vā́ ṛ́ṣīṇāṁ hótāsā́thaitát sádo 'suratamasám abhípupruve tá ṛ́ṣayó 'trim abruvann éhi pratyáṅṅ idáṃ támó 'pajahī́ti sá etát támó 'pāhan

Then reverently approaching (him) thus, he (the Yajamāna) gives gold to the Ātreya. Where then they (usually) recite the Prātaranuvaka, they once were reciting. Atri was the Hotar of the ṛṣis. Then the darkness of the Asuras floated into the Sadas. The ṛṣis said to Atri, "Come back here. Smash away this darkness." He smashed away this darkness.

Although Svarbhānu, the act of wounding, and even the sun itself are not mentioned in either passage, it is hard to escape the conclusion that the Svarbhānu story lies behind this ritualized variant, given the close parallels in action and diction to some Svarbhānu passages. The darkness in the ŚBM passage is qualified as asuratamasá- 'the darkness of the Asuras': āsura 'descendant of the Asuras' is Svarbhānu's patronymic. The sun can be discerned in the guise of the gold given to the Ātreya—recall that gold can stand for the sun. How close the

[75]So Eggeling, ŚBM IV.3.4.21, n. 2.

[76]Eggeling (ŚB IV.3.4.21, n. 2) suggests supplying this verb for the Kāṇva text (note that the question is lacking in ŚBM) and for KātyŚS X.2.21. BŚS (VIII.6) has the same procedure, but with the question ka ātreya iti 'who is the Ātreya?', which makes better sense (and for this reason could be a correction). As in ŚBK and KātyŚS the question is asked three times in BŚS. The answer is always ayam aham 'I am he.'

BŚS VIII.6 athaiṣa ātreyo 'greṇa sada āste . . . athainam utkramya pṛcchati ka ātreya ity ayam aham itītaraḥ pratyāha taṃ tathaiva dvitīyam utkramya pṛcchati ka ātreya ity ayam aham ity evetaraḥ pratyāha taṃ tathaiva tṛtīyam utkramya pṛcchati ka ātreya ity ayam aham ity evetaraḥ pratyāha tasya pāṇau hiraṇyam ādadāti

Then the Ātreya sits in the Sadas (shed) at the front. . . . Then he (the Adhvaryu) goes up to him and asks, "Who is the Ātreya?" "I am he," the other replies. Going up to him a second time, he asks, "Who is the Ātreya?" "I am he," the other replies. Going up to him a third time, he asks, "Who is the Ātreya?" "I am he," the other replies. He puts gold in his (the Ātreya's) palm.

identification is between the gold and the sun in this particular case we will see further on. The signature verb of the Svarbhānu story, apa √han 'smash away', appears here as well in the phrase (found in both passages) támo 'pa √han 'smash away the darkness', which is identical to that in the explicitly Svarbhānu passages. And the dialogue between the ṛṣis and Atri is very close to that of the gods and ṛṣis with Atri in JB I.80, a Svarbhānu passage.

> ŚBM tá ṛ́ṣayó 'trim abruvann éhi pratyáṅṅ idáṃ támó 'pajahī́ti sá etát támó 'pāhan
>
> The ṛṣis said to Atri, "Come back here. Smash away this darkness." He smashed away this darkness.
>
> JB I.80 svarbhānur vā āsura ādityaṃ tamasāvidhyat / taṃ devāś carṣayaś cābhiṣajyan / *te 'trim abruvann ṛṣe tvam idam apajahīti / tatheti / tad atrir apāhan* . . .
>
> Svarbhānu Āsura pierced the Āditya with darkness. The gods and seers healed him. *They said to Atri, "Seer, smash this (darkness) away." (Saying) yes, he smashed it away.* . . .

We can construct a composite picture of the procedure for healing the sun. The gods are the first to become aware of the darkening of the sun, but to remedy the situation they must enlist the aid of the ṛṣi Atri. Together they restore the sun. Into this composite we can fit the passages where the gods alone are mentioned (MS II.5.2, etc.), where the gods and ṛṣis work in partnership (JB II.390, etc.; note that Atri is Hotar of the ṛṣis in ŚB), where Atri apparently works alone (MS IV.8.3, etc.), as well as the fuller form where the gods seek Atri's help (JB I.80, etc.).[77] Note that all the texts that have versions involving the

[77]It does not account for the Soma-Rudra passages, which I still do not fully understand. However, Rudra's hidden involvement in the Svarbhānu story we will discuss below, and this may be somehow reflected in the Soma-Rudra passages here. Moreover, M. Witzel has pointed out to me that in the Kaṭha Āraṇyaka in the Pravargya ceremony, which forms part of the soma sacrifice, *Rudra* is identified with the sun:

> KaṭhĀ II.89 asaú vā́ ādityó rudró mahāvīráḥ
>
> Rudra Mahāvīra is yonder Āditya [= the sun].

and is in fact addressed with a mantra containing our signature word sūryatvác- 'sun-skinned':

> KaṭhĀ II.100 diví pṛṣṭó yajatás *sūryatvák*

gods alone also know an Atri version.[78] For those accustomed to Brāhmaṇic discourse, it is not surprising that one or the other of the participants should be focussed on in any particular telling of the myth, depending on its particular ritual application: this focus does not mean that the other participants are unknown to the teller.[79]

Now this configuration—Atri assisted by the gods and the other ṛṣis—is precisely the one found in the RVic Svarbhānu hymn. The myth begins and ends by assigning the feat to Atri or the Atris:

RV V.40.6	. . . sū́ryam . . . avindad átriḥ	Atri found the sun.
.8	átriḥ sū́ryasya diví cákṣur ā-dhāt	Atri placed the eye of the sun in heaven.
.9	átrayas tám ánv avindan	The Atris found him.

But the help of the gods is also mentioned: Indra in vs. 6, Varuṇa (and possibly Indra[80]) in vs. 7. (Note: no Soma or Rudra.)

Atri also holds the same position as rescuer of the sun in the AV references to this myth.

AV XIII.2.4 . . . yám átrir dívam unninā́ya

(The sun), whom Atri led up into heaven . . .

AV XIII.2.12 diví tvā́trir adhārayat, sū́rya . . .

Atri supported thee in heaven, O Sun.

Touching heaven [so Witzel: 'Den Himmel berührend' → *spr̥ṣṭó], worship-worthy, *sun-skinned*

which is immediately paraphrased with the adjective ādityávarṇa- 'having the color of the Āditya [= sun]':

KaṭhĀ II.100 rudrám . . . ādityávarṇam.

(See Witzel 1972, pp. 37–39.) Thus, the association of Rudra with the sun in this mystical ceremony may have given Rudra the power to rescue the sun.

[78]Except the TS, which has only one explicit Svarbhānu passage.

[79]We discussed this more fully above, apropos of the versions of the Yati story with and without Indra.

[80]Or Mitra: see Chap. 10, D.

AV XIII.2.36 páśyāma tvā savitā́raṃ yám āhúr, ájasraṃ jyótir *yád ávindad átriḥ*

May we look upon thee, whom they call Savitar, the imperishable light, *which Atri found.*

Note the echo of RV V.40.6 in vs. 36.

Given the usually immense power of the gods, their need of the human or originally human Atri in this myth, the concentration on Atri in so many versions of the myth, suggests that he was uniquely qualified to restore the sun. Indeed, the very last pāda of the RVic myth says just this:

RV V.40.9 (átrayas tám ánv avindan,) nahy ànyé áśaknuvan

(The Atris found him,) for no others were able.[81]

Why is Atri the only person for the job, as it were? To determine this, we must examine both the character of Atri elsewhere and the means used to restore the sun. This entails something of a digression, designed to reveal exactly what the full remedy for the darkening of the sun actually is.

B. The Rebirth and Failed Birth of the Sun

The phraseology of the mythic remedy shows that the rescue of the sun is conceived on quite a different model from his wounding: the remedy for the darkened sun is conceived of as a type of childbirth.

1. *The Rebirth of the Sun*

The first piece of direct, if minor, evidence for this is an alternative verb for the removal of the sun's darkness. In two KS passages the verb is not the usual apa √han 'smash off', but instead is apa √lup 'rip/strip off', though the sentence otherwise conforms to the stereotypical for-

[81] As I have shown elsewhere (forthcoming, b), this sentence must be so interpreted syntactically. It cannot mean 'for the others [= the gods] were not able', though that might seem a semantic possibility, given the prose versions of this myth.

mulation. Compare the apa √lup passage(s) with one of the more typical formulations (also containing an ablative):

KS XII.13 (= XXVII.2) tásmād devā́s *támó 'pālumpan*

The gods stripped off the darkness from him.

KS XI.5 táyāsmāt *támó 'pāghnan*

With this (Iṣṭi) they smashed the darkness from him.

The lexeme apa √lup is not particularly common in Vedic, and it seems at least partially specialized as an idiom with úlbam 'caul (embryo cover, amnion)': 'to strip off the caul'; for example,

MS I.6.5 agnír vaí sṛṣṭá *úlbam apalúmpaṃ* nā́śaknot tásya prajā́patiḥ . . . *úlbam ápālumpat*

Agni, (when first) created, could not strip off his caul. Prajāpati stripped off his caul.

(Cf. also MS I.6.4.) Since a or the usual object of ápa √lup in Vedic is the caul (expression úlbam ápa √lup), in the phrase támó 'pālumpan in KS XII.13 (= XXVII.2), támas fills the place of úlbam and imposes the identification támas = úlbam, darkness = caul.

úlbam ápa √lup	MS I.6.5 etc.	'strip off caul'
támas ápa √lup	KS XII.13	'strip off darkness'

Hence, támas 'darkness' = úlbam 'caul'

Much stronger support for this identification is found in JB III.334–5, which not only exemplifies this identification (darkness = caul), but suggests further identifications. It presents the story of a different birth, the result of an apparent coupling of Mind and Speech,[82] both created by Prajāpati. But, though the myth is different from that of Svarbhānu, as are the results, the procedure is uncannily the same. The birth of the child here is described in the exact same manner as the uncovering of the sun in Svarbhānu.

[82]For more on this, see Chap. 9, B, below.

JB III.334 so 'yaṃ garbho 'jāyata / taṃ jātam amr̥jan yathā vatsaṃ jātaṃ mātā lihyād evam

This embryo was born. They wiped him (just) born, exactly as a mother might lick a newborn calf.

.335 tasya yat prathamam ulbam apālumpaṃs tat kr̥ṣṇāyas samabhavat / yad dvitīyam ulbam apālumpaṃs tad rajatam abhavat / yat tr̥tīyam ulbam apālumpaṃs tad dharitam abhavat

The first caul of his they stripped off became black-metal (iron). The second caul they stripped off became silver. The third caul they stripped off became gold.

This is almost identical with the following Svarbhānu passage:

KS XII.13 tásmād devā́s támó 'pālumpan yát prathamám apā́lumpan sā́viṣ kr̥ṣṇā́bhavad yád dvitī́yam̐ sā́ phalgúr yát tr̥tī́yam̐ sā́ balakṣī́

The gods stripped off the darkness from him. The first darkness they stripped off became a black ewe. The second a reddish one. The third a white one.

The only differences are that it is támas- 'darkness' that is being stripped off in the KS passage and that the three swipes produce various colored sheep, not different metals.[83] But the production of metals from the processes of birth (or abortion) finds a parallel in KS VIII.5, which we will discuss below.

In other words, the removal of darkness from the sun is told in words appropriate for birth—the sun in some literal sense is being reborn. Comparison between JB III.334–5 and KS XII.13 (etc.) makes this conclusion hard to avoid. Let us look more minutely at the parallelism. Note first that the JB passage is very explicitly about birth, from the first sentence so 'yam garbho 'jāyata 'this embryo was born'. When the removals are described, JB provides the overt object ulbam 'caul', which we can then supply in KS XII.13. Moreover, in both the Svarbhānu myth and the JB passage, the three removals produce increasingly brighter substances.

[83]The other Svarbhānu passages that describe the production of sheep also follow this pattern, but with the less explicit verb apa √han, rather than apa √lup.

JB III.335	KS XII.13
tasya yat prathamam ulbam apālumpaṃs tat kṛṣṇāyas samabhavat	yát prathamám apā́lumpan sā́viṣ kṛṣṇā́bhavat
The first caul of his they stripped off became black-metal (iron).	The first darkness they stripped off became a black ewe.
yad dvitīyam ulbam apālumpaṃs tad rajatam abhavat	yád dvitī́yaṁ sā́ phalgúḥ
The second caul they stripped off became silver.	The second a reddish one.
yat tṛtīyam ulbam apālumpaṃs tad dharitam abhavat	yát tṛtī́yaṁ sā́ balakṣī́
The third caul they stripped off became gold.	The third a white one.

The production of metals from the embryo covers in the JB is peculiar, but it is paralleled elsewhere. Though this issue appears at first to be only tenuously connected to the rebirth of the sun in the Svarbhānu myth, pursuing the question will yield yet one more support for our interpretation of the rescue of the sun as a birth.

2. *Other Mythic Descriptions of Birth*

KS VIII.5 describes a coupling, probably illicit, between Agni and the wives of Varuṇa (varuṇānīs), who are identified with the waters (āpas). This union seems to result in pregnancy, in a garbha- 'embryo', of whom we hear no more. Various metals are produced from the encounter: Agni's retas- (semen, seed) becomes gold (specifically, harita- [hiraṇya-] 'yellow(ish) [gold]'); the waters' [seed (?!)] becomes silver (rajata- [hiraṇya-], lit. 'white(ish) [gold]'); and the 'śamala of the embryo' (garbhasya śamalam) also becomes a metal,[84] called durvarṇa

[84]Recall that śamala is also compared with a metal in KS X.4 (see Chap. 6, B.1). On this myth, see (briefly) Heesterman 1957, p. 87; on metals as embryo covers, ibid., p. 112.

(lit. 'ill-colored'), possibly another kind of silver, perhaps a different alloy, or possibly iron.[85]

> KS VIII.5 agnir vai varuṇānīr abhyakāmayata tasya tejaḥ parāpatat[86] tad dhiraṇyam abhavat . . . agniṃ vai varuṇānīr abhyakāmayanta tās samabhavad āpo varuṇānīr yad agne reto 'sicyata tad dharitam abhavad yad apāṃ tad rajataṃ tasmād dharitarajatābhyām ubhayā hiraṇyo[87] yad garbhasya śamalaṃ tad durvarṇaṃ tasmād brāhmaṇena durvarṇaṃ na bhartavyaṁ śamalaṁ hi tad

> Agni desired the wives of Varuṇa. His splendor 'flew forth'. It became gold. . . . The wives of Varuṇa desired Agni. He united with them. The wives of Varuna are (really) the waters. What seed of Agni's was discharged, that became gold. What (seed) of the waters [i.e., the wives of Varuṇa], that (became) silver. Therefore gold (hiraṇya) is (named) in both ways, by both "harita" and "rajata." What was the "blemish of the embryo", that (became) "ill-colored" (metal). Therefore, "ill-colored" (metal) is not to be carried (worn?) by a Brahman, for it is a blemish.

[85]The referents for these words for metals are not wholly clear. Híraṇya-, the ordinary word for 'gold', is sometimes qualified both as hárita- 'yellowish (gold)' and rajatá- 'whitish (gold)', often contrastively in the same passage (e.g., KS X.4). These phrases are plausibly taken (cf., e.g., Macdonell and Keith 1912, sub hiraṇya; Rau 1973, p. 18) as referring to gold (harita hiraṇya) and silver (rajata hiraṇya), respectively, rather than to two varieties of gold.

But if our passage already contains gold and silver (haritam and rajatam), then what is durvarṇam? BR gives this as a lexical word for 'silver'. This would make sense, as a term coined in opposition to suvárṇa- 'gold' (lit. 'having good color', already, e.g., MS I.6.4 híraṇyaṁ suvárṇam). Indeed, in TB II.2.4.5 a two-way contrast is set up between durvárṇaṁ híraṇyam, which was created from the Asuras, and suvárṇaṁ híraṇyam, which was created from the gods. In such a two-way split, an interpretation of 'silver' and 'gold' imposes itself.

However, in our passage the 'silver' slot is already filled. Perhaps it refers to an alloy of silver, different from (and inferior to) rajata? However, durvarṇa may instead refer to iron, based on the parallelism of JB III.335 with KS VIII.5. Because JB and KS agree on gold (both haritam) and silver (both rajatam) in this sequence, durvarṇam in the KS passage may be 'iron', equivalent to the remaining JB term kr̥ṣṇāyas- ('iron', lit. 'black metal'). But this is of no moment for the overall interpretation of the passage. Rau (1973, p. 18, n. 2) implicitly notes the three-way contrast in our passage and translates durvárṇam as 'unedles Metall' (base metal), but he does not make an attempt to identify this third substance more closely.

[86]On this verb, see above, Chap. 3, C.1.

[87]Both von Schroeder in his edition of KS and Raghu Vira in the KapS parallel (VII.1) print ubhayāhiraṇyo, as if this were a compound of the type ubhayā́dant- 'having teeth in both jaws', but it seems more sensible to take ubhayā as a separate adverb 'in both ways', identical with RV X.108.6 ubhayā́.

As in JB III.335 cited above, the three substances removed become metals in the KS passage, though in the opposite order: JB III.335 from dimmest to brightest (kr̥ṣṇāyas 'black-metal' → rajatam 'silver' → haritam 'gold'), KS VIII.5 vice versa (haritam 'gold' → rajatam 'silver' → durvarṇam 'iron'?)

JB III.335	KS VIII.5 (in reverse)	KS XII.13
kr̥ṣṇāyas 'iron'	durvarṇam 'iron'	áviṣ kr̥ṣṇā́ 'black ewe'
rajatam 'silver'	rajatam 'silver'	(áviḥ) phalgúḥ 'reddish'
haritam 'gold'	haritam 'gold'	(ávir) balakṣī́ 'white'

Let us now examine another feature of KS VIII.5: what are the three substances from which the metals arose? The 'seed' (retas) of Agni is either his semen or the embryo resulting from it. The 'seed' (retas) of the waters is not clear, but I would suggest that it might be the 'breaking of the waters' signalling the beginning of labor and birth.[88]

And what about the third term, the garbhasya śamala 'blemish of the embryo'? I have found no parallel formulations to this puzzling phrase. I think, however, that it may refer to the úlba-, the 'caul' or 'embryo cover',[89] or to the combination of úlba- and jarā́yu-, the 'placenta', that is, to the 'caul and placenta' or to the 'amnion and chorion'. In other words, the garbhasya śamala 'blemish of the embryo' would be the accessory parts of the birth—the matter that protects and nourishes the embryo in the womb but is discarded after birth.

The first piece of evidence for this is simply a passage in which the caul and placenta together with the śleṣmán- 'mucus' of the embryo are equated with evil:

> ŚB VII.2.1.5 tásya yáḥ pāpmā́ yáḥ śleṣmā́ yád úlbaṃ yáj jarā́yu tád asyaitā́bhir ápāghnan
>
> What of him (the embryo) (was) evil, what mucus, what caul, what placenta—that of his they smashed off [note the verb] with these (bricks).[90]

[88]This might suggest more strongly that the retas of Agni is the embryo, not the semen.

[89]Filliozat 1949: 'membranes embryonnaires'. However, the ulba- is usually compared with a garment, not with metal (e.g., MS IV.4.3).

[90]On this passage see also Heesterman 1957, p. 17.

Identifying these parts as evil (pāpmán-) is rather like calling them a blemish (śamala).

A stronger piece of evidence for the identification of garbhasya śamala and the ulba (caul) comes from a story of Agni and Varuṇa's wife in MS I.6.12, which is parallel to (though rather different from) the tale of Agni and Varuṇa's wives in KS VIII.5. In this passage Agni is Varuṇa's student and commits the egregious crime of sexual connection with his teacher's wife.[91] They seem to be interrupted in the middle of their congress by Varuṇa, the cuckolded husband. Other details are not entirely clear, partly because of the rarity of the words used. What is important for us is that this passage, like KS VIII.5, treats of transformations (this time into trees). The two elements transformed are rétas- 'seed' (as in KS VIII.5) and úlba- 'caul'. Thus the úlba- fits the same structural slot in this passage as the garbhasya śamala in the KS passage (with the middle slot of KS—the retas of the waters—unfilled).

KS VIII.5	MS I.6.12
agne retas 'seed of Agni'	rétas 'seed'
apām (retas) '(seed) of the waters'	—
garbhasya śamalam 'blemish of the embryo'	úlbam 'caul'
Hence, śamalam 'blemish' = úlbam 'caul'	

MS I.6.12 agnír vaí várunaṃ brahmacáryam ā́gachat pravā́santaṃ tásya jāyā́ṁ sámabhavat tā́ṃ purástād āyántaṃ pratikśā́ya pratyáṅ níradravat sò 'vet sárvaṁ vā́ indriyā́ṃ nṛmṇaṁ réto nirlúpya haratī́ti tád anuparāhā́ya níralumpad yád rétā ā́sīt sò 'śvatthá ārohò 'bhavad yád úlbaṁ sā́ śamī́

Agni went for his studentship to Varuṇa, who was (temporarily) away from home. He (Agni) united with his (Varuṇa's) wife. On seeing him (Varuṇa) returning in front (of him), he (Agni) ran out in the back/opposite direction.[92] She (Varuṇa's wife) knew, "He (Varuṇa), after ripping out all this Indriyan, manly seed, will take it (away = steal it?)." She (Varuṇa's wife), having let (it) drop by the way, ripped it out (herself).

[91] On the dreadful punishments this conduct merits, see, e.g., ĀpDS I.25.1. There the offender cuts off his sexual organs and walks off with them in his hands until he falls down and dies. Cf. also I.25.2; GautDS XXIII.8–12; VāsDS XX.13–15.

[92] This probably has sexual connotations.

The seed became a "mounted" fig tree.[93] The caul (embryo cover) became a śamī tree.

As I interpret this passage, Varuṇa's wife, afraid that Varuṇa will forcibly pull out (nir √lup) the fetus resulting from her guilty liaison with Agni and take it away, performs an abortion on herself. The premature fetus becomes one plant (the aśvattha tree), its surrounding caul another (the śamī). However, the interpretation of the passage is not entirely clear.

There are two types of uncertainty in the passage. (1) It is hard to know which of the principal characters, Agni, Varuṇa, or Varuṇa's wife, is subject of any particular verb. Change of subject is not overtly signalled. I have considered all the possibilities; what I have arrived at makes the most sense to me. (2) The vocabulary, especially the lexemes nir √lup and anu-parā √hā, is rare and ambiguous. Nir √lup occurs only in this passage in the Saṃhitās and Brāhmaṇas, as far as I know. However, since the related idiom apa √lup (lit., 'rip off/away') is connected with the removal of the embryo cover, nir √lup (lit. 'rip out') can well also have become semantically specialized in the domain of childbirth, to mean 'abort' or the like.

Anu-parā √hā seems to occur only here in the Saṃhitās and Brāhmaṇas. However, parā √hā occurs once, in the TS, and clearly must mean 'drop', 'shed' or the like.

TS V.4.3.3 sā́ śócantī parṇám párājihīta sò 'rkò 'bhavat

She, in pain, dropped a feather. It became the Arka plant.

One remaining puzzlement, at least to modern ears, is that what is 'ripped out' (nir √lup) is the seed or semen (rétas), which seems to have been just deposited, and that this seed already has a 'caul' (ulba). This might seem to telescope the moment of sexual intercourse (involving deposit of semen) with later stages of pregnancy and birth, in which there is a developed embryo (garbha) with a caul (ulba). But rétas has a broader meaning in Sanskrit than 'semen' in English. This word refers not only to semen but also the resulting embryo. The semen deposited

93 The term ārohá- 'mounted, a rider' must refer to the growth habit of the aśvattha tree (*Ficus religiosa*): "The seeds . . . are carried by birds and lodging in a tree, germinate and grow" (Cowen 1965, p. 69). The roots then grow downward from this seat in the branches of the host until they reach the ground (usually killing the host in the process).

in the female is/becomes the embryo; it is not modified by the female but only protected[94] in her until the time of birth. 'Seed' is then a more telling translation than 'semen'. For example:

RV V.83.1 vr̥ṣabháḥ . . . *réto* dadhāty óṣadhīṣu *gárbham*

The bull (Parjanya) places his *seed* (as) *embryo* in the plants.

Thus it would make perfect sense for the rétas- 'seed' → 'embryo' to have a caul 'embryo cover', presumably supplied by the female.

Now if śamala (lit. 'blemish') can be used in the semantic realm of childbirth, where it seems to refer to the caul (= embryo cover, ulba) plus or minus the placenta (jarāyu), then the śamala that is removed from the sun in MS II.1.5 can also be seen as an embryo cover.

MS II.1.5 svàrbhānur vā́ āsuráḥ sū́ryaṃ támasāvidhyat tám̐ sómārudrā́ abhiṣajyatāṃ tásya vā́ eténaivá *śámalam* apā́hatām

Svarbhānu Āsura pierced the sun with darkness. Soma and Rudra healed him. With this (worship?) they smashed away his *blemish*.

The use of the word here evokes the image of the removal of the embryo cover (ulba), also called śamala. In other words, the usual darkness (tamas) of the sun in this myth may be implicitly identified with the caul (ulba) by the mediation of the metaphoric term common to both of them, that is, śamala 'blemish'. Again the image hidden in the vocabulary describing the freeing of the sun is that of a birth.

3. *The Fourth Sheep*

So, JB III.334–5 (with the support of KS VIII.5) imposes a new interpretation on the dénouement of the Svarbhānu myth—that the 'darknesses' removed from the sun are embryo covers/cauls and that the process thus mimics a birth. We seem to have two mythic patterns combined here. On the one hand we have the apparently adult sun being punished for a serious infraction,[95] 'pierced with darkness', as with a weapon. But the sun, darkened by this hostile encounter, is rescued by a process that conforms to a very different pattern of ac-

[94] For the limits and dangers of this 'protection', see Chap. 8, D.3., below.

[95] As we will see, Chap. 10, E.

tivity and diction, that of birth and especially of the removal of the protective membranes that envelop the embryo in the womb.[96] The sun is now an embryo, a garbha, and the darkness that was a weapon in the beginning of the myth is now likened to the nurturing embryo covers that must be removed for the full beauty of the newborn to be revealed.

Proceeding on the assumption that the remedy is likened to a birth allows us to explain two other puzzling features, one a textual problem in some versions of the myth, the other a related myth sometimes told in conjunction with the Svarbhānu tale.

First the textual problem: the source of the fourth sheep. Three BYV versions of the myth that present the full transformation of darkness into sheep parallel each other relatively closely.[97]

> TS II.1.2.2–3 tásya yát prathamáṃ támo 'pā́ghnant sā́ kṛṣṇā́vir abhavad yád dvitī́yaṁ sā́ phálgunī yát tṛtī́yaṁ sā́ balakṣī́ *yád adhyasthā́d apā́kṛntant sā́vir vaśā́ // sám abhavat*
>
> The first darkness they smashed off became a black ewe. The second a reddish one. The third a white one. *What they cut off from the ______ became a vaśā ewe:*
>
> KS XII.13 yát prathamám apā́lumpan sā́viṣ kṛṣṇā́bhavad yád dvitī́yaṁ sā́ phalgúr yát tṛtī́yaṁ sā́ balakṣī́ *yád adhyasthā́d apā́lumpan sā́vir vaśā́bhavat.*
>
> The first darkness they stripped off became a black ewe. The second a reddish one. The third a white one. *What they stripped off from the ______ became a vaśā ewe.*
>
> MS II.5.2 yát prathamáṃ támo 'pā́ghnant sā́viḥ kṛṣṇā́bhavad yád dvitī́yaṁ sā́ lóhinī yát tṛtī́yaṁ sā́ balakṣī́ *yád adhyastā́d apā́kṛntat [→ *apā́kṛntant?]*[98] *sā́vir vaśā́bhavat*
>
> The first darkness they smashed away became a black ewe. The second a reddish one. The third a white one. *What he [→ *they] cut off from the ______ became a vaśā ewe.*

[96]For a possible way to reconcile these two images, see Chap. 10, B.

[97]Two more (KS XXVII.2, MS IV.5.7) present only the first three sheep.

[98]There is no clear reason why apā́kṛntat should be singular here. I am tempted to read *apā́kṛntant, with dissimilatory loss of the second *n*.

They differ only in the choice of verb (TS/MS vs. KS), the order of ávi- and kr̥ṣṇā́- (MS/KS vs. TS), in what color the second sheep is (TS ~ KS vs. MS), *and* in the source for the fourth animal (TS/KS vs. MS).[99] In either version this last phrase is puzzling and unprecedented. Keith translates the TS passage "what they cut from the upper part of the bone," but this hardly fits the context: no bones have been mentioned, and it is somewhat difficult to imagine the sun having any. Caland's interpretation "'upper bone', 'cranium' (?)" suffers from the same difficulty, as does Wackernagel-Debrunner's 'Oberfläche eines Knochens' (surface of a bone).[100] The compound (adhi-asth-a) occurs nowhere else that I am aware of.

Keith comments, "The phrase is a curious one, but the tradition is uniform." But, in fact, the larger BYV tradition is not uniform: the MS has adhyastā́t (not adhyas*thā́*t), with no variants noted by von Schroeder. The MS reading together with the JB parallel gives the clue to the interpretation of this phrase.

Let us return to JB III.334–5, in which the removal of the embryo covers uncannily recalls the removal of darkness from the sun; what follows the first three removals is now our concern.

> .335 tasya yat prathamam ulbam apālumpaṃs tat kr̥ṣṇāyas samabhavat / yad dvitīyam ulbam apālumpaṃs tad rajatam abhavat / yat tr̥tīyam ulbam apālumpaṃs tad dharitam abhavat / tasmāt tat tviṣimattamam / tat tad dhy asyādhyātmam āsīd *atha yaj jarāyu nāḍyām āsīt* / tal loham abhavat

> The first caul of his they stripped off became black-metal (iron). The second caul they stripped off became silver. The third caul they stripped off became gold. Therefore it (gold) is the most sparkling. For it was his own self (or, was that which was on his self?). *Then the placenta that was in the (birth)canal (?)* became copper.

As in the BYV version there are three identical swipes, which produce increasingly brighter animals (or metals) each time; as in the BYV there is a fourth element different from these three. Here it is straighforwardly named as the placenta, jarāyu.

99PB VI.6.8 and JB I.81 also tell the story of the sheep, but the colors are different, and the source for the fourth sheep is quite different in PB (see immediately below). JB has no fourth sheep.

100 Keith 1914, ad loc.; Caland 1931, ad PB VI.6.8; Wackernagel-Debrunner, *AIG*, vol. 2.1, p. 311.

The placenta makes sense as the source of the fourth sheep in the BYV versions as well. The MS form adhyastá- can easily be interpreted as 'placenta', 'afterbirth'; it can be analyzed as the past passive participle to adhi √as, lit. 'cast forth, expelled *in addition*', a perfect designation for the afterbirth. Though adhi √as seems not to have this meaning elsewhere in Vedic, the idiom is uncommon. Other compounds with √as do refer to birth processes: remember nir √as in the Yati story for the horse's excreting/giving birth to Syūmaraśmi;[101] parā √as already in RV X.72.8 seems to mean 'miscarry.'[102]

RV X.72.8 aṣṭaú putrā́so áditer, yé jātā́s tanvàs pári
devā́m̐ úpa praít saptábhiḥ, *párā* mārtāṇḍám *āsyat*

Eight (were) the sons of Aditi who were born from her body. She approached the gods with seven. She '*threw aside*' Mārtāṇḍa.

Moreover, in JB II.441 the bitch Saramā, Indra's canine confidante, finds (and eats) a placenta apāstam 'cast down' (idiom ápa √as):

JB II.441 sā ha jarāyv *apāstaṃ* viveda / tad dha cakhāda

She found an *expelled/cast down* placenta (and) ate it.[103]

It is possible that apāstam here simply means 'discarded, thrown out', though I favor the other interpretation, which connects the idiom specifically with the processes of birth. A passage in an AV hymn for safe childbirth suggests that dogs (of which Saramā is one) regularly or characteristically eat the just-expelled placenta:

AV I.11.4 ávaitu pṛ́śni śévalaṃ, *śúne* jarā́yv *áttavé,* 'va jarā́yu padyatām

Let the spotted, slimy (?) placenta come down *for the dog to eat*. Let the placenta fall down.

[101]KS VIII.5, discussed in Chap. 4, A.1. This section also treats Agni's affair with the wives of Varuṇa.

[102]In reference to the Mārtāṇḍa myth, for which see below; cf. Geldner, ad loc. Possibly (but less likely) rather 'discard after birth, expose'. Cf. n. 131. Hoffmann instead interprets parā √as as having its literal meaning, 'lay/throw aside' ('beiseitelegen'), in this and other passages. See 1957, p. 95, n. 29 (1976, p. 431, n. 29).

[103] Another echo of adhi √as + placenta *may* possibly be found in the JB passage we began with (III.335). The phrase tad dhy asyādhyātmam āsīt 'for it was his own self'(?), referring to gold, makes little sense, and it may be considerably corrupted from *adhyasta- or *adhyāsyat. However, since its position, as well as its form, is wrong, I advance this possibility only very tentatively.

Thus, a mysterious reference to an 'overbone' (adhyasthá-, TS, KS) can be understood if we instead follow the MS reading (adhyastá-) and interpret it in the context of birth, which is strongly suggested by what precedes.

Just one of the sheep passages seems to suggest a different source for the fourth sheep; however, even this one may be indirectly linked with birth. PB VI.6.8 follows the standard pattern for the removal of darkness, up to the fourth transformation.

> PB VI.6.8 te 'trim upādhāvaṁs tasyātrir bhāsena tamo 'pāhan yat prathamam apāhan sā kr̥ṣṇāvir abhavad yad dvitīyaṁ sā rajatā yat tr̥tīyaṁ sā lohinī yayā varṇam abhyatr̥ṇat sā śuklāsīt

> They resorted to Atri. Atri smashed away his darkness with the Bhāsa (Sāman). The first (darkness) he smashed away became a black ewe. The second a silvery one. The third a reddish one. With which [*fem.*] he bored through to (his) color, that became a bright/white one.

Caland translates yayā varṇam abhyatr̥ṇat sā śuklāsīt 'with what (arrow) he set free its original appearance (colour), that was a white sheep', commenting "the fem. yayā is somewhat doubtful; I suppose that iṣuṇā [arrow] is to be supplied. . . . If my interpretation is right, we have to imagine Atri as shooting with arrows towards the sun to drive away the daemon of darkness."

This picture of Atri's activity is far from the one we have just drawn; moreover, it immediately disappears when we look at other instances in Vedic of the lexeme abhi √tr̥d, lit. 'drill/bore to', the verb with which the mysterious yayā ('with which [feminine]') is to be construed. Abhí √tr̥d is used of penetrating through some protective covering to lay bare a desirable thing. In the RV it is several times used of reaching a stream or a source of water (e.g., II.24.4, IX.110.5). Indeed in prose the action of abhí √tr̥d seems more specialized than in the RV: it is almost always used as the final action of digging. One digs for something (√khan) and finally uncovers it (abhí √tr̥d).

> ŚB II.3.2.14 yáthāpó vābhikhánann anyád vānnā́dyaṃ tát kṣiprè 'bhitr̥ndyā́t

> (It is) as if in digging for water or some other food, he would lay it bare in an instant.

(This is contrasted with the situation where "in digging . . .", sá sāmí nivárteta 'he would turn away prematurely'.)

The instrument one uses with this verb is a spade, ábhri, a feminine noun. The ŚB passage just quoted continues:

> ŚB II.3.2.15 ábhrayo ha vā́ etā́ annā́dyasya yád ā́hutayaḥ / abhí haivaítád annā́dyaṃ tr̥ṇatti
>
> These offerings are the spades (for the digging) of food. In this way he lays bare food.

(Cf. also AiĀr I.3.1.)

Thus the noun to be supplied with yayā in PB VI.6.8 must be abhri- 'spade', and the last sentence (yayā varṇam abhyatr̥ṇat sā śuklāsīt) should be rendered '(The spade) with which he dug through to/laid bare his (true) color became a white ewe'. This probably reflects a slightly different vision of the obscuring darknesses; rather than being embryo covers as they seem to be in the versions just examined, they may be seen as layers of earth to be dug away, until the true surface of the sun is revealed again. The conceptual similarity between those two things is clear, as well as their conceptual distance from shooting arrows at the sun to drive away the darkness demon.[104]

C. Some Other Failed Births of the Sun

1. *Saving the Sun from Miscarriage*

In the other myth illumined by the interpretation of the rescue of the sun as a description of birth, the gods fear that the sun will fall from heaven, and they prop it up with various means. This story is once told in conjunction with Svarbhānu (in PB IV.5.9–12; Svarbhānu in IV.5.2), three times independently (KS XXXIII.6, TB I.2.4.2, AB IV.19).

[104]Moreover, it is worth noting (though perhaps not pursuing) the actual character of the ábhri- 'spade'. The mantra constantly addressed to her (e.g., KS XVI.1, MS II.7.1, ŚB III.6.1.4) is ábhrir asi nā́ry asi (/nā́rir asi) 'Thou art spade; thou art woman'. Not only is the spade feminine in gender, but she is typed as a female being. Once in a discussion of the characteristics of the ábhri-, the material from which she is made, bamboo, is called the yoni (womb) of Agni and his safe birth is discussed (ŚB VI.3.1.32). Thus the ábhri- is, however tangentially, connected with the birth process. Hence, digging with the spade to uncover the sun in PB VI.6.8 could be a metaphorical equivalent of removing the cauls from the sun in the other passages. In addition, the ábhri- is several times (e.g., ŚB VI.4.1.5) identified with speech, vā́c-, and so the spade in PB VI.6.8 might be an oblique reference to the fourth formulation (bráhman-, unfortunately neuter in gender) with which Atri rescues the sun in RV V.40.6. (For more on this, see below, Chap. 9, C.2.)

KS XXXIII.6 devā vā ādityasya svargāl lokād avapādād abibhayus taṃ triṣu svargeṣu lokeṣv ādadhus tasya parāco 'tipādād abibhayus taṃ parastāt tribhis svargair lokaiḥ pratyastabhnuvan sa eṣa ubhayataṣ ṣaṭsu svargeṣu lokeṣu pratiṣṭhito dhṛtyai pratiṣṭhāyā anavapādāyānatipādāya

The gods feared the falling down of the Āditya from the heavenly world. They placed it in three heavenly worlds. They feared its falling beyond on the far side (of the heavenly world). They propped it up beyond with three heavenly worlds. It is (now) established on both sides in six heavenly worlds, for firmness, for firm standing, for not falling down or beyond.

The other passages are very similar, differing primarily in the means used to secure the sun.[105] As in the KS passage, the idiom for 'fall down' is ava √pad (except in AB IV.19, which has the virtual homonym ava √pat). Ava √pad frequently has simply its literal, additive sense 'fall' (√pad) 'down' (ava), and it is used of the sun already in the RV:

RV I.105.3 mó ṣú deva adáḥ svàr, *áva pādi* divás pári

O god, let not yonder sun *fall down* from heaven.

But áva √pad also has well-established idiomatic meanings in the realm of birth. It can refer to the normal expulsion of the placenta in childbirth (as in the cited refrain in AV I.11.4–6 áva jarā́yu padyatām 'Let the placenta fall down'). More important for us, it is commonly used to mean 'miscarry'.[106]

TS V.5.1.6 yáthā sāmí gárbho 'vapádyate . . .

As when an embryo '*falls down*' prematurely . . .

which is contrasted with

TS V.5.1.6–7 yáthā saṃvatsarám āptvā́ // kālá ā́gate vijā́yate . . .

[105] TB I.2.4.4 reverses the order: they fear first the falling beyond, then the falling down.

[106] The idiom is found already in the AV (V.17.7, VIII.6.20); cf. also MS I.6.12, JB I.306 ≅ PB XV.5.16.

As when (the embryo) having attained a year, its time having come, is born . . .

JB II.2 yo vai māsyo garbho 'vapadyate 'srāvīd iti vai tam āhuḥ

When a month-old embryo '*falls down*', they say about it, "It was miscarried."[107]

So, in the story about the gods' fears for the sun, though the literal meaning of áva √pad 'fall down' is obviously present, the idiomatic meaning 'miscarry' is probably also there. The gods see the sun as an embryo that must be supported until the proper time for a proper birth. Further parallels strengthen this likely association. In several of the versions of the falling down of the sun (TB I.2.4.4, AB IV.19), the gods support him with five reins.

AB IV.19 tasya vai devā ādityasya svargāl lokād avapātād abibhayus tam pañcabhī raśmibhir udavayan

The gods were afraid of this Āditya falling from the heavenly world. They fastened him up with five reins.

This has a conceptual parallel in passages concerning miscarriages in which the umbilical cord is seen as the leash that keeps the embryo from falling out of the womb.

JB I.306 (≅ PB XV.5.16) nābhyo ha vai dhṛtā garbhā avācīnabilebhyo nāvapadyante

Embryos, held firm from the navel, do not 'fall down' from (their wombs) (despite) having their (wombs') openings downward.

2. *Mārtāṇḍa/Vivasvant*

Now the gods have reason to worry about a miscarriage of the sun. A well-known YV myth relates the birth of Aditi's (eight) children.[108] The first seven are born without incident, but the last miscarries (or is aborted by his brothers; cf. KS XI.6, MS I.6.12) and is expelled as a shapeless mass or as an egg (hence his name, Mārtāṇḍa 'stemming

[107]On asrāvīt see Narten 1964, pp. 282f.
[108]TS VI.5.6.1, MS I.6.12, KS XI.6, ŚB III.1.3.3–4.

from a mortal/dead egg'). We have already met this story briefly in a RVic version (X.72.8),

RV X.72.8 aṣṭaú putrā́so áditer, yé jātā́s tanvàs pári
devā́m̐ úpa praít saptábhiḥ, párā mārtāṇḍám āsyat

Eight (were) the sons of Aditi who were born from her body. She approached the gods with seven. She 'threw aside' Mārtāṇḍa.

but the myth is treated more extensively in YV prose.[109] Here is one version:

MS I.6.12 áditir vaí prajā́kāmaudanám apacat sóñśiṣṭam āśnāt tásyā dhātā́ cāryamā́ cājāyetām̐ sā́param apacat sóñśiṣṭam āśnāt tásyā mitrā́ś ca váruṇaś cājāyetām̐ sā́param apacat sóñśiṣṭam āśnāt tásyā ám̐śaś ca bhágaś cājāyetām̐ sā́param apacat saíkṣatóñśiṣṭaṃ me 'śnatyā́ dvaú-dvau jā́yete itó nūnáṃ me śréyaḥ syād yát purástād aśnīyā́m íti sā́ purástād aśitvópāharat tā́ antár evá gárbhaḥ sántā avadatām āvám idáṃ bhaviṣyāvo yád ādityā́ íti táyor ādityā́ nirhantā́ram aicham̐s tā́ ám̐śaś ca bhágaś ca nírahatām . . . sá vā́ índra ūrdhvá evá prāṇám[110] anudáśrayata mṛtám ítaram āṇḍám ávāpadyata sá vā́vá mārtāṇḍó yásyemé manuṣyā̀ḥ prajā́ sā́ vā́ áditir ādityā́n úpādhāvad ástv evá ma idáṃ mā́ ma idáṃ moghé párāpaptad íti tè 'bruvann áthaiṣò 'smā́kam evá bravātai ná nó 'timanyātā íti sá vā́vá vívasvān ādityáḥ

Aditi, having desire for offspring, cooked an odana (rice mess). She ate the leftovers [after offering to the gods]. Dhātar and Aryaman were born from her. She cooked another and ate the leftovers. Mitra and Varuṇa were born from her. She cooked another and ate the leftovers. Am̐śa and Bhaga were born from her. She cooked another. She saw, "Of me eating the leftover, (offspring) are born in pairs. From now on it would be (even) better for me if I ate beforehand." Having eaten beforehand, she offered. The two, (though still) being embryos within, said, "We two will thrive here, as the Ādityas (do)." The Ādityas sought a striker-forth (abortionist) of these two. Am̐śa and Bhaga struck them forth. . . . Indra stood erect, according to/because of his breath. The other egg 'fell down' dead. This was Mārtāṇḍa, whose offspring are these men. Aditi ran to the Ādityas, (saying), "Let this of mine exist. Let this of mine not

[109]These YV passages have been translated and discussed thoroughly and illuminatingly by Hoffmann (1957 [1976, pp. 422–38]). Accordingly, I will present only one passage in full, and indicate some matters on which I disagree with Hoffmann.

[110]For this emendation and its translation, cf. Hoffmann 1957, pp. 88f., 102f. (1976, pp. 424f., 437f.).

'fly forth' in vain." They said, "Then he shall call himself (one) of us. He shall not disdain us." This one (became) Vivasvant Āditya.

This Vivasvant is thus the result of an abnormal birth, specifically in MS/KS an abortion. The KS/MS passages express the abortion and its results quite vividly:

KS XI.6 táṃ níraghnan sá nírasto 'śayat

They (the brothers) smashed him forth. Expelled[111] he lay (there).

MS I.6.12 táyor ādityā́ nirhantā́ram aichaṁś tā́ áṁśaś ca bhágaś ca nírahatām . . . mr̥tám ítaram āṇḍám ávāpadyata

The Ādityas sought a striker-forth (abortionist) of these two. Aṁśa and Bhāga struck them forth. . . . The other egg 'fell down' [note áva √pad again] dead.

The other versions do not provide the reason for the miscarriage/abortion, but its results are nonetheless starkly presented:

TS VI.5.6.1 tásyai vyr̥̀ddham āṇḍám ajāyata

A 'failed' egg was born to her.

ŚB III.1.3.3 ávikr̥taṁ hāṣṭamā́ṃ janayā́ṃ cakāra mārtāṇḍáṁ saṃdeghó haivā́sa yā́vān evórdhvás tā́vāṃs tiryáṅ

She bore an eighth, unshaped: Mārtāṇḍa. He was a lump, as broad as he was tall.

Although in the MS and TS versions the process that transforms the 'dead egg' into Vivasvant is not described, KS and ŚB treat it with some care. The aborted fetus is fixed up by cutting away the dead parts and discarding them; what is left becomes vivasvant- āditya-, the "'shining-forth' (vi √vas) son of Aditi."

KS XI.6 táṁ sámaskurvaṁs tásya yán mr̥tám ā́sīt tád ápākr̥ntan sá hasty àbhavad yáj jīváṁ sá vivásvāṁ ādityáḥ

[111] N.B. nir √as 'throw forth', as in Syūmaraśmi's birth/excretion from the horse discussed above, Chap. 4, A.1.

They fixed him up. What of him was dead they cut away; that became the elephant. What was alive (became) Vivasvant Āditya.

ŚB III.1.3.4 hántemáṃ vikarávāméti táṃ vícakrur yáthāyáṃ púruṣo víkr̥tas tásya yā́ni māṁsā́ni saṃkŕ̥tya saṃnyāsús táto hastī́ sámabhavat . . . yám u ha tád vicakrúḥ sá vívasvān ādityáḥ

(The Ādityas said,) "Come on, let us shape him." They shaped him as man here (on earth) is shaped. What flesh of his they cut off and threw down in a heap, from that the elephant came into being. . . . What they shaped (became) Vivasvant Āditya.

Note especially in the KS versions the verb apa √kr̥t 'cut off'. This is the same expression we saw above used for the cutting away of the placenta in TS II.1.2.2 and MS II.5.2 (e.g., TS II.1.2.2–3 yád adhyasthā́d *apā́kr̥ntant* sā́vir vaśā́ sám abhavat 'What they *cut off* from the expelled (placenta) became a vaśā sheep'). It seems in both those passages and here to describe the shaping of a proper man from the various products of birth.

Now Vivasvant is a common name of the sun in post-Vedic literature, and it is commonly supposed to refer to the sun already in Vedic, even in the RV.[112] If this is so, then the failed birth of the sun as Vivasvant/Mārtāṇḍa in the passages just discussed would give the gods reason to worry about another miscarriage of Sūrya in the passages noted above (KS XXXIII.6, etc).

Hoffmann, however, rejects this identification of Vivasvant with Sūrya for the Vedic period,[113] though he does not seem to give strong arguments for this opinion. He simply says that the identification has no textual support ("keine Stütze", n. 30). As I understand his view, he thinks the identification has simply been assumed for Vedic by later commentators, based on the undeniable post-Vedic identification of the two. This post-Vedic identification has arisen because Sūrya 'the sun' is often called Āditya 'son/descendant of Aditi' already in the RV, and Vivasvant/Mārtāṇḍa is also a son of Aditi.

But, first of all, there is some textual support for the identification already in Vedic. In the latish ŚB the equation is quite explicit:

ŚB X.5.2.4 asaú vā́ ādityó vívasvān

[112]Cf., e.g., Hillebrandt 1927–29, vol. 1, p. 18; vol. 2, pp. 343ff.

[113]Hoffmann 1957, pp. 94–96 (esp. n. 30), 100 (1976, pp. 430–31 [esp. n. 30], 435).

Vivasvant is really yonder Āditya.

(Remember that asaú ādityáḥ 'yonder Āditya' is an unambiguous designation of the sun throughout Vedic prose.)

Moreover, Hoffmann does not address the question of why the sun is called āditya/āditeya already in the RV, if it is not because of such an identification. Since the sun is considered to be the son of Aditi, and one of Aditi's sons has a transparently celestial epithet, Vivasvant 'having the shining forth', it is hard to believe that the Vedic mind, which was trained to make far more exotic identifications than this, would have failed, for half a millennium or so, to equate the two. Although the equation may not date back to the *Rig* Vedic period, I think it must be accepted as potential already for the older prose Saṃhitās, in other words for the time of the Vivasvant birth story in MS/KS/TS. The fact that the birth/abortion of the sun is a concern in our myth too would lend further support to this view.

3. *Agni and Sūrya in the Womb*

Another story seems to allude to a possible miscarriage of the sun. Though the elements in this story are suggestively similar to those in the kernel of the Svarbhānu story, the episode is cryptic, and I have so far found no parallels outside MS/KS (KapS). In this tale Sūrya is with Agni in the same womb.

> MS I.8.2 sahá vā́ etā́ āstām agníś ca sū́ryaś ca samāné yónā áyasi lóhite sá ādityá ūrdhvá údadravat tásya rétaḥ párāpatat tád agnír yóninópāgṛhṇāt tád enaṁ vyàdahat tásmād áyo 'trapú prátidhuk kṣīráṁ ví dahati

> Agni and Sūrya were together in the same womb (made of) reddish metal [= copper]. The Āditya (Sūrya) ran straight up. His seed/embryo flew forth. Agni gathered it up with the womb. It [= seed? (tád) or yóni? unexpressed] burned him (/it?).[114] Therefore untinned copper burns milk just milked.

[114] There is a textual problem here. The conclusion of the passage suggests that the receptacle (yóni-/copper pan) burns the liquid (rétas-/milk). But, as the passage stands, enam in the previous sentence ought to refer to Agni, not to the seed, as the form is masculine, not neuter, requiring a rather senseless interpretation: 'the seed or yoni burned *Agni*'. Hence I am inclined to emend this to neuter enat, to allow an interpretation: 'the womb burned the seed/embryo'. Rau (1973) accepts the text and translates,

KS VI.3 (≅ KapS IV.6) samāne vai yonā āstām̐ sūryaś cāgniś ca tatas sūrya ūrdhva udadrav̀at tasya retaḥ parāpatat tad agnir yoninopágr̥hṇād ayasā tad akrūḍayat tat krūḍyamānaṃ gavi nyadadhāt tad idaṃ payas tasmād atrapv ayaḥ pātraṃ pratidhuk krūḍayati

Sūrya and Agni were in the same womb. From there Sūrya ran straight up. His seed/embryo flew forth. Agni gathered it up with the copper womb. It (the womb) curdled (?)[115] it (the seed). He put it, curdled, in the cow. That is this milk. Therefore an untinned copper pot curdles fresh milk.

These passages are both intriguingly suggestive and frustratingly puzzling. Rather than attempt a thorough exegesis of them, which I would find impossible at this time, I will simply list some of their interesting and aggravating features.

Note first in MS I.8.2 the womb (yóni-) made of áyas- lóhita- 'reddish metal' or 'copper'. This reminds us of the birth description in JB III.335 in which the placenta becomes copper (atha yaj jarāyu nāḍyām āsīt / tal loham abhavat 'Then the placenta that was in the (birth)canal became copper'), but this parallel does not advance us very far.

A central crux of the two passages resides in the word rétas- and the idiom ūrdhvá údadravat. As we have already seen, though rétas ordinarily means 'seed, semen', it can also refer to what we might call the next stage of the semen, namely, the embryo deposited in the womb. Therefore what happens in the womb in these two passages can either be (*a*) that Sūrya released semen while still a fetus, and Agni collected it, or (*b*) that Sūrya the embryo underwent or began to undergo an unnatural and premature birth, and Agni collected the remains of it. I am inclined to the latter view.

One might expect that the idiom describing Sūrya's action, ūrdhvá údadravat, would allow us to decide between the two scenarios sketched above, and in fact it does help. Despite appearances, (ūrdhvá-) úd √dru does not seem to have sexual connotations. Ordinarily it has either a literal, additive meaning 'run [√dru] up [úd]' or it is used in ritual passages to mean 'recite quickly'. However, in one context it

"Der [d.h. der Samen] verdarb ihn [d.h. den Mutterschoss] durch Hitze" (It [i.e., the seed] destroyed it [i.e., the womb] with heat). But given the following sentence, this reversal does not make sense to me.

[115]The verb krūḍayati occurs only here in Sanskrit, as far as I know. Rau's translation (1973, p. 19) is similar to mine: "brachte [den Samen] zum Gerinnen" (brought the (seed) to coagulation, curdled the seed).

refers to an unnatural birth, as here, in a story of the birth of Agni from Prajāpati. Prajāpati wishes to emit Agni from his mouth, but Agni disdains this and crashes through the top of his head. The KS/MS version is fairly minimal, but the JB fills in more of the details:

> KS VI.1 prajā́patir vā́ idám āsīt tásmād agnír ádhyasr̥jyata sò 'sya mūrdhná ūrdhvá údadravat tásya yál lóhitam ā́sīt tád ápāmr̥ṣṭa tád bhū́myāṃ nyàmārṭ
>
> Prajāpati was (all) this. From him Agni was created. He ran straight up from his head. He (?) wiped off the blood and wiped it on the ground.[116]
>
> JB I.73 prajāpatiḥ prajā asr̥jata / so 'gnim api mukhād asisr̥kṣata / so 'gnir mukhād bībhatsamāna ūrdhva uddrutya mastiṣkam [→ *mastakam?[117]) uddhatyāsr̥jyata / taṃ devāś carṣayaś copasametyābruvan vitunno 'yaṃ mastiṣko (/*mastako) māmuyā bhūt karavāmemaṃ kasyāṃ *cid ācitīti
>
> Prajāpati emitted the creatures. He was about to / wanted to emit Agni from his mouth. Agni, feeling aversion to the mouth, (instead) having run straight up and slammed into the brain (?*skull), was born. The gods and r̥ṣis, coming up, said, "Let this brain (/*skull), (though) bored through, not be lost. Let us put it in (our) care."[118]

The use of ud √dru in the Agni-Sūrya myth just given, also in a birth context, suggests that rétas in MS I.8.2/KS VI.3 refers to the embryo Sūrya, and that Sūrya experienced a similar birth through the top of the head. Indeed in the PB equivalent of JB I.73 (= PB VI.5.1), it is the sun who is born from Prajāpati's head, though not through the medium of this verb.

> PB VI.5.1 prajāpatir akāmayata bahu syāṃ prajāyeyeti so 'śocat tasya śocata ādityo mūrdhno 'sr̥jyata so 'sya mūrdhānam udahan
>
> Prajāpati desired, "Might I be more, might I be reproduced." He burned/was pained, and out of the head of him who burned/was pained (yonder) Āditya [= the sun] was emitted. This (sun) smashed up (through) his head.

[116]Similarly MS I.8.1, with asr̥jata 'emitted' rather than ūrdhvá údadravat.

[117]So Caland 1919, ad loc., and 1931, ad PB VI.5.1.

[118]The translation of this last sentence more or less follows that of Bodewitz 1977, p. 150. Caland (1919, no. 9) reads ācitrīti and translates (approximately), "Let us make it into something lovely."

If Sūrya is experiencing a similar difficult birth in our passages, this helps explain Agni's collecting the material in a womb/copper pot. Agni seems to be reassembling the embryo sun in another? womb, which, however, burns Sūrya rather than protecting him. These details have telling parallels in other myths about miscarriage and potential miscarriage.[119]

Though we can construct a relatively self-consistent and sensible plot line for these two passages, it is still difficult to understand the larger connections and concerns of this episode. For example: Is Agni hostile or friendly in gathering up Sūrya? How is Sūrya affected by the burning; is he ever reborn, as Atri is? What about the 'curdled' milk in the cow?

Thus, several stories of the birth of the sun (or a form of the sun, Vivasvant Āditya) make him the patched-up result of a miscarriage; this makes it all the more important that his (re)birth after injury should be accomplished in the prescribed manner, with orderly disposal of the caul and placenta: the process hidden in the words of our Svarbhānu story.

[119]As we will see in Chap. 8, D.3.

CHAPTER 8

Failed Birth and Rebirth of Atri

A. Atri and Miscarriage

A miscarriage befalls another of the principal actors in our myth, Atri, the rescuer and restorer of the sun. The story of his unfortunate birth is told quite straightforwardly in the ŚB. It begins with the common tale of the rivalry between Mind (Manas) and Speech (Vāc);[120] the two, as usual, go to Prajāpati for a judgement on which is better. Prajāpati finds in favor of Mind; Speech is angry and refuses to bear oblations for Prajāpati anymore. Following is an abbreviation of this sequence from ŚBK:

> ŚBK II.4.2.12 mánaś ca ha vaí vā́k cāhám̐ bhádra ūdāte . . .
> .14 . . .taú hā́sam̐pādayantau prajā́patim̐ praśnám ā́jagmatuḥ sá ha prajā́patir mánasa evā́dhyuvāca

> Mind and Speech were (both) saying, "I am excellent." . . . They, not agreeing, went to ask Prajāpati. Prajāpati spoke in favor of Mind.

So much is familiar from the other versions of this tale, but the ŚB version continues with an unexpected consequence of this disappointment to Speech. She miscarries, and her fetus is unceremoniously gathered up and stuffed into a container by the gods. This assemblage of aborted material reminds us of the story of Agni and Sūrya, in

[120]Cf., e.g., TS II.5.11.4, MS IV.6.4.

which Agni collects the 'seed' of Sūrya after he apparently experiences a failed birth.

The Atri story continues in the slightly clearer ŚBK version:

> ŚBK II.4.2.14 (cf. ŚBM I.4.5.12) sā́ ha pároktā vā́g vísiṣmiye tásyā gárbhaḥ papāta . . .
>
> Speech, thus contradicted, was astonished. Her embryo 'fell/flew' [= miscarried].
>
> .15 . . .tád u hedā́ṃ devā́ rétaḥ siktā́ṃ cármaṇi vā kumbhyā́ṃ vā babhrus tád dha sma pr̥cchanty átraivá tā́3d íty átraivéti tátó 'triḥ sā́ṃbabhūva tásmād ápi stríyātréyyainasvī́ty āhur etásyā hí sá yóṣāyā devátāyā vācáḥ sā́ṃbhūta íti
>
> The gods then collected/bore this poured-out seed in a skin or a pot. They (kept) ask(ing), "Is it (all?) here (atra)?" "It is (all?) here," (they said). So it became Atri. Therefore they say, "He is guilty with an ātreyī woman." For he (Atri) was produced from this woman, from the divinity Speech.

B. The Ātreyī

Before we examine the substance of this story, we must embark on a digression to understand its moral: tásmād ápi stríyātréyyainasvī́ty āhur. This phrase is puzzling. I have rendered it for the moment literally (and incomprehensibly) as 'Therefore they say, "He is guilty with an ātreyī woman"'. Eggeling translates the equivalent phrase in ŚBM I.4.5.13 (tásmād ápy ātreyyā́ yoṣítainasvī́) as 'For the same reason one becomes guilty by (intercourse) with a woman who has just miscarried'. This is largely based on Sāyaṇa's comment on this passage:

> Sāy. on ŚBM I.4.5.13 tasmāt sr̥tagarbhā rajasvalā strī nāmnātreyīty ākhyāyate tayā yoṣitā saha saṃbhāṣaṇādikaṃ kurvan puruṣa enasvī bhavati
>
> Therefore a woman who has (just) miscarried (and is now) menstruating is called an ātreyī. A man making conversation and so forth with this woman becomes guilty.

But Sāyaṇa's comment seems a desperate attempt to reconcile this particular context regarding Atri's birth with the later lexical meaning of the word ātreyī/ātreyikā, namely, 'a menstruating woman' (cf., e.g., Amarakośa 2.6.1.20). We need to look further at this word to determine how it is used in this particular passage.

1. *The Ātreyī in Legal Texts*

Ātreyī occurs twice elsewhere in the Brāhmaṇas, once in the JB as a patronymic of Apālā, once in JB II.219. The latter passage also concerns Atri—this time his successful wish for children.

> JB II.219 athākāmayatātrir bhūyiṣṭhā ma ṛṣayaḥ prajāyām ājāyerann iti / sa etaṃ triṇavaṃ stomam apaśyat / tam āharat / tenāyajata / . . . / tato vai tasya bhūyiṣṭhā ṛṣayaḥ prajāyām ājāyanta parassahasrā hāsya prajāyāṃ mantrakṛta āsur api hāsya striyo mantrakṛta āsuḥ / *tasmād yo 'py ātreyīṃ striyaṃ hanti taṃ pary eva cakṣate*

> Then Atri desired, "Might abundant ṛṣis be born in my line." He saw this Triṇava Stoma. He took it. He worshipped with it. . . . Thereupon abundant seers were born in his line. More than a thousand mantra-makers were in his line; there were also female mantra-makers in his (line). *Therefore they condemn one who hits/ kills an ātreyī woman.*

The JB passage does not directly reveal anything further about the meaning of ātreyī, but it provides us with the means for approaching it, for the JB sentence is a close paraphrase of a provision that occurs frequently in the Dharma Sūtras concerning the punishment for the killing of an ātreyī.[121] Vasiṣṭha gives a most convenient definition of ātreyī (differing from the definitions of the lexica):

> VāsDS XX.34 brāhmaṇīṃ cātreyīṃ hatvā . . .
> .35 ātreyīṃ vakṣyāmo rajasvalām ṛtusnātām ātreyīm āhuḥ
> .36 atra hy eṣyad apatyaṃ bhavatīti

> (One) having killed a Brāhmaṇa woman (who is) ātreyī (incurs the aforementioned penalty). . . .
> We will explain "ātreyī": a (recently) menstruating woman who has

[121] ĀpDS 1.24.9, GautDS XXII.12, VāsDS XX.34–36, Vi.Smṛ L.9, Yājñ.Smṛ III.251, Manu (MDŚ) XI.87.

taken her periodic bath[122] [i.e., the bath following menstruation] they call an ātreyī.

For offspring is *going to come* [future of √i] *then/there* (atra). [atra + √i → atre-].[123]

That ātreyī in these texts is not a menstruating woman (as the lexical texts would have it) but one soon after her period, hence more likely to conceive, is also suggested by Viṣṇu Smṛti L.8–9 gurviṇīṃ rajasvalāṃ *vā* / atrigotrāṃ *vā* nārīm, which introduces a disjunction: '(one who kills) a pregnant woman *or* a menstruating woman *or* a woman of the Atri family [= an ātreyī].' If ātreyī were synonymous with rajasvalā 'menstruating', it would not be opposed to that term with the vā . . . vā (or . . . or) construction.

The time thus defined by VāsDS, that immediately after a woman's period, is considered the best for procreation already in the TS.

TS II.5.1.5. tásmād ṛ́tviyāt stríyaḥ prajā́ṃ vindante

Therefore women get offspring after their period.

Also ĀpGS, which is more explicit about proper days:

ĀpGS III.9.1 caturthaprabhṛtyā ṣoḍaśīm uttarām-uttarāṃ yugmāṃ prajāniḥśreyasam ṛtugamana ity upadiśanti

Each following night with an even number, from the fourth (after the beginning of her monthly illness) till the sixteenth, brings more excellent offspring to them, if chosen for the (first) cohabiting after her illness; this it is said.[124]

The second half of the month is less auspicious for procreation than the first.[125]

It is for this reason that the killing of an ātreyī is accorded separate treatment in the dharma literature and that the punishment for it is

[122]Or as Bühler (1898, ad loc.) delicately (if offensively) puts it "she who has bathed after *temporary uncleanness*" (my italics). Cf. also Oldenberg's "monthly illness" below.

[123]The text and translation of .36 more or less follow Kane (1946, p. 527, n. 970) rather than the standard text of Führer (1883) and the standard translation of Bühler (1898). Otherwise, I am not convinced by Kane's interpretation of the meaning of ātreyī.

[124]The translation is Oldenberg's (1892, ad loc.).

[125]Cf. Gonda 1980, p. 246, with references.

ordinarily more severe than for the killing of a woman not in this condition. For example, in Baudhāyana Dharma Sūtra though the killing of a woman is otherwise punished like the killing of a śūdra (the lowest of the four major divisions of society and the only non-Aryan one)—or a cow—the killing of an ātreyī is equivalent to the killing of a kṣatriya (the second highest division) or even that of a brahman (the highest division).

BDS I.10.19.3 śūdravadhena strīvadho govadhaś ca vyākhyāto 'nyatrātreyyā vadhāt . . .
.5 ātreyyā vadhaḥ kṣatriyavadhena vyākhyātaḥ

(The punishment for) the killing of a woman—except for the killing of an ātreyī—and the killing of a cow have been explained by (the provision about) the killing of a śūdra. . . .
(The punishment for) the killing of an ātreyī has been explained by (the provision about) the killing of a kṣatriya.

BDS II.1.1.10 saṃvatsaraṃ śūdrasya
.11 striyāś ca
.12 brāhmaṇavad ātreyyāḥ

(The penalty for the striking/killing) of a śūdra is (to perform the penance) for a year.
Similarly (for the striking/killing) of a woman.
(But) (the penalty for the striking/killing) of an ātreyī is like that (for the striking/killing) of a brahman [twelve years].

The ātreyī merits special treatment precisely because of her peculiar fitness for conception. Since she is in the state most conducive to conceiving, killing her is tantamount to killing an embryo as well. It is equivalent to (and may possibly be) abortion. That preventing potential pregnancies is legally as serious as aborting real ones can be seen in the marriage provisions recently discussed by H.-P. Schmidt,[126] whereby a father who does not marry off his daughter as soon as possible after menarche is guilty of bhrūṇahatyā (abortion, embryo-killing) for each opportunity missed (i.e., for each menstrual period allowed to go by while the girl remains unpaired). Thus, it is not for herself that an ātreyī is valued but as a potential vessel for a fetus.

The reason that ātreyī means 'a woman after her period' is not

[126]Schmidt 1987, pp. 78ff.

entirely clear to me. On the one hand, the dharma literature considers the word a transparent vṛddhi derivative of Atri-, meaning 'a (female) descendant of Atri'. Otherwise atrigotrā- 'a (female) member of the Atri family' could not substitute for ātreyī in Vi. Smṛ L.9 just quoted. But in its legal usage, the word ātreyī seems to have merely a technical or scientific meaning. It refers to a part of the female cycle; it seems to have no semantic connection with the mythological figure of Atri. In other words, the word appears formally to be a proper noun, but in meaning and use a common noun. This is, of course, a commonplace situation in etymology: consider words like *quisling* and *boycott*. Without precise historical information the reason for the transference from proper to common noun is impossible to discern, since it depends on associating a particular, named individual in particular circumstances with a more general semantic notion; it is the ultimate arbitrary linguistic sign.

The historical context for this transference of ātreyī seems certainly to have been lost by the time of the legal texts; note that the VāsDS quoted provides it with a competing, synchronic folk etymology: atra + √i 'go there' (= 'approach'), to account for the form of ātreyī.

2. *Legal Reflections in the Brāhmaṇas*

The situation in the JB and the ŚB is less clear. The word ātreyī must have had the common meaning 'woman after her period' already, and the legal provision about the ātreyī in dharma literature must have been already current in some form in the Brāhmaṇa period (as I will argue shortly). But both ŚB and JB attempt to explain the meaning of ātreyī and its occurrence in this legal provision by recourse to a historical or pseudohistorical account, each telling a different story involving Atri and birth. Yet neither story adequately accounts for the meaning of ātreyī and its legal usage, so that these "historical" explanations seem at first almost as ad hoc as the VāsDS folk etymology.

In order to understand the connection between the legal meaning of ātreyī and the stories supposedly explaining it, we must first be clear on what the Brāhmaṇic passages actually say about the ātreyī. As it turns out, this question is also worth pursuing because of the light it unexpectedly sheds on the history of Indian legal language. Let us first compare the formulations concerning the ātreyī in JB and ŚB:

ŚBK II.4.2.15 tásmād ápi stríyātréyyainasvī́ty āhuḥ
ŚBM I.4.5.13 tásmād ápy ātreyyā́ yoṣítainasvī́

JB II.219 tasmād yo 'py ātreyīṃ striyaṃ hanti taṃ pary eva cakṣate

Lit. ŚBK: Therefore they say, "He is guilty with an ātreyī woman."
ŚBM: Therefore he is guilty with an ātreyī woman.

JB: Therefore they condemn one who hits/kills an ātreyī woman.

The versions in the two texts are superficially very different: all that they have in common are the words tasmād, api, and ātreyī. Indeed, if we follow Sāyaṇa and Eggeling, they refer to entirely different things, the JB to murder, but the ŚB to sex. As we saw above, Sāyaṇa and Eggeling interpret the ŚB passage as referring to intercourse (sexual or otherwise) with an ātreyī, a rather different proposition from the otherwise universal one (in JB and dharma texts) concerning killing or striking her. But, if the word ātreyī means what it does in the dharma literature, this interpretation of the ŚB passage does not make sense, unless the guilty man in question is specified as *not* her husband, since sexual union with an ātreyī should give rise to children, a desirable outcome. Moreover, it would seem odd that only one text (the ŚB) would deviate so markedly from the thoroughly stereotyped contexts in which ātreyī otherwise appears, especially since, like the others, the ŚB passage concerns wrongdoing in regard to the ātreyī.

It therefore seems best to try to reconcile the ŚB passage with the other ones. Indeed, I think that the JB and the ŚB versions refer to the same action, and that the JB version is the fuller statement of it, while the ŚB gives an abbreviated reference to it according to a Vedic syntactic rule not previously noticed (as far as I know).

The kinship of the two passages is first suggested by a small detail, the api positioned identically in both.

ŚBK II.4.2.15 tásmād *ápi* stríyātréyyainasvī́ty āhuḥ
ŚBM I.4.5.13 tásmād *ápy* ātreyyā́ yoṣítainasvī́
JB II.219 tasmād yo '*py* ātreyīṃ striyaṃ hanti taṃ pary eva cakṣate

Though the function of this word is not entirely clear, its unexpected presence in both passages suggests that the two are variants on a single original formulation. I think that api here is an adverb, meaning 'also, in addition', and that its appearance indicates that the provision had been extracted from a list of similar formulations, such as

(Such and such a penalty for one who *x*s, and one who *y*s,) *and also* one who strikes an ātreyī.[127]

Such lists are common in the law texts, and indeed the ātreyī provision is in such a list wherever it appears, though not introduced by api.[128]

But we must still reconcile the remainder of the two Brāhmaṇic provisions. I consider the ŚB statement to be a shorthand version of the one in JB. Rather than spelling out the offense against the ātreyī, the ŚB simply makes global reference to the law, by using the instrumental case: "Therefore one incurs guilt by reason of (the well-known legal provision about) the ātreyī woman"—namely, that one should not strike her.

Although this use of the instrumental does not seem to be described for Vedic proper, it is the standard way of citing laws in the dharma literature, for example, in the BDS passage cited above:

BDS I.10.19.3 *śūdravadhena* strīvadho govadhaś ca vyākhyāto 'nyatrātreyyā vadhāt . . .
.5 ātreyyā vadhaḥ *kṣatriyavadhena* vyākhyātaḥ

(The punishment for) the killing of a woman—except for the killing of an ātreyī—and the killing of a cow have been explained *by (the provision about) the killing of a śūdra*.. . .

(The punishment for) the killing of an ātreyī has been explained *by (the provision about) the killing of a kṣatriya*.

[127]Or alternatively: '(for one who) strikes (x) and also (strikes) an ātreyī'.

[128]The other possibility is that api is a preverb in tmesis, part of a compound verb api √han. This possibility is semantically attractive because api √han in half (MS III.10.4, IV.7.4; KS XII.5; TS II.1.5.3) of its relatively rare occurrences in Vedic has the idiomatic value 'destroy the pregnancy or fertility (of a female)', as in

TS II.1.5.3 óṣadhayaḥ khálu vā́ etásyai sū́tum ápi ghnanti yā́ vehád bhávati

The plants indeed destroy the childbearing of her who becomes barren.

Since the value of the ātreyī is her fitness for conception, and since the story told in ŚB I.4.5.12–13 involves a miscarriage, this idiom fits well. However, the later dharma texts do not understand it this way (having only √han without preverb). Moreover, api appears to be in the wrong syntactic position for a preverb in tmesis in this period. In an informal collection of approximately seventy-five examples of tmesis in Vedic prose (both BYV Saṃhitās and Brāhmaṇas, including both ŚB and JB), the preverb is always in first position in its clause (unless preceded by a vocative, which by its nature is extraclausal). So, an interpretation with api simply as adverb may be preferable, despite the semantic fit of the lexeme api √han. (For further discussion of this lexeme, cf. Bodewitz 1977, p. 155 and n. 13.)

But, more interestingly, this proposed use of the instrumental to make reference to a well-known legal provision seems to be found already in the BYV Saṃhitās.

> MS IV.6.4. (≅ KS XXVII.9) tásmād ávijñātena gárbheṇa bhrūṇahā́
> [Lit.] Therefore (he is) an embryo killer with an unknown embryo.

This statement makes little literal sense, but it is immediately clear if it is understood as a citation of the legal provision concerning the killer of an 'embryo of unknown (sex)', a provision adjacent to the one about the ātreyī in several law texts.[129]

> MDŚ XI.87 hatvā garbham avijñātam etad eva vrataṃ caret . . . ātreyīm eva ca striyam
>
> Having killed/struck an embryo of unknown (sex) (or) an ātreyī woman, he should perform the (aforementioned) penance.[130]

One can then translate the MS/KS passage:

> Therefore (one is known/condemned as) an embryo killer/abortionist, by (the legal provision about) an embryo of unknown (sex).[131]

The rhetorical structure, as in the ŚB passage, gives the abbreviated law in the instrumental, representing the victim, and the charge against the perpetrator in the nominative.

[129]Notice also that the provision is found in the section of the MS that contains the story of the rivalry of Speech and Mind, a story that concludes in the ŚB with Atri's abortion.

[130]Also ĀpDS I.24.8, GautDS XXII.13.

[131]Though this pursuit is not strictly relevant to our mythological concerns, it might be useful to clarify what this curious provision about an 'embryo of unknown (sex)' is about. The reference must be to aborting a child that is still in the womb, hence (in those days before amniocentesis) of unknown sex. This is implicitly contrasted with killing a child immediately after birth, when its sex has been revealed. Needless to say, the children killed at that later point would be girls, and (at least in the BYV Saṃhitās) there seems to be little or no guilt attached to the act. In both the KS and the MS passages just cited, tásmād ávijñātena gárbheṇa bhrūṇahā́ (Therefore (one is known/condemned as) an embryo-killer (/an abortionist), by (the legal provision about) an embryo of unknown (sex)) is soon followed (within one or two lines) by the statement

> tásmāt stríyaṃ jātā́ṃ parā́syanti ná púmāṁsam
>
> Therefore they throw away [expose] a newborn female, (but) not a male.

Abortion is condemned because it risks destroying a boy, not because of a general "pro-life" stance.

Note that if legal citations can be made with this shorthand economy already in the MS/KS, a legal code of fairly rigid formulation must have been in existence and well-known already at the time of the composition of early Vedic prose. This conclusion, though not surprising in itself, could have some influence on our views of the later dharma texts and their relation to other Indian literature.

3. The Ātreyī in Atri's Mythology

We are now in a better position to understand how the patronymic ātreyī came to have the peculiar value 'woman after her period'. First, note that the word is used only in one context, that of killing: she is always cheated not only of her life but also of her fertility. In the ŚB the legal provision regarding her is introduced by a story about the seer Atri's bungled birth by miscarriage. The Vādhūla Sūtra version of this story (the only other one existing, as far as I know), though garbled, is even more explicitly violent. Speech seems to have been forcibly aborted by Mind.

> VādhS no. 79 [= *AO* 6, p. 195] vāk ca ha vai manaś ca yajñaṃ parigr̥hṇānāv aitāṃ tasyai ha vāco manasā paryāptāyā apriyeṇa garbho 'sraṃsata so 'trir r̥ṣir abravīt [→ *abhavat] sā devān abravīd imaṃ me bhiṣajyateti . . .

> Speech and Mind went grasping the worship around. Of her, Speech, encompassed/surrounded (?) by Mind in an unfriendly act (or 'by her enemy Mind'?), the embryo 'fell'. It *became the r̥ṣi Atri. She said to the gods, "Heal him for me!" . . .

As we will shortly see, Atri is in fact the very symbol of an aborted fetus. Given this, it is not surprising that his mother could be the corresponding symbol of the aborting miscarrying mother. Now remember that killing an ātreyī is so bad because it is robbing her family of her power to conceive, and that even keeping a pubescent girl unmarried is tantamount to abortion. Therefore, it is reasonable that Atri's mother, as the symbol of aborted motherhood, should come to stand for a woman in this situation.[132]

[132]We need now to account for why ātreyī seems to mean literally '*descendant* of Atri'. Remember that there is no shorthand way of referring to one's parents; so all we need is to flip generations, as well as reading the vr̥ddhi in a more liberal light 'belonging/relating to Atri'.

The semantic channel for this change from proper to common noun[133] must be something like the following: Originally ātreyī was a term applied to women particularly fit for conception and childbearing whose fertility was violently interfered with—just like Atri's mother. The term became particularly associated with a legal provision, a provision that condemns the violence against such a woman. This could be verbosely paraphrased as "one should not strike/ kill a woman (so that she becomes) an ātreyī/like Atri's mother." Then, since the violence against the woman is explicit in the wording of the law (e.g., JB II.219 yaḥ . . . hanti 'who strikes/kills [the ātreyī]'), it is possible to reinterpret ātreyī as a neutral term referring to a potentially fertile woman—not to a woman whose potential fertility has been destroyed, as the original mythological locus requires. Except in the later lexica ātreyī never appears in a neutral context in which the potential fertility has any chance of reaching fruition, but only in the context of violence to it.

The meaning of the common noun ātreyī and its mythic associations add a special resonance to the one other occurrence of this word in Vedic. Recall that Apālā is so called in the JB account of her distress:

JB I.220 *apālā* ha vā *ātreyī* tilakāvā rucchvasā vāpy āsa

Apālā Ātreyī . . .

On the one hand, the word is simply a straightforward patronymic here: 'Apālā, daughter of Atri', a genetic filiation that ties her to Atri's mythic cure for skin disease and the production of hair. But, taken in its legal meaning, it pointedly underlines the troubling situation Apālā finds herself in. As an adolescent girl, Apālā asks for the outward signs of womanhood; she also yearns for fertility and, albeit hesitantly, for a husband. But, if Apālā has reached menarche and is still husbandless, then she is truly ātreyī, in the legal meaning of the term; her fertility is cheated every month, since not marrying off a daughter once she has started menstruating is equivalent to monthly abortion. Given the rarity of the word ātreyī in this period and its highly charged contexts,

[133]Notice that in its earliest appearances in this meaning the word is actually an adjective: 'an ātreyī woman': ātreyī strī (ŚBK II.4.2.15 tásmād ápi *stríyātréyya*inasvī́ty āhuḥ; JB II.219 tasmād yo 'py *ātreyīṃ striyaṃ* hanti); ātreyī yoṣit (ŚBM I.4.5.13 tásmād ápy *ātreyyā́ yoṣíta*inasvī́). The adjectival use suggests that it is the *quality* or *experience* of some particular woman or group of women that is being identified, not a woman herself.

I think we must allow for a lurking reference to the dharmic meaning of the word in this apparently innocent patronymic applied to Apālā.

Although Atri's dangerous birth is related straightforwardly only here (as far as I know), in the two ŚB passages and the Vādhūla Sūtra passage just cited, the story must have been extremely well known and in fact emblematic for the word ātreyī to acquire the meaning it has. Indeed, disguised yet powerful echoes of Atri's birth are found elsewhere, notably already in the RV, as well as in the Śrauta Sūtras.

C. Atri as Symbol of Abortion in the Śrauta Sūtras

The Ātreya-brahman figures in two places in the ritual as set forth in the Śrauta Sūtras. We have already mentioned his receiving of gold as Dakṣiṇā at the midday pressing of the soma sacrifice.[134] His other role is far more peculiar.

At the end of the Aśvamedha, after the purificatory bath (Avabhṛtha), a man is hired, often at an extravagant price (one hundred, two hundred, or even a thousand cows, plus or minus a wagon),[135] and driven into a river or the bath. Libations are poured on his head, sometimes of the blood of the dead horse, and then he is often driven away. The man chosen is required to be almost monstrously deformed, ugly, and diseased, and the mantras accompanying the libations are very curious. Although not all of the treatments of this episode mention the identity of the man, a number of the Śrauta Sūtras specify an Ātreya, a 'descendant of Atri'.[136] A relatively restrained description of this event follows:[137]

> ĀpŚS XX.22.6 avabhṛthena pracaryātreyaṃ śipiviṣṭaṃ khalatiṃ viklidhaṃ śuklaṃ piṅgākṣaṃ tilakāvalam avabhṛtham abhyavanīya tasya mūrdhañ juhoti mṛtyave svāhā bhrūṇahatyāyai svāhā jumbakāya svāheti tisraḥ

[134]See also Chap. 9, C.1.

[135]100: ĀpŚS, BŚS, HirŚS, VādhS. 200: alternative in ĀpŚS, HirŚS. 1000: ŚāṅkhŚS. Wagon: ĀpŚS, BŚS, HirŚS.

[136]So BŚS, ĀpŚS, and HirŚS, belonging to the TS, and ŚāṅkhŚS, belonging to the RV. Not all of the Śrauta Sūtras specify an Ātreya; he is not found, for example, in the TB, which treats the procedure relatively fully (III.9.15.1–3). The minimal treatments of MŚS and VārŚS also fail to mention an Ātreya.

[137]Cf. BŚS XV.37, ŚāṅkhŚS XVI.18.18ff., KātyŚS XX.8.16ff., HirŚS XIV.5.3–8, VādhS 99 (*AO* IV, pp. 202f.), VārŚS III.4.5.17, MŚS IX.2.5.25, ŚB XIII.3.6.5, TB III.9.15.2.

After the final bath, he leads an Ātreya (who is) śipiviṣṭa (?), bald, viklidha,[138] white (with leprosy? or leukoderma?), yellow-eyed, spotted, into the bath and pours three (libations) on his head, (saying), "To death, hail! To abortion (embryo killing), hail! To Jumbaka, hail!"

The Śrauta Sūtras differ on the exact description of this monstrous creature. Baudhāyana and Śāṅkhāyana are especially extravagant in their adjectives, but most treatments agree on the following core adjectives, all of which are found in the Āpastambha passage just quoted:

śukla- 'whitish' or 'afflicted with white leprosy' (?)
viklidha- 'leprous' (?Caland)/'having projecting teeth' (?Lüders)
piṅgākṣa- 'yellow-eyed'
khalati- 'bald'

These adjectives are found in almost all of the texts that treat the episode to any significant extent. Another description, 'spotted, having a skin disease' (tilakāvala- / tilakavant-), is also found in about half of the texts.[139]

The mantras also contribute to the disturbing mood: "Hail to Death. Hail to abortion (lit. embryo killing). Hail to Jumbaka." This last, Jumbaka, is said to be a name of Varuṇa by both ŚB (XIII.3.6.5) and TB (III.9.15.3), but there is no way to evaluate this identification, since the name or epithet occurs only in this invocation, as far as I know, and it has no satisfactory etymology.[140]

[138]The meaning of viklidha is not entirely clear. Caland renders it as 'leprous' (ad loc.), while Lüders (1938, pp. 142ff.) interprets it as meaning 'with protruding teeth'.

[139]Tilakāvala- (ĀpŚS, HirŚS, ŚāṅkhŚS); tilakavant- (BŚS).

[140]The ŚB passage:

ŚB XIII.3.6.5 jumbakā́ya svā́héty avabhr̥thá uttamā́m ā́hutiṃ juhoti váruṇo vaí jumbakáḥ sākṣā́d evá váruṇam ávayajate śuklásya khalatér viklidhásya piṅgākṣásya mūrdháni juhoty etád vaí váruṇasya rūpám

(Saying) "Hail to Jumbaka," he offers the last oblation at the final bath. Jumbaka is really Varuṇa. Thus by worship he banishes Varuṇa in bodily form. He offers on the head of (a man, who is) white (with leukoderma), bald, viklidha, yellow-eyed. For that is the form of Varuṇa.

This identification of Jumbaka, and by extension of the (Ātreya) victim, with Varuṇa has been extensively discussed by Kuiper 1979, pp. 213–22 (with further literature). He points out (p. 220) the striking similarity between the traits of the victim in our ritual and those of the curious stock figure, the Vidūṣaka, in later Sanskrit drama, and suggests (p. 221) that "both the character and the traditional (but theoretical) outward appearance of the vidūṣaka date back to Vedic ritual. . . . In its origin the deformity of

It is probably not surprising that a procedure so liberally provided with startling features has attracted attention before now. Hillebrandt sees it as a remnant of human sacrifice: the new king used to kill the old king at the end of his reign, but now he hires a substitute for this ceremonial role in the form of an image of Varuṇa.[141] Keith disputes Hillebrandt's interpretation, with reason, I believe.[142] In turn, he suggests that this is a purificatory ritual: the hideous Ātreya functions as a scapegoat and takes on the sins of the village outcasts. There is more textual support for this view than for Hillebrandt's. As Keith points out, several texts do suggest that sin is removed by the ritual.

ŚāṅkhŚS XVI.18.21 niḥṣiddhapāpmāno 'pagrāmā bhavantīti

"Those who have been expelled out of their community are . . . freed of their bad lot," (they say).[143]

---

the vidūṣaka had no connection whatsoever with dramatic performance but was simply the deformity of the Vedic scapegoat" (i.e., the victim in our ritual).

This suggested connection seems quite convincing: it would not be surprising for so peculiar a figure as our victim to be represented in the later tradition. What I am less certain about is the identification with Varuṇa, which rests on the mysterious Jumbaka and his supposed equivalence with Varuṇa. According to Kuiper, "The Vedic jumbaka was not ridiculed for his corporeal defects, which were considered a varuṇa-lakṣanam (TĀ) [mark of Varuṇa]. His deformity was due to being a human image of Varuṇa." Though Kuiper's theory fits with the dedication to Jumbaka and the ŚB/TB naming of Jumbaka as Varuṇa, it cannot explain the two other mantras ('To death, hail; to abortion, hail') or the identity of the victim as an Ātreya. And in fact Kuiper does not actually address these issues.

Moreover, the evidence that Varuṇa was conceived of as hideous rests primarily on the ŚB/TB passages just cited, as well as the TĀr passage mentioned by Kuiper, which is clearly derivative of the other two:

TĀr I.2.3 paṭáro víklidhaḥ piṅgáḥ / etád varuṇalákṣaṇam

Paṭara (?), viklidha, yellow(-eyed). That is the mark of Varuṇa.

As Stanley Insler has pointed out (pers. comm.), the term varuṇa-lákṣaṇam 'mark of Varuṇa' need not refer to Varuṇa's appearance, but to a mark he puts on others (like the mark of Zorro). Otherwise, as Lüders admits (1938, p. 143, n. 4), citing Caland, Varuṇa's epithets do not suggest a demonic appearance.

Because of the tenuousness of the link between Varuṇa and the Ātreya victim in this ritual, it seems likely to me that the principal association was between the victim and Atri of Vedic mythology, though secondarily Varuṇa may have become part of this complex because of his fearsome aspects.

141 Hillebrandt 1929, vol. 2, p. 28, n. 4. Even if this interpretation fit the described action better than it does, one might think this would be more appropriate for the Rājasūya (royal consecration ritual).

142 Keith 1925, pp. 262f.

143 Caland's translation (1953, ad loc.). Cf. also KātyŚS XX.8.17–18.

Moreover, in a number of texts the victim is driven away, and/or warned not to remain anymore in the territory (presumably of the Yajamāna).

> VādhS no. 99[144] tasmā anoyuktaṃ ca śataṃ ca dattvāha kṣattar etad etasmā upa kurv athainaṃ nirvaha mā me vijite vātsīr iti
>
> Having given him a yoked wagon and a hundred (cows), he (the Yajamāna?) says, "Attendant, furnish this (payment) to him; then convey him forth, (saying), 'Do not abide in the (territory) conquered by me.'"

This banishment of the hideous victim does suggest some sort of purification (though by no means necessarily a scapegoat ritual), but before it is possible to address the larger questions the action raises, one must look at some apparently minor and very specific points. Why is this man an Ātreya, and what relevance do the mantras have to his appearance and family membership? Focussing on these details in this ritual vignette will help explain why this bizarre, seemingly self-contained episode was apparently grafted onto the Aśvamedha. The episode appears to be a sort of ritualized playlet, dramatizing parts of several myths that center on the figure of Atri. The two myths most relevant are that of Apālā Ātreyī and that of the birth of Atri himself.

The Apālā myth helps explain some details of the appearance of the Ātreya in the ritual skit. As we saw above, the maiden Apālā performs a private soma sacrifice to Indra, asking in return that her skin should become clear and that 'hair' should grow in three places: on her father's head, on her belly, and, as grain, in the fields.

In the JB version, Apālā's skin affliction is described thus: JB I.220 apālā ha vā ātreyī *tilakāvā rucchvasā vāpy* āsa. Though the second word appears to be corrupt, the first, tilakāvā, is exactly the word that describes the blemished victim in the Śrauta Sūtras. Similarly, the JB describes Apālā's father as khalati- 'bald', the same word as in the ŚSs (JB I.220 khalatir hāsyai pitāsa / taṃ hākhalatiṃ cakāra 'Her father was bald: he made him not bald'). Since Apālā's patronymic is Ātreyī, her father is (or can be) Atri. Though our ritual treatment telescopes into one person, the Ātreya victim, the attributes of two people in the Apālā myth (Apālā's skin and her father's baldness), the verbal and thematic

[144]Caland 1926b (*AO* IV), pp. 202f. Similar BŚS, ŚāṅkhŚS.

echoes in the ritual material seem to me a striking reference to the Apālā Ātreyī story.

The story of Atri's birth is even more dramatically encoded in the ritual action. As we just saw, Atri is, in fact, the result of a miscarriage or abortion. Now we already know the Vedic view of miscarried fetuses: they do not have a human form. In a parallel myth we examined above, the aborted or miscarried last son of Aditi, Mārtāṇḍa, is described in the following terms:

> ŚB III.1.3.3 ávikr̥taṁ hāṣṭamáṃ janayā́ṃ cakāra mārtāṇḍáṁ saṃdeghó haivā́sa yā́vān evórdhvás tā́vāṃs tiryáṅ
>
> She bore an eighth, unshaped: Mārtāṇḍa. He was (just) a lump, as broad as he was tall.

In order to make him human, the dead parts must be cut off (apa √kr̥t) and the remaining material shaped (vi √kr̥).[145]

If the Aśvamedha ritual fragment under consideration actually makes indirect reference to Atri's failed birth, then the dreadful, almost inhuman appearance of the Ātreya victim makes sense. He represents the miscarried/aborted fetus; his appearance reflects the unformed or deformed shape of an embryo not brought to term. And now, in this context, the terrible invocations, mr̥tyave svāhā bhrūṇahatyāyai svāhā 'To death, hail, to abortion, hail!', also make sense. These are said as libations are poured on the head of the Ātreya, on the symbolic product of the abortion that is being verbally celebrated. The deformed Ātreya in the ritual physically represents, in all his ugliness, the aborted Atri of the myth.

But why should this appalling spectacle be appended to one of the great Vedic rituals, whose purpose is to affirm and extend the power and position of the sacrificer who ordered it? The answer again lies in the mythic background. Both stories—Apālā Ātreyī and the birth of Atri—have a larger purpose and a successful issue. Apālā desires and acquires sexual maturity and fertility. Similarly, Atri achieves, as we will see, the result of fertility, a successful birth—though only the second time around. This second birth effectively neutralizes the bad effects of the first one. I would suggest that the grisly ceremony embedded in the Aśvamedha, with its shocking invocations, is a way of

[145]See KS XI.6, ŚB III.1.3.4, quoted above.

recognizing and controlling the terrible consequences of fertility and gestatation gone awry—the aborted, inhuman fetus rather than the full-term, perfectly formed infant. By invoking abortion they acknowledge its power, *but* by invoking it while libating an *Ātreya,* they undercut its power. After all Atri survived an abortion and lived to tell the tale. So, indeed, does his 'descendant', the Ātreya, who emerges from the water some hundred or more cows the richer. True, he is driven off: sympathetic magic cannot remove his physical blemishes. But he carries away the gruesome power of abortion, leaving behind only the positive powers of fertility, as they have been expressed elsewhere in the Aśvamedha (for example, in the notorious coupling of the king's wife with the dead horse).

So, this minor episode in one of the great Vedic rituals embodies in disguised form most of the major elements in the myths clustered around Atri, Apālā, and Svarbhānu. The Ātreya-victim has the blemished skin and baldness that are found in both the Apālā and the Svarbhānu myths and that need to be healed: the skin of Apālā and of the sun, the baldness of Apālā's father (Atri) and of the earth. And he is addressed with a mantra that recalls his ill-managed birth. He is addressed three times, just as Apālā's skin is removed three times and the sun's darkness is smashed away three times,[146] and he is immersed in water, indeed, according to some texts,[147] in the final bath (Avabhṛtha-), which removes impurities just as the wiping of Apālā/Sūrya does. The neatness with which the ritual details, unintelligible in themselves, represent crucial elements in a complex set of myths seems to me a textbook example of the interpenetration of myth and ritual in these texts.

D. Atri's Second Birth

1. *Atri's Kettle in the RV*

In the RV Atri is known principally for two things—he rescues the sun in the Svarbhānu hymn and, far more frequently, he is himself rescued from confinement, usually by the Aśvins. The place of his confinement is variously described. It is sometimes called dark (támas-) and narrow (áṃhas-), as in

[146]Though, since three is a standard number in myth and folktale, one cannot invest too much importance in this.

[147]E.g., ŚB XIII.3.6.5, ĀpŚS XX.22.6, VārŚS III.4.5.17.

RV VII.71.5 nír áṃhasas támasa spartam átrim

You two (Aśvins) won Atri forth from narrowness, from darkness.

But it is most commonly characterized as 'heated' (taptá-),[148] and the place itself is either a 'kettle' (gharmá-)[149] or an ṛbī́sa-. The latter word is almost confined to the RV and to Atri's predicament, and, though sometimes taken as 'stove, oven', it seems better interpreted with Baunack as 'glühend heisse Erdvertiefung', a 'glowing, hot cleft in the earth' (presumably emitting steam and so forth).[150] Following are passages with Atri both in the gharmá- and in the ṛbī́sa-:

RV X.80.3 agnír átriṃ gharmá uruṣyad antáḥ

[148]Támas-: RV VI.50.10, VII.71.5; áṃhas-: I.117.3, VII.71.5; taptá-: I.112.7, I.118.7, I.119.6, X.39.9.

[149]Gharmá- of course has several meanings besides 'kettle', including 'heat' itself and the hot drink warmed in the gharma-kettle. The interpretation of the Atri myth is considerably complicated by the fact that gharma- as 'hot drink' also figures importantly in the story. The Aśvins both *rescue* Atri *from* the gharma-kettle and *give to* him a gharma-drink, as in

RV V.73.6 yuvór átriś ciketati, nárā sumnéna cétasā
gharmáṃ yád vām arepásaṃ, nā́satyāsnā́ bhuraṇyáti

Atri thinks of you two with benevolent sense, O men, when he eagerly seeks your flawless gharma(-drink) with his mouth, O Nāsatyas [=Aśvins].

The double role of gharmá- in this tale has been recognized at least since Bergaigne (1878–83, vol. 2, pp. 470ff.); cf. also Geldner (e.g., ad V.73.6a), Renou (*ÉVP* vol. 16, ad VIII.73.3, though with less conviction). Velankar's attempt (1962, pp. 228–37) to render all examples of gharmá- in this story as 'hot drink' often does violence to the text and requires interpreting other lexical items and syntactic constructions in perverse or extremely vague fashion.

For the record, I take the gharmá- of at least X.80.3, I.112.7, I.119.6, VIII.73.7 as referring to the kettle, rather than the drink. For a taptá- gharmá- 'heated gharmá-' clearly meaning 'kettle' (not in an Atri episode), cf. RV V.30.15 gharmáś cit taptáḥ. . . ayasmáyaḥ 'the heated kettle made of metal'.

[150]ṛbī́sa-: RV I.116.8, I.117.3, V.78.4, X.39.9. 'Stove, oven': Geldner, ad I.116.8; Mayrhofer, *KEWA, EWA*, s.v. 'Earth-cleft': Baunack 1896, pp. 280–84; cf. Debrunner, *Nachträge* to Wackernagel-Debrunner, *AIG*, vol. 1, p. 130; also Grassmann, Monier-Williams both s.v. An alternative interpretation is that an ṛbī́sa is a man-made? trench or ditch in which ashes (still live) are deposited (cf. e.g, Roth, cited by Baunack 1896, p. 282; Mayrhofer, *EWA*). For our purposes this would make no difference. Velankar (1962, pp. 230f.) interprets ṛbī́sa as meaning "a big hollow in a very old and big tree, reaching down deep in the bowels of the earth." Though he gives no arguments for this bizarre gloss, I assume it rests on verses like RV V.78.5–6, in which the Aśvins open up a tree for Saptavadhri, a figure who may (or may not) be identical to Atri. I think we are wiser to treat that episode separately.

Agni released (lit. made wideness for) Atri in the kettle.

RV I.116.8 r̥bī́se átrim aśvinā́vanītam, únninyathuḥ . . .

You two (Aśvins) led up Atri, who had descended into the earth-cleft.

RV X.39.9 yuvám r̥bī́sam utá taptám átraya, ómanvantaṃ
cakrathuḥ . . .

You two (Aśvins) made the heated earth-cleft cool[151] for Atri.

The remedy provided to Atri is sometimes characterized as omán-, ománvant-, omyā́vant-, which Geldner renders as 'Schutzmittel' (means of protection). This accords well with some other occurrences of omán- and its derivatives, as well as with a root etymology to √av 'help, favor'. But it is nonetheless tempting to follow Neisser in seeing in some occurrences of omán- and its derivatives a homonym (to omán- 'help, favor') meaning 'coldness'.[152] Since the problem Atri faces is heat, a specific solution—'coolness'—seems preferable to a general one—'favor, help'. Indeed, the usual solution specified is that the Aśvins neutralized the heat 'with snow.'[153]

RV VIII.73.3 úpa str̥ṇītam átraye, hiména gharmám aśvinā

O Aśvins, you bestrewed the kettle with snow, for Atri.

[151]The gender of r̥bī́sa- is given as neuter (cf. Grassmann; Monier-Williams; Mayrhofer, *KEWA, EWA* s.v. [following the Naighaṇṭuka, as Baunack points out, 1896, p. 267]). If this were the case, the usual interpretation of X.39.9 would not be possible, as ománvantam is masculine in form but would be modifying the neuter accusative r̥bī́sam. But there are no diagnostic passages in the RV for the gender of r̥bī́sa-: the two occurrences of r̥bī́sam (V.78.4, X.39.9) are both syntactically accusative and therefore ambiguous in gender between masculine and neuter. Baunack (loc. cit.) has already suggested that for Vedic at least we must reckon (also?) with a masculine stem.

[152]Omán-: I.118.7, VII.68.5; ománvant-: X.39.9; omyā́vant-: I.112.7. 'Schutzmittel': e.g., Geldner's translation of X.39.9—"Ihr versahet für Atri den glühenden Ofen mit einem Schutzmittel" (You outfitted the stove/oven with a means of protection for Atri). 'Coldness': Neisser 1891, pp. 244ff.; in substantial agreement, Renou Introduction générale to Wackernagel-Debrunner, *AIG,* vol. 1, p. 53, n. 70, with literature; Oldenberg, *Noten,* ad I.112.7; Mayrhofer, *KEWA,* sub omā́ (but in *EWA,* sub omán-, he rejects a second omán 'coldness' as unnecessary).

[153]Cf. I.116.8, I.119.6, VIII.73.3.

The passages with omán(vant)- 'coolness' would simply allude to the same solution.[154]

Now so far this tale about Atri conforms to the usual pattern of scattered, semicomprehensible allusions to the Aśvins' good deeds, but recalls very little about Atri's birth in the ŚB. The only potential link, so far, is the kettle: the aborted fetus of Atri is placed in a skin or a kettle in ŚBK:

> ŚBK II.4.2.15 tád u hedáṃ devā́ rétaḥ siktáṃ cármaṇi vā *kumbhyā́ṃ vā* babhruḥ
>
> The gods then collected/carried this poured-out seed in a skin *or a pot*.[155]

2. *A Disguised Parallel in the JB*

The semantic connection between the RVic allusions and the ŚB tale is found in a JB passage already cited by Geldner (ad RV I.116.8) as parallel to the RVic Atri saga. This is a story of the mortal world, and the identity of the participants is quite different from the RV/ŚB. But the stories are parallel in outline, and, in particular, the mainspring of the action involves a descent into, and rescue from, an arvīṣa-, clearly a phonologically normalized form of RVic ṛbī́sa-.[156] The four occurrences of ṛbī́sa- in the RV and the occurrences of arvīṣa- in JB I.151 are the only attestations of these two related words in the Saṃhitās and Brāhmaṇas,[157] this shared isolation would be enough to suggest a connection, even if the stories were not otherwise so similar.

In this tale two brothers on a journey are approached by a woman with a feverish child. She asks them to heal her child. Unaccountably

[154]Geldner recognizes this de facto by equating the Schutzmittel of I.118.7 with Schnee 'snow' in his notes.

[155]ŚBM is vaguer: I.4.5.13 rétaś cárman vā yásmin vā babhruḥ 'They carried the seed in a skin or something'.

[156]Both the plain (rather than retroflexed) *s* after *ī* and the plain (rather than aspirated) *b* of ṛbī́sa- give the word a markedly non-Sanskritic appearance.

[157]Ṛbīsa is found marginally in the ŚSūtras, in the compound ṛbīsapakva- 'cooked by/in an ṛbīsa'.

> ĀpŚS V.25.6 narbīsapakvasyāśnīyāt
>
> He shouldn't eat (anything) cooked by/in an ṛbīsa.

(≅MŚS I.5.6.14, HirŚS VI.5.24, BhārŚS V.6.19, etc.; cf. VārŚS I.4.3.42.)

angry, they contemptuously order her to throw the child into a cleft, and she does so. On their return they find the child still in the cleft and, feeling contrite, raise the child and heal him:

JB I.151 paurumīḍhaṃ dakṣonidhanam āyuṣkāmaḥ kurvīta / tarantapurumīḍhau vai vaitadaśvī māheyau mahyā ārcanānasyai putrau / tau ha yantau strī paryetyovāca putrasya vai tyasyā upatapati / taṃ sma me cikitsatam iti /tau ha krudhyantāv ivocatuḥ kathaṃ nāv itthaṃ brūyād iti taṃ vā arvīṣa upavapeti / sā heyaṃ strī śraddhāya devarṣī mā mantrakr̥tāv avocatām ity arvīṣa upovāpa / tau ha punar āyantau paretyovāca yaṃ vai kumāram avocatam arvīṣa upavapety ayaṃ vai so 'rvīṣa upoptaś śeta iti / tau hāsādhv iva kr̥tvā menāte / tāv akāmayetām ud ita iyāva gātuṃ nāthaṃ vindevahi sam ayaṃ kumāro jīved[158] iti / sa etat purumīḍhas sāmāpaśyat / tenāstuta *agnim īḷiṣvāvase, gāthābhiś śīraśociṣam / agniṃ rāye purumīḍha śrutaṃ naraḥ* // ko nāma kumāra iti /sudītir nāmeti /tam agnis sudītaye chardir ity evābhyamr̥śat / sa tānto niravartata / tam etena nidhanena samairayad dakṣāyā iti

One desiring a (full) lifetime should perform the Paurumīḍha (Sāman) with (the word) dakṣa as finale. Taranta[159] and Purumīḍha Vaitadaśvi [= patronymic] Māheya [= metronymic] were the (two) sons of Mahī Ārcanāna [= their mother]. A woman, coming up to the two as they were going, said, "My son has a fever. Heal him for me." They as if angry said, "How can (anyone) talk to us in this way? Throw him in an earth-cleft." The woman, having trust, (thinking), "Divine seers, mantra-makers, said (this) to me," threw him into an earth-cleft.

Going up to them on their return, she said, "The boy you said 'throw (him) in a cleft' is (still) lying there, thrown into the cleft." They thought they had acted pretty ignobly, and wished, "Let us come up out of this; let us find a way out, a help. Let this boy live." Purumīḍha saw this sāman. He praised with it: "Call upon sharp-flamed Agni for help, with songs. / Agni the famed for wealth, O Purumīḍha. Men . . ." [= RV VIII.71.14abc]. (He said), "What is the boy's name?" "Sudīti" (lit. 'Very Bright'). He touched him, (saying), "Agni/fire (should be) a protection for the bright one/for Sudīti."[160] He (Sudīti) came out (of the cleft), (but

[158]Following Caland 1919. Crit. Ed. prints jīvad.

[159]On the Indo-European connections of this name, cf. Watkins, forthcoming.

[160]This sentence, "Agni (should be) a protection for the bright one (/for Sudīti)", which fits the story so well, is only a slight alteration of the final pāda of the verse quoted immediately above (as set to the sāman):

RV VIII.71.14d agníṃ sudītáye chardíḥ

(Men [supply from pāda c]) call upon) Agni (as) a protection for the Bright One,

he was still) fainted away/benighted. With the final passage (of the sāman) "for ability" (dakṣāyai), he fixed him up/reinvigorated him.[161]

The RVic echoes are obvious: most clearly, the two men asked to heal (cikitsatam) the child are the representatives of the Aśvins, the heavenly twin physicians who rescue Atri in the RV. Indeed, one of the two men in the JB passage, Purumīḍha, is mentioned in the RV as connected both with the Aśvins *and* with Atri:

RV I.183.5 *yuvā́ṃ* gótamaḥ *purumīḷhó átrir,* dásrā hávaté 'vase havíṣmān
. . . nāsatyā . . .

You two, O masters, O Nāsatyas [= Aśvins], (did) Gotama, *Purumīdha, Atri,* call upon; (you) (does) the offerer call upon for help.

As in the RV there is a dangerous descent into the cleft (ṛbī́sa-/ arvīṣa-). Though the cleft is not explicitly heated in the JB passage, the child himself *is:* he is suffering from a fever (upatapati). The element of heat has just been differently assigned. Even the condition of the child on coming out of the cleft, tānta-, may recall a feature of Atri's RVic experience. Tānta- is the past participle to root √tam (pres. tāmyati); though specialized to mean 'be faint, swoon', its etymological connection to támas- 'darkness'[162] remains synchronically clear, and 'bedimmed' or 'benighted' may suggest the appropriate nuance. Remember that Atri is released also from darkness (támas-) in the RV (VI.50.10, VII.71.5). In this context the child's name Sudīti 'Very Bright' (more lit. 'having good brilliance') is wishful thinking, designed to banish his mental and physical darkness.[163]

But what is this story about? I would submit that the ŚB/VādhS descriptions of Atri's birth furnish the key. In these Atri's mother miscarries or aborts; the JB simply presents an even more violent

---

with accusative agním, rather than the nominative agnis that serves as subject in the JB climax.

[161]This passage has been translated by Caland (1919, sec. 44) and O'Flaherty (1985a, p. 80). The latter renders arvīṣa as 'ditch', which fails to capture the sinister nature of the place, and tāntaḥ as 'in that very condition' (mistaking it for tāvān/tāvat or tathā?). She also classifies it with tales expressing "fear of the father," a connection that I fail to see.

[162]Cf. Mayrhofer, *KEWA,* vol. 1, sub tā́myati.

[163]Though it is also, of course, extracted from Purumīḍha's sāman. See n. 160.

version of this: the child's mother casts him into a cleft.[164] This cleft corresponds to the skin or kettle of the ŚB—and both function as a second surrogate womb from which the child can emerge by a more successful birth. Now if the cleft (arvīṣa) in the JB is a surrogate womb, and the child's emergence from it is a second birth, then the cleft (r̥bī́sa) in which Atri is confined in the RV can also be seen as such a womb, and his rescue from it also a second birth.

The Vedic Indians also interpreted the cryptic RVic references to Atri's ordeal as a symbolic birth, as RV V.78 shows. This is a nine-versed Aśvin hymn of a particular shape: the first three verses invoke the Aśvins with simplicity; the second three allude to rescues they have performed; and the third set is a charm for safe childbirth. Verse 4 tells of Atri's ordeal, and is most closely tied to the final charm, since it compares Atri to a woman in need (i.e., at delivery).[165]

RV V.78.4 átrir yád vām avaróhann r̥bī́sam, ájohavīn nā́dhamāneva yóṣā

When Atri, descending into the cleft, invoked you two (Aśvins) like a woman in need.

The similarity between Atri's confinement in the r̥bī́sa and the embryo's delivery from the womb has not escaped commentators. Baunack elaborates on the parallels with sensitivity; his ultimate interpretation, however, is that an aged Atri dies (or dies symbolically) and is reborn as a young man.[166] O'Flaherty comments, "The Aśvins 'delivered' Atri from a pit as the child is delivered from the womb."[167]

[164]There is, in fact, a striking emphasis on motherhood in the JB passage. In addition to the sick child's mother, we hear far more than usual about the mother of the two young men. Taranta and Purumīḍha are first identified by their patronymic (vaitadaśvī) in common fashion, but then they are not only given a metronymic (māheyau 'descendants of Mahī'), but that metronymic is pleonastically expanded: mahyā ārcanānasyai putrau 'the two sons of Mahī, descendant of Arcanānas'. Their mother's name, Mahī, literally means 'the Great One'. This focus on the mother may be a disguised reminder of the inherent importance of Atri's mother, Vāc 'Speech', in the ŚB versions. O'Flaherty (1985a, pp. 80f.) also notes this uncommon emphasis on the mothers and comments, "Into this tale . . . the Jaiminīya has introduced two interesting women," though we learn nothing more of the mother of the two young men than her name.

[165]Cf. e.g., Geldner, ad loc.

[166]Baunack 1896, p. 286. In other words, the Aśvins make him young just as they made the old man Cyavana young in another well-known Aśvin exploit.

[167]Baunack 1896, p. 285; O'Flaherty 1981, p. 186. O'Flaherty's account of the rest of the myth, particularly her statement that Atri was locked away from his wife every

I would simply say that the situations are not merely similar, but actually identical, that Atri's successful second birth, after his perilous miscarriage, is meant to serve as pattern for a less eventful normal birth, as described in the last verse of the hymn:

RV V.78.9 dáśa mā́sāñ chaśayānáḥ, kumāró ádhi mātári
niraítu jīvó ákṣato, jīvó jī́vantyā ádhi

The child lying for ten months in his mother—
Let him come forth live, unharmed—live from her (also) being alive.

It is worth noting, in passing, that this hymn shares noteworthy formal features with RV V.40, the Svarbhānu hymn.[168] Both are, of course, found in the 5th Maṇḍala, the book of the Atri family, and together collect the known mythological exploits of their eponymous ancestor and employ them as charms.

Thus, according to the ŚB and Vādhūla Sūtra, Atri resulted from a miscarriage or abortion. The premature fetus is placed in a pot or a skin. The ŚB version of Atri's birth ends rather abruptly with the gods' makeshift assembling of the aborted material in this container. We do not know what becomes of it later, though Atri the seer is the ultimate happy result. The RV tells of Atri's release from a pot or cleft, once in the explicit context of childbirth. Here the *first* half of the story is missing. Seen from the perspective of the ŚB miscarriage tale, we can view Atri's "release" in the RV as a second birth from a surrogate womb, though in the RV the abortion/miscarriage is not mentioned. The JB story just quoted, though not explicitly about Atri, brings together the two halves of the story: the violent casting into a cleft of a child by its own mother (rather like an abortion) and its later release by an Aśvin-like pair. Atri (or in JB an Atri-like figure) is first miscarried and later successfully reborn from an artificial womb.

3. *Wombs and Their Substitutes*

Let us now examine some of the details in these variant tales that support this interpretation. The physical characteristics of Atri's place

night and released in the morning, has no textual support in Vedic that I know of, but rather rests on Sāyaṇa's introductory story to RV V.78.5. A different explanatory story is told in Bṛhaddev. V.82–84. Neither of these seems to be anything but a later rationalization of the cryptic hints given in the RV.

[168]Cf. Oldenberg 1888, p. 198f., and *Noten,* ad locc.

of confinement in the RV—narrowness and darkness—are certainly appropriate for a womb. And the skin (carman-) in which Atri's miscarried remains are placed in both ŚB versions is likewise appropriate for this later ritualistic text, for a skin figures prominently in the consecration (Dīkṣā) of the sacrificer in Vedic ritual, a ceremony often compared to a second birth. The consecrated one (Dīkṣita-) is wrapped in the skin (carman-) of a black antelope (kr̥ṣṇājina-), which is often identified with some part of the birth apparatus.

> AB 1.3 vāsasā prorṇuvanty ulbaṃ vā etad dīkṣitasya yad vāsa ulbenaivainaṃ tat prorṇuvanti kr̥ṣṇājinam uttaram bhavaty uttaraṃ vā ulbāj jarāyu jarāyuṇaivainaṃ tat prorṇuvanti . . . unmucya kr̥ṣṇājinam avabhr̥tham abhyavaiti tasmān muktā garbhā jarāyor jāyante

> They cover (the consecrated one) with a garment. This garment is the caul of the consecrated one. Thus they cover him with a caul. The black antelope (skin)[169] is on top. The placenta is on top of the caul. Thus they cover him with a placenta. . . . Releasing the black antelope (skin), he goes down into the bath. Therefore, released from the placenta, embryos are born.

Both the pot and the earth-cleft as places for a second gestation also have parallels elsewhere in a far better known Vedic story, that of Manu and the flood (ŚBM I.81. ≅ ŚBK II.7.3), and in several episodes in the MBh. At the beginning of the Manu tale, a small defenseless fish appears in Manu's handwashing water. He promises to save Manu from the great flood to come if Manu will raise him. Indeed, his first words to Manu are strikingly like those of the Yatis to Indra in the episode of the survivors:[170] the fish says simply *bibhr̥hí mā* 'Raise/bear me!' (ŚBM I.8.1.2, ŚBK II.7.3.1), which, as we saw, is a formula with coercive power. When Manu inquires how to do this (ŚBK II.7.3.2 katháṃ bhā́ryo 'si 'how are you to be raised?'; ŚBM katháṃ te bhŕ̥tiḥ 'how is your raising?'), the fish replies:

> ŚBM I.8.1.3 (≅ ŚBK II.7.3.2) yā́vad vaí kṣullakā́ bhávāmo bahvī́ vaí nas tā́van nāṣṭrā́ bhavaty utá mátsya evá mátsyaṃ gilati [ŚBK girati] *kumbhyā́ṃ* mā́gre bibharāsi sá yadā́ tā́m ativárdhā átha *karṣū́ṃ* khātvā́ tásyāṃ mā bibharāsi sá yadā́ tā́m ativárdhā átha mā samudrám abhyávaharāsi tárhi vā́ atināṣṭró bhavitā́smi

[169]The word cárman- 'skin' is often omitted in these passages, but that this word is to be supplied is clear from passages like ŚB III.2.1.8 (concerning this same stage in the consecration), where cárman- 'skin' is punningly identified with śárman- 'refuge'.
[170]See above Chap. 4, B.

As long as we're itty-bitty, there's a lot of destruction for us, and fish swallows[171] fish. You will keep/raise me *in a jar* at first. When I will outgrow this, having dug *a trench*, you will keep me in that. When I will outgrow that, then you will take me down to the ocean. Then I will be beyond destruction.[172]

The kumbhí- 'pot' is exactly the same vessel that holds Atri in the ŚBK version of his miscarriage. Though karṣū́- 'trench' is not verbally identical with the ṛbī́sa-/arvīṣa- 'earth-cleft' of the RV/JB, it seems semantically a man-made equivalent of that natural feature. Thus, just like Atri, the fish, too small to survive on its own, takes refuge in, or is raised in, two womblike containers until he can successfully reenter his natural medium.[173]

The MBh. presents a number of remarkably similar stories in which pots or other womblike enclosures are used to incubate not-yet-viable embryos. For example, the warrior Droṇa is so called because the spilled seed of his father Bharadvāja was placed in a trough or bucket (droṇī), whence he was born (see, e.g., MBh. I.57.89).

The eggs laid by the two sisters Kadrū and Vinatā were placed in 'sweating pots' for five hundred years:

MBh. I.14.13 tayor aṇḍāni nidadhuḥ . . .
sopasvedeṣu bhāṇḍeṣu, pañca varṣaśatāni ca

The eggs of these two they (the servants) deposited in sweating pots for five hundred years.

Kadrū's thousand sons hatch normally after this period, but when Vinatā breaks one of her two eggs in curiosity and anxiety, she finds a half-formed creature, like a fetus not brought to term.

Even closer to our Atri tale are two stories involving miscarriage or

[171]Note the same root √gir 'swallow, devour' as in the climactic plea of the sun in RV V.40.7 mā́ mā́m . . . ní *gārīt* 'Let him not swallow me'.

[172]Though this story occurs only in the ŚB, hence relatively late in Vedic, at least this portion looks linguistically earlier, because the subjunctive appears in its early Vedic usage. At this point the second-person subjunctive (as in bibharāsi, abhyavaharāsi) should have virtually disappeared, and the first person (as in ativardhai) should have imperative value. (Cf. Jamison 1987b, p. 173.)

Needless to say, this myth has been frequently treated in the secondary literature; see, e.g., Heesterman 1985, pp. 59–69.

[173]I am not suggesting that Atri had *two* second gestations, merely that both a pot and a trench suggest themselves to the Vedic mind as surrogate wombs.

abortion and a second gestation in a vessel. Vaidarbhī, wife of King Sagara, gives birth to a 'bottle-gourd embryo':

MBh. III.104.18 tataḥ kālena vaidarbhī garbhālābum vyajāyata

Then, after a time, Vaidarbhī brought forth a bottle-gourd embryo.

Sagara is about to discard this monstrous production, but is enjoined by a divine voice to remove the seeds from the gourd and keep each in a 'sweating pot':

MBh. III.104.20 alābumadhyān niṣkṛṣya, bījaṃ yatnena gopyatām
.21 sopasvedeṣu pātreṣu, ghṛtapūrṇeṣu bhāgaśaḥ

[The voice from heaven:] "Having extracted (the seeds) from the middle of the gourd, let (each) seed individually be guarded carefully
In sweating pots full of ghee."

Sixty thousand warlike sons are the ultimate result.

Most remarkably like the Atri story is the tale of Gāndhārī, Dhṛtaraṣṭra's wife. Pregnant for two years with no result, she finally *aborts* herself:

MBh. I.107.11 . . . yatnena mahatā tataḥ
sodaraṃ pātayām āsa, gāndhārī duḥkhamūrchitā

With great effort then, Gāndhārī, contorted with pain, aborted herself (lit. caused [the contents of] her womb to fall).

The result is an unformed ball of flesh, which she prepares to discard:

MBh. I.107.12 tato jajñe māṃsapeśī, lohāṣṭhīleva saṃhatā
dvivarṣasaṃbhṛtāṃ kukṣau, tām utsraṣṭum pracakrame

Then was born a hunk of flesh like a congealed globule of blood.
This, (which she had) carried in her belly for two years, she set out to throw away.

But, as in the case of Vaidarbhī and Sagara, there is divine (or semi-divine) intervention, and another course is counselled. The seer

Dvaipāyana Vyāsa, the legendary composer of the Mahābhārata, who had promised Gāndhārī one hundred sons, tells her to prepare one hundred pots filled with ghee and to sprinkle the aborted flesh with cold water. The ball then divides into one hundred tiny embryos, which are kept in the pots. When they develop sufficiently, the pots are to be broken open.

MBh. I.107.18 ghṛtapūrṇaṃ kuṇḍaśataṃ, kṣipram eva vidhīyatām
śītābhir adbhir aṣṭhīlām, imāṃ ca pariṣiñcata
.19 sā sicyamānā aṣṭhīlā, abhavac chatadhā tadā
aṅguṣṭhaparvamātrāṇāṃ, garbhāṇāṃ pṛthag eva tu. . . .
.21 tatas tāṃs teṣu kuṇḍeṣu, garbhān avadadhe tadā . . .
.22 śaśāsa caiva bhagavān, kālenaitāvatā punaḥ
vighaṭṭanīyāny etāni, kuṇḍānīti sma saubalīm

.18 [Vyāsa:] "Let one hundred pots filled with ghee be prepared. And sprinkle this globule with cool water."
.19 The globule, being sprinkled, became one hundred separate embryos the size of a finger joint. . . .
.21 Then (Vyāsa) placed these embryos in the pots . . .
.22 And the blessed one instructed the daughter of Subala (Gāndhārī) after how much time these pots were to be broken open.

One hundred sons and one daughter reach term and are duly extracted from the pots.

In discussing these MBh. stories, I am not suggesting that there is genetic affiliation between them and the Vedic Atri story, that is, that these are cryptic retellings of Atri's birth. My point is rather that the theme of abortion/miscarriage and a second incubation in a vessel seems to be a widespread one in Indian literature, explicitly presented several times in the MBh. Though the Vedic Atri story is less straightforwardly narrated, the existence of these clearer parallels lends support to my reconstruction of the Atri plot line.[174]

[174]The MBh. stories share several features absent from the Atri story, which I will not pursue here. One is that all of these second gestations result in exaggeratedly multiple births (except for Vinatā, who only produces two offspring). The other theme is the rivalry between two women, one of whom produces a perfect child. Vaidarbhī's co-wife Śaibhyā has a beautiful son when Vaidarbhī produces a bottle gourd. Gāndhārī aborts herself in despair after hearing that her sister-in-law Kuntī has borne a splendid son. And, in a slight reversal, when Kadrū's one thousand sons hatch properly after five hundred years' incubation, her sister and co-wife Vinatā breaks open one of her two eggs prematurely to find a half-formed embryo.

One feature of Atri's confinement that I do not entirely understand is the emphasis on heat and cooling in the RV (and to an extent in the JB). However, I *tentatively* suggest that this is illumined by a very curious mantra found in a number of Vedic texts:[175]

himásya tvā jarā́yuṇā, śā́le [AV] pári vyayāmasi
ágne [TS, etc.]

With a placenta of snow/cold we envelop thee, O house.
O Agni.

Recall that Atri is several times protected 'with snow' (hiména) in the RV and that the kettle/cleft in which he finds himself may be 'made cool'. Vedic Indians may have conceived of the fetus (or of some fetuses, perhaps the results of certain types of conception) as potentially exposed to, or surrounded by, damaging fire, liable to burn up, and that they considered the various embryo covers as cooling protectors against this fire—only in this way does a phrase like 'himásya . . . jarā́yuṇā 'with a placenta of snow' make sense. An MS passage presents a somewhat similar notion, the burning up of rétas- (the semen or embryo):

MS III.1.3 agnír vā́ etásyā́gre sṛṣṭásya yóne réto níradahat

At first Agni burned up the seed from/of the womb of this (ass) just created.

The story of Agni and Sūrya in the same womb also seems to involve this conception: the container with which Agni gathers up Sūrya's fetal remains 'burns him':

MS I.8.2. tásya rétaḥ párāpatat tád agnír yóninópāgṛhṇāt tád enaṁ vyàdahat

His (Sūrya's) seed/embryo flew forth. Agni gathered it up with the womb. It (the womb) burned him.

This heated container, apparently the second in which Sūrya resides,

[175]AV VI.106.3 ≅ TS IV.6.1.1, MS II.10.1, KS XVII.17, VS XVII.5, ŚB IX.1.2.27.

seems exactly parallel to the second heated surrogate womb in which Atri is confined.[176]

Heat and cooling are also present, at least tangentially, in the MBh. stories as well. The flesh-lump of Gāndhārī must be sprinkled with *cool* water to re-form as embryos, and the *sweating* (sopasveda-) pots of the Vinatā/Kadrū and Vaidarbhī episodes probably have this quality because they are heated.[177]

The fire itself may well be the "fire" of digestion inside everyone. That food is digested by an internal fire is stated explicitly in BĀU (V.9.1) and possibly as early as RV or AV.[178] So Atri in his second womb is perhaps being protected from the enclosing digestive fire with cooling embryo covers.

> RV I.116.8 himénāgníṃ ghraṃsám avārayethām
>
> You two (Aśvins) obstructed (from Atri) the fire (and) the heat with snow,

which parallels the versions of the above mantra containing the vocative Agni:

> TS IV.6.1.1, etc. himásya tvā jarā́yuṇā, ágne pári vyayāmasi
>
> With a placenta of snow/cold we envelop thee, O Agni.

In another RV passage a protective *house* appears, as in the AV variant (śā́le 'O house'):

> RV VIII.73.3 úpa stṛṇītam átraye, hiména gharmám aśvinā
> .7 *ávantam* átraye *gṛhám*, kṛṇutáṃ yuvám aśvinā
> .8 várethe agním ātápaḥ, . . . átraye
>
> You two bestrewed the kettle with snow for Atri, O Aśvins.
> You made *a protecting house* for Atri, O Aśvins.
> You obstructed fire from burning (him) for Atri.

[176]The hazards of gestation and the potential danger for the fetus posed even by the embryo covers have been discussed by Heesterman 1957, passim, esp. pp. 17ff., 39, and 56 with n. 41. Cf. p. 56: "Now the embryonic state is one in which danger is imminent; the embryonic covers are not only protective but may also harm the embryo."

[177]Van Buitenen (1973, 1975, ad locc.) in fact translates 'steaming' in both cases.

[178]Cf. Filliozat 1949, p. 48.

To summarize, Atri, the rescuer of the sun in the Svarbhānu myth, has a complex past. He is the child of Speech and Mind. His birth was violently interrupted, and he required a second gestation, which only the intervention of the Aśvins brought to a successful conclusion. This history may be of relevance to his part in the Svarbhānu story.

CHAPTER 9

Atri's Qualifications and Means for Rescuing the Sun

A. The Rescue of the Sun: Why Atri?

The RV makes a particularly strong statement about Atri's fitness for his task: he is not only the rescuer of the sun, but he is the only one who *can* do so. What makes Atri uniquely fitted to perform this service? There seem to be a number of possible factors.

First, why should it matter that Atri's birth parallels that of the sun, that both have experienced miscarriage and a second successful birth? It hardly needs to be reiterated that in Vedic ritual in general the human microcosm is manipulated in order to produce results in the divine macrocosm through various types of sophisticated sympathetic magic, both physical and verbal. It seems reasonable to extend this principle to the mythological sphere by assuming that, to the Vedic mind, parallel experience between a human and a god would make that human especially qualified to act in the divine realm, to manipulate the god whose experience matches his own. The efficacy of sympathetic magic depends on homologies: only by exploiting such often mystical or cryptic similarities can man use his weak means to control forces far more powerful than his. If I am correct, Atri's botched birth is not merely coincidentally similar to the sun's, but is the episode that empowers him to engage with the sun. It gives him potential power over the life of the sun greater than that possessed by the ordinarily much more powerful gods. This is why they must ask him for his help.

There are two other major reasons that I think Atri is the only appropriate rescuer. The first concerns his birth and parentage and the one remaining role his descendant, the Ātreya priest, plays in the later ritual. The second, also dependent on his parentage, concerns the verbal powers Atri can command.

B. Atri's Parentage

Let us return to a passage we examined in another connection,[179] JB III.335, which describes the stripping off of the embryo covers of a newborn child in exactly the same manner as the removal of the darknesses from the sun. But now let us consider that the embryo thus revealed is the offspring of Mind and Speech.

The story is this: Prajāpati, as often in Vedic was alone, and wished for offspring. By thinking he produces Mind, and Mind in turn, by austerities, produces Speech:

> JB III.334 tan mano 'manuta / . . . / tad anena manasā sahātapyata . . . tat tapyamānaṃ vācam asṛjata
>
> He thought up this Mind. . . . Then together with this Mind he 'heated up' (performed austerities). It (Mind), being 'heated', produced Speech.

Thus created, the pair, Mind and Speech, are then transformed into other of the standard Vedic pairings. These transformations seem nonsexual.

> JB III.334 (cont.) tāv evaitau stomāv abhavatāṃ parāṅ ca pūrvāṅ ca / tau prāṇāpānau te 'horātre . . . tad daivyaṃ mithunaṃ yad idaṃ kiṃ ca dvandvaṃ tad abhavatām
>
> These two became the two stomas, following and preceding; they (became) prāṇa(-breath) and apāna(-breath); they (became) day and night [etc.]. This (is) the divine couple. Whatever pairs there are, these they became.

But they then appear to have a sexual episode:

> tad idaṃ mano vācam askandat / sa hiraṇmayo garbho 'dhīyatāmṛtaḥ

[179] Chap. 7, B.1.

Then Mind spilled this (seed) on Speech.[180] The immortal golden embryo was deposited (in her).

This is the child who is later delivered in exact parallel to the removal of darkness from the sun.

Now in the ŚB version of Atri's birth, we are certain of half his parentage: his mother is Speech. Moreover, there is a strong presumption that Mind is his father, since the only actors in that little drama are the squabbling pair, Mind and Speech, and Prajāpati, to whom they appeal for judgement. There is more than a hint of domestic bickering in that myth, in which Mind and Speech say antiphonally to each other 'aham bhadraḥ' 'I am excellent'.

ŚBK II.4.2.12 mánaś ca ha vaí vā́k cāhám̐ bhádra ūdāte . . .
.14 . . . taú hā́sam̐pādayantau prajā́patim̐ praśnám ā́jagmatuḥ sá ha prajā́patir mánasa evā́dhyuvāca

Mind and Speech were (both) saying, "I am excellent." . . .
They, not agreeing, went to ask Prajāpati. Prajāpati spoke in favor of Mind.[181]

If Atri is the child of Speech and Mind in the ŚB episode, then he can be identified with the hiraṇmaya garbha (golden embryo) of JB III.334–5,[182] and the birth so meticulously described there would in fact be Atri's. Again we see the exact duplication of experience between Atri and the sun, in this case told in almost identical words. It is this parallelism that gives Atri the ability to operate in the sun's realm.

[180]Skand is a standard verb for the release of semen (rétas-), though often an accidental release.

ŚB I.7.4.3 tásya sāmí rétaḥ prácaskanda

Half his seed spilled.

In JB III.334 I take idam as a demonstrative with retas to be supplied. However, if idam is taken with manas, very little is changed: 'this Mind spilled (seed) on Speech'.

[181]The MS version is even more querulous:

MS IV.6.4 vā́k ca mánaś cāvadetām ahám̐ śréyān asmy ahám̐ śréyān asmī́ti

Speech and Mind were contending: "I am better." "(No) *I* am better."

[182]Of course, later the hiraṇyagarbha is identified with Brahman, and even in Vedic there is a hiraṇyagarbha that functions as a sort of Ur-kind (original child), but the particular birth we are discussing seems, at least in part, distinct from that mythic complex.

Moreover, note the epithet of our putative Atri. He is a 'golden' embryo; in other words he possesses one of the principal characteristics of the sun itself—its color. He is thus crucially linked to the sun's sphere by this joint quality. He is, to use a term much-abused in older treatments of Vedic mythology, solar.

That Atri is 'golden' helps explain another detail concerning the Ātreya priest in the ritual, that he is ordinarily associated with gold. Gold (called *atri*hiraṇya 'Atri gold' in KS XXVIII.4; JB I.80) is the prescribed sacrificial gift for this officiant.[183] The reason usually given for this gift is that Atri banished the darkness and found the sun's light (= gold).

> MS IV.8.3 yád ātreyā́ya híraṇyaṃ dádāti táma evā́pahaté 'tho jyótir upáriṣṭād dadhāti
>
> When he gives gold to the Ātreya (priest), he thus smashes away darkness; moreover, he establishes light up above.

But it may rather (or also) be that it was because of his own golden nature that Atri had the power to find the sun.

C. Atri's Means

1. *The Ritual*

Further evidence for the appropriateness of Atri to be rescuer of the sun comes from an examination of the means used by Atri to 'smash away' the sun's darkness. In most of the YV versions of the myth, no particular means is specified. Only in one passage do we find even the slightest hint of a means:

> KS XI.5 tám etáyéṣṭyāyājayan
>
> They had him worship with this Iṣṭi.[184]

The Sāma Veda Brāhmaṇas and the KB usually do specify a means, one of the named sāmans endemic to these texts, especially the Svara Sāmans:

[183]Cf. MS IV.8.3, KS XXVIII.4, ŚB IV.3.4.21, PB VI.6.11, JB I.80, GB II.3.19.

[184]The Iṣṭi in question seems to be the same one being practiced in the Svarbhānu passage in MS II.1.5, involving a caru of white rice for Soma and Rudra.

PB IV.5.2 taṃ devāḥ svarair aspṛṇvan

The gods won him with the Svara (Sāmans),

or the Bhāsa (Sāman):[185]

PB VI.6.8 (= XIV.11.14) tasyātrir bhāsena tamo 'pāhan

Atri smashed away his darkness with the Bhāsa (Sāman).

This is the typical remedy in these Brāhmaṇas and, as such, usually unhelpful for interpretation of the adjoining myth: the sāmans to be employed are usually suggested by some coincidence of sound (*svara*- / *bhāsa*-: svar-bhānu) or sense (*divā*-kīrtya PB IV.6.13 'to be recited *by day*').[186]

It is the RVic version that gives us the most extensive account of Atri's means, and the most striking feature of these means is that they are entirely ritual. There are no feats of strength, cleverness, or trick-

[185]Svara Sāmans: PB IV.5.2, JB II.386, KB XXIV.3; Bhāsa Sāman: PB VI.6.8, XIV.11.14.

[186]Hopkins in his discussion of Svarbhānu (1909, p. 35) denies that svara- and bhāsa- are names of sāmans. Instead he interprets the words literally (as 'noise' and 'lightning', respectively) and sees them as tools of "barbarous magic," "the simplest form of all for driving away the eclipse demon." "The gods won the sun back by making noises" (svarās) is Hopkins's translation of PB IV.5.2 taṃ devāḥ svarair aspṛṇvan; "by a lightning Atri drove off the darkness" of PB VI.6.8 (= XIV.11.14) tasyātrir bhāsena tamo 'pāhan (tentatively followed by Caland 1931, ad loc.). But this ignores the contexts, which make it clear that sāmans are involved (the actual word sāman is very commonly omitted in these circumstances), the well-nigh universal tendency of this text to use sāmans and other ritual utterances as cure of choice, and the fact that the parallels identify at least the svaras as sāmans.

JB II.386 ta etāni svarāṇy apaśyan / tair etam aspṛṇvan

The (gods and ṛṣis) saw these Svara (Sāmans). With them they won him. [One regularly 'sees' *x*-sāman; one obviously does not 'see' noises.]

KB XXIV.3 tān vai svarasāmāna iti ācakṣate / etair ha vā atraya ādityaṃ tamaso 'spṛṇvata

These they call the Svarasāman (Days). With them the Atris won the sun away from darkness.

In this instance Hopkins seems to be imposing a "primitive," nonritualistic interpretation despite all textual evidence to the contrary. Below we will see a case where, in reverse, he removes an interesting mythic detail by a rationalistic textual interpretation.

ery. He effects the rescue of the sun entirely by religious performance.[187] Two verses mention these means:

RV V.40.6 . . . sū́ryam . . ., turī́yeṇa bráhmaṇā́vindad átriḥ

Atri found the sun with the 'fourth formulation'.

.8 grā́vṇo brahmā́ yuyujānáḥ saparyán, kīríṇā devā́n námasopaśíkṣan
átriḥ sū́ryasya diví cákṣur ā́dhāt

The Brahman (Atri), yoking the pressing stones [for pressing soma], serving the gods with plain/mere reverence, seeking to win (the sun),[188] Atri placed the eye of the sun in heaven.

This material suggests several questions. What ritual or part of a ritual is he performing? What is the 'fourth formulation'? Why is his reverence (námas) 'mere' or 'plain' (kīrí-)?

The answer to the first question is, on the surface, obvious, but it allows a further and less obvious refinement to be added. The obvious answer is that he is performing a soma ritual, and we see him as he begins to press the soma, hence the 'yoking' of the pressing stones. But we can be more precise than this; in fact, the hymn itself gives us the answer. The hymn in which the Svarbhānu myth is told is a hybrid affair: its last five verses (5–9) comprise the Svarbhānu story, neatly packaged as a unit by the nearly identical first halves of vss. 5 and 9. The first four verses are addressed to Indra. There is no clear relation

[187]For a strikingly similar situation, compare the well-known and widespread Vala myth, in which Indra and the Aṅgirases release cows confined in a cave. As Schmidt (1968, p. 237) remarks, "Die Waffen, mit denen die Höhle geöffnet wird, sind priestlicher Natur: Gedichte, Lieder, Gesänge, die ihre Macht der magischen Kraft der Wahrheit verdanken" (The weapons with which the cave is opened are of a priestly nature: poems, songs, hymns that owe their strength to the magical power of Truth). This is all the more remarkable, as Schmidt notes, because Indra is generally associated with brute force rather than prayer.

[188]This translation differs from the usual translation of this verse, which takes kīríṇā devā́n námasā with upaśíkṣan (as well as saparyán). Geldner: "Atri . . . mit blosser Verbeugung die Götter ehrt and zu gewinnen sucht" (Atri with merest reverence honored and sought to win the gods). Similar, Lüders (1959, vol. 2, p. 542). O'Flaherty (1981, p. 188): "honoured the gods with devout obeisance, seeking to win their protection" ("protection" is not in the text). This interpretation perhaps accords slightly better with the pāda break than mine, but it is less satisfactory in sense: the object of Atri's desire is the sun; that is the reason he embarks on the ritual.

between the two parts.[189] Though Oldenberg compares V.78 for this type of structure and calls both "Zauberspruch" (charms or magic spells), he also sees no natural connection in V.40 (unlike V.78) between the introductory verses and the charm proper.[190] But let us look at the final pādas of vs. 4, the last introductory verse.

RV V.40.4cd yuktvā́ háribhyām úpa yāsad arvā́ṅ, mā́dhyaṃdine sávane matsad índraḥ

Having yoked (them), he (Indra) will come hither with his two bay steeds. Indra will become exhilarated (on soma) at the midday pressing.

Mā́dhyaṃdina- sávana- 'midday pressing' is a technical term in the ritual (already attested nine times in the RV), referring to the second of the three daily pressings at the soma sacrifice. The precision of the term is the key here. Remember the function of the Ātreya 'descendant of Atri' in the later ritual books. Other than his curious role as victim in the Aśvamedha, he shows up *only* at the Mādhyaṃdina Savana, this same midday pressing, where, as a nonofficiating spectator, he is given gold. This gift of gold (sometimes called atrihiraṇyam 'the gold of Atri') is justified in various Vedic prose texts by telling the Svarbhānu myth. The Ātreya is given gold, a symbol of the sun, because Atri freed the sun from darkness.[191] So, circumstantial evidence suggests that the Svarbhānu myth is introduced at this point in RV V.40 because it is an appropriate tale to narrate at the Midday Pressing; that is, the mention of the midday pressing in vs. 4 evoked the apparently unrelated vss. 5–9. And this suggests that Atri's soma pressing in vs. 8 is the midday pressing as well, in other words, that it was by the performance of the midday pressing that Atri freed the sun.

The appropriateness of the Svarbhānu myth for the midday pressing is suggested by another ritual detail, namely, that there is a barely disguised ritual encoding of the freeing of the sun performed at the

[189]Cf., e.g., Geldner: "Ein innerer Zusammenhang zwischen diesen beiden Teilen ist nicht ersichtlich" (An internal connection between these two parts is not obvious).

[190]Oldenberg, *Noten*, ad loc. We have already examined V.78, Chap. 8, D.2. Both Lüders (1959, vol. 2, p. 543) and O'Flaherty (1981, quoting Sāyaṇa) suggest that the compiler considered the first four verses the 'fourth bráhman' alluded to in vs. 6, but why attach Svarbhānu to this rather than to some other four-versed hymn?

[191]Cf. MS IV.8.3, KS XXVIII.4, PB VI.6.11, JB I.80. The ŚB instead tells the related story of Atri banishing darkness from the shed at this point (ŚBM IV.3.4.21 ≅ ŚBK V.4.1.16–17); cf. above, Chap. 7, A.

midday pressing. At this pressing, before the distribution of the Dakṣiṇās (including the gold for the Ātreya), the so-called Dākṣiṇa libations (libations related to the Dakṣiṇā) are made. To modern ears the procedure at these libations sounds a little awkward; it involves juggling a ghee-soaked fringe wrapped around a piece of gold. But the physical awkwardness has a ritual point.

> BŚS VIII.5 tasyaitasya vasanasyāntamāyāṃ daśāyāṃ hiraṇyaśalkaḥ pragrathito bhavati . . . sruci caturgr̥hītaṃ gr̥hītvā vasanasyāntaṁ srugdaṇḍa upasaṃgr̥hya saurībhyām r̥gbhyāṃ gārhapatye juhoti . . . atha divaṃ gaccha suvaḥ pateti hiraṇyaṁ hr̥tvodgr̥hṇāti
>
> A piece of gold is wrapped in the fringed end of this (just mentioned garment). . . . Having dipped (ghee) four times in the spoon, he (puts the wrapped gold down into the ghee),[192] wrapping the fringed end around the spoon handle, and offers into the Gārhapatya fire with two verses to the Sun [= RV I.50.1, 115.1, see below]. . . . Then he takes out the gold, saying, "Go to heaven. Fly to the sun."[193]

This action seems a brief ritual reenactment of the Svarbhānu myth. The brilliance of the gold/sun is obscured by the enveloping garment (like the darknesses/embryo covers stripped off the sun) and by submersion in the ghee, but it is then released. The connection between the gold and the sun is emphasized by the recitation of two RVic verses addressed to Sūrya, the sun, as well as by the envoi ('Go to heaven. Fly to the sun') when the gold is removed.

> RV I.50.1 úd u tyáṃ jātávedasaṃ, deváṃ vahanti ketávaḥ
> dr̥śé víśvāya sū́ryam
>
> The beacons carry up this god, Jātavedas—the Sun/Sūrya for all to see.
>
> RV I.115.1 citráṃ devā́nām úd agād ánīkaṃ, cákṣur mitrásya váruṇasyāgnéḥ
> ā́prā dyā́vāpr̥thivī́ antárikṣaṃ, sū́rya ātmā́ jágatas tasthúṣaś ca
>
> The bright front of the gods has arisen, the eye of Mitra, Varuṇa, and Agni.

[192]For this detail, cf., e.g., ĀpŚS XIII.5.7 ghr̥te 'vadhāya 'putting (it) down into the ghee'.

[193]Cf. also ŚB IV.3.4.6, MŚS II.4.5.1ff., ĀpŚS XIII.5.6–8.

He has filled heaven, earth, and the atmosphere—Sūrya, the soul of the moving and the still.

Gold is shortly thereafter given to the Ātreya, whose ancestor is the mythical effector of the release that has just been ritually reenacted. The purpose of the gift is stated clearly in the ŚB:

ŚB IV.3.4.8 támasā vā́ asaú lokò 'ntárhitaḥ sá eténa jyótiṣā támo 'pahátya svargáṃ lokám upasáṃkrāmati

Yonder world is obscured by darkness. Having smashed away [note apa √han] the darkness with this light [= the gold], he goes to the heavenly world.

2. *'Mere' Reverence and the Fourth Formulation*

We have thus far established that Atri performs his release of the sun by ritual means, and we have more narrowly localized this ritual activity, to the midday pressing, where not only is the myth reenacted in disguised form but the mortal representative of Atri receives gold as a token of his part in the myth, as the texts often directly explain.

But the other two questions remain so far obscure—what is the 'fourth formulation' and why is the reverence Atri offers kīrí- 'mere, small, plain'? These two questions can perhaps best be treated together, if only to highlight thereby a potentially troubling paradox.

The word kīrí- used to be taken as 'praiser, praising', but its contexts suggest rather the meaning 'humble, mere'.[194] Yet 'humble, mere' reverence seems unlikely means for Atri to use to rescue the sun, when the gods themselves have been unable to do so. Another RVic passage, also from the Atri Maṇḍala, may help illuminate what actually is meant by kīríṇā námasā.

RV V.4.9c ágne atriván námasā gṛṇānáḥ . . .
.10ab yás tvā hṛdā́ kīríṇā mányamānó, 'martyam mártyo jóhavīmi

O Agni, being hymned (by me) with reverence like Atri's . . .
(By me) who, thinking about you with merest heart, strongly invoke you, (I) a mortal (to you) an immortal.

194'Praiser': e.g., Grassmann, Monier-Williams, s.v. 'Humble': Geldner, ad V.40.8; Mayrhofer, *KEWA*, s.v. Cf. also Pischel in Pischel and Geldner 1889, pp. 216–28: 'elend, arm' (wretched, poor).

Geldner translates hr̥dā́ kīríṇā 'mit dem blossen Herzen' (with plain/mere heart) and suggests reasonably that this means "ohne viele Worte oder Opfergaben" (without many words or offerings). Indeed, the mányamānaḥ 'thinking' suggests that he thinks his devotion rather than speaking it, but—the poet seems to be boasting—even his mere thought amounts to a particularly strong invocation: jóhavīmi 'I invoke' is an intensive verbal form; the unmarked alternative would be hváyāmi or hváye. The poet seems to be implying that his thoughts are stronger than others' words. Now the presence in the preceding verse of atrivát 'like Atri' and námasā, the word in V.40.8 that is modified by kīrí-, suggests that the poet's[195] devotional approach to the god is modelled on that of Atri, and therefore that Atri's 'mere reverence', kīríṇā . . . námasā, in V.40.8 also involves few words or offerings. Perhaps his sincerity or his fervor or some inborn power makes his slightest ritual thought or gesture more efficacious than those of others.

It is in this context that we should examine the phrase (also in the instrumental) turī́yeṇa bráhmaṇā 'with the fourth formulation', of V.40.6. Bráhman- is obviously a highly charged word in Vedic (and, of course, in later literature), and 'formulation, holy speech' is only a dim approximation at a translation.[196] In V.40.8, the ritual verse, Atri is named as a brahmán-, literally, a 'possessor of the formulation, a formulator'. This is no mere verse filler or honorific and interchangeable title: it is his mastery of the formulation that must be crucial to his recovery of the sun.

Atri's eloquence is mentioned elsewhere. Once the Aśvins give aid to the 'agreeably speaking' Atri:

RV VIII.73.8 várethe agním ātápo, vádate valgv átraye

You hindered Agni from burning (him), for the agreeably speaking Atri.

And in RV V.2.6 it is exactly the 'formulations of Atri' (bráhmāṇy átreḥ) that are efficacious.

RV V.2.6 vaśā́ṃ rā́jānaṃ vasatíṃ jánānām, árātayo ní dadhur mártyeṣu
bráhmāṇy átrer áva táṃ sr̥jantu

[195]He would be an Ātreya.

[196]Cf., e.g., Renou 1949; Thieme 1952 (1984, pp. 100–137).

The king of dwellings, the dwelling place of men [i.e., Agni] did the demons deposit [= hide] among mortals.
Let *the formulations of Atri* release him.

Though the being whom 'the formulations of Atri' release here is Agni, a similar process may be envisioned for the sun.

It is quite clear why Atri should be characterized by his control of the bráhman. He is the son of Speech, as we learned in the ŚB account of his birth, and indeed he is identified as speech in the later ŚB (= BĀU), though not for a reason one might expect:

ŚB XIV.5.2.6 (= BĀU(M) II.2.4) vā́g evā́trir vācā́ hy ánnam adyáté 'ttir ha vaí nā́maitád yád átrir íti

Atri is speech. For by speech food is eaten. Indeed 'eating' (attí-) is his name, that is, 'Atri'.

Yet the passages we have just seen imply that Atri's most successful worship involves few words. This is one paradox.

Let us examine another one, the 'fourth formulation'.[197] One might expect that the 'fourth formulation' would be the perfected formulation, the best fashioned, since it accomplished the release of the sun. And indeed the only other early Vedic occurrence of the phrase[198] also

[197]A reminiscence of Atri's 'fourth formulation' seems to be found in the importance of four in Atri's life history presented later. In TS VII.1.8.1 Atri, praying for offspring, sees the 'four-night ritual' (sá etáṃ catūrātrám apaśyat) and four sons are born to him (táto vaí tásya catvā́ro vīrā́ ā́jāyanta). In section 2 of the same passage he wants the vīryā̀ṇi (manly qualities) that are eluding him; he sees four soma offerings with four stomas (sá etā́ṁś catúraś cátuṣṭomānt sómān apaśyat) and obtains what he desires. The catūrātra of Atri also appears in PB XXI.9, JB II.281.

[198]JB I.81 has turyeṇa brāhmaṇā in a mantra. Though it occurs soon after a Svarbhānu passage, it is unclear and adds nothing to the debate (as far as I can see).

JB I.81 rājānam ānayati / tam abhimantrayate sa pavasva sudhāmā devānām abhi priyāṇi dhāma // trir devebhyo 'pavathās trir ādityebhyas trir aṅgirobhyaḥ // yena turyeṇa brahmaṇā bṛhaspataye 'pavathās tena mahyaṃ pavasva

He leads up the king; he addresses him with mantras: "Become purified (as) one having good foundation, to the dear foundations of the gods. Three times you became purified for the gods; three times for the Ādityas; three times for the Aṅgirases. By which fourth formulation you became purified for Bṛhaspati, by that become purified for me."

Given the word triḥ 'three times', it seems likely that the turyeṇa brahmaṇā here refers to the 'fourth *repetition* of a formula', rather than to the fourth progressive stage of formulation, as I interpret turī́yeṇa (bráhmaṇā) in RV V.40.6 and AV VII.1.1. The phrase in this JB passage thus would have nothing semantically to do with our phrase.

seems to have a special effectiveness—though the passage is somewhat obscure.

AV VII.1.1 dhītī́ vā yé ánayan vācó ágram̥, mánasā vā yé 'vadann r̥tā́ni
tr̥tī́yeṇa bráhmaṇā vāvr̥dhānā́s, turī́yeṇāmanvata nā́ma dhenóḥ

Whitney: They either who by meditation led the beginning of speech, or who by mind spoke righteous things—
They, increasing with the third incantation, perceived with the fourth the name of the milch-cow.

This passage has received considerable attention from some eminent twentieth-century Vedicists;[199] the consensus is that the 'fourth bráhman' represents the perfected end product of a process of progressively sharpening the thought or formulation, so that pādas a, b, c, d each express one of the bráhman(s) in the series, culminating in d, the fourth bráhman, which gives access to the 'name of the cow'—"a mystical expression for 'literary formulation of hidden truth'" (Thieme, "mystische Ausdrucksweise für 'dichterische Formulierung einer geheimen Wahrheit'") or, more simply, the "open Sesame" for the release of the cows in the Vala myth (Lüders).[200]

There may be another covert reference to the 'fourth formulation' in the RV, in the opening of a hymn to Br̥haspati:

RV X.67.1 imā́m̥ dhíyam̥ saptáśīrṣṇīm pitā́ na, r̥táprajātām br̥hatī́m avindat
turī́yam̥ svij janayad viśvájanyo, 'yā́sya ukthám índrāya śám̥san

Our father found this seven-headed thought, born from truth, lofty.
The energetic one belonging to all men gave birth to the fourth ______, chanting a hymn to Indra.

Schmidt (1968, p. 224) supplies bráhman with turī́yam here and cites other discussions of the concept. Whether or not this is the intent of the passage, the context is too cryptic to be of much use.

[199]Cf., e.g., Renou 1949; Thieme 1952, p. 106 (1984, p. 115); Lüders 1959, vol. 2, p. 543.

[200]I would follow Thieme, whose discussion of this AV verse (1952, p. 106 [1984, p. 115]) is especially worthy of study. Puhvel (1987, p. 153) suggests in passing that the "Fourth Brahman" is really "silent meditation": "Elsewhere it appears that this mysterious 'fourth' was silent meditation, as opposed to varieties of the articulated word (*vāc-*), and that Atri thus rescued the sun by the mystic power of silence." Although this is an intriguing idea and might fit well with Atri's kīríṇā . . . námasā 'merest reverence' in V.40.8, he cites no evidence for the "elsewhere," and so it is an idea difficult to judge. Is his support amanvata 'he thought' (Whitney: 'he perceived') in AV VII.1.1?

3. *The Fourth (Part of) Speech*

I find this convincing and true as far as it goes, but it does not account for a prominent ambiguity in the notion of 'fourth', especially with regard to speech. Because vā́c- 'speech' and bráhman- 'ritual formulation' are so closely tied, one cannot ignore the fact that the 'fourth (part) of speech' is a prominent topos in Vedic. As to 'fourth' in general, on the one hand, as here, 'the fourth' represents the outcome of a process of refinement; on the other, it is associated with the mortal and imperfect as opposed to the first three quarters, which belong to the divine and perfected sphere.[201]

The fourth of something in Vedic often seems to be somehow left-over, at loose ends, presumably as a consequence of the common division of things into threes (the three worlds, the three pressings in the soma sacrifice, the three fires of the śrauta ritual, the three seasonal rites, the three twice-borne castes, etc.). As an afterthought, it often belongs to the mortal realm. Consider, for example, the fourth, mortal bridegroom in the marriage hymn. The first three are gods:

RV X.85.40 sómaḥ prathamó vivide, gandharvó vivida úttaraḥ
tr̥tī́yo agníṣ ṭe pátis, turī́yas te manuṣyajā́ḥ

Soma acquired (you) first; the Gandharva acquired (you) next.
Agni was your third husband; your fourth is born of man.

A particularly common division of this sort is that of speech (vā́c), of which three parts ordinarily belong together, with the fourth (and last) apart. No doubt the first expression of this is in a famous passage in the RVic riddle hymn:

RV I.164.45 catvā́ri vā́k párimitā padā́ni, tā́ni vidur brāhmaṇā́ yé manīṣíṇaḥ
gúhā trī́ṇi níhitā néṅgayanti, turī́yaṃ vācó manuṣyà vadanti

Speech is divided into four quarters. These the Brahmans know, who are wise.
The three deposited in hiding they do not make stir. The fourth (part) of speech men speak.

[201]For other discussions of "the fourth" in Vedic, cf. Bodewitz 1982; 1983, pp. 37ff.; Falk 1987, pp. 112f.

But the division of speech into four parts is told a number of times in the BYV, with the first three parts associated with the three worlds, the fourth with men or with paśus ('beasts, animals', among whom man is often classified).

> KS XIV.5 (≅ MS I.11.5) sā vāg *sṛṣṭā[202] caturdhā vyabhavad eṣu lokeṣu trīṇi turīyāṇi paśuṣu turīyaṃ yā divi sā bṛhati sā stanayitnau yāntarikṣe sā vāte sā vāmadevye yā pṛthivyāṁ sāgnau sā rathantare yā paśuṣu tasyā yad atyaricyata tāṃ brāhmaṇe nyadadhus tasmād brāhmaṇa ubhe vācau vadati daivīṃ ca mānuṣīṃ ca

> Speech, (once) created, divided into four: three quarters (entered) into these worlds, one quarter in the animals. The (part) in heaven is in the Bṛhat (Sāman) and the thunder; that in the atmosphere is in the wind and the Vāmadevya (Sāman); that on earth is in the fire and the Rathantara (Sāman). What was left over from the part in the animals they established in the Brahman. Therefore a Brahman speaks both (kinds of) speech, both divine and human.

Though the passage seems designed to give the Brahman special powers of speech through access to a divine part of it, this conclusion does not follow logically from the rest of the passage. Since he presumably already received a share in the fourth part of speech allotted to the paśus, getting the leftovers simply endows him with a little extra of what he already has. In this case I think the composers are fudging, but the division into four remains unmistakable.

Another KS passage (VI.7 = KapS IV.6) describes the division of speech in a rather shocking fashion. I cite the KapS parallel, as the KS is somewhat corrupt.

> KapS IV.6 vācā vai saha manuṣyā ajāyanta / ṛte vāco devāś cāsurāś ca / te yan manuṣyā avadaṁs tad evābhavan / te devāś cāsurāś ca prajāpatim abruvann ime vāvedam abhūvann iti / sa vācaḥ satyaṃ niramimīta bhūr bhuvaḥ svar iti / yat turīyam anṛtaṃ tan manuṣyeṣu nyadadhāt / etad vai vāco 'nṛtaṃ yan manuṣyā vadanti

> Men were born with speech; the gods and Asuras without speech. When men spoke, they throve. The gods and Asuras said to Prajāpati: "These (men) have thriven here." He created truth from speech, (say-

[202]Von Schroeder prints dṛṣṭā here, but this is surely to be emended to sṛṣṭā, following MS I.11.5.

ing), "Bhūr bhuvaḥ svar." The fourth (part of speech) was untruth. He put (it) in men. This is the untruth(ful part) of speech, which men speak.

4. *Creative Imperfection*

If men's quarter share in speech is untruth, then even the most perfected of human speech, even the 'fourth brahman' with which the 'fourth (part of) speech' invites comparison, is fundamentally flawed in comparison with the rest of speech distributed in other spheres.[203] Yet it is finally the fourth brahman, rather than the gods' efforts, that works to free the sun. It may not be entirely farfetched to suggest that it is the flaws in human speech that makes it so effective in this case. Perhaps because it is not inherently and effortlessly perfect and true, any approach to perfection and truth in human speech gives it an extra power. Also perhaps the blemishes in the sun itself are best healed by a flawed, not a flawless medium.

I advance this hypothesis rather reluctantly, as it smacks of the Christian felix culpa, the "fortunate fall" of Adam and Eve, which set in motion the redemption of mankind by the son of God—a notion quite distant from the Vedic milieu. But I nonetheless do advance it, for there is other evidence to lend it support. First remember that though Atri is the child of Vāc, he is the *miscarried* child, an imperfect product with, presumably, an imperfect command of his mother's qualities.

Then let us look at another story of the division of speech, this time from PB/JB. This episode feeds into a version of the hairless-earth story, a variant of the same story that ends several versions of Svarbhānu. In this story Prajāpati divides speech into *three* parts, which become the three worlds:

> JB II.244 (≅ PB XX.14.5) prajāpatir vā idam agra ekākṣarāṃ vācaṃ tredhā vyabhajat / ta ime lokā abhavann ṛkṣā anupajīvanīyāḥ/ . . . sa aikṣata katham ime lokā loma gṛhṇīyuḥ katham upajīvanavanta syur iti

> In the beginning Prajāpati divided speech, (which) has one syllable, into three parts.[204] It became these (three) worlds. (They were) bald and

[203]For the division of speech elsewhere, see MS III.6.8, IV.4.9, IV.5.8; ŚB IV.1.3.16; PB V.7.1 ≅ IX.2.3 (the latter with brahman instead of vāc); and cf. also Brereton 1988, pp. 3, 6f.

[204]This is a pun. Vāc- 'speech' (a word containing one syllable) is divided into 'syllables' akṣara- (a word containing three syllables), as the preceding part of the passage shows. On this sort of syllable counting, see Jamison 1986, esp. p. 171.

> not livable upon. . . . He sought "How might these worlds get hair? How might they acquire the means for subsistence?"

As in the BYV passages (especially KS XIV.5 [≅ MS I.11.5] above), three parts of speech become the three worlds, but in their perfection they are sterile, devoid of life; they seem to be in need of the fourth part of speech, the imperfect, untruthful part that men speak. Even as the blemishes of the sun become the hair on the earth in the Svarbhānu myth, so would this flawed speech become hair, endow the earth with life, in this myth. In any event that is how *I* would have completed the myth; unfortunately, the composers of JB/PB did not. Instead, Prajāpati sees the three-night worship (Trirātra Yajña) and works the changes this way. Despite the disappointing failure of the Brāhmaṇas to conform to my plot, I think that my proposed denouement is lurking behind the story as told. We have already noted the tendency of the Sāmaveda Brāhmaṇas to short-circuit a mythological remedy to a story by supplying a strictly ritual one. I would maintain that this happened here, given the parallelism of the Svarbhānu/barren-earth story *and* one final piece of evidence.

In the Svarbhānu/barren-earth story, each wiping off of the darkness produces another color of sheep, but the fourth action in the BYV versions (MS II.5.2, KS XII.13, TS II.1.2.2–3)[205] produces not a different color of sheep, but a different type entirely—an avi *vaśā*.

> MS II.5.2 yát prathamáṃ támo 'pā́ghnant sā́viḥ kr̥ṣṇā́bhavad yád dvitī́yaṁ sā́ lóhinī yát tr̥tī́yaṁ sā́ balakṣī́ yád adhyastā́d apā́kr̥ntat [→ *apā́kr̥ntant?] sā́vir vaśā́bhavat . . .
>
> The first darkness they smashed away became a black ewe. The second a reddish one. The third a white one. *What he [→ *they] cut off from the cast-out (placenta) became a vaśā ewe. . . .*

Vaśā is usually translated as 'barren', but the semantics of this word must be more complex than that, as is shown by a passage like the following:

> ŚB IV.5.2.1 vaśā́m ā́labhante . . . anumárśaṃ gárbham éṣṭavaí brūyāt

[205]The exception is MS IV.5.7, where there is no fourth action.

They take (as sacrificial victim) a vaśā. . . . (Having killed her and cut her open,) he should tell (them) to seek gropingly for an embryo.

One would hardly make such a search in an animal definitely known to be barren. As H. Falk has elegantly shown,[206] the vaśā is a cow (or other female domestic animal) that has been bred but has not calved; she may yet calve or she may indeed be barren.[207] In the Svarbhānu story, it is this vaśā, cut out from the placenta, that is offered in order to acquire hair for the earth. Again, as in the fourth part of speech, it is the imperfect thing, which nonetheless has the possibility of improving, that is successful. Moreover, in this story it is the fourth animal produced; interestingly enough, the vaśā is also called 'the fourth' elsewhere, and is seen as fulfilling the sacrificer's objectives.

TS III.4.2.2 (= KS XIII.11) tvám̥ turī́yā vaśínī vaśā́si, sakŕ̥d yát tvā mánasā gárbha ā́śayat
vaśā́ tvám̥ vaśínī gacha devā́nt, satyā́ḥ santu yájamānasya kā́māḥ

Thou art the fourth—the willing vaśā, since suddenly/at once an embryo lay in you (fathered?) with/by mind (?!).[208]
Do thou vaśā go willing to the gods. Let the wishes of the worshipper come true.

Geldner[209] has suggested that the four darknesses in the prose Svarbhānu story are equivalent to the four formulations of RV V.40. It would follow from this that the fourth brahman (turī́ya- bráhman-) of RV V.40.6 is identified with the animal produced from the fourth darkness, that is, the vaśā. This identification of the fourth formulation with the vaśā is supported by the features they share. Each is an imperfect object: the human fourth formulation or portion of speech in comparison with the three parts of divine speech, the potentially barren vaśā in comparison with female animals that have already pro-

[206]Falk 1982, p. 175.
[207]As such, the vaśā reminds us somewhat of Apālā, who, though having presumably reached the age of womanhood, still does not have its visible marks.
[208]I do not understand this pāda at all. Could it possibly be an occult reference to the pairing of Speech (Vāc [= the vaśā here]) with Mind (Manas)? Or does it somehow mean that the vaśā has a mental, though not a physical, embryo?
[209]Ad loc.; cf. Lüders 1959, vol. 2, p. 542.

duced. Yet perhaps because of this imperfection, each is the tool that accomplishes a major cosmic task: the fourth brahman in restoring the sun to heaven, the sacrificed vaśā in giving the earth 'hair'. And each, of course, is the fourth in its series, a spot apparently reserved for the human and imperfect.

To summarize, Atri is the proper, indeed the only one to free the sun, not so much because of his excellences as because of his failings. He shares the failed birth of the sun, and though as son of Speech, he is master of holy words (brahmán), it is mastery only of imperfect, human speech. His reverence is kīrí- 'humble, mere'. Yet it is effective because the sun itself is flawed, marked with darkness, which, as we will see, results from moral failings. Moreover, it is effective because flaws and blemishes, not sterile perfection, can fructify and enliven the world. It is the darknesses from the sun that produce the 'hair' on the earth, just as (if I am right) the fourth part of speech belonging to mortals does. And this is symbolized by the use of the *fourth* brahman, as perfected a formulation as mortal speech can produce, and the (fourth) vaśā, an animal that has so far failed (to produce offspring) but may yet succeed.

5. *Pied Beauty*

Let us now consider the products of the smashing off of darkness, the various animals. We have just examined the avi vaśā, the 'possibly barren ewe', which is the most interesting and the most important. Most important because this is the animal actually sacrificed to produce hair/plants on earth. Most interesting because of the uncertainty of her qualities—her as-yet-disappointing performance in bearing young, but potential for doing so in the future. The vaśā is repeatedly praised in Vedic, especially in two long hymns in the AV, which Whitney entitles "Extolling the cow (vaśā́)" (X.10) and "The cow (vaśā́) as belonging exclusively to the Brahmins" (XII.4). Her condition was obviously of great interest, and the uncertainty surrounding her may have made her a more mythically powerful figure than a reliably fertile female could be.[210]

[210]As Falk has said, in a slightly different connection (1984, p. 117, n. 10): "Gerade wer seine generativen Kraft entweder freiwillig als Asket, gezwungener massen als Kastrat oder aufgrund angeborener Sterilität zurückhält, der steht im Ruf, ein besonders intensives Verhältnis zur Fruchbarkeit. [Whoever holds his(/her) generative power in check—either voluntarily like an ascetic, perforce like a castrate, or because of inherent sterility—is considered to have an especially intense connection with fertility.]"

Yet the whole series of animals in Svarbhānu is worth investigating. First let us note that in all versions all the animals are sheep (/ewes [avi-]). This has been explained away by Hopkins as a textual error "that converted āvir abhavat ['it became visible'] to avir abhavat ['it became a sheep']" by misunderstanding of the sandhi in kr̥ṣṇāvir abhavat.[211] But as Hopkins to some extent notes, the "error" would have to be very old, since it occurs in all versions of the story that contain this episode, and the sacrificial offering of the avi vaśā shows that an animal is clearly understood. Here Hopkins tries to impoverish the mythic richness of the tale by explaining away the apparently puzzling and dreamlike transformation: darkness → sheep.

But in the context of the myth this particular transformation makes perfect sense. Sheep are the hairy animal par excellence. As in Apālā and in the AV charm discussed above, the skin affliction of the sun is transformed into hair—the hair/wool of the sheep—which in turn undergoes a further transformation into the 'hair' of the earth, namely, plants.

The sequence of colors makes sense, too. Whatever the particular color terms chosen, the series progresses from dark to light, as the darknesses are successively purged from the sun, and we get closer to his true brilliance. The various series are as follows:

	1st	2nd	3rd	4th
MS II.5.2 IV.5.7	kr̥ṣṇā́ 'black'	lóhinī 'reddish'	balakṣī́ 'white'	[vaśā́]
KS XII.13 XXVII.2	kr̥ṣṇā́	phalgúḥ 'reddish'	balakṣī́	[vaśā́]
TS II.1.2.2	kr̥ṣṇā́	phálgunī 'reddish'	balakṣī́	[vaśā́]
PB VI.6.8	kr̥ṣṇā	rajatā 'shining'	lohinī 'reddish'	śuklā 'bright'
JB I.81	kr̥ṣṇā	dhūmrā 'smoky'	phālgunī 'reddish'	—

All of the sequences start with 'black', understandably. The BYV and the SV Brāhmaṇas form separate groups, the former with black, reddish, white, the latter inserting another term between black and red-

[211]Hopkins 1909, p. 35; tentatively accepted ("may well be right") by Caland 1931, ad PB VI.6.8.

dish and moving the white ewe into the fourth slot, where the other texts have vaśā́. Given the position of phālgunī 'reddish' in the third slot in JB I.81, it seems likely that the series is incomplete here: we should expect a final 'white/bright' sheep to symbolize the complete restoration of the sun, as in PB VI.6.8.

These particular colors may themselves have significance. First, these same colors, which after all represent the skin affliction removed from the sun, are the colors of skin blemishes (apa-cit-) in an AV charm to remove these spots.[212]

AV VI.83.2 ény ékā śyény ékā, kṛṣṇaíkā róhiṇī dvé

One (apacit) is variegated; one white, one black, two reddish.

But this collection of colors can have a larger significance. Here the problem is to limit the possibilities, not search for them, since color symbolism is very common in Vedic in far more elaborate systems than this. For example, lists of sacrificial victims, such as those for the Aśvamedha, exhaustively list the colors and markings of the various animals.[213] For our three colors in particular, note Gonda's statement: "It appears that in ancient India just as in other countries three basic colours black, red, and white (mentioned together, e.g., Kauś. 18.17) were usually clearly distinguished. These three continue to play a part in attempts at classifying various provinces of reality".[214] In other words, the first three ewes produced from the sun's darkness may in some sense constitute a complete set, a collection that stands for a unity—the world of beasts, perhaps, or even the world of living things.[215] In this connection one can compare a passage like the following from the GobhGS concerning the proper siting of a house:

GobhGS IV.7.5 gaurapām̐su brāhmaṇasya
.6 lohitapām̐su kṣatriyasya
.7 kṛṣṇapām̐su vaiśyasya

.5 The earth (should be) white, (if he is a) brāhmaṇa.
.6 Red, (if he is a) kṣatriya.
.7 Black, (if he is a) vaiśya,

[212]Cf. Zysk 1985, p. 87f.
[213]Cf., e.g., VS XXIV, esp. 1–19.
[214]Gonda 1980, p. 46; for color symbolism in general, see pp. 26–28, 44–48, and passim. Cf. also Hiltebeitel 1976, pp. 69–74, 283f.
[215]Note that this is a triad, like the other triads mentioned above.

where these three colors define the set of Aryans.[216] The order of superiority in these colors (with vaiśya/black the lowest) also corresponds to the order in the Svarbhānu story. It is possible, then, that the removal of the sun's darkness produced not only the plants on the earth, in the form of the vaśā that is sacrified, but also the totality of beings that subsists on them, namely, the Aryan tripartition.

There may also be a simple connection between a variety of colors and the fertility subsequently created on the earth. In another story of the 'bald earth', the earth invokes a dappled (pr̥śni) cow, and various colors enter her. Plants then arise.

> AB V.23 iyaṃ vā alomikevāgra āsīt saitam mantram apaśyad āyaṃ gauḥ pr̥śnir akramīd iti tām ayam pr̥śnir varṇa āviśan nānārūpo yaṃ-yaṃ kāmam akāmayata yad idaṃ kiṃ cauṣadhayo vanaspatayaḥ sarvāṇi rūpāṇi
>
> This (earth) was 'hairless', as it were, in the beginning. She saw this mantra: "This dappled cow has come hither." This dappled, variegated color entered her. Whatever she desired, whatever plants, trees[217]—all forms—(then entered her).[218]

According to a passage like this, it is the *fact* of variety, of whatever sort (such as a mixture of colors), that is life-giving. Unity is sterile.[219]

[216]Cf. Puhvel (1987, p. 159f.) on "the canonic colors of the Indo-European three social classes, white for the priests, red for the warriors, and green/blue for the productive class." This last, of course, does not fit here. Puhvel believes that the cost of producing white and red garments (by bleaching and by expensive dyes, respectively) explains their "privileged" status, but surely color symbolism has more to do with it: white for light and purity, red for blood?

[217]Keith (1920, ad loc.) unaccountably translates vanaspatayaḥ as 'birds'!

[218]Cf. also ŚB V.1.3.3.

[219]It is difficult not to be reminded here of the poetry of G. M. Hopkins, despite the great gulf between their traditions, especially "Pied Beauty," which begins "Glory be to God for dappled things."

CHAPTER 10

The Wounding of the Sun

We now know how the sun was freed from its untoward darkening and what good came of it. The questions remain: how did the sun get into this predicament in the first place, and who is Svarbhānu, the supposed villain of the myth, who put him there?

A. Who Is Svarbhānu?

The name in Vedic occurs only in this context, indeed only in the inflexible initial sentence of the myth (and in two subsequent verses of the RVic version, both times in the phrase svàrbhānoḥ . . . māyā́ḥ 'the magical powers of S.' [V.40.6, 8]). This character inflicts the fateful wound and disappears from the story, so the only clue we have to him is his name. It is, of course, notoriously difficult and dangerous to etymologize proper names, but in this case the etymology is obvious. Svàrbhānu is simply a nominalized epithet, a bahuvrīhi (possessive compound) meaning 'having the light of the sun' (cf. svàr-cakṣas- 'having the appearance of the sun', svàr-mīḍha- 'having the reward of the sun', or for that matter Apālā's epithet sū́rya-tvac- 'sun-skinned', lit. 'having the skin of the sun').[220] This has traditionally been consid-

[220]O'Flaherty rather curiously compares the phrase svàrbhānur āsuráḥ (her 'sunlight demon') with the American television character Cookie Monster ("he eats sunlight as the monster eats cookies" [1981, p. 189, n. 3]), as if this phrase were instead a compound (*svarbhānv-āsura-) and as if āsura- were capable of governing an object. Clever, but grammatically impossible and semantically distorting.

ered what we might call a proleptic name: he is called Svarbhānu because by his action in the myth he *gets possession* of the sun's light. As Lanman put it: "I trust it will not be deemed a forcing of the Bahuvrīhi idea if I interpret *Súvar-bhānu* as 'having, *i.e.* keeping *or* withholding the sun's beams'."[221] But, as we have seen, the myth itself gives no reason to believe that Svarbhānu himself actually gets the light. Rather it seems that the light remains in the sun, covered by various kinds of darkness, and shines forth again when the coverings are removed. So he must be one 'having the sun's light' for some other reason.

At this point it is worthwhile asking who or what else besides the sun has "bhānu-" and who or what else (if anything) can have the bhānu- of the sun. It is at this point that things become very clear. In the RV bhānu is posited occasionally of various beings and entities, such as the Maruts (e.g., V.59.1) or the Aśvins' chariot (VI.62.2). It is regularly attributed to the sun and to Uṣas 'Dawn'. But the being whose bhānu is most consistently mentioned is Agni, by a large margin (there are approximately forty such passages in the RV). Even more important, Agni's bhānu is on a number of occasions compared with the sun's. This comparison is made of no other being.

RV II.2.8 *svàr ṇá* dīded aruṣéṇa *bhānúnā*

Like the sun he shone with ruddy light.

RV II.8.4 ā́ yáḥ *svàr ṇá bhānúnā,* citró vibhā́ty arcíṣā

Who shines forth widely with his light like the sun, bright with his beam.[222]

In other words, to anyone familiar with the traditional phraseology of the RV, the epithet svàrbhānu would automatically evoke Agni. So, unless we can find good reasons to dispute this, for a Vedic audience by far the most likely candidate to be Svarbhānu is the fire god Agni.

One might object that the other constant epithet of Svarbhānu is Āsura- 'Asuryan' or 'Son of Asura' and that this designation would prevent or hinder the identification of Agni and Svarbhānu, since in the Brāhmaṇas the Asuras are the implacable foes of the Devas, the gods (among whom Agni is numbered). However, as is well known, the

[221]Lanman 1893, p. 190; similarly Macdonell 1897, p. 160.
[222]Cf. also V.26.2, VI.4.6, VII.3.6, X.43.9.

position of the Asuras and of the word ásura- is different in the RV from that in the Brāhmaṇas. The Asuras are not automatically the villainous opponents of the Devas in this early text.[223] In fact Agni is on a number of occasions called ásura- or compared to an ásura- — more than any other god in the Family Books (seven times—no other god is so called there more than two or three times).[224]

The same is true of the rarer word āsurá- in the RV. Āsurá- is found five times in the RV, twice in our hymn (svàrbhānu- āsurá-). In the late RV it is used once of Indra's enemy Namuci (X.131.4), but in its other two occurrences it refers to two gods of the highest respectability, once to Varuṇa (V.85.5) *and* once to Agni (III.29.11) in a passage that is a virtual glossary of Agni's other epithets:

RV III.29.11 tánūnápād ucyate gárbha *āsuró*,[225] nárāśáṃso bhavati
yád vijā́yate
mātaríśvā yád ámimīta mātári, vā́tasya sárgo abhavat
sárīmaṇi

He is called "Tanūnapāt *Āsura*" as an embryo; he becomes
"Narāśaṃsa" when he is brought forth.
"Mātariśvan" when he was created in his mother; he became "Gust of
Wind" (?) in his streaming.

Hale sees āsura- in the Svarbhānu passages as problematic or at least unusual,[226] but of course if Svarbhānu is really Agni, the difficulty disappears: the use of āsura- here would conform to the common usage of ásura as epithet of Agni.

It is possible that (Agni) Svarbhānu always has the epithet āsura as a

[223]For a careful consideration of ásura- and its derivatives and compounds in early Vedic, see W. E. Hale 1986.

[224]By Hale's count (1986, pp. 51f.); cf. also pp. 66 (derivatives in the Family Books), 80 (ásura- in RV I, VIII–X), 102 (ásura- in AV).

[225]Notice that this passage shows the same distraction of epithet and patronymic as the RV Svarbhānu passages V.40.5 and .9:

. . . svàrbhānuḥ, . . . āsuráḥ #

with āsuráḥ occurring at the end of the pāda as here:

tánūnápāt . . . āsuráḥ #

This provides another small piece of support for the identification of Svarbhānu as Agni.

[226]"For the first time in this study a derivative of ásura- appears in relation to a demonic being" (Hale 1986, p. 64).

sort of pun: āsurá- phonologically approximates asūryá- 'sunless', an adjective whose only occurrence in the RV, indeed in all of early Vedic, is also in the fifth (Atri) Maṇḍala, also in an Indra hymn, here of a monstrous enemy of Indra. (Notice also our signature word 'darkness' [támas].)

RV V.32.6 tyáṃ cid . . . śáyānam, asūryé támasi vāvṛdhānám

Even this one (did Indra smash)—(him) lying, growing in sunless darkness.

Since Svarbhānu makes the world 'sunless', the pun would be appropriate.

B. What Did Svarbhānu Do to the Sun?

1. *The Piercing of the Sun*

With Agni as Svarbhānu, we are now in a better position to understand the actual physical manifestations of Svarbhānu's attack. We can begin with the first sentence: svàrbhānur vá̄ āsuráḥ sū́ryaṃ támasāvidhyat 'Svarbhānu Āsura pierced the sun with darkness'. The action of the root √vyadh is accomplished by a particular type of physical object, which is always expressed in the instrumental case. Támasā in our passage is such a weapon.[227] Typical weapons with √vyadh include a 'sharpened arrow or spear' (śáru-),

RV X.87.6 tám ástā vidhya śárvā śíśānaḥ

[227]Támas- 'darkness' is found twice in the RV, outside of the Svarbhānu passages, with √vyadh (compounded with prá), but in the locative. Prá √vyadh means literally 'wound forth', hence something like 'violently throw forth in(to)'.

RV VII.104.3 índrāsomā duṣkṛ́taḥ . . . támasi prá vidhyatam

O Indra and Soma, wound the evildoers forth into darkness.

Similar is I.182.6. Prá is not otherwise found with √vyadh in the RV. Given the idiomatic preverb and the variant case usage, these two passages seem unconnected with the usage in the Svarbhānu passages, where támasā fills the grammatical slot of the weapon. (For more on instrumental weapons, see Watkins 1986.) In later texts támasā occurs on several occasions with √vyadh outside of Svarbhānu, but presumably influenced by this widespread mythic formulation. Cf. AV III.2.5, 6 (on these passages, see further below, Chap. 10, E.3), XVI.7.1; TS VI.1.10.4; JB I.76.

(As) an archer, pierce him with your arrow/spear, sharpening (it).

and immediately following in this hymn:

RV X.87.13 śaravyā̀ . . . yā́, táyā vidhya hŕ̥daye yātudhā́nān

What is (your) arrow/spear, with that pierce the sorcerers in the heart.

a 'sharp weapon',

RV II.30.9 . . . táṃ tigiténa vidhya

Pierce him with a sharp ____

and 'lightning',

RV I.86.9 vídhyatā vidyútā rákṣaḥ[228]

Pierce the demon with lightning.

Consider also X.87.4, where íṣu- 'arrow' appears to be the antecedent of tā́bhir (vidhya):

RV X.87.4 yajñaír íṣūḥ saṃnámamāno agne, vācā́ śalyā́m̐
aśánibhir dihānáḥ
tā́bhir vidhya hŕ̥daye yātudhā́nān

O Agni [note the aggressor], bending (your?) arrows around with (our) worships [= polishing or preparing them?], rubbing (your?) arrow-points with (our) speech, (as if) with stones [= sharpening them?],
With these (arrows?) pierce the sorcerers in the heart.[229]

In post-RVic texts the weapon is almost always an arrow (íṣu-).[230]
Besides these clearly sharp or pointed implements we find in the RV

[228]Note the phonological play here—vídhyatā: vidyútā—two words of entirely different etymology and grammatical identity (second plural imperative verb vs. instrumental singular noun), but differing phonologically only in accent, aspiration of the second consonant, and color of the second vowel.

[229]The exact interpretation of this passage is difficult because the participles saṃnámamāno and dihānáḥ are unclear in this context. But the point remains: the weapons here appear to be sharp.

[230]Cf., e.g., AV I.19.2, III.25.1–3, V.18.15; TS VI.5.5.2.

weapons of less well defined shape, for example, héṣas- 'missile' (X.89.12) or áśman- 'stone' (II.30.4 and cf. X.89.12, with nominative). Several of the weapons are qualified as 'hot' or 'flaming':

RV X.89.12 . . . vidhya . . ., tápiṣṭhena héṣasā dróghamitrān

Pierce the contract breakers with the hottest missile.

RV IV.4.1 ástāsi vídhya rakṣásas tápiṣṭhaiḥ

You are an archer. Pierce the demons with the hottest (arrows?) [cf. X.87.6 above].

RV II.30.4 . . .tápuṣā́śneva vidhya, . . . vīrā́n

Pierce the warriors with your heat/flame, as with a stone.

RV X.87.17 tám . . . arcíṣā vidhya . . .

Pierce him with your flame.

RV VII.104.5 agnitaptébhir yuvám áśmahanmabhiḥ / tápurvadhebhir ajárebhir atríṇo, ní . . . vidhyatam . . .

Do ye two, with fire-/Agni-heated, stone-weaponed, heat-/flame-weaponed, unaging (flames) pierce the Atrins.[231]

The only weapon mentioned in the RV, besides darkness, that does not fall into these categories of sharp and/or heated substances is himá- 'snow' in VIII.32.26 himénāvidhyad árbudam '(Indra) pierced Arbuda with snow'. Unfortunately, this one of Indra's exploits is otherwise obscure (though he harms Arbuda with other means in the RV). Perhaps it involves a trick, like the slaying of Namuci. Or perhaps hiména 'snow, cold' is meant to evoke by direct semantic opposition the *hot* weapons we have just examined.[232] In any case the metrical and grammatical parallelism between

[231]Despite the similarity of name, the Atrins have nothing to do with Atri that I can determine.

[232]For another case in which a RVic poet uses a semantically opposite term to evoke a common formula, consider

RV I.103.7 yát sasántaṃ vájreṇā́bodhayó 'him

támasā́vidhyat – ∪ x in the Svarbhānu passages and
himénāvidhyat – ∪ x here

is striking. This particular configuration—instrumental (weapon) with the imperfect of √vyadh in pāda initial position—is not found elsewhere in the RV.

Thus the ideal weapon with √vyadh appears to be both pointed and hot, like lightning or tongues of flame. As we just saw, flames—the very characteristic of Agni—are several times explicitly (X.87.17) or implicitly (VII.104.5) the weapons. Moreover, in Agni's epithet svàrbhānu we may see an almost teasing reference to the weapon with which he wounds the sun. Though bhānú- itself is not found as an instrumental weapon with √vyadh, it qualifies or is qualified by words related to these weapons. For example, compare

RV X.3.5 . . .yás téjiṣṭhaiḥ . . . bhānúbhir nákṣati dyā́m

(Agni), who with his sharpest brilliance(s) reaches heaven . . .

containing *téjiṣṭha-* . . . (bhānú-) 'sharpest (brilliance)' to RV II.30.9 (above) containing *tigiténa* 'with a sharp (weapon)'. (Téjiṣṭha- and tigitá- are, of course, derived from the same root.) Compare also

RV VI.4.6 ā́ sū́ryo ná bhānumádbhir arkaír, ágne tatántha ródasī ví bhāsā́

O Agni, like the sun with brilliant rays/flames, you have stretched across the two worlds with light,

containing bhānumánt- *arká-* '(brilliant) ray/flame', to RV X.87.17 (above) containing *arcíṣā* 'with flame'.

When you (Indra) "awakened" the sleeping serpent with your cudgel . . .

As I have discussed elsewhere (1982/83, pp. 10ff.), ábodhayaḥ is a substitute for the usual verb in this formula: asvāpayaḥ 'you "put to sleep" [= killed]'. The mnemonic force of formula is so powerful that this type of semantic pun is possible. It is as if, in formal linguistics, one switched the plus/minus value of a semantic feature: [+ make to sleep] → [− make to sleep], that is, 'awaken'; or [+ hot] → [− hot], that is, 'cold' in VIII.32.26 quoted in the text. Negating the feature does not remove it from the semantic complex. Thus, the underlying meaning of VIII.32.26 '(Indra) pierced Arbuda with "snow"' might be someting like '(Indra) pierced Arbuda with a heated (weapon)'. This relation between heat (tápas-, etc.) and 'snow/cold' (himá-) reminds us of the Aśvins aiding Atri in the *hot* earth-cleft *with snow* (hiména, as here), but I can see no precise further connection.

Agni himself is often the subject of √vyadh,[233] in fact is so more often than any other god, including Indra. He is subject principally in two hymns IV.4 and X.87, directed, in Geldner's words, "An Agni den Unholdtöter" (To Agni the demon killer) and "An Agni den Rakṣastöter" (To Agni the Rakṣas [= type of demon] killer), respectively. So the root √vyadh is especially characteristic of Agni and especially in his righteously punishing aspect.

Thus, already in the first sentence of the myth, the epithet Svarbhānu, the verb √vyadh, and the characteristic weapons found with √vyadh would all immediately evoke Agni to the listening Vedic adept and could conjure up a particular visual image: the sharpened, searing flames leaping towards the sky to pierce the sun and leave burnt and blackened spots on the surface of his perfect skin.

2. *The Māyā́ of Svarbhānu*

Another image is evoked in other parts of the RVic version.

RV V.40.5cd áksetravid yáthā mugdhó, bhúvanāny adīdhayuḥ

The creatures perceived like a bewildered one, not knowing the place.

.6 abc svàrbhānor ádha yád indra māyā́, avó divó vártamānā avā́han
gūḷhā́ṃ sū́ryaṃ támasā

Then, O Indra, when you smashed down from heaven the circling 'magic spells' of Svarbhānu, (Atri found) the sun, hidden by darkness.

.8d svàrbhānor ápa māyā́ aghukṣat

(Atri) has hidden away the 'magic spells' of Svarbhānu.

Here we have a sun not 'pierced' but 'hidden' by darkness, a swirling māyā́ (magic spell), which is so encompassing that men on earth cannot see where they are. If we take phraseology seriously—and it is, of course, the whole point of my approach that we must, always, and not

[233]RV IV.4.1, 5; IV.8.8; X.87.4, 6, 13, 17 (all but IV.4.5 and IV.8.8 quoted above passim).

merely when it is convenient—then this image seems incompatible with the first: the piercing with sharp darkness and the hiding of the sun by swirling darkness are different pictures. Though as images they are incompatible, they can be reconciled: as separate aspects of the attacker, Svarbhānu / Agni. Accompanying the pointed flames of the fire are thick clouds of smoke, which can obscure the sky from those on earth, indeed make even earthly features invisible. It is this other 'weapon', this māyā́ or magic effect of Agni's, that must be involved in the passages just quoted.

Elsewhere in the RV the flame of Agni and his smoke are frequently juxtaposed or played off against each other, allowing an easy paradox: he who is bright yet dark. Following is a simple example, where bhānú- and dhūmá- 'smoke' appear in sequence, both in the instrumental:

RV VI.48.6 ā́ yáḥ papraú *bhānúnā* ródasī ubhé, *dhūména* dhāvate diví

(Agni,) who filled both worlds with his *brilliance,* flows to heaven with his *smoke.*

It is often stated that smoke reaches to heaven.

RV V.11.3 dhūmás te ketúr abhavad diví śritáḥ

Your smoke became a banner stretched to heaven.[234]

This passage is especially striking because it allows comparison with a passage of almost identical phraseology, but in which 'smoke' is replaced by māyā́.

RV V.63.4 māyā́ vām mitrāvaruṇā diví śritā́, sū́ryo jyótiś carati citrám ā́yudham
tám abhréṇa vr̥ṣṭyā́ gū́hatho diví

O Mitra and Varuṇa, your māyā́ is stretched to/in the sky. The sun [N.B.!], the light wanders (as) a bright weapon, (but) you hide him in the sky with a cloud, with rain.

Though the māyā́ hiding the sun here is a rain cloud, the identity of the phrasing between V.63.4 and V.11.3:

[234]Cf. IV.6.2, VI.2.6, VII.3.3, VII.16.3.

RV V.63.4 māyā́ . . . diví śritā́
RV V.11.3 dhūmā́ḥ . . . diví śritā́ḥ

allows us to make the equation māyā́ = dhūmá '(cloud of) smoke'. The māyā́ in V.63.4 interposes an impenetrable visual barrior, hides the sun. So also the māyā́ of V.40.6 and 8 in the Svarbhānu hymn. (Notice that all passages now under discussion come from the same Maṇḍala, hence the same family of poets.) That the māyā́ of V.40.6 are vártamāna- 'turning, swirling, circling' (as smoke does) adds a further touch of visual verisimilitude.

Thus the darkness in this myth has two aspects, both physical manifestations of Agni. It is, on the one hand, a weapon, piercing the sun: Agni's sharp flame (or rather its result, the burnt and blackened spots where the flame has penetrated); but, on the other, it is also the enveloping clouds of smoke that hide the sun from the sight of those below. The deliverance of the sun must therefore also have two aspects. The clouds must be removed ('smashed down' áva √han V.40.6; 'hidden away' ápa √guh V.40.8), so the wounded sun can be found, and then the wound must be healed. This helps explain the variant ways in which the deliverance of the sun is described.

3. Smoke in the Skin-Disease Charm?

The identification of māyā́ with smoke may also explain another detail we left aside long ago: the āsurī in the AV skin-disease charm.[235] Recall the problem: in AV I.24 a cure for skin disease is made from a dark substance transformed into trees.

AV I.24.1 suparṇó jātáḥ prathamás, tásya tvám̐ pittám āsitha
tád āsurī́ yudhā́ jitā́, rūpám̐ cakre vánaspátīn

The 'well-winged' (sun) was born first; of it thou wast the gall. This the Āsurī, conquered in battle (?), gave form to as trees.

AV I.24.2 āsurī́ cakre prathamédám̐ kilāsabheṣajám idám̐ kilāsanā́śanam
ánīnaśat kilā́sam̐ sárūpām akarat tvácam

The Āsurī first made this a cure for kilāsa, a destroyer of kilāsa.
She destroyed the kilāsa (and) made the skin of even color/form.

[235]See Chap. 6, B.3.

As we saw above, the elements of this charm look very like those in both the Svarbhānu myth and the Apālā myth: something removed from the sun both becomes vegetation and cures a skin disease. The problem lies in the creator of this cure: it is an Āsurī (female Āsura), who ought to be unfavorably viewed, and moreover she is 'conquered in battle' (yudhā́ jitā́, vs. 1) and should therefore not have the power to accomplish cures. We noted above the struggles commentators have had with this problem.

Who is the āsurī? The feminine form of this adjective is relatively rare in Vedic; it most commonly occurs in a widespread mantra where it modifies māyā́ 'magic power' and implicitly applies to the earth:

> VS XI.69 (= TS IV.1.9.2; MS II.7.7; III.1.9; KS XVI.7; ŚB VI.6.2.6)
> dŕ̥m̐hasva devi pr̥thivi svastáya, āsurī́ māyā́ svadháyā kr̥tā́si

> Be firm, O goddess earth, for well-being. Thou art the asuryan magic power, created by your own power.

I will not attempt to interpret the purport of this mantra, but simply suggest that with the āsurī́ of AV I.24.1 we supply māyā́ as well.[236]

If we do this, we are immediately reminded of the māyā́ of Svarbhānu (Āsura) in the RVic Svarbhānu hymn:

> RV V.40.6ab *svàrbhānor* ádha yád indra *māyā́,* avó divó vártamānā avā́han

> Then, O Indra, when you smashed down from heaven the circling magic spells of Svarbhānu (Āsura).

> .8d svàrbhānor ápa māyā́ aghukṣat

> He hid the magic spells of Svarbhānu (Āsura).

Here we have the asuryan māyā́ defeated, as in AV I.24.1. Moreover, we have identified these māyā́ in RV V.40 as clouds of Agni's smoke. This veil of smoke referred to by māyā́ is the darkness that is removed

[236]This seems to some extent to be Sāyaṇa's solution, who glosses āsurī́ of AV I.24.1 with asurāṇām māyā kā cana strī (the māyā of the Asuras, some woman or other). Cf. Bloomfield 1897, ad loc.

from the sun and that in other versions of the story becomes vegetation.[237]

What relevance does this have to the AV skin-disease charm? A multistep process of identifications will help illuminate the mythological background of this charm. We supply māyā́ with āsurī́ in the charm on the basis of VS XI.69 (etc.) just quoted; we then identify this supplied māyā́ with the māyā́ of Svarbhānu Āsura in RV V.40. Since we interpreted the māyā́ in that hymn as referring to clouds of smoke (on the basis of the similarity between RV V.11.3 and V.63.4, as well as our identification of Svarbhānu as Agni), we can interpret the āsurī́ (māyā́) of AV I.24 as 'smoke', as well. The circle is completed, and the charm makes sense.

The skin-disease charm has as its mythological mainspring the legend of Svarbhānu, seen, as it were, from the asuryan side: the asuryan māyā́/smoke is defeated and transformed into trees (= 'hair'), yielding thereby a cure for skin disease, just as the sun was cured of its skin disease by the removal of this same māyā́, which became the 'hair' of the earth. I would therefore translate I.24.1cd tád āsurī́ yudhā́ jitā́, rūpáṃ cakre vánaspátīn as 'Then the asuryan (māyā́/smoke) conquered in battle was made into the form (of) trees' and I.24.2ab āsurī́ cakre prathamédáṃ kilāsabheṣajám as 'The asuryan (māyā́/smoke) was first made into this cure for kilāsa'.

I have spelled out the identifications that underlie this interpretation heavy-handedly, even though I believe the actual process for the audience was lighter, quicker, and less conscious than I, of necessity, have portrayed it. This process of chaining identifications may seem tortuous, and because of the many links in the chain, the results—in this case the interpretation of the mythological basis of the skin-disease charm—may seem fragile, suspect. However, I think this is our impression only because we are not of the culture that made these particular connections. Even in our own more heterogeneous and less verbally acute culture, the mention of a peripheral but salient detail can evoke without effort a whole narrative complex associated with it. For exam-

[237]In AV I.24 it is also equated with the sun's gall (pittám). Pittám is not a particularly well-defined substance in Vedic, but it is worth noting that it is identified with Agni in a well-attested mantra (AV XVIII.3.5 ≅ VS XVII.6, TS IV.6.1.2, MS II.10.1, KS XVII.17, ŚB IX.1.2.27) ágne pittám apā́m asi 'O Agni, thou art the gall of the waters'. Cf. Filliozat 1949, p. 137, for this identification in Ayurvedic medicine. This gives us another indirect connection between the cure of the skin disease kilāsa and Agni.

ple, a trail of bread crumbs conjures up a witch, an oven, a gingerbread house, and two children; the mention of porridge does the same for three bears, three beds, and a girl with golden hair. The links in these chains are forged so early and so firmly that we are not aware of the oddity of these associative connections.

C. The Svarbhānu Myth as Reflecting the Physical World

1. *Catastrophic Events*

Let us return to the Svarbhānu myth proper and look briefly at real world analogies to these mythical events: what in the physical world could suggest a crisis of such cosmic dimensions that the sun itself needs to be rescued? The answer given in the past has always been an eclipse, but this makes sense neither physically nor mythically.

The obscuring of the sun by smoke could be a relatively common occurrence. A sufficiently serious fire of the dimensions of a forest fire will produce a blanket of smoke through which the sun temporarily cannot penetrate. What about the darkness that pierces the sun? This question yields a more speculative—and more interesting—possibility. When I first presented the Svarbhānu myth as a paper,[238] I had considered and rejected the possibility that the myth depicts sunspots, since I had assumed that sunspots are invisible to the naked eye and therefore had not been discovered before the invention of the telescope. However, at the presentation of the paper H. Scharfe suggested the possibility of sunspots and has since kindly supplied me with a wealth of material concerning ancient observations of sunspots, primarily by the Chinese, but also intermittently elsewhere.[239] Indeed, I think it quite

[238]At the American Oriental Society Annual Meeting, Los Angeles, Spring 1987.

[239]Following are excerpts from Professor Scharfe's extensive communication to me on the history of sunspot observation, along with the references he supplied me.

"Was it physically possible for the Vedic Indians or, for that matter, premodern man in general to observe sunspots?

"There is overwhelming evidence that this was indeed possible or even likely. While it is normally not advisable to look at the sun for any length of time, the sun can often be observed with impunity during sunrise and sunset, especially when the air is hazy; it can also be observed *through the haze of forest fires* (my italics) or reflected in water. . . .

"The earliest recording of sunspots may be ascribed to Theophrastos (370–290 B.C.), the learned disciple of Aristotle. . . . But the idea that the sun may not be pure after all was repugnant to Europeans, and thus various observations of sunspots were neglected or explained away as passings of one of the interior planets. The death of Charlemagne in A.D. 814 was preceded either in 807 or 814 by a large sunspot that could be seen for seven or eight days. . . .

likely that sunspots *are* the physical model for the myth. Given the importance of the sun in Vedic religion, seeing such a serious and inexplicable blemish on it would surely have provoked a mythological and ritual response. Since, as Scharfe has suggested (see n. 239), sunspots could be detected relatively easily through a haze of smoke, the association of fire and smoke with the phenomenon is not surprising.[240]

I do not want to imply by this that the Svarbhānu myth is, in simple nature-mythology fashion, primarily or only "about" sunspots. Merely that this remarkable and presumably unsettling phenomenon has been incorporated into the mythology and, along with the other "issues" found in myth, dealt with.

2. *Cyclical Events*

Although I believe that, insofar as this myth makes reference to ["is about"] natural phenomena, it refers to sunspots, I also think that the myth has been incorporated (co-opted) into a more routine and predictable part of the ritual cycle. Observable sunspots, after all, are rare and (at least for premodern astronomers) unexpected phenomena—

"There are a number of observations of sunspots by Arab and European authorities before Galilei; Galilei observed sunspots with the aid of a telescope and projection on paper.

"The primary tradition in the observation of sunspots was, however, in China. The first clear reference goes back to the year 28 B.C., and careful records were kept from then on. 122 major sunspots are recorded in the years from 28 B.C. to 1638 A.D. . . . The observation of sunspots goes probably way back beyond 28 B.C. Sunspots were called *wu* which means 'crow' as well as 'black,' and the myth of a crow in the sun was traditional in the time of the Chou and early Han dynasties. A silk painting showing a crow in the sun was excavated from a tomb dating from the middle of the second century B.C. . . ."

(References: Sarton 1947, pp. 69–71; Needham 1959, pp. 434–36; Bray and Loughhead 1964, p. 1; Roy 1982, p. 495.)

A report in the *Boston Globe* (Alan M. MacRobert, "Sun Sure to Produce More Dazzling Light Shows," April 3, 1989) also confirms the visibility of some sunspots: "Early in March, a gigantic dark spot appeared on the face of the sun. Unlike most sunspots it was so big that it could easily be seen with no optical aid other than a suitable filter." See also Schove 1950; 1983, pp. xi, 2, 36–38, 39, 51–69; Clark and Stephenson 1978; Eddy 1980; Bicknell 1968 (I am grateful to Robert Burkhardt for this last reference). Sunspot activity occurs in eleven-year cycles, but I have not found any mythic or ritual consciousness of this fact in Svarbhānu.

[240]Indeed, "in medieval Russia in 1365 and 1371 the smoke from forest fires made the sun appear 'bloody' and sunspots are clearly described in, e.g., the Niconovsky chronicle" (Schove 1950, p. 22 [1983, p. 36]).

unsettling for precisely this reason—and the vast, creaking machine of ritual would not provide a regular place to "deal" with them. But other things *regularly* happen to the sun; most disturbing perhaps is the gradual shortening of the day after the summer solstice as the sun progresses southwards from its northernmost point. It should come as no surprise that this yearly progress is treated, and thereby controlled, by a ritual.

This is the year-long Sattra ('session') known as the Gavāmayana or (literally) 'progress of the cows'.[241] The whole design of the Sattra mimics the shape of the year, with the endpoints the two solstices; this design is explicitly recognized by the Brāhmaṇic commentators. The Sattra begins at the beginning of the new year, at the time of the winter solstice, and the year is divided into two complementary periods of six months. In general, the ritual activities of the second period exactly reverse the actions of the first, producing a sort of bilateral symmetry.[242] Two especially important days are celebrated: the Viṣuvant Day (also known as the Divākīrtya Day, after the name of its first sāman) between the two six-month periods and the Mahāvrata Day at the end. In accounts of this ritual, both ancient and modern, the Viṣuvant Day has been overshadowed by the Mahāvrata Day, the latter including as it does harp, lutes, drums, singing and dancing female slaves, and in some versions ritual copulation (see, e.g., MŚS VII.2.7). But it is the Viṣuvant Day that will engage our attention here.

Viṣuvant- means 'having equal sides', 'midmost', and it must refer to the summer solstice, surrounded by exactly equivalent halves of the year.[243] This is implied by the complementarity of the six-month halves of ritual observance and is in fact explicitly stated in the KB:

> KB XXV.1 sa ṣaṇ māsān udaṅṅ eti ṣaḍ āvṛttāṃs tasmāt sattriṇaḥ ṣaḍ evordhvān māso yanti ṣaḍ āvṛttān

[241]Cf. Hillebrandt 1897, p. 157; Eggeling, ŚB II.426f.; BŚS XVI.13–23; ĀpŚS XXI.15–23; MŚS VII.2.4.13–VII.2.8; VārŚS III.2.3, etc.

[242]This bilateral arrangement gives rise to a predictable metaphor, of the Sattra as a man, with the central Viṣuvant Day as his trunk and the two six-month periods as his limbs.

> PB IV.7.1 ātmā vā eṣa saṃvatsarasya yad viṣuvān pakṣāv etāv abhito bhavataḥ
>
> The Viṣuvant (Day) is the body (/the trunk) of the year; on both sides of it are these two halves (/wings).

Cf. also AB IV.22, ŚB XII.2.3.6.

[243]It could, of course, theoretically also refer to the winter solstice, but that is impossible here, given that the Sattra begins at that time.

It (the sun) goes north for six months, then six months reversed; therefore the performers go for six months forward, then for six months reversed.

The period immediately surrounding the Viṣuvant Day is characterized by more concentrated ritual activity than the relatively tranquil months before and after. Right before and right after this day are two periods of three Svarasāman Days, which are themselves sandwiched by an Abhijit Day (before) and a Viśvajit Day (afterwards). All this seems designed to mark out the Viṣuvant Day for special notice. On this day itself the complementarity characterizing the entire Sattra is emphasized by making the offerings first in the usual order and then reversed.

ĀpŚS XXI.21.6 tān ūrdhvān āvṛttāṃś ca viṣuvati

On the Viṣuvant (Day) (they offer) them ascending [i.e., in the usual order] and reversed.

Between these two sets of offerings, an extra one is made—to Sūrya, with a particular verse—as we see in the immediately following passage:

ĀpŚS XXI.21.7 teṣāṃ madhye sauryam ud u tyaṃ jātavedasam iti

In the middle of these (offerings) (they offer) one to Sūrya, [with the verse RV I.50.1] "Up (they carry) this Jātavedas . . . "

Moreover, there is an extra victim sacrificed, an unblemished white goat, again to Sūrya.[244]

AB IV.19 sauryam paśum anyaṅgaśvetam savanīyasyopālambhyam ālabheran sūryadevatyaṃ hy etad ahaḥ

They should sacrifice an unmarked white animal to Sūrya in addition to the (normal) one for the pressing day. For this day has Sūrya as its deity.

244 Cf. MŚS VII.2.5.4, ĀpŚS XXI.23.1, BŚS XVI.14, VārŚS III.2.3.23, ŚāṅkhŚS XI.13.8–9.

The verses accompanying this victim are RV I.115.1–6, beginning with vs. 1 citrám devā́nām úd agād ánīkam 'The bright face of the gods has arisen'.[245]

All of this ought to bring to mind a number of details we have already learned about the Svarbhānu myth. It ought to, because the Svarbhānu myth is explicitly linked to the Viṣuvant Day (and/or its surrounding Svarasāman Days) in most of its tellings in PB, JB, and KB.[246] In some of these passages the Svarasāman Days are the remedy used to free the sun, in others the Divākīrtya Sāmans;[247] as just noted, both the Svarasāman Days and Divākīrtya Sāmans are prominent parts of the Gavāmayana ritual. The white goat sacrificed for Sūrya reminds us of the white ewe that is the final result of the wiping away of the sun's darkness. Moreover, the verses that accompany the extra libation to Sūrya (RV I.50.1) and the sacrifice of the goat (RV I.115.1) are exactly the same verses we saw above recited at the midday pressing, as the gold piece/sun is brought up from the ghee and unwrapped—just before gold is given to the Ātreya priest.[248]

In other words, it seems that the Svarbhānu myth, though originally concerning something else, that is, sunspots, was regularly associated with, and narrated at, the summer solstice, and some of its mythic details have been incorporated into the ritual, just as some of the ritual details of the Viṣuvant Day have been plugged into some versions of the myth. Why?

The other myth regularly told at this point in the Gavāmayana is one we have already examined:[249] the gods fear the sun will fall from the

[245]According to ŚāṅkhŚS XI.13.9.

[246]I.e., the Brāhmaṇas of the Sāma and Rig Vedas: PB IV.5.2, IV.6.13, as well as XXIII.16.2; JB II.386, 390; KB XXIV.3. PB XXIII.16.2 is not in the Gavāmayana section proper, as the other two passages cited are, but in a section concerning the second 21-day rite. However, this 21-day rite is clearly simply an abbreviated Gavāmayana taking place around the summer solstice. It includes as its centerpiece three Svarasāman Days, a Divākīrtya (= Viṣuvant) Day, and three more Svarasāman Days (PB XXIII.16.1), just as the Gavāmayana does. It is specifically prescribed for the summer, when the sun is hottest, as we saw above.

PB XXIII.16.8 naidāghīya upeyuḥ
.9 tad dhy eṣa pratitejiṣṭhaṃ tapati

.8 They should undertake (this rite) in summer.
.9 For at that time this (sun) heats most sharply.

[247]Svarasāman Days: PB IV.5.2, JB II.386, KB XXIV.3; Divākīrtya Sāmans: PB IV.6.13, JB II.390.

[248]See Chap. 9, C.1.

[249]See Chap. 7, C.1.

sky, and they secure it on all sides (viṣuvant- seeming an appropriate term here). The telling of both myths seems a sort of preventive measure: the sun is at its strongest and highest. Though one might think this would lead to celebration, it may at the same time give rise to anxiety and depression[250] about the long inevitable progress to the comparative weakness and darkness at the winter solstice. By reminding the hearers that the sun has been released from worse darkness before, it may allay their fears as the yearly darkness begins, ever so slowly, to return.

Notice also that the appropriate place in the soma sacrifice both to tell and to reenact this myth is what we might term the *daily* equivalent of the summer solstice, namely, the midday pressing, when the sun is at its highest during the day.

D. What Did the Sun Say? RV V.40.7

A few problems in the myth of Svarbhānu remain to unravel. The identification of Svarbhānu as Agni may cast some light on the most obscure verse of the RVic treatment of this myth, vs. 7—a verse I confess I am still not completely certain about.

RV V.40.7 mā́ mā́m imā́ṃ táva sántam atra, irasyā́ drugdhó bhiyásā
ní gārīt
tvám mitró asi satyárādhās, taú mehā́vataṃ váruṇaś ca rā́jā

[The sun:] "O Atri, let him not, deceived/misled by envy (?) and
fear, swallow me, being this one of yours.
You are an ally[251]/Mitra, whose gifts are true; do you
two, (you) and King Varuṇa, help me here."

This is the one piece of direct speech in this hymn, always presumed to be, no doubt rightly, the words of Sūrya, the sun.[252] It is the exact centerpiece of the myth as well, lying between vss. 5–6 and 8–9, and it is the centerpiece of the eclipse theory as well. The famous phrase mā́

[250]A feeling I confess to having at the summer solstice: it's all downhill from now on.

[251]My translation of the common noun mitrá- (masc.) as 'ally' (rather than 'friend') follows that of Brereton 1981; see esp. pp. 25ff. for discussion.

[252]Since this verse comes immediately after the statement (vs. 6d) turī́yeṇa bráhmaṇāvindad átriḥ 'Atri found (it) with the fourth formulation', it is tempting to see the verse as being the fourth formulation, but this makes no sense in context.

mā́m . . . nígārīt 'Let him not swallow me' is the evidence that allows the Svarbhānu myth to be compared with the later Rāhu myth, in which Rāhu swallows the sun. It is also, I hasten to add, the only piece of such evidence in Vedic,[253] and, as it turns out, the phrase can easily be understood in the context of the Vedic myth as we have reconstructed it. It is indeed the easiest part of this verse to understand.

If Svarbhānu is Agni, the sun's fear of being swallowed is justified, for Agni is one of the most voracious beings in the RV. In his benevolent guise as ritual fire, he 'eats' the oblations offered him; as uncontrolled and destructive fire, he 'eats' anything in his path. In either case he is one of the most common subjects of the root √ad 'eat' in the RV, and also appears once as subject of the relatively rare root √gir 'swallow', the root found in (ní) gārīt:

RV X.27.13 pattó jagāra pratyáñcam atti

(Agni)[254] swallowed (him) from the foot (up); he eats him from behind.

Another passage graphically illustrates the pitiless devouring nature even of the *ritual* fire:

RV X.79.4 jā́yamāno mātárā gárbho atti

(Even) while being born, the embryo [= Agni] eats its parents [i.e., the kindling sticks].

So, by saying 'let him not swallow me' in V.40.7, the sun is simply expressing fear of one of Agni's well-known devastating characteristics.

There may also be here a semantic pun on the name of Atri, who is addressed at the end of pāda a. (Note that (ní)gārīt ends pāda b: their shared position puts these two words in perceivable relation to each other.) Atri is derived by most ancient and modern etymologies from

[253]Except, potentially, for ápavratena, for which see below.

[254]On fire as subject here, cf. Geldner, ad loc. The other occurrences of √gir tend to be riddling and mysterious (as indeed is V.40.7) and are not terribly helpful for interpreting V.40.7. However, compare the occurrence of the root in the flood story above (ŚBM I.8.1.3 [≅ ŚBK II.7.3.2]), in which the verb expresses the inescapable violence of creatures against their own kind: utá mátsyo evá mátsyaṃ gilati [ŚBK girati] 'And fish swallows/devours fish'.

the root √ad 'to eat' (via *ad-tri-).[255] For an explicit statement of this derivation of the name, we must wait till the BĀU, in a passage we have already examined.

> ŚB XIV.5.2.6 (= BĀU(M) II.2.4) vā́g evā́trir vācā́ hy ánnam adyáté 'ttir ha vaí nā́maitád yád átrir íti

> Atri is speech. For by speech food is eaten. So "Atri" is really "atti" (eating) by name.

However, already in early Vedic prose the adjective atrí-, always feminine and always modifying prajā́- 'creature', clearly means 'eating, devouring', always in opposition to ādyá- 'to be eaten, devoured', as in a passage we examined in another context:

> MS I.10.13 yéyám úttarā védir yā́ *atrī́ḥ prajā́s* tā́sām eṣā́ yóniḥ . . . yéyáṃ dákṣiṇā védir yā́ ādyā̀ḥ prajā́s tā́sām eṣā́ yóniḥ

> The northern altar is the womb of the *devouring creatures*. . . . The southern altar is the womb of the creatures to be devoured.[256]

Though this potentially negative characteristic of our hero Atri oddly enough seems not to figure in his mythology, there are a set of evil beings named atrín-, already well attested in the RV, who can reasonably be translated 'devourers'.[257] The synchronic derivation of Atri's name would certainly be obvious to a Vedic speaker.

In RV V.40.7 then, the concept 'swallow' may have occurred to the sun (rather than some other kind of fiery destruction) as a sort of ironic reference to the name of his rescuer: 'you (an ally, though also) a devourer (atri), keep *him* from devouring me'.

This leaves us the rest of the verse to deal with, and it is far more intractable. Here are the questions it raises: (1) Why is Svarbhānu '*misled* by jealousy and fear'? (2) Are both halves of the verse addressed to Atri, or is the second half addressed to someone else? If the latter,

[255] Cf. Bergaigne, 1878–83, vol. 2, pp. 467–68; Macdonell 1897, p. 145; Wackernagel-Debrunner, *AIG*, 2.2, p. 710; Mayrhofer, *KEWA*, s.v. However, Mayrhofer, *KEWA*, vol. 3, Nachtr., p. 626, and *EWA* I, p. 59, has become less certain of this etymology. Note also Oldenberg's skepticism (*Noten*, ad II.8.5). Even if this is not the correct diachronic etymology, the perceived synchronic connection would allow such a pun to be made.

[256] Also MS IV.5.1, 6.3; KS XXVII.8, XXVIII.10, XXXVI.7; TS VI.4.10.4–5.

[257] Cf., e.g., RV VII.104.5, in Chap. 10, B.1, and n. 255.

who is it? (3) Why does the sun 'belong' to Atri, and why is this expressed the way it is? I have only partial answers to these questions.

Let us begin with the first question, for which I have some speculative answers (which so far lack complete textual support). By attributing Svarbhānu's actions to his being irasyā́ drugdhó bhiyásā 'misled by jealousy and fear', the sun may be trying to put the best face on things. With drugdhá- 'misled', he seems to be implying that the alleged grounds for Svarbhānu's attack are untrue. If I am right about what these are, he is disputing the accuracy of the accusation of a truly heinous crime. With the words irasyā́ and bhiyásā 'by/with jealousy and fear',[258] he is perhaps imputing other motives to Agni, motives that make sense given the relation between the sun and the fire.

These two beings are in a sense rivals and brothers, being the twin lights of the universe—Sūrya in heaven, Agni on earth. Indeed, as we saw above, in at least one story, the two are together in the same womb before birth and may be rivals. But Sūrya is more powerful, since he is entirely outside human control, and more important to men, since life on earth depends on his continued rising. Agni may be jealous of Sūrya's greater eminence and also fearful of being overwhelmed by him, fearful, too, perhaps of the cosmic consequences of Sūrya's unpunished crime.[259] But I advance these speculations without complete confidence, and think that the significance of irasyā́ drugdhó bhiyásā[260] may rest on parts of the myth that are for us unrecoverable.

Other parts of the verse are more amenable to investigation. To whom is this verse addressed? It is generally assumed that Atri is the addressee throughout,[261] given the vocative atre in pāda a; in this case

[258]It is syntactically possible that drugdháḥ is not to be construed with the two instrumentals, which would then be instrumentals of cause: 'let him, misled/deceived, not swallow me *because of* jealousy and fear'. This alternative does not appreciably change the meaning or improve our ability to understand the verse. Furthermore, the placement of these instrumentals, flanking the past participle, suggests a close syntactic connection with that word. Lanman (1893, p. 188f.) construes bhiyásā with the sun: "I am thine, yet sore affrighted," but RVic word order does not seem to me to be *that* free.

[259]The references to Agni and Sūrya in Vedic literature are so extensive that I have not been able to go through all of them systematically. However, I would not be surprised to find other references to rivalry and fear in their relationship.

[260]One of the problems with this phrase is that our usual method of examining verbal parallels offers little help; in fact, it creates some more puzzlement in the usage of drugdhá-. The linguistic details of this problem I will treat elsewhere.

[261]This interpretation is clear in O'Flaherty's translation (1981, p. 188): "for I am yours, Atri. You are my friend, whose favour is real. I hope that both you and King Varuṇa will help me now." The interpretation is not entirely explicit in Geldner, but it seems the most likely way to interpret his translation and note.

pāda c, tvám mitró asi, is ordinarily translated 'you [= Atri] are a friend . . . ' rather than the otherwise possible 'you are Mitra'. It is undoubtedly the case that the first half of the verse is addressed to Atri. However, for reasons of syntax and vocabulary, I think the second half is directed elsewhere.

Pāda d is a sort of disguised vā́yav índraś ca construction, a construction in which two beings are subjects of a second-person dual verb, one of them addressed in the vocative and the other appended in the nominative (type 'do ye two—you, O *X*, and (that fellow) *Y*' (e.g., vāyav [voc., 'O Vāyu'] indraś [nom., '(that) Indra'] ca).

RV V.40.7cd *tvám* mitró asi . . ., taú mehā́vataṃ *váruṇaś ca* rā́jā

You are an ally. . . . Do ye two, (you, O *X*) and king Varuṇa, help me here.

This syntactic fact, the vā́yav índraś ca construction, has an important, indeed inescapable, *semantic* implication. All vā́yav índraś ca constructions involve already well-established pairs of beings, pairs that enter into substantially attested dvandvas (pair compounds), for example, índrā-víṣṇū, mitrā́-váruṇā, and so forth.[262] Chance pairs of gods or men do not occur in this construction. Yet the standard interpretation of V.40.7 would require a pair váruṇā-átrī- (or átrī-váruṇā-), which would be unprecedented in the construction.

So, in pāda c it seems better to supply as referent of tvám a god who is regularly associated with Varuṇa and can enter into a dvandva with him. The obvious answer might seem to be Mitra (the dvandva mitrā́-váruṇā being extremely well attested), especially given the statement in c tvám mitró asi (you are Mitra/an ally), yielding a translation of cd 'you are Mitra; do ye two, (you) and king Varuṇa, help me here'.

Brereton (1981, pp. 42f.) singles out this passage as showing an unprecedented, or at least unusual, relation between gods and men: "It is primarily the responsibility of gods to help men which is emphasized. There is, however, at least one example of a god pleading with a man for help in accordance with an alliance. This is V.40.7, in which the sun calls upon Atri to rescue him from the evil Svarbhānu." Brereton translates pāda c as "You are an ally whose care is true." If, as I argue, the addressee of this pāda is Indra, then the anomaly that Brereton perceives disappears; Sūrya is calling on another god for help, not on a mortal. Note, in addition, that, according to Brereton, Indra is one of the gods who most characteristically enters into mitrá-s 'alliances' (pp. 34, 39).

For other translations of this passage and further discussion, see Jamison 1988, n. 36.

[262]As I have shown elsewhere (Jamison 1988). Consult this article for further discussion of the construction and of the substantial earlier literature on the subject.

However, I think the answer is more likely Indra, who also frequently appears in a dvandva with Varuṇa (índrā-váruṇā, over forty times). Mitra has not otherwise been mentioned in the hymn, but Indra has already been identified as aiding the rescue of the sun in the previous verse and, indeed, in the vocative.

RV V.40.6ab svàrbhānor ádha yád indra māyā́, avó divó vártamānā avā́han

When, O Indra, you smashed down from heaven the circling magic powers of Svarbhānu . . .

Moreover, the other epithet of the being addressed in 7c is satyárādhas- 'whose gifts are true'. In every other occurrence of this word in the RV except one,[263] it is applied to Indra (six times total).

RV IV.24.2 sá súṣṭuta índraḥ satyárādhāḥ

The well-praised Indra, whose gifts are true . . .

It is a characteristic epithet of Indra and would evoke him in this context.

Verse 7 then is addressed to two different beings, both mentioned in the previous verse. Sūrya first speaks to Atri, then turns to Indra, mentioning also his companion Varuṇa. This change of addressees may well be signalled by the use of the personal pronoun tvám at the beginning of pāda c.[264] Unfortunately neither Indra nor Varuṇa figures in the later Svarbhānu stories, and we only know of Indra's precise role from RV V.40.6ab, just quoted. It is useful to remember, however, that Indra is often credited with 'finding the sun' in cosmogonic contexts, so his aid in this later solar crisis would be likely to be solicited. Among many passages, consider

RV III.39.5 satyáṃ tád índro daśábhir dáśagvaiḥ, sū́ryaṃ viveda támasi kṣiyántam

This is true: Indra, along with the ten Daśagvas, found the sun, (which was) dwelling in darkness.

[263]VII.41.3, where the referent is Bhaga, the 'Distributor'.

[264]For the use of personal pronouns in direct speech for deixis and disambiguation, see Jamison, forthcoming, a; also Insler's comments on that paper in the same volume.

The last puzzle of RV V.50.7 is the phrase mā́m imáṃ táva sántam . . . (lit. 'me, being this one of yours')—puzzling as to both meaning and syntax. Why does the sun say he is Atri's and why does he express it this way? There is no textual evidence for the sun's belonging to Atri, certainly none for his belonging to Atri prior to this event (though their experiences are parallel, as we saw). The only way this can be sensibly interpreted is that Sūrya is making a promise or a proposition: 'I *will be* yours, *if* you help me'. One would expect a subjunctive in such a statement (*asāni tava), but in combining the two clauses, the putative subjunctive was converted into a present participle (there being, of course, no modal participles and no future at all to the verb √as 'to be').[265]

But why the imám 'this one here'? This use of the demonstrative with the personal pronoun (mā́m imáṃ, lit. 'this me') is quite unprecedented, but the sun, of course, is in an unprecedented situation and must make use of extreme verbal measures. I think that the added imám is to emphasize the here and now of the sun's declaration, the specificity of his promise of fealty to Atri.[266] "I, this (sun) here and now, will be yours, O Atri, [if you help me]." It is perhaps like the "hereby" of English performative verbs" "I hereby promise. . . ."[267]

This immediacy may also be signalled by a pun[268] on the vocative atre at the end of the pāda. This vocative appears as atra in sandhi (before i-):

RV V.40.7 mā́ mā́m imáṃ táva sántam *atra,* (irasyā́ . . .)

[265]We might work with a different semantic possibility suggested by sántam. The present participle of the verb √as 'to be', especially in the nominative, is often a concessive, roughly meaning 'although'; this value is not unknown for oblique cases of this participle as well.

RV X.114.5 suparṇáṃ víprāḥ kaváyo vácobhir, *ékaṃ sántam* bahudhā́ kalpayanti

The seers, the poets arrange the bird, (though) being (only) one, in many ways, with their words.

However, taking sántam in this way in V.40.7 seems to me only to cause more problems in interpretation: 'Let him not swallow me, *although* I am yours (?!)'.

[266]The linguistic argumentation leading to this conclusion is complex, and I will present it elsewhere.

[267]A *performative verb* is one which by simply being uttered performs the action expressed by the verb. Examples include verbs like "promise," "warn." A common informal test for performatives in English is whether "hereby" can be appropriately inserted into the utterance.

[268]Different from the pun on the name just discussed.

This atra is identical, save for lack of accent, with the adverb átra 'here'. Hence, atra may be interpreted not merely as the sun's urgent address to his potential rescuer Atri, but also as a sign, along with imám, of the "presentness" of his promise. Recall that the same pun on átra 'here' is responsible for Atri's name in the ŚB account of his birth, when the gods, having gathered up the aborted remains, keep saying, átraivá tā́3d 'Is it (all) here?'.

Thus, in RV V.40.7, the centerpiece of the Svarbhānu hymn, the sun makes this strong statement and pledge of possession, that the sun *will be* Atri's. This then is acted out ritually by the gift of gold to the Ātreya at the midday pressing,[269] since gold is equivalent to the sun. This gold, remember, is often called atri-hiraṇya- 'the gold of Atri', and is closely connected to the ritual enactment of the freeing of the sun at this same pressing.

I do not claim to have solved all the problems in this difficult verse; the notorious allusive difficulty of dialogue in the RV is here compounded by having just a snatch of it, from only one mouth. But it does seem clear that this verse can be interpreted consistently with the myth as we have thus far constructed it, even with the identification of Agni with Svarbhānu.

E. What Did the Sun Do Wrong?

Now we arrive at the last major crux in our myth. If Svarbhānu is not the Eclipse Demon or some other wicked Asura, but our familiar and basically virtuous Agni, then we must revise our ideas of the whole mainspring of the action. It no longer appears that the innocent sun is wounded in a wanton act of violence, a kind of celestial mugging. If Agni attacked him, then Agni may have had a reason—the sun may have deserved it. In fact, there is a good deal of evidence that he did. On several occasions he is said to need a Prā́yaścitti- an 'expiation'.

> KS XI.5 (≅ TS II.1.2.2, PB XXIII.16.2) svàrbhānur vā́ āsurás sū́ryaṃ támasāvidhyat sá ná vyàrocata tásmai devā́ḥ prā́yaścittim aichan

> Svarbhānu Āsura pierced the sun with darkness. He did not shine forth. The gods sought an expiation for him.

[269] See Chap. 9, C and C.1.

Now, of course, a Prā́yaścitti is necessary for all sorts of mistakes, including minor and often unavoidable or unintentional infractions of the myriad ritual prescriptions; it does not necessarily imply that a major breach of the moral code has been committed. It may be that by its unavoidable inability to shine, the sun incurred the need for an expiation. But it could well be something more serious. Indeed in an AV passage clearly alluding to this myth, the sun has to be freed from énas-, a word about as close to 'sin' as we get in Vedic.

AV II.10.8 sū́ryam r̥tám̐ támaso grā́hyā ádhi, devā́ muñcánto asr̥jan nír énasaḥ

The gods, freeing the sun (and the truth?)[270] from the seizure of darkness, released (him) from sin.[271]

What is this énas? Bloomfield dismisses it: "The moralizing cause of the sun's mishap, his énas- (sin), is not expressed distinctly anywhere, nor is it to be taken au grand sérieux."[272] However, though there seems to be no outright legal indictment[273] of the sun for this énas- in Vedic, there are some strong indications as to the nature of the deed, and it *is* serious.

1. *Prajāpati's Incest*

Let us turn to another extremely familiar tale in Brāhamaṇic mythology, Prajāpati's incest with his daughter, Uṣas. The opening of this

[270]The interpretation of r̥tá- in this verse is not clear. Whitney (AV, ad loc., seemingly followed by Lüders 1959, vol. 2, p. 635, n. 1) takes it as a functioning past participle of the root √r̥ (pres. r̥ṇóti, etc.) and translates: "The Gods, releasing from the seizure of darkness the sun *whom it had befallen,* let him loose from sin" (my italics). But I think it highly unlikely that the composer of this hymn could have had any reasonable expectation that his hearers would interpret an r̥tá- as anything but the extremely common and semantically crucial word r̥tá- 'truth'. In other words, though a real past participle r̥-tá- could have been easily formed, I very much doubt that anyone would have formed it in competition with the semantically specialized r̥tá- already existent. There would simply be too much possibility of confusion. Thus, I think it best to take it as belonging to the familiar r̥tá- 'truth', though this otherwise does not figure in the myth. So Bloomfield (1897, ad loc.).

[271]The AV makes another connection between grā́hi- 'seizure' and támas- 'darkness', this time with our verb √vyadh 'pierce', in

AV III.2.5 grā́hyāmítrām̐ṣ támasā vidhya śátrūn

Pierce the enemies with "seizure", the rivals with darkness.

[272]Bloomfield 1897, p. 294.

[273]Like the indrasya kilbiṣāni passages discussed above, Chap. 2, A.3.

myth is not as rigid as Svarbhānu, but it generally has a form like the following:

> MS III.6.5 prajā́patir vaí svā́ṃ duhitáram ádhyaid uṣásam
>
> Prajāpati 'approached' his own daughter, Dawn (Uṣas).

The relevant passages are the following:[274]

> MS III.6.5 prajā́patir vaí svā́ṃ duhitáram ádhyaid uṣásaṃ tásya rétaḥ párāpatat té devā́ abhisámagachanta . . . tád údagr̥bhṇan . . . téna yajñám atanvanta
>
> Prajāpati 'approached' his own daughter, Dawn (Uṣas). His seed flew forth.[275] The gods approached (it) together (. . . and) picked it up. . . . With it they stretched the worship.
>
> MS IV.2.12 prajā́patir vaí svā́ṃ duhitáram abhyàkāmayatoṣásaṁ sā́ rohíd abhavat tā́m ŕ̥śyo bhūtvā́dhyait tásmā ápavratam achadayat tám ā́yatayābhiparyā́vartata tásmād vā́ ábibhet sò 'bravīt paśūnā́ṃ tvā pátiṃ karomy átha me mā́ sthā íti . . . tám abhyāyátyāvidhyat sò 'rodīt tád vā́ asyaitán nā́ma rudrá íti . . . táto yát prathamáṁ rétaḥ parā́patat tád agnínā páryainddha . . . táto yád atyásravat tád bŕ̥haspátir úpāgr̥hṇāt
>
> Prajāpati desired his own daughter, Dawn (Uṣas). She became a red doe.[276] He, having become a buck, 'approached' her. It seemed 'against

[274]A very abbreviated version is found in PB VIII.2.10.

[275]On párā √pat 'fly forth', see above, Chap. 3, C.1.

[276]The transformation of Uṣas and Prajāpati into red doe (rohít-) and buck (ŕ̥śya-), respectively, happens in several versions (MS IV.2.12, AB III.33, JB III.262 [where Prajāpati becomes rather a pr̥ṣata- 'speckled deer']). This may seem irrelevant to the story as a whole, but the transformations carry with them an associative baggage of their own. First, the transformation of a woman into a rohít is used in another tale as a stratagem to escape unwanted sexual advances. In the TS a woman effects this change to run away from the Gandharvas, this time with success.

> TS VI.1.6.5–6 (té devā́ abruvant strī́kāmā vaí gandharvā́ striyā́ níṣ krīṇāméti té vā́caṁ stríyam ékahāyanīṃ kr̥tvā́ táyā nír akrīṇant) sā́ rohíd rūpáṃ kr̥tvā́ gandharvébhyaḥ // apakrámyātiṣṭhat
>
> (The gods said, "The Gandharvas are fond of women. Let's ransom (the soma) with a woman." They, having made Speech into a woman one year old, ransomed (soma) with her.) She, having made herself a red doe in form, having run away from the Gandharvas, (just) stood (there).

On the other hand, the coupling of rohít- and ŕ̥śya- seems to have been something of a byword for sexual activity (like 'rabbits' in modern English?), as in a verse occurring in two AVic hymns devoted to the curing of impotence:

commandment' to him (Rudra). He (Rudra) turned toward him (Prajāpati) with an outstretched (arrow).[277] He (Prajāpati) feared him (Rudra) and said, "I will make you lord of beasts, but don't stand against me." . . . (Rudra), on taking aim, pierced him. He cried out (*arodīt*). And that is his name: *Rud*ra. . . . The first seed that flew forth was kindled by the fire. . . . The (seed) that overflowed Bṛhaspati collected.

ŚB I.7.4.1 (≅ ŚBK II.7.2.1–2) prajā́patir ha vaí svā́ṃ duhitáram abhídadhyau / dívaṃ voṣásaṃ vā mithuny ènayā syām íti tā́ṁ sáṃ babhūva

.2 tád vaí devā́nām ā́ga āsa / yá itthám̐ svā́ṃ duhitáram asmā́kam̐ svásāraṃ karótī́ti

.3 té ha devā́ ūcuḥ / yò 'yáṃ deváḥ paśūnā́m ī́ṣṭe 'tisaṃdháṃ vā́ ayáṃ carati yá itthám̐ svā́ṃ duhitáram asmā́kam̐ svásāraṃ karóti vídhyemám íti tám̐ rudrò 'bhyāyátya vivyādha tásya sāmí rétaḥ prácaskanda . . .

.1 Prajāpati longed for his own daughter, either Heaven or Dawn. Thinking, "Might I make a pair with her," he united with her.

.2 To the gods this was a sin: "Who does thus to his own daughter, our sister (commits a sin)."

.3 The gods said to this god who is Master of Beasts (Rudra), "This one violates custom(ary law) who does thus to his own daughter, our sister. Pierce him!" Rudra, on taking aim, pierced him. Half of his seed spilled forth.

AB III.33 prajāpatir vai svāṃ duhitaram abhyadhyāyad divam ity anya āhur uṣasam ity anye tām ṛśyo bhūtvā rohitam bhūtām abhyait taṃ devā apaśyann akṛtaṃ vai prajāpatiḥ karotīti te tam aichan ya enam āriṣyaty etam anyonyasmin nāvindaṃs teṣāṃ yā eva ghoratamās tanva āsaṃs tā ekadhā samabharaṃs tāḥ sambhṛtā eṣa devo 'bhavat . . . taṃ devā abruvann ayaṃ vai prajāpatir akṛtam akar imaṃ vidhyeti . . . tam abhyāyatyāvidhyat sa viddha ūrdhva udaprapatat . . . tad vā idam prajāpate retaḥ siktam adhāvat

Prajāpati longed for his own daughter—some say "Heaven", others "Dawn". Having become a buck, he 'approached' her, who had become

---

AV IV.4.7 (= VI.101.3) ā́háṃ tanomi te páso, ádhi jyā́m iva dhánvani
kramasvárśya* [for -rśa; see Whitney, ad loc.] iva
rohítam, ánavaglāyatā sádā

I stretch your penis, like a bowstring on a bow.
Mount (her) like a buck a doe, always untiringly.

Cf. also JB II.87.

[277] So Delbrück 1888, p. 9.

a red doe. The gods saw, "Prajāpati does (something) not to be done." They sought one who would harm him. They did not find anyone among themselves. They collected together into one their own most dreadful bodies. Thus collected, they became this god [= Rudra]. . . . The gods said to him, "This Prajāpati has done (something) not to be done. Pierce him!" . . . Having taken aim, he pierced him. Pierced, he flew straight up. . . . The seed, (which had) poured out from Prajāpati, flowed.

In the JB version the creation of Rudra happens *before* Prajāpati's transgression.[278]

JB III.262 devā vai sattram upayanto 'bruvan / yan naḥ krūram ātmanas tan nirmimāmahai / mā sakrūrā apagāmeti / . . . / tata eṣo 'khalo devo 'jāyata / . . . / eṣa ha vāva so 'gnir jajñe / . . . / sa devān abravīt kasmai mām ajījanateti / aupadraṣṭryāyety abruvan yo 'tipādayāt taṃ hanāsā iti/

prajāpatir hoṣasaṃ svāṃ duhitaram abhyadhyāyat / sāsmai rohid bhūtvātiṣṭhat / tāṃ pr̥ṣato bhūtvāskandat / sa aikṣatāsmai vai māṃ devā ajījanann aupadraṣṭryāya / ati vā ayaṃ pādayati hantainaṃ vidhyānīti / tam avidhyat / sa viddha etad rūpaṃ pratyasyordhva udakrāmat . . .
.263 . . .tasya viddhasya retaḥ parāpatat

The gods, undertaking a (sacrificial) session, said, "What is cruel of ourselves, that let us 'measure out'. Let us not, (still) possessed of cruelty, undertake (this session)." Thereupon this "noninjurious"[279] god was born. . . . It was Agni that was really born thus. . . . He said to the gods, "For what did you create me?" "For overseeing/witnessing," they said. "Who(ever) will transgress, him you will smash."

Prajāpati longed for his own daughter, Dawn. She, having become a red doe, stood (still?) for him. He, having become a speckled deer, spilled (his seed) on her. He (the "noninjurious god") saw, "For this did

[278]As it does also in MS IV.2.12. Just preceding the passage quoted in the text is

MS IV.2.12 prajā́patir vaí trī́n mahimnò 'sr̥jatāgníṁ vāyúṁ sū́ryaṃ té catvā́raḥ pitāputrā́ḥ sattrám āsata té svédaṁ samávaukṣaṁs tád ábhavat

Prajāpati created three (sons) from his greatness, Agni, Vāyu, Sūrya. These four, father (and) sons, sat a session. They dripped down sweat. It came into existence [as Rudra].

The being thus created is said to have 'two cruel and unpeaceful names' (nā́manī krūré áśānte), which, of course, points to Rudra(-Śiva), but the reason for his creation is not explicitly given, as it is in JB III.262. Note here Agni and Sūrya as brothers; cf. Chap. 7, C.3.

[279]A euphemistic name, like Śiva 'the kind one', for Rudra.

the gods create me, for overseeing. This one transgresses. Well, I will pierce him." He pierced him. He (Prajāpati), pierced, having thrown away this form, strode straight up. . . . Of him, pierced, the seed flew forth.

2. *The Participants*

This is clearly a moral breach. The gods consider it an ā́gas- (much like énas- a 'sin') in the ŚB (ŚB I.7.4.2 tád vaí devā́nām ā́ga āsa 'this was a sin to the gods') and also a 'violation of agreement or custom' (ŚB I.7.4.3 atisaṃdhā́ṃ vā́ ayā́ṃ carati 'this one commits a violation of agreement'), something 'not to be done' in the AB (AB III.33 taṃ devā apaśyann akṛtaṃ vai prajāpatiḥ karotīti 'The gods saw, "Prajāpati does something not to be done." '), a transgression in the JB (sa aikṣata . . . aty vā ayaṃ pādayati 'He saw, . . . "This one transgresses." ') and, interestingly enough, something ápavrata- 'contrary to commandment' in the MS (MS IV.2.12 tásmā ápavratam achadayat 'It seemed to him (something) contrary to commandment'; cf. also atisaṃdhá- above). They seek and ultimately find or create someone to punish Prajāpati, namely, Rudra, and he wounds the offender.

This myth must be simply a later variant of an older form, *with Prajāpati substituting for Sūrya*. Prajāpati doesn't cut much of a figure in the RV and certainly not as the father of Uṣas. The word prajā́pati- occurs only six times in the RV, and only in the late RV as a god in his own right. In the two earlier occurrences, prajā́pati is an epithet of other gods, once of Soma (IX.5.9) *and* once of Savitar (IV.53.2). It is worth nothing that Savitar (lit. 'the Impeller') is often considered to be an aspect of the sun,[280] as in a Svarbhānu passage already quoted:

AV XIII.2.36 páśyāma tvā savitā́raṃ yám āhúr, ájasraṃ jyótir yád ávindad átriḥ

May we look upon thee (the sun), whom they call Savitar, the imperishable light, which Atri found.

Moreover, the RVic passage with Prajāpati as epithet of Savitar (RV IV.53.2) especially endows Savitar with attributes of the sun.[281] So Prajāpati in his earliest appearance is in some sense associated with, or identified with, the sun.

[280]Macdonell 1897, pp. 32–33; Hillebrandt 1927–29, vol. 2, pp. 106ff., etc.
[281]See Geldner, ad loc.

The real, old father of Dawn is given often (about thirty-five times in the RV) as 'heaven' (divó duhitár- ≈ duhitár- diváḥ), but sometimes (eleven times in the RV) as the sun (sū́ryasya duhitár- ≈ sū́ro duhitár-). The doubling of terms for her father might suggest that Sūrya and heaven are equivalent in this instance. Thus, if a more likely original father to Uṣas is, as it were, plugged into this story, we have *Sūrya committing incest with Uṣas,* surely enough of an énas (sin) to deserve the punishment described.

Indeed there is a certain amount of circumstantial evidence in the RV itself for this constellation of beings and events. As just noted, Uṣas is called 'daughter of Sūrya / the sun'; she is given this epithet especially when as bride she is mounting the chariot of the Aśvins, her bridegrooms.

RV I.117.13 yuvó rátham̱ duhitā́ sū́ryasya, sahá śriyā́ nāsatyāvṛṇīta

Your chariot, O Nāsatyas [= Aśvins], the daughter of the sun has chosen, along with your beauty.[282]

But Sūrya also appears as a *suitor* of Dawn in the RV.

RV I.115.2 sū́ryo devī́m uṣásam̱ rócamānām, máryo ná yóṣām abhyèti paścā́t

Sūrya goes along behind the shining goddess Dawn, like a suitor after a maiden.[283]

So, the text presents Sūrya in two different roles with regard to Uṣas, both father and wooer, the combination of which would suggest an incestuous relation.

Moreover, this incest seems to be known to the RV. A case of cosmic incest is graphically if glancingly alluded to in several RVic passages.[284]

RV X.61.7ab pitā́ yát svā́m̱ duhitáram adhiṣkán, kṣmayā́ rétaḥ sam̱jagmānó ní ṣiñcat

[282]Cf. I.118.5, IV.43.2, etc.

[283]Cf. I.123.10 and I.92.11 with I.113.9.

[284]I.71.5, 8; X.61.5–7; possibly III.31.1f.; cf. Geldner, ad. loc.; Oldenberg, *Noten,* ad loc.; Schmidt 1968, pp. 44ff.

When the father 'sprang upon' his own daughter, uniting (with her),
he poured down seed upon the earth.

Though no names are named here, the passage is preceded by a formulaic reference to Dawn:[285]

RV X.61.4a kṛṣṇā́ yád góṣv aruṇī́ṣu sī́dat

When Black (Night) sat among the ruddy cows (of Dawn) . . .

and Geldner suggests that this allusion to Dawn leads directly into the tale of incest.[286] Certainly in later texts the passage is considered to refer to Prajāpati's incest with Uṣas, since it is quoted in ŚB I.7.4.4 immediately after the recital of that story:

ŚB I.7.4.3 [tám̐ rudrò 'bhyāyátya vivyādha tásya sāmí rétaḥ prácaskanda táthén nūnáṃ tád āsa]
.4 tásmād etád ṛ́ṣiṇābhyánūktam / pitā́ yát svā́ṃ duhitáram . . .

[.3 Rudra, on taking aim, pierced him. Half of his seed spilled forth. Even so was it as now (?).]
.4 Therefore it was said by the seer, "When the father his own daughter . . . [= RV X.61.7]."

The passages are sexually explicit, indeed violent.[287] This is no gentle mingling of cosmic essences taking place offstage.

RV X.61.5 práthiṣṭa yásya vīrákarmam iṣṇád, ánuṣṭhitaṃ nú náryo ápauhat
púnas tád ā́ vṛhati yát kanā́yā, duhitúr ā́ ánubhṛtam anarvā́

[285]Cf. Geldner; Oldenberg, *Noten;* Renou, *ÉVP,* vol. 16.; all ad locc.

[286]*RV* III, p. 226. However, in RV I.71.5a, 8b, the male seems to be identified with Heaven, not the Sun specifically (5a mahé . . . pitré . . . divé 'for great Father Heaven'; 8b dyaúḥ 'Heaven'). This may be a poetic broadening of the Sun to refer to his domain (cf. the dual fatherhood of Uṣas just described). Or it may be an admixture of another, very similar incest motif, that of Heaven with Earth. That the Sūrya-Uṣas incest is at least partially referred to is clear from its aftermath, described in I.71.5cd, which is quoted in the text.

[287]The passages are otherwise obscure in many ways, and I am not certain (perhaps fortunately) of some of the details.

(The one) whose (penis, which) performs the manly work,[288] stretched out, discharging (the seed)[289]—that one, the manly one, then pulled away (his penis, which had been) 'attending on/following' (her).
He tore out again from the maiden, his daughter, what (had been) thrust in [290]—he the unmastered.

These graphic descriptions do not exist merely for their own titillating sake (though there is some of that). The cruel and violent immediacy of the portrayal shows the deed as one requiring punishment. The consequences of the act—its punishment—are also known to the RV.

RV I.71.5cd sṛjád ástā dhṛṣatā́ didyúm asmai, svā́yāṃ devó duhitári tvíṣiṃ dhāt

The Archer boldly released a missile at him, (when) the god placed his 'brilliance'[291] in his own daughter.

This passage bears a strong resemblance to the later descriptions of Rudra's punishment of Prajāpati *and* to the wounding of the sun by Svarbhānu.

Let us now turn to the Avenger. In the later versions it is Rudra, though often referred to by one of his less fearful epithets, such as paśupati 'lord of beasts' or akhala 'noninjurious'.[292] But *Rudra* is in fact constantly identified as *Agni*.

MS I.6.6 eṣá hí rudró yád agníḥ

[288]On this bahuvrīhi (possessive compound) vīrákarma-, an obvious designation for 'penis', cf. Oldenberg, *Noten*, Renou, *ÉVP*, vol. 16, ad loc.

[289]Oldenberg (*Noten*, ad loc.) suggests supplying rétas 'seed' with the participle iṣṇát.

[290]On the sexual connotations of ánu √bhṛ, see Jamison 1981[82], esp. p. 59. Note that the preverb ánu also occurs in ánuṣṭhitam in pāda b, which in context must also be a sexual idiom. One of the difficulties with the interpretation of these and other sexual passages is that the idioms found there are rare in Vedic (which does not ordinarily treat sexual matters with great vividness).

[291]Tvíṣi- 'brilliance' is associated elsewhere with the sun, not surprisingly. Cf. IX.71.9 ádhi tvíṣīr adhita sū́ryasya '(Soma) has put on the brilliance of the sun', and IX.39.3, which seems to present the same image, though without an explicit sū́rya-. Also X.89.2. This is another piece of evidence that the incest of I.71 is at least partly that of Sūrya and Uṣas.

[292]Paśupati: ŚB I.7.4.3 yó 'yáṃ deváḥ paśūnā́m ī́ṣṭe 'this god who is master of the beasts'; also MS IV.2.12, AB III.33. Akhala: JB III.262 ('not wicked', so Caland 1931, ad PB VIII.2.10).

For this Rudra is (really) Agni.[293]

And in the relevant JB passage:

JB III.262 tata eṣo 'khalo devo 'jāyata / . . . /eṣa ha vāva so 'gnir jajñe / na hainam eṣa hinasti ya evaṃ veda

Thereupon this noninjurious god was born. . . . *Agni was really the one who was born.* He (the god) does not harm him who know thus.

And indeed S. Insler has suggested (pers. comm.) that Rudra was originally just a fearful epithet of Agni, as it is several times in the RV.

RV IV.3.1 ā́ vo rā́jānam adhvarásya *rudráṃ,* hótāraṃ satyayájaṃ
ródasyoḥ
agním . . .

(Him) the king of your ceremony, the *fierce* one, the truly
worshipping Hotar of the two worlds,
Agni . . .

With this easy substitution we have our avenger: (Rudra-)Agni is the punisher of the incestuous father of Uṣas; (Svarbhānu-)Agni is the punisher of the Sun. The two stories can be superimposed: the motive for the Svarbhānu violence is found in the shocking incestuous encounter narrated in the other story.

3. *Verbal Parallels between the Myths*

There are verbal parallels as well. In the RV version of Svarbhānu, the sun is described as (V.40.6c) gūḷháṃ sū́ryaṃ támasā́pavratena. This is usually translated 'the sun hidden by "unlawful" darkness' or the like.[294] This is in fact one of the principal supports for the eclipse

[293]Also I.6.7, I.6.11; II.1.10; III.9.1, etc. Note that ásura- is used early as an epithet of Rudra (two or three times in RV Family Books; Hale 1986, pp. 51f.; cf. also pp. 66, 80). This establishes another, albeit not terribly strong, link between Agni and Rudra as being identified with Svarbhānu Āsura.

[294]Geldner: 'von der ungesetzlichen Finsternis' (by unlawful darkness); Schmidt (1958, p. 96): 'von der dem Gelübde abgewandten Finsternis' (by darkness turned away from the vow/oath); O'Flaherty: 'darkness pitted against the sacred order'. O'Flaherty comments (1981, p. 189), "The sacred law or order (ṛta), the way of nature, would not have made the sun dark at that time." I do not know if she has misread ápavratena for an *ápa-ṛteṇa, or if she is asserting a special link between vratá- and ṛtá-.

theory: the darkness is unseasonable, against natural law. However, given the MS passage above, it could mean as well 'hidden by darkness *because of* (an action) contrary to commandment'.[295] This would be very like the instrumental of legal provision we discussed above with regard to ātreyī.[296]

The word ápa-vrata- is quite rare in Vedic. It occurs twice elsewhere in the RV (I.51.9, V.42.9),[297] once quite close to this passage, applied to people, enemies 'without (or) contrary to commandment'.[298]

RV V.42.9 ápavratān prasavé vāvr̥dhānā́n, brahmadvíṣaḥ sū́ryād yāvayasva

Keep away from the sun (!) those without commandment, grown (strong) in impulsion, hostile to the formulation.

Notice the presence of parallel brahma-dvíṣ- 'hating the brahman/formulation'. The enemy are defined by their lack of the verbal formulae ('commandment' and 'holy formulation') that define the Aryan community.

Another occurrence of ápavrata- is in a widespread mantra, in fact in exactly our phrase támasā́pavratena. But this passage is so clearly based on the Svarbhānu passage that it cannot be taken as independent evidence.[299]

AV(Ś) III.2.6 asaú yā́ sénā marutaḥ páreṣām, asmā́n aíty abhy ójasā spárdhamānā
tā́m vidhyata támasā́pavratena, yáthaiṣām anyó anyáṃ ná jānā́t

O Maruts, that army of adversaries that comes against us, contending with might—

[295]My translation of vrata- in this compound as 'commandment' (rather than the 'vow, oath' it comes to mean later) follows that of Brereton 1981; see pp. 70ff., with extensive discussion of the copious earlier literature.

[296]Chap. 8, B.2.

[297]And once in a Khila verse appended to RV X.103. See below.

[298]Schmidt (1958, p. 93) allows only the former meaning, commenting (apropos of RV I.51.9), "Die genannte Feinde haben das Gelübde nicht gebrochen, sie haben es vielmehrs niemals geleistet" (The enemies mentioned have not broken the oath/vow; rather they have never taken it). But it is hard to see, for example, how Prajāpati in the incest story could be considered outside of the Aryan community bound by oath/commandment, rather than as a transgressor of that oath/commandment.

[299]The preceding verse also recalls the phraseology of this myth. Cf. n. 227.

Pierce it with apavrata darkness, so that no one of them may know the other.[300]

Note the reminiscences of our passage. The phrase támasā́pavratena occurs at the end of the (third) pāda, as in RV V.40.6 (6c gūḷhám̐ sū́ryam̐ támasā́pavratena). The verb in c, whether vidhyata or gūhata, is a prominent verb in Svarbhānu: vidhyata of course recalls avidhyat, *the* verb of the myth; gūhata recalls the gūḷhám that begins V.40.6c as well as aghukṣat in vs. 8 (svàrbhānor ápa māyā́ aghukṣat 'he hid away the māyā́ of Svarbhānu'). Finally, the last pāda (yáthaiṣām anyó anyám̐ ná jānā́t 'so that no one of them may know the other') seems a rather flat-footed recasting of the last pādas of the preceding verse in RVic Svarbhānu:

RV V.40.5cd ákṣetravid yáthā mugdhó, bhúvanāny adīdhayuḥ

The creatures perceived like a bewildered man who does not know the place.

The only other attestation of ápavrata- (that I know of) in all of Vedic is the one just cited in the Prajāpati incest passage:

MS IV.2.12 tásmā ápavratam achadayat

It appeared to him (something) contrary to commandment.

The shared isolation of these occurrences suggests a semantic connection between the passages.

Moreover, past tense verb forms of the root vyadh[301] (imperfect avidhyat, perfect vivyādha, past participle viddhá-) are found primarily in two contexts in Vedic prose: in the Svarbhānu passages and in the punishment of Prajāpati. The verb seems to have come to signal this particular act of punishment. For example, of eleven occurrences of avidhyat in the BYV, nine apply to Svarbhānu, one of the two others to Prajāpati; of approximately twenty such forms in the Brāhmaṇas (including perfect vivyādha), eleven are in the Svarbhānu myth, four in the Prajāpati incest episode, and the rest in assorted nonrelated pas-

[300]The other variants (RV Kh III.21.1 [to X.103], SV II.1210, VS XVII.47, AVP III.5.6) have gūhata 'hide' rather than vidhyata (as well as minor variations in pāda b).

[301]I speak here only of *un*compounded forms of this root, those without preverbs.

sages. The past participle viddhá- does not appear in BYV prose, but in the Brāhmaṇas, of eleven occurrences, three are in the Svarbhānu episode, four in the Prajāpati incest episode. Two examples from the Prajāpati/Uṣas story follow:[302]

MS IV.2.12 prajā́patir vaí svā́ṃ duhitáram abhyàkāmayatoṣásam . . . tásmā ápavratam achadayat . . . tám abhyāyátyā*vidhyat*

Prajāpati desired his own daughter Uṣas. . . . It seemed contrary to commandment to him [= Rudra]. . . . Aiming (at him) he pierced him.

JB III.262 ati vā ayaṃ pādayati hantainaṃ *vidhyān*īti / tam *avidhyat* / sa *viddha* etad rūpaṃ pratyasyordhva udakrāmat
.263 . . . tasya *viddhasya* retaḥ parāpatat

(Rudra thought) "This one transgresses. Well, I will *pierce* him." He *pierced* him. He, *pierced*, throwing off this form, strode straight up.[303]
. . . of him, *pierced*, the seed 'flew forth'.

4. *Why Heal the Sun?*

Given the dreadful nature of the deed, we must ask why the sun is healed—why does the greater part of the version identified with Svarbhānu concern the remedy for the wounding? Surely the incestuous father deserves his wound. Here there are two answers, one given in the very first verse of the RVic Svarbhānu treatment just quoted. Without sunlight, the creatures cannot see. No matter how badly the sun has behaved, the world is lost without him.

Moreover, the semen spilled in this forbidden act has (as seems often to be the case in these mythological matters) produced fertility for the

[302]Cf. also AB III.33; ŚB I.7.4.3 (≅ ŚBK II.7.2.2), II.1.2.9 (≅ ŚBK I.1.2.6); and for viddhá- AB III.33; ŚBK I.1.2.6, II.7.2.2.

[303]This action is the same as that in ŚB II.1.2.9 sá etác chárīram ajahāt 'Then he left his body' and AB III.33 sa viddha ūrdhva udaprapatat 'He, wounded, flew forth erect'. All of these narratives explain the creation of the asterism called Mr̥ga 'the Deer' or Mr̥gaśīrṣa 'Head of the Deer', and therefore Prajāpati must end the tale by rising to heaven to become this asterism.

In contrast to the reading given in Raghu Vira and Lokesh Chandra's JB edition (reproduced above), Caland (1919, no. 207) reads sa etarūpaṃ paryasya 'he putting on the form of an antelope [eta-]'. But this appears to be more distant even from his manuscript readings than etad rūpaṃ pratyasya, and furthermore the ŚB passage just quoted (II.1.2.9) supports an abandonment of the body (pratyasya) rather than the assumption of a new shape (paryasya).

earth and its inhabitants. These effects are already prominent in the RV; in fact, some of the RVic passages concerning the incest approach the deed with a certain cavalier amorality—almost glorying in hard-core description of the act and benevolently regarding its consequences.

RV I.71.8 ā́ yád iṣé nṛpátiṃ téja ā́naṭ, chúci réto níṣiktaṃ dyaúr abhī́ke
agníḥ śárdham anavadyáṃ yúvānaṃ, svādhyàṃ janayat sūdáyac ca

When the 'ardor'[304] reached the lord of men for release—Heaven (discharged) the pure seed spilled (when Heaven engaged) in (sexual) encounter,
Agni engendered the faultless young flock (of Aṅgirases), of good thought, and sweetened it.

RV X.61.7 pitā́ yát svā́ṃ duhitáram adhiṣkán, kṣmayā́ rétaḥ saṃjagmānó ní ṣiñcat
svādhyò 'janayan bráhma devā́, vā́stoṣ pátiṃ vratapā́ṃ nír atakṣan

When the father 'sprang upon' his own daughter, uniting (with her), he poured down seed upon the earth.
The gods of good thought engendered the formulation and fashioned from (it) Vastoṣpati, the protector of commandments.[305]

In all the prose accounts of the incest the outcome is also further creation. In one MS passage the seed, which the gods gather up (MS III.6.5 tád údagṛbhṇan)—this action rather reminds us of the gods collecting the aborted Atri and of Agni gathering up Sūrya's retas in the womb[306]—is used to 'stretch' the worship for its initial performance (MS III.6.5 téna yajñám atanvanta[307]); in PB VIII.2.10 it becomes cattle (paśu), as also (after some intermediate transformations) in MS IV.2.12, JB III.263, and AB III.34, along with various supernatural beings.

[304]Cf. Renou 'l'ardeur (génitale)' (*ÉVP*, vol. 12, ad loc.).

[305]An ironic outcome, to produce the 'protector of commandments' (vratapā́) from an action that was 'contrary to commandment' (ápavrata-).

[306]However, as we noted in the discussion of that episode (Chap. 7, C.3), the retas there appears to be an embryo, not semen as here.

[307]atanvanta: *sic* (von Schroeder in his edition gives no variants), a seemingly isolated thematicization of tanóti, not noted by Whitney, *Roots*, etc. Nearby MS III.7.1 has the expected athematic form in an almost identical expression: devā́ yajñám atanvata.

The ŚB feels constrained to explain, or at least comment on, the gods' change of heart: after having essentially hired a hit man (Rudra) to punish Prajāpati for his unnatural sexual behavior, they are now behaving quite tenderly toward him and his spilt semen.

> ŚB I.7.4.4 téṣāṃ yadā́ devā́nāṃ kródho vyaíd átha prajā́patim abhiṣajyaṃs tásya táṁ́ śalyáṃ nírakr̥ntan

> When the anger of the gods went away, then they healed Prajāpati and cut out his dart [with which Rudra had wounded him].

In the same way the gods seek a remedy for Sūrya in the Svarbhānu versions. Their eagerness to heal him does not mean that they did not instigate his punishment.

Thus, circumstantial evidence suggests that Sūrya was 'pierced with darkness' by Agni for a serious offense, incest with his daughter, but that once ritually expiated, the sin and its punishment, like most of the truly horrible episodes in Vedic mythology, brought positive and fructifying results to the world of man, in the form of the growth of vegetation. At some later, but still relatively early date, the incest theme seems to have been, for whatever reason, excised from the Svarbhānu-Sūrya myth and attributed to Prajāpati, forming a different complex of sin, punishment, expiation, and creation.

We are now in a position to reassemble the constituents of the Svarbhānu myth: Sūrya, the sun, committed incestuous rape against his daughter, Dawn. On behalf of the gods, Agni, in his fierce aspect as Rudra and bearing the punning epithet Svar-bhānu (possessing the light of the sun) Āsura, punished the sun for this violation of law and custom. The punishment took two complementary forms, showing two sides of Agni's character. The sun was 'pierced with darkness', that is, pierced by Agni's sharp flames that left holes burnt on the sun's surface, and he was covered over, 'hidden', by darkness, that is, swirling clouds of Agni's smoke.

But the gods, having so punished the sun that he did not 'shine forth', needed him again and sought to heal the sun by removing the darknesses. This removal of the darknesses is conceived of in two, partially overlapping ways, each of which has connections with other mythic complexes. On the one hand, the spots pierced on the sun's surface are transformed into the 'hair' (vegetation) of the earth, through the mediation of hairy sheep. This connects with the mythic complex relating skin disease, hair, and fertility that we also meet in the story of Apālā and elsewhere. On the other hand, the enveloping smoky darknesses that obscure the sun are removed in the same fashion as embryo covers from a newborn, thereby portraying the healing of the sun as equivalent to a second birth. This in turn brings to mind other stories relating miscarriages, feared or real, of the sun, and it also suggests the appropriate healer of the sun, namely, the seer Atri, who endured both a failed birth and a later successful rebirth, just like the sun. These two methods of healing are closer than we might think at first, for the pivotal figure in the second, Atri, is also Apālā's father, and the issue of fertility—longed for, cheated, and ultimately fulfilled—unites the two mythic strains.

We have come a long way from Eclipse Demons.

Vedic literature abounds in such tantalizing mythic fragments. Some, I fear, must remain forever beyond our understanding because too little related or explanatory material has been preserved in the storehouse of ancient Indian literature. Others, however, can be illuminated, set in context, even "explained," if we are willing to burrow meticulously through the great bulk of Vedic literature in search of verbal echoes, thematic parallels, ritual encodings—and if we are willing to recreate imaginatively the shared culture of the narrator and the audience of these myths. I hope to have done this for two myths, to have shown how these misleadingly brief and starkly told tales nestle in the complex web of Vedic myth and ritual and reflect the serious concerns of their society about both cosmic and quotidian matters—the progress of the heavens, the progress of the ritual, the progress of the life cycle. Much remains to be done in the field of Vedic myth and ritual, and the investigation amply repays anyone willing to accept its discipline.

Glossary of Technical Terms in Vedic Ritual and Religion

Long vowels follow the corresponding short vowels; *ś* follows *s*.

Adhvaryu	The chief priest of the Yajur Veda, responsible for ritual action.
Agni	'Fire'. One of the chief gods of the Vedic pantheon.
Agnicayana	'Piling of the fire altar'. A ritual involving a special preparation of an altar for soma sacrifices.
Agnihotra	'Fire offering'. The twice-daily offering of milk products into the fire.
Agniṣṭoma	The most basic form of soma sacrifice.
Agnyādheya	'Establishment of the fires'. The ritual initially establishing the three śrauta fires necessary to become an Āhitāgni.
amedhya	Unfit for contact with worship.
Aṅgirases	A priestly family.
Anukramaṇī	RV index; gives for each hymn its meter, the god to whom it is dedicated, and its putative author.
Aryaman	An Āditya, god of custom.
Aryans	The Indo-European invaders of India.
Asuras	The traditional enemies of the gods (Devas) in the Brāhmaṇas
Aśvamedha	'Horse sacrifice'. A ritual performed by a king to consolidate and extend his power, involving the sacrifice of a horse.
Aśvins	Twin deities who characteristically heal and rescue those in distress.
Atharvans	A priestly family.
Avabhṛtha	The final bath, which purifies the Yajamāna after the ritual and releases him from his Dīkṣā.

Ādityas — 'Sons of Aditi'. A group of gods (of varying number) born of the goddess Aditi.

Āgrayaṇa — 'First fruits'. A harvest ritual.

Āhavanīya — The fire 'to be offered into'. One of the three fires of the śrauta ritual and the one into which the oblations are poured.

Āhitāgni — One 'having established fires'. A person having established the three fires, hence a person eligible to perform the śrauta rituals.

Āpas — 'Waters'. A group of goddesses.

Āraṇyaka — 'Forest Book'. A type of mystical text.

barhis — Grass strewn on the Vedi for the gods to sit on.

Bhaga — Deified 'Portion'.

Bhṛgus — A priestly family.

bhūr bhuvaḥ svaḥ — A common ritual cry.

Brahmacārin — Student of a priest.

bráhman — A sacred 'formulation'.

brahmán — The possessor or creator of a bráhman.

Brāhmaṇa — (1) A prose text explaining the ritual. (2) A member of the priestly class, one of the three classes of the Aryans.

Camasādhvaryu — 'Cup-adhvaryu' or 'priest of the drinking vessels'. A minor assistant of the Adhvaryu.

caru — A sort of porridge of grain cooked with milk and butter and offered as an oblation.

Cāturmāsyāni — 'Four-monthly' or seasonal sacrifices.

Classical Sanskrit — The language as codified by the grammarian Pāṇini. A later variety than Vedic Sanskrit.

Dakṣiṇā — 'Priestly gift'. The present or fee given the priests officiating at a ritual by the sacrificer who arranged or ordered the ritual (Yajamāna).

Dakṣiṇāgni — 'Southern fire'. One of the three fires at a śrauta ritual.

Dakṣiṇā Vedi — 'Southern altar'. A second altar used in a few rituals and constructed south of the Mahāvedi.

Darśapūrṇamāsa — Ritual regularly performed at the time of the 'new (and) full moon'.

Dākṣiṇa — 'Relating to the dakṣiṇā'; a set of libations at the Madhyaṃdina Savana.

Devas — The 'gods'.

Dharma Sūtras — Texts codifying customary law.

Dīkṣā — Consecration of the sacrificer (Yajamāna) before the performance of the soma sacrifice.

Dīkṣita — The one consecrated in the dīkṣā.

Dyaus — Deified 'Heaven, Sky' (also Dyaus Pitar 'Father Sky').

Ekāha — 'One-day' soma sacrifice.

Epic Sanskrit — The language of the great epics, the Mahābhārata and the Rāmāyaṇa.

Family Books — Books (or Maṇḍalas) II–VII of the Rig Veda, each ascribed to a single bardic family.

First function — In trifunctional interpretations, the sphere of the priest (brāhmaṇa).

Gandharva — A sort of demigod, ordinarily referred to collectively. They are often characterized as musicians and lovers of women.

garbha — 'Embryo.'

Gavāmayana — 'Progress of the cows'. A year-long ritual (or Sattra) beginning at the winter solstice and focussed around the summer solstice.

Gārhapatya — 'Householder's fire'. One of the three fires necessary for śrauta ritual.

ghee — 'Clarified butter.' Melted, it is one of the most common offerings poured into the fire at the ritual.

Gr̥hya Sūtras — Texts concerning the domestic (gr̥hya) cult, simpler rituals than the solemn (śrauta) cult and requiring only one fire.

Haviryajñas — Rituals involving primarily agricultural offerings.

Hotar — The priest associated with the Rig Veda, who recites verses from this text at the ritual.

Indra — The great warrior god.

Iṣṭi — A type of ritual, involving only agricultural offerings, not animal sacrifice or soma.

Jātakarman — Rites for the newborn in the domestic or gr̥hya cult.

Kārīrī Iṣṭi — A particular Kāmyā Iṣṭi performed for rain.

Kāmyā Iṣṭi — 'Wish offering'. Cover term for various rituals performed for particular desires.

Khila — Additional, apocryphal hymns of the Rig Veda.

kilāsa — A particular skin affliction, probably leukoderma.

kṣatriya — The second or 'warrior' class of Aryans, also called rājanya.

Mahāvedi — 'Great altar'. An enlargement of the ritual ground for soma sacrifices (and a few others).

maṇḍala — 'Circle'. The designation of the books of the Rig Veda.

manthin — 'Stirred' oblation. A particular oblation of soma mixed with milk.

mantra — Holy formulation used in the ritual (both in verse and in prose).

Manu — The first man and the first sacrificer.

Maruts — A group of young warrior gods, frequently associated with Indra.

Mādhyaṃdina Savana — 'Midday pressing'. The second of the three pressings of soma on the pressing day of a soma sacrifice.

māyā — Magic power.

Mitra	Deified 'Alliance', an Āditya.
odana	'Rice mess'. A type of oblation.
Parjanya	Deified 'Thunder'.
paśu	Cover term for beast or animal, often (but not always) referring specifically to domestic animals.
Paśubandha	'Animal sacrifice'. A ritual in which one or more animals is sacrificed.
Pāṇini	The great grammarian who codified the rules of Sanskrit, c. 500 B.C.
pragātha	A type of stanza.
Prajāpati	'Lord of Creatures'. The ultimate creator, a god tied to the ritual who emerges fully only in the Brāhmaṇas.
prasarpaka	Nonofficiating priests, spectators at the ritual.
Pratiprasthātar	A priest who acts as assistant to the Adhvaryu.
Pravargya	A subsidiary ceremony in the preliminaries to the soma sacrifice, in which a hot drink of milk and ghee is prepared in a clay pot, the Mahāvīra.
Prātaḥsavana	'Early-morning pressing'. The first of the three pressings of soma on the pressing day of the soma sacrifice.
Prātaranuvāka	'Early-morning recitation'. One of the first acts of the pressing day of a soma sacrifice.
Prāyaścitti	'Expiation'. An action to counter mistakes, intentional or not, made in the performance of a ritual.
Pṛthivī	Deified 'Earth', a goddess.
puroḍāśa	An offering cake.
Pūṣan	A god who guards prosperity.
Rāhu	The 'eclipse demon' of later Sanskrit, who swallows the sun and moon during eclipses.
rājanya	An alternate name for the second or 'warrior' class of the Aryans. (Cf. kṣatriya.)
Rājasūya	'Consecration of the king'. An elaborate ritual.
retas	'Seed'.
Rudra	A fierce and often punishing god.
ṛc	'Verse'. Form of sacral utterance collected in the Rig Veda.
ṛṣi	'Seer'. Originally mortal composers of hymns.
ṛta	'Truth'.
Sadas	'Shed'. A temporary structure erected for certain rituals.
Saṃhitā	'Collection'. Cover term for the canonic texts collecting the ritual formulae.
Sattras	'Sittings' or 'sessions'. Rituals that last twelve days or more.
Sautrāmaṇī	A healing ritual.
Savanīya-puroḍāśa	'The pressing cakes'. A set of offerings at the soma pressing.
Savitar	Deified 'Impeller', often identified with the sun.
Sākamedha	The third of the Cāturmāsyāni ('four-monthly') or seasonal rituals. Performed in the autumn.

sāman	Tune to which verses are set to be sung or chanted in the ritual. Contained in the Sāma Veda.
Sāyaṇā	A famed medieval commentator on the Rig Veda, among other texts.
Second function	In trifunctional interpretations, the sphere of the warrior (kṣatriya).
smṛti	'Remembered' or traditional lore, as opposed to śruti.
soma	The drink, whose exact identity is not certain, offered at the soma sacrifices. Also the drink deified.
somapītha	'Soma-drink'. (1) The soma draught itself. (2) The privilege of partaking of soma.
Soma sacrifice	Any of the rituals in which the drink soma is prepared and offered to the gods. The most solemn and elaborate set of rituals.
stotra	A group of verses chanted to a sāman.
surā	An intoxicating drink usually forbidden to Brahmans, but used in certain rituals.
Sūrya	Deified 'Sun'.
śastra	Group of verses chanted together.
Śākhā	'Branch'. Cover term for different schools that preserved and interpreted the Vedas.
śrauta	Referring to the solemn ritual and texts associated with it. Pertaining to received and divinely inspired texts, rather than those composed by men.
Śrauta Sūtras	Texts setting forth the exact performance of the śrauta rituals.
śruti	Divinely inspired or revealed texts, as opposed to smṛti.
śūdra	The lowest of the four major divisions of society and the only non-Aryan one.
tejas	'Splendor'.
Third function	In trifunctional interpretations, the sphere of the agriculturist (vaiśya).
Tīvra Soma	'Sharp' or 'bitter' soma. A ritual for healing those who have become sick on soma.
trifunctional	An interpretation of Indo-European and Indo-Iranian religious, social, and political structures as reflecting the tripartition of social classes in India. A theory especially associated with G. Dumézil.
tṛca	A set of three verses.
Tṛtīya Savana	'Third [or evening] pressing'. The third and final pressing on the pressing day of the soma sacrifice.
Tvaṣṭar	Deified 'Fashioner'.
Udgātar	Priest associated with the Sāma Veda, who chants the sāmans.
Upaniṣads	Late Vedic mystical texts.
Uṣas	Deified 'Dawn', a Goddess.

Uttaravedi	'Further' or 'upper' altar. Altar constructed on the Mahāvedi for the soma sacrifices (and a few other rituals), on which the new Āhavanīya fire is placed.
Uttarā Vedi	'Northern altar'. Altar constructed on the Mahāvedi. *Cf.* Dakṣiṇā Vedi.
Vaiśvadeva	First of the Cāturmāsyāni or seasonal rituals. Performed in the spring.
vaiśya	'Clansman, villager'. Third (and lowest) of the Aryan classes.
vajra	'Cudgel'. Indra's most characteristic weapon.
Vala	One of Indra's most celebrated opponents.
vapā	'Omentum' (peritoneal folds). The first and most important part of a sacrificed animal cooked and offered to the gods.
Varuṇa	The great ethical god, guardian of commandments, an Āditya.
Varuṇapraghāsa	The second of the Cāturmāsyāni or seasonal rituals. Performed in the rainy season.
Vasus	A group of gods.
vaśā	A cow (or other female animal) that has been mated but has not yet produced offspring.
Vāc	Deified 'Speech', a goddess.
Vāta	Same as Vāyu.
Vāyu	Deified 'Wind'.
Veda	'Knowledge'. Text (one of four) collecting the sacred utterances and lore of the ritual.
Vedi	'Altar'.
Viṣṇu	A god, famed in Vedic primarily for his 'three strides', which won the worlds for the gods.
Viśve Devās	'All the gods' or the 'All-gods'.
Vṛtra	'Obstacle'. The most famous of the adversaries defeated by Indra in perhaps the most often told myth in Vedic.
Yajamāna	'Sacrificer' or 'one sacrificing for himself'. The person who contracts and pays for the ritual and to whom the benefit from the ritual accrues.
yajña	'Worship'.
yajus	The form of sacral utterance collected in the Yajur Veda, usually serving to address or dedicate items used in the ritual.
yoni	'Womb'.
Yūpa	Post to which the sacrificial victim is tied.

A Note on Sanskrit Pronunciation

This section gives approximate English equivalents to the various Sanskrit sounds and some discussion of the production of unfamiliar sounds.

Vowels

Short and long *a* differ in length and quality.

a	*a* corresponds to the vowel in b*u*t
ā	*ā* that in f*a*ther

But short and long *i* and *u* differ only in length.

i	The *i*'s resemble the vowel of b*ea*t.
ī	
u	The *u*'s resemble the vowel of b*oo*t.
ū	

e	= b*ai*t
ai	= b*i*te
o	= b*oa*t
au	= b*ou*t

These four (e, ai, o, au) count as "long" vowels or diphthongs, just as ā, ī, and ū do.

r̥	('syllabic r') is equivalent to the final syllable of fath*er* or the interior sound of p*er*t. There is also, rarely, a long syllabic r̥̄.

Consonants:

Stops: Sanskrit stops come in four varieties, plain voiceless (vl., e.g., *t*), voiceless aspirate (vl. asp., e.g., *th*), plain voiced (vd., e.g., *d*), and voiced aspirate (vd. asp., e.g., *dh*). They are further classified into five series by where they are made in the mouth.

	vl.	*vl. asp.*	*vd.*	*vd. asp.*
velar	k	kh	g	gh
palatal	c	ch	j	jh
retroflex	ṭ	ṭh	ḍ	ḍh
dental	t	th	d	dh
labial	p	ph	b	bh

Remarks on the vertical columns: The aspirated stops (columns 2 and 4) differ from their plain counterparts in that a small puff of air follows the articulation of the stop. The voiceless aspirates (column 2) are closest in sound to English voiceless stops that are initial in their words. For example, Skt. *th* is equivalent to the *t* in English *t*en. It is important to remember that Skt. *th* is *not* equivalent to *th* in English words like *th*in, *th*ought, or like *th*at. Similarly, Skt. *ph* equals English *p* in *p*en, not the *ph* in *ph*iloso*ph*y.

For our rough and ready purposes, the plain voiceless set (column 1) can be pronounced like the voiceless aspirates (column 2), though a more exact equivalent would be the type of consonant that appears after *s* in English words: English s*t*op contains a Skt. *t*, but a *t*op a Sanskrit *th*.

The plain voiced set (column 3) is equivalent to English voiced stops (d, etc.), while the voiced aspirates (column 4) have a little breathy murmur after the articulation of the stop. There is no English equivalent of the voiced aspirates, and for our purposes we can pronounce the voiced aspirates much like plain voiced stops.

One should remember that the two aspirate sets (columns 2 and 4) contain single consonants, not combinations of two consonants. Each is written with one letter in devanāgarī (the usual writing system of Sanskrit now), not two as in their English transliterations.

Remarks on the horizontal rows: The *k*/g series is equivalent to English velars *k* and *g* (e.g., *k*eep, *g*uess), also spelled with the so-called hard c in such words as *c*at. English *g*'s in words like *g*em are *not* equivalent.

The *c*/*j* series is equivalent to English *ch* (e.g., *ch*eese, *ch*at) and *j* (e.g., *j*udge, *j*eep; also English *g*'s in words like *g*em).

The *ṭ/ḍ* series, the retroflexes, are pronounced like *t/d*, but with the tongue tip pointed back toward the roof of the mouth. There is no equivalent in English.

The *t/d* series corresponds roughly to English *t/d* (and better to their French equivalents).

The *p/b* series corresponds to English *p/b*.

There are also five different *nasal* consonants corresponding to the five horizontal rows:

velar	ṅ
palatal	ñ
retroflex	ṇ
dental	n
labial	m

ṅ corresponds to English *ng* in si*ng*, etc.

ñ is rather like the *ny* in words like ca*ny*on (or, better, the Spanish *ñ*).

There is no English equivalent to retroflex *ṇ;* it is also pronounced with the tongue tip turned back.

n and *m* are like English *n* and *m*.

Other consonants: y, r, l, and *v* are pronounced like their English counterparts.

There are three types of sibilants: palatal *ś*, retroflex *ṣ*, and dental *s*. The last corresponds to English *s*, while the other two can both be pronounced like English *sh* (*sh*ould, *sh*e), as English does not make a distinction between palatal and retroflex sibilants.

The Skt. *h* is a voiced *h*, with no English equivalent. The *ḥ* ('visarga'), occurring ordinarily at the end of words, is voiceless, like the English *h*, and is now often pronounced with a brief vowel following it, which echoes the vowel that precedes it (e.g., devaḥ would end *aha*, but agniḥ *ihi*).

ṃ ('anusvāra') may conveniently be pronounced as nasalization of the preceding vowel (e.g., French vin, son).

Accent: The accents marked in the Vedic passages in this work are pitch accents, not accents of intensity, but the complexities of the Vedic accent need not detail us here. In current practice, Sanskrit words are conventionally pronounced as if following the "Latin" rules: Words whose penultimate syllable is long (that is, contains a long vowel or a short vowel followed by two consonants) are accented on that syllable (e.g., svarbhā́nu, salavṛkéya; vadánti). Those that have a short penultimate syllable are accented on the third syllable from the end (e.g., váruṇa). Words of two syllables are accented on the initial syllable, whether it is short or long (e.g., ágni, íti). (N.B. The accents just marked on these examples are for illustration only and do not reflect the actual inherited pitch accent found in Vedic.)

References

Baunack, T. 1896. "Über einige Wunderthaten der Aśvin." *ZDMG* 50:263–87.

Bergaigne, A. 1878–83. *La religion védique*. 3 vols. (Bibliothèque de l'École des Hautes Études 36, 53, 54.) Paris.

Bhide, V. V. 1972. "The Use of the Karīra in the Vedic Sacrifice." *Proceedings of the All-India Oriental Conference, 24th Session, Varanasi, 1968*, pp. 215–20. Poona.

Bicknell, P. J. 1968. "Did Anaxagoras Observe a Sunspot in 467 B.C.?" *ISIS* 59:87–90.

Bloomfield, M. 1889. *The Kauśika Sūtra of Atharva Veda. JAOS* 14. Repr. Delhi, 1972.

——. 1893. "Contributions to the Interpretation of the Veda." *JAOS* 15:143–88.

——. 1897. *Hymns of the Atharva-Veda*. (Sacred Books of the East 42.) Oxford. Repr. Delhi, 1964.

Bodewitz, H. W. 1977. "Notes on the Jaiminīya Brāhmaṇa." *JRAS* (1977): 150–57.

——. 1982. "The Waters in Vedic Cosmic Classifications." *Indologica Taurinensia* 10:45–54.

——. 1983. "The Fourth Priest (the *Brahmán*) in Vedic Ritual." *Studies in the History of Religions* 45:33–68.

——. 1984. "What Did Indra Do with the Yatis?" In *Amṛtadhārā* [Fs. Dandekar], pp. 65–72, ed. S. D. Joshi. Delhi.

BR = O. Böhtlingk and R. Roth. *Sanskrit-Wörterbuch, herausgegeben von der Kaiserlichen Akademie der Wissenschaften*. 7 vols. St. Petersburg, 1879–89.

Bray, R. J., and R. E. Loughhead. 1964. *Sunspots*. London.

Brereton, J. P. 1981. *The Ṛgvedic Ādityas*. (American Oriental Series 63.) New Haven, Conn.

——. 1988. "Unsounded Speech: Problems in the Interpretation of BU(M) I.5.10 = BU(K) 1.5.3." *IIJ* 31:1–10.

Brown, N. 1965. "Theories of Creation in the Rig Veda." *JAOS* 85:23–34.

Bühler, G. 1886. *The Laws of Manu*. (Sacred Books of the East 25.) Oxford.

———. 1898. *The Sacred Laws of the Āryas*. Pt. 1, *Āpastamba and Gautama*, 2d ed. Pt. 2, *Vasiṣṭha and Baudhāyana*. (American edition of Sacred Books of the East 2, 14.) New York.

Buitenen, J. A. B. van. 1973. *The Mahābhārata. 1, The Book of the Beginning*. Chicago.

———. 1975. *The Mahābhārata. 2, The Book of the Assembly Hall. 3, The Book of the Forest*. Chicago.

Caland, W. 1900. *Altindisches Zauberritual*. Amsterdam.

———. 1904–13. *The Baudhāyana Śrauta Sūtra Belonging to the Taittirīya Saṃhitā*. 3 vols. (Bibliotheca Indica 163.) Calcutta. 2d ed., New Delhi, 1982.

———. 1908. *Altindische Zauberei: Darstellung der altindischen "Wunschopfer."* Amsterdam.

———. 1919. *Das Jaiminīya-Brāhmaṇa in Auswahl*. (Verhandelingen der Koninklijke Akademie van Wetenschappen te Amsterdam, Afd. Lett., N. R. 19.4.) Amsterdam. Repr. Wiesbaden, 1970.

———. 1921–28. *Das Śrautasūtra des Āpastambha*. 3 vols. Göttingen-Leipzig, 1921; Amsterdam, 1924, 1928. Repr. Wiesbaden, 1969.

———. 1926a. *The Śatapatha Brāhmaṇa in the Kāṇvīya Recension*. Revised by Raghu Vira. Lahore. Repr. Delhi, 1983.

———. 1926b. "Eine dritte Mitteilung über das Vādhūlasūtra." *AO* 4:1–41, 161–213.

———. 1926c. "Rāhu im Veda." In *Beiträge zur Literaturwissenschaft und Geistesgeschichte Indiens* [Fs. Jacobi], pp. 240–41, ed. W. Kirfel. Bonn.

———. 1931. *Pañcaviṃśa-Brāhmaṇa: The Brāhmaṇa of Twenty Five Chapters*. (Bibliotheca Indica 255.) Calcutta. Repr. Delhi, 1982.

———. 1953. *Śāṅkhāyana-Śrautasūtra*. Ed. Lokesh Chandra. Nagpur.

Clark, D. H., and F. R. Stephenson. 1978. "An Interpretation of the Pre-telescopic Sunspot Records from the Orient." *Royal Astronomical Society Quarterly Journal* 19:387–410. Excerpted in Schove 1983, pp. 51–69.

Cowen, D. V. 1965. *Flowering Trees and Shrubs in India*. 4th ed. Bombay.

Dange, S. A. 1980–81. "Religious Suicide in the Vedic Period (?)." *Ind. Taur.* 8–9:113–121.

Delbrück, B. 1888. *Altindische Syntax*. (Syntactische Forschungen V.) Halle an der Saale. Repr. Darmstadt, 1968.

Dumézil, G. 1956. *Aspects de la fonction guerriére chez les Indo-Européens*. Paris.

———. 1968. *Mythe et épopée* 1. Paris.

———. 1985. *Heur et malheur de guerrier*. 2d ed. Paris.

Eddy, J. A. 1980. "The Historical Record of Solar Activity." In R. O. Pepin, J. A. Eddy, and R. B. Merrill 1980, pp. 119–34.

Eggeling, J. 1882–1900. *The Śatapatha Brāhmaṇa According to the Text of the Mādhyandina School*. 5 vols. (Sacred Books of the East 12, 26, 41, 43, 44.) Oxford. Repr. Delhi, 1963.

Einoo, S. 1988. *Die Cāturmāsya oder die altindischen Tertialopfer dargestellt nach den Vorschriften der Brāhmaṇas und der Śrautasūtras*. (Monumenta Serindica 18.) Tokyo.

Ernout, A., and A. Meillet. 1959. *Dictionnaire étymologique de la langue latine: Histoire des mots.* 4th ed. (1st ed. 1932.) Paris.

Ettinghausen, R. 1955. "The Snake-eating Stag in the East." In *Late Classical and Medieval Studies in Honor of Albert Mathias Friend,* pp. 272–86, ed. K. Weitzmann. Princeton. Reprinted in R. Ettinghausen, 1984, *Islamic Art and Archaeology: Collected Papers,* pp. 674–92, ed. Myriam Rosen Ayalon. Berlin.

Falk, H. 1982. "Zur Tiersucht im alten Indien." *IIJ* 24:169–80.

——. 1984. "Die Legende von Śunaḥśepa vor ihrem rituellen Hintergrund." *ZDMG* 134:115–35.

——. 1987. "Viṣṇu im Veda." In *Hinduismus und Buddhismus* [Fs. U. Schneider], pp. 112–33, ed. H. Falk. Freiburg.

Filliozat, J. 1949. *La doctrine classique de la médecine indienne.* Paris. Repr. 1975.

Führer, A. A. 1883. *Śrīvāsiṣṭhadharmaśāstram: Aphorisms on the Sacred Laws of the Āryas, as Taught in the School of Vasiṣṭha.* (Bombay Sanskrit and Prakrit Series 23.) Bombay.

Gelder, J. M. van. 1961–63. *The Mānava Śrautasūtra Belonging to the Maitrāyaṇī Saṃhitā.* 2 vols. (Śatapiṭaka Series 17, 27.) New Delhi. Repr. Delhi, 1985.

Geldner, K. F. 1951. *Der Rigveda: Aus dem Sanskrit ins Deutsche übersetzt und mit einem laufenden Kommentar versehen.* 3 vols. (Harvard Oriental Series 33, 34, 35.) Cambridge, Mass.

Gonda, J. 1976. *Triads in the Veda.* Amsterdam.

——. 1980. *Vedic Ritual: The Non-Solemn Rites.* Leiden.

Grassmann, H. 1872–75. *Wörterbuch zum Rig-Veda.* Leipzig.

Griffith, R. T. H. 1899. *The Hymns of the Yajur-Veda.* Benares.

Grzimek, B. 1975. *Animal Life Encyclopedia.* Vol. 12, *Mammals III.* New York.

Hale, M. Forthcoming. "Some Observations on Intersentential Pronominalization in the Language of the Taittirīya Saṃhitā." In *Sense and Syntax in Vedic: Panels of the VIIth World Sanskrit Conference* (gen. ed.: Johannes Bronkhorst), vol. 3, ed. J. P. Brereton and S. W. Jamison. Leiden.

Hale, W. E. 1986. *Asura in Early Vedic Religion.* Delhi.

Heesterman, J. C. 1957. *The Ancient Indian Royal Consecration.* The Hague.

——. 1985. *The Inner Conflict of Tradition: Essays in Indian Ritual, Kinship, and Society.* Chicago.

Hillebrandt, A. 1897. *Ritualliteratur.* Strassburg.

——. 1927–29. *Vedische Mythologie.* 2d ed. 2 vols. Breslau. Repr. Hildesheim, 1965.

Hiltebeitel, A. 1976. *The Ritual of Battle: Krishna in the Mahābhārata.* Ithaca, N.Y.

Hock, H. H. 1982. "Clitic Verbs in PIE or Discourse-based Verb Fronting? Sanskrit *sá hovāca gārgyaḥ* and Congeners in Avestan and Homeric Greek." *Studies in the Linguistic Sciences* 12, no. 2:1–38.

Hoffmann, K. 1957. "Mārtāṇḍa und Gayōmart." *MSS* 11:85–103.

——. 1960a. "Textkritisches zum Jaiminīya-Brāhmaṇa." *IIJ* 4:1–36.

——. 1960b. "Der vedische Typus *menāmenam.*" *KZ* 76:242–48.

——. 1967. *Der Injunktiv im Veda.* Heidelberg.

——. 1975, 1976. *Aufsätze zur Indoiranistik.* (Kleine Schriften.) Ed. J. Narten. 2 vols. Wiesbaden.

Hopkins, E. W. 1907. "The Sniff-Kiss in Ancient India." *JAOS* 28:120–34.

———. 1909. "Gods and Saints of the Great Brāhmaṇa." *Transactions of the Connecticut Academy of Arts and Sciences* 15:19–69.

Hubert, H., and M. Mauss. 1898. "Essai sur la nature et la fonction du sacrifice." *L'année sociologique*, 29–138. (English trans., W. D. Halls, 1964, *Sacrifice: Its Nature and Function*. Chicago.)

Ilani, G. 1975. "Hyenas in Israel." *Israel—Land and Nature* 1:10–18.

Insler, S. 1987. "The Vedic Causative Type *jāpáyati*." In *Studies in Memory of Warren Cowgill (1929–1985)*, pp. 54–65, ed. C. Watkins. Berlin.

Jamison, S. W. 1981[82]. "A Vedic Sexual Pun: *ástobhayat, anubhartrī́*, and RV I.88.6." *AO* 42:55–63.

———. 1982/83. "'Sleep' in Vedic and Indo-European." *KZ* 96:6–16.

———. 1986. "Brāhmaṇa Syllable Counting, Vedic *tvác-* 'Skin', and a Sanskrit Expression for the Canonical Creature." *IIJ* 29:161–81.

———. 1987a. "Linguistic and Philological Remarks on Some Vedic Body Parts" (pt. 2, 'kukṣí', pp. 71–81). In *Studies in Memory of Warren Cowgill (1929–1985)*, pp. 66–91, ed. C. Watkins. Berlin.

———. 1987b. "Mantra Glosses in the Śatapatha Brāhmaṇa: More Light on the Development of the Vedic Verbal System." In *Festschrift for Henry Hoenigswald*, pp. 169–75, ed. G. Cardona and N. H. Zide. Tübingen.

———. 1988. "Vāyav Indraś ca Revisited." *MSS* 49:13–59.

———. Forthcoming, a. "The Syntax of Direct Speech in Vedic." In *Sense and Syntax in Vedic: Panels of the VIIth World Sanskrit Conference* (gen. ed.: Johannes Bronkhorst), vol. 3, ed. J. P. Brereton and S. W. Jamison. Leiden. Also to appear in *Studies in Sanskrit Syntax*, ed. H. H. Hock. Delhi.

———. Forthcoming, b. "Notes on Negatives and Indefinites in Vedic." In *Proceedings of the Eighth East Coast Indo-European Conference, Harvard University, June 1989*. Cambridge, Mass.

Kane, P. V. 1946. *History of Dharmaśāstra*. Vol. 3. Poona.

Keith, A. B. 1914. *The Veda of the Black Yajus School Entitled Taittiriya Sanhita*. 2 vols. (Harvard Oriental Series 18, 19.) Cambridge, Mass. Repr. Delhi, 1967.

———. 1920. *Rigveda Brāhmaṇas: The Aitareya and Kauṣītaki Brāhmaṇas of the Rigveda*. (Harvard Oriental Series 25.) Cambridge, Mass. Repr. Delhi, 1971.

———. 1925. *The Religion and Philosophy of the Vedas and Upanishads*. 2 vols. (Harvard Oriental Series 31, 32.) Cambridge, Mass. Repr. Delhi, 1970.

Krishnan, M. 1972. "An Ecological Survey of the Larger Mammals of Peninsular India." *Journal of the Bombay Natural History Society* 69:26–54.

Kruuk, H. 1972. *The Spotted Hyaena*. Chicago.

———. 1975. *Hyaena*. London.

———. 1976. "Feeding and Social Behavior of the Striped Hyaena (*Hyaena vulgaris* Demarest)." *East African Wildlife Journal* 14:91–112.

Kuiper, F. B. J. 1979. *Varuṇa and Vidūṣaka: On the Origin of Sanskrit Drama*. Amsterdam.

Lanman, C. R. 1893. "Rigveda V.40 and Its Buddhist Parallel." In *Festgruss an Rudolf von Roth zum Doktor-jubiläum von seinen Freunden und Schülern*. [Fs. Roth], pp. 187–90. Stuttgart. Ed. W. Kohlhammer.

Lawick-Goodall, H. van, and J. van Lawick-Goodall. 1971. *Innocent Killers*. Boston.

Lévi, S. 1898. *La doctrine du sacrifice dans les Brāhmaṇas*. Paris. Repr. 1966.

Lincoln, B. 1986. *Myth, Cosmos, and Society*. Cambridge, Mass.

Littleton, C. S. 1982. *The New Comparative Mythology*. 3d ed. Berkeley, Calif.

Lüders, H. 1938. "Sk kaḍāra—viklidha." *AO* 16:131–45.

——. 1951, 1959. *Varuṇa*. 2 vols. Ed. L. Alsdorf. Göttingen.

Macdonald, D. 1984. *Encyclopedia of Mammals*. New York.

Macdonald, D. W. 1978. "Observations on the Behavior and Ecology of the Striped Hyaena *Hyaena hyaena* in Israel." *Israel Journal of Zoology* 27:189–98.

Macdonell, A. A. 1897. *The Vedic Mythology*. (Grundriss der indo-arischen Philologie und Altertumskunde III/1A.) Strassburg.

Macdonell, A. A., and A. B. Keith. 1912. *Vedic Index of Names and Subjects*. 2 vols. London. Repr. Delhi, 1958.

Mayrhofer, *EWA* = M. Mayrhofer. *Etymologisches Wörterbuch des Altindoarischen*. 1986–. Heidelberg.

Mayrhofer, *KEWA* = M. Mayrhofer. *Kurzgefasstes etymologisches Wörterbuch des Altindischen*. 4 vols. 1956–80. Heidelberg.

Meulenbeld, G. J. 1974. *The Mādhavanidāna and Its Chief Commentary, Chapters 1–10*. Leiden.

Minkowsky, C. Z. 1989. "The Rathakāra's Eligibility to Sacrifice." *IIJ* 32:177–94.

Monier-Williams, M. 1899. *A Sanskrit-English Dictionary*. 2d ed. Oxford. Repr. 1956.

Nagy, G. 1990. *Greek Mythology and Poetics*. Ithaca, N.Y.

Narten, J. 1964. *Die sigmatischen Aoriste im Veda*. Wiesbaden.

Needham, J. 1959. *Science and Civilisation in China*. Vol. 3, *Mathematics and the Sciences of the Heaven and the Earth*. Cambridge.

Neisser, W. 1891. "Vorvedisches im Veda." *BB* 17:244–56.

Oertel, H. 1897. "Contributions from the *Jaiminīya Brāhmaṇa* to the History of the Brāhmaṇa Literature, First Series." *JAOS* 18:15–48.

——. 1898. "Contributions from the *Jaiminīya Brāhmaṇa* to the History of the Brāhmaṇa Literature, Second Series." *JAOS* 19:97–125.

——. 1899. "The Jaiminiya Brahmana Version of the Dirghajihvi Legend." In *Actes du Onzième Congrès International des Orientalistes, Paris, 1897*, vol. 1, *Langues et archéologie des pays ariens*, pp. 225–39. Paris.

O'Flaherty, W. D. 1981. *The Rig Veda: An Anthology*. Harmondsworth, U.K.

——. 1985a. *Tales of Sex and Violence. Folklore, Sacrifice, and Danger in the Jaiminīya Brāhmaṇa*. Chicago.

——. 1985b. "The Case of the Stallion's Wife: Indra and Vr̥ṣaṇaśva in the R̥g Veda and the Brāhmaṇas." *JAOS* 105:485–98

Oldenberg, *Noten* = H. Oldenberg. 1909, 1912. R̥gveda: Textkritische und exegetische Noten. (Abhandlungen der königlichen Gesellschaft der Wissenschaften zu Göttingen 11, 13.) Berlin. Repr. Göttingen, 1970.

Oldenberg, H. 1885. "Ākhyāna-Hymnen im Rigveda." *ZDMG* 39:52–90.

——. 1886, 1892. *The Gr̥hya-Sūtras*. 2 vols. (Sacred Books of the East 29, 30.) Oxford. Repr. Delhi, 1964.

——. 1888. *Metrische und textgeschichtliche Prolegomena zu einer kritischen Rigveda-Ausgabe*. Berlin. Repr. Wiesbaden, 1982.

——. 1893. "Indra und Namuci." Nachrichten, Göttingen Akademie der Wissenschaft, pp. 342–49.

——. 1906. "Vedische Untersuchungen." *ZDMG* 60:115–64.

——. 1917. *Die Religion des Veda*. 2d ed. Stuttgart. Repr. Darmstadt, 1970.

Owens, M., and D. Owens. 1984. *Cry of the Kalahari*. Boston.

Pepin, R. O., J. A. Eddy, and R. B. Merrill, eds. 1980. *The Ancient Sun*. New York.

Pischel, R., and K. Geldner. 1889. *Vedische Studien* 1. Stuttgart.

Puhvel, J. 1987. *Comparative Mythology*. Baltimore.

Raghu Vira and Lokesh Chandra. 1954. *Jaiminīya-Brāhmaṇa of the Sāmaveda*. (Sarasvati-Vihara Series 31.) Nagpur. 2d rev. ed., Delhi, 1986.

Rau, W. 1973. *Metalle und Metallgeräte im vedischen Indien*. (Abhandlungen der Akademie der Wissenschaften und der Literatur, Mainz: Geistes- und Sozialwissenschaftliche Klasse, 1973, no. 8.) Wiesbaden.

Renou, *ÉVP* = L. Renou. 1955–69. *Études védiques et pāṇinéennes*. 17 vols. (Publications de l'Institut de Civilisation Indienne, Fasc. 1, 2, 4, 6, 9, 10, 12, 14, 16, 17, 18, 20, 22, 23, 26, 27, 30.) Paris.

——. 1947. *Les écoles védiques et la formation du Veda*. (Cahiers Société Asiatique 9.) Paris.

——. 1949. "Sur la notion de *bráhman*." *Journal Asiatique* (1949):7–46.

——. 1954. *Vocabulaire du rituel védique*. Paris.

Rieger, I. 1979. "A Review of the Biology of Striped Hyaenas *Hyaena hyaena* (Linné, 1758)." *Säugetier-kundliche Mitteilungen* 27:81–95.

Roy, J.-R. 1982. *L'astronomie et son histoire*. Quebec. [non vidi.]

Sarton, G. 1947. "Query No. 111: Early Observations of Sunspots?" *ISIS* 37:69–71.

Schmidt, H.-P. 1958. *Vedisch* vratá *und awestisch* urvăta. Hamburg.

——. 1968. *Bṛhaspati und Indra*. Wiesbaden.

——. 1984. "Akūpārā." In *Amṛtadhārā* (Fs. Dandekar), pp. 377–81, ed. S. D. Joshi. Delhi.

——. 1987. *Some Women's Rites and Rights in the Veda*. Poona.

Schove, D. J. 1950. "The Earliest Dated Sunspot." *British Astronomical Association Journal* 61:22–25. Excerpted in Schove 1983, pp. 36–38.

——, ed. 1983. *Sunspot Cycles*. (Benchmark Papers in Geology 68.) Stroudsburg, Pa.

Schroeder, L. von. 1881–86. *Maitrāyaṇī Saṃhitā*. 4 vols. Leipzig.

——. 1900–1910. *Kāṭhakam: Die Saṃhitā der Kaṭha-Śākhā*. 3 vols. Leipzig.

——. 1908. "Das Apālā-lied." *WZKM* 22:223–44.

——. 1909a. "Göttertanz und Weltentstehung." *WZKM* 23:1–17.

——. 1909b. "Nachträge zum Apālālied." *WZKM* 23:270–72.

Skinner, J. D., and G. Ilani. 1979. "The Striped Hyaena *Hyaena hyaena* of the Judean and Negev Deserts and a Comparison with the Brown Hyaena *H. brunnea*." *Israel Journal of Zoology* 28:229–32.

Sörensen, S. 1904. *An Index to the Names in the Mahābhārata, with Short Explanations and a Concordance to the Bombay and Calcutta Editions and P.C. Roy's Translation.* London.

Speijer, J. S. 1886. *Sanskrit Syntax.* Leiden. Repr. Delhi, 1973.

Speyer, J. S. (= Speijer, J. S.) 1896. *Vedische und Sanskrit-Syntax.* (Grundriss der indo-arischen Philologie und Altertumskunde I.6.) Strassburg. Repr. Graz, 1974.

Staal, F. 1979. "The Meaninglessness of Ritual." *Numen* 26:2–22.

Thieme, P. 1952. "Bráhman." *ZDMG* 102:91–129.

——. 1954. *Die Heimat der indogermanischen Gemeinsprache.* Wiesbaden.

——. 1963. "'Jungfrauengatte'. Sanskrit kaumārah̤ patih̤—Homer. κουρίδιος πόσις—lat. maritus." *KZ* 78:161–248.

——. 1984. *Kleine Schriften.* 2d ed. Wiesbaden.

Varenne, J. 1982. *Cosmogonies védiques.* Paris.

Velankar, H. D. 1962. "Gharma and Oman in the Atri Legend." In *Indological Studies in Honor of W. Norman Brown* [Fs. W. Normal Brown], pp. 228–37 (American Oriental Series 47), ed. E. Bender. New Haven, Conn.

Wackernagel-Debrunner, *AIG* = *Altindische Grammatik.* Göttingen.

Vol. 1. 1896. *Lautlehre.* J. Wackernagel. Repr. 1957, with Intro. by L. Renou.

Vol. 2.1. 1905. *Einleitung zur Wortlehre. Nominalkomposition.* J. Wackernagel. Repr. 1957.

Vol. 2.2. 1954. *Die Nominalsuffixe.* A. Debrunner.

Vol. 3. 1930. *Nominalflexion—Zahlwort—Pronomen.* A. Debrunner and J. Wackernagel.

Walker, E. P. 1983. *Mammals of the World.* 4th ed. Baltimore.

Watkins, C. 1986. "The Name of Meleager." In *o-o-pe-ro-si* [Fs. E. Risch], pp. 320–28, ed. A. M. Etter. Berlin.

——. 1987. "How to Kill a Dragon in Indo-European." In *Studies in Memory of Warren Cowgill (1929–1985),* pp. 270–99, ed. C. Watkins. Berlin.

——. Forthcoming. "Latin *tarentum Accas,* the *Ludi Saeculares,* and Indo-European Eschatology." In *Proceedings of the Leningrad Indo-European Conference (June 1988),* ed. E. Polomé.

Weber, A. 1850. "Analyse der in Anquetil du Perron's Übersetzung enthaltenen Upanishad." *Ind. Stud.* 1:380–456.

——. 1855. "Einiges über das Kāṭhakam." *Ind. Stud.* 3:451–79.

——. 1858. "Das erste Buch des Atharvaveda." *Ind. Stud.* 4:393–430.

——. 1873. "Zweites Buch des Atharva-Saṃhitā." *Ind. Stud.* 13:129–216.

——. 1893. *Über die Königsweihe, den Rājasūya.* (Abh. Preuss. Akad. d. Wiss.) Berlin.

Whitfield, P., ed. 1984. *Macmillan Illustrated Animal Encyclopedia.* New York.

Whitney, *Roots* = W. D. Whitney. 1885. *The Roots, Verb-Forms, and Primary Derivatives of the Sanskrit Language.* Leipzig.

——. 1905. *Atharva-Veda-Saṃhitā.* Revised and Edited by Charles Rockwell Lanman. 2 vols. (Harvard Oriental Series 7, 8.) Cambridge, Mass. Repr. Delhi, 1962.

Witzel, M. 1972. *Das Kaṭha Āraṇyaka*. (Inaugural-Dissertation, Erlangen-Nürnberg.) Erlangen.

———. 1987. "On the Localisation of Vedic Texts and Schools." In *India and the Ancient World* (Fs. Eggermont), pp. 173–213, ed. G. Pollet. Leuven.

———. 1989. "Tracing the Vedic Dialects." In *Dialectes dans les littératures indo-aryennes*, pp. 97–265, ed. C. Caillat. Paris.

Zysk, K. 1985. *Religious Healing in the Veda*. (Transactions of the American Philosophical Society 75.7.) Philadelphia.

Index of Passages Cited

The order given here and in the General Index is that of the Roman alphabet, with long vowels following the corresponding short vowels and *ś* following *s*.

Index of Sanskrit Terms

The order given here is that of the Devanāgarī alphabet.

General Index

Long vowels follow the corresponding short vowels; *ś* follows *s*. PN denotes a personal name.

Library of Congress Cataloging-in-Publication Data

Jamison, Stephanie W.
The ravenous hyenas and the wounded sun : myth and ritual in ancient India / Stephanie W. Jamison.
p. cm. — (Myth and poetics)
Includes bibliographical references and index.
ISBN 0-8014-2433-X (alk. paper)
1. Mythology, Hindu—Case studies. 2. Hinduism—Rituals–Case studies. 3. Indra (Hindu deity) 4. Svarbhānu (Hindu deity) 5. Vedas—Criticism, interpretation, etc. 6. Brahmanas—Criticism, interpretation, etc. 7. India—Religious life and customs. I. Title. II. Series.
BL 1212.2.J35 1991
294.5'13—dc20 90-55723

"ਅਸਲੀਲ ਵਾਕ"

aślīla vāk

CPSIA information can be obtained at www.ICGtesting.com
Printed in the USA
BVOW072148040412

286896BV00001B/158/P